Meriwether Lewis

Meriwether Lewis

THOMAS C. DANISI &
JOHN C. JACKSON

Foreword by ROBERT J. MOORE JR., PhD

 **Prometheus Books**

59 John Glenn Drive
Amherst, New York 14228–2119

921
LEWIS
B

Published 2009 by Prometheus Books

Meriwether Lewis. Copyright © 2009 by Thomas C. Danisi and John C. Jackson. All rights reserved. No part of this publication may be reproduced, stored in a retrieval system, or transmitted in any form or by any means, digital, electronic, mechanical, photocopying, recording, or otherwise, or conveyed via the Internet or a Web site without prior written permission of the publisher, except in the case of brief quotations embodied in critical articles and reviews.

Inquiries should be addressed to
Prometheus Books
59 John Glenn Drive
Amherst, New York 14228–2119
VOICE: 716–691–0133, ext. 210
FAX: 716–691–0137
WWW.PROMETHEUSBOOKS.COM

13 12 11 10 09   5 4 3 2 1

Library of Congress Cataloging-in-Publication Data

Danisi, Thomas, 1951–
    Meriwether Lewis / Thomas C. Danisi and John C. Jackson.
        p. cm.
    Includes bibliographical references and index.
    ISBN 978–1–59102–702–7 (cloth : acid-free paper)
    1. Lewis, Meriwether, 1774–1809. 2. Lewis and Clark Expedition (1804–1806)
3. West (U.S.)—Description and travel. 4. West (U.S.)—Discovery and exploration.
5. Explorers—West (U.S.)—Biography. 6. Clark, William, 1770–1838. I. Jackson,
John C., 1931– II. Title.

F592.7.L42D36 2009
917.804'2092—dc22
[B]

                                                                2008054728

Printed in the United States of America on acid-free paper

Contents

Foreword

ROBERT J. MOORE JR., PHD

Meriwether Lewis, explorer, soldier, and territorial governor, remains a controversial figure, even after two hundred years. The bicentennial of his explorations to the Pacific Ocean between 1804 and 1806 whipped up a frenzy of controversy between those who saw Lewis as a hero, and those, particularly Native Americans, who saw him as the leading edge of American westward expansion and the destruction of their way of life. The events surrounding Lewis's death, at least within some circles of historians, are as hotly debated as the assassination of President John F. Kennedy, with very partisan adherents to two major theories: murder or suicide.

Because Lewis is so controversial, it is amazing that up to the publication of this volume there were just two biographies of the man, the 1965 account by Richard Dillon, and the best-selling *Undaunted Courage* written by Stephen Ambrose in 1996. Both concentrate on just two aspects of Lewis's life, the expedition for which he is famous and his controversial death. Very little space is devoted to his youth and background, his career in the army, his duties as personal secretary to President Jefferson, and most especially to his tenure as governor of the Louisiana Territory. When these events are briefly discussed in Dillon, Ambrose, and countless articles and books on the expedition, they are always in the context of trying to prefigure or foreshadow Lewis's supposed mental breakdown and suicide. More troubling to a historian is the fact that the Dillon biography has no footnotes or references to support any of its information, and that the Ambrose biography often cites Dillon as its source material!

What was sorely needed in the case of a true biography of Meriwether Lewis was not to rehash the well-known story of the expedition to the Pacific but to discuss those other areas of Lewis's life that formed his character and made him an important and controversial figure, even in his own time. Even the well-worn tale of Lewis's demise receives fresh treatment in this volume, due to its reliance on primary sources and the larger context of health and medicine of the period. Startlingly, this book presents a third possibility regarding Lewis's death, grounded in both historical and scientific evidence, avoiding the clichéd, partisan arguments for either murder or conventional suicide. At this late date and with such paltry remaining evidence from the "crime scene" or in period documents, we will probably never know the answer to the question "how did Meriwether Lewis die?" but in this book Thomas Danisi and John Jackson provide a plausible third scenario. The Danisi and Jackson version of Lewis's death satisfies several problems with the two "conventional" tellings of the story. It is difficult to believe that Thomas Jefferson or William Clark, the two men who knew Lewis best, had reason to cover up Lewis's death (as the murder advocates would have it) by cloaking it in the guise of a suicide, or that they were complicit in a conspiracy against him. Since they both stated that they believed Lewis had taken his own life, it is difficult not to accept these statements to be genuine. Yet it is also difficult to believe that Lewis suffered from such a severe mental illness that he would kill himself. As you will see, Danisi and Jackson have found a plausible middle ground that satisfies these questions. But before readers go quickly thumbing to the final chapter to read about Lewis's death, first consider the new information this book can provide on Lewis's life and achievements.

This biography discusses, perhaps for the first time in any detail, Lewis's important tenure as territorial governor. Since some historians partially attribute the death of Lewis to his inability to function adequately in this post, it is important to take a close look at these years. Was Lewis appointed to a position for which he was ill-suited? Or is it just in hindsight, because of the widely accepted belief that he committed suicide, that his efforts appear to be a failure? In fact, after his return from the West, Lewis was a major figure in the process of remaking the lands he "discovered" between 1804 and 1806 into a mirror image of the East Coast of the United States.[1]

Meriwether Lewis was stridently righteous, narrowly elitist, and in a later time period would have been called a "jingo." He believed in the superiority of American culture and the democratic form of government as it had evolved in the United States. He was a racialist; not a racist, but a racialist, meaning he felt that his culture was superior to all others, and that he had not only a right but a duty and an obligation to enlighten and improve those on a lower racial and cultural rung than himself. Rather than working with the other cultural groups in Upper Louisiana to share the best aspects of the lifeways of all, Lewis looked toward changing the laws and the peoples of the region. He believed that by imposing the economic system, Indian policies, and land laws favored by the United States, he would enlighten the inhabitants and better their lives by bringing democracy and order to the frontier.

In 1808, when Meriwether Lewis arrived in St. Louis to take up his duties as governor, President Thomas Jefferson was just ending his second term as chief executive. His proudest achievement was the successful purchase of the Louisiana Territory from the French, assuring him of the eventual growth of American democracy to the West. Although Jefferson believed in states' rights and distrusted a strong central government, he came to realize during his presidency that staving off the nation's monarchal enemies would take a determined leadership and that the survival of the nation depended upon the spread of democracy throughout the Americas. The first step was to push westward, into the purchased lands that provided space to grow for the young nation.[2] The town of St. Louis would be the logical control center for the American takeover of the trans-Mississippi West. With the arrival of the Americans, the simpler days of the little French-speaking town were gone forever. St. Louis hung onto its French traditions for a time, but in the end overwhelming waves of non-French settlers from Europe and the eastern United States moved in.[3]

The appointment of Meriwether Lewis as governor of the Louisiana Territory and of William Clark as Indian agent for the Far West and general of the territorial militia were more than mere rewards. These two men knew the West better than any other American of their time. They were government employees, continuing to carry out the will of the policymakers, particularly Thomas Jefferson, in Washington, just as they had on their expedition. Now, after surveying the West, the two men could facilitate the absorption of the West into the American sphere of influence.

On March 8, 1808, Meriwether Lewis returned to St. Louis, accompanied by his brother, Reuben, to assume his new office. Being governor of the sprawling Upper Louisiana Territory proved challenging. In 1808 St. Louis was still a rowdy frontier town on the edge of a "wilderness." Lewis was often opposed by factions in St. Louis, many of whom were interested in wresting land from the former French inhabitants. As governor, Lewis set out to accomplish three major goals: revise and codify the laws of Louisiana; facilitate the westward expansion and settlement of Anglo-Americans by obtaining land from and moving native peoples; and safeguarding US property and land laws in the region by building a strong militia, by ensuring the proper placement of installations and troops, and by securing alliances with powerful tribal groups like the Osage.[4] Lewis brought printer and editor Joseph Charless to St. Louis in 1808 to publish the laws of the territory and to counteract propaganda put forth by Lewis's political enemies. Charless founded the *Missouri Gazette*, which became the official mouthpiece for Lewis.[5]

The new laws established by Lewis were heavily influenced by English common law as practiced in Virginia, Lewis's home state, and reflected the overall goals and values of the United States. The laws constituted a radical departure from Spanish laws, under which the territory had formerly been governed. The right of slaves to purchase their freedom, the right of married women to make contracts, and the rights of citizens granted land charters by the king of Spain were all nullified. After 1804 lawyers set up courts with jury trials and the legal representation of both sides.[6]

It was up to Lewis and Clark to organize areas to the west of St. Louis where, it was planned, Indian tribes would be moved. Thomas Jefferson saw American Indians as undeveloped people who could be slowly introduced to "superior" Western culture. He believed that assimilation was possible, but he also came to believe that the process might take a long period of time. It would be better to move the tribes beyond the Mississippi River, Jefferson felt, where their assimilation process could take place gradually and friction with their Euro-American neighbors would be lessened. This was the essence of Jeffersonian Indian policy; to woo or threaten Indian tribes east of the Mississippi and "encourage" them to move west of the river, therefore giving them time to assimilate to the ways of the whites. In contrast with eastern tribes already weakened and vulnerable, the western tribes showed themselves to be less compliant to US desires. Tribal trading partners among the Missouri River tribes were carefully cultivated, while the government also held out the hope of patching relations with the Lakota Sioux and Arikara. These tribes had to accept the idea of allowing transplanted eastern tribes to live in their midst, and also might be coerced into becoming allies of the United States rather than England or Spain. The western tribes were wooed primarily with the carrot, but Lewis never relinquished the threat to use force against them as well. When the Osage defied US authority, he halted trade with them, declared that they no longer enjoyed US protection, and invited their enemies to wage war on them.[7]

Governor Lewis supported the land policies and property rights of individuals under the Anglo-American and the Franco-Spanish regimes but saw the status of Indian lands as one in which various degrees of arm-twisting and offers of annuities and presents could be used to gain clear title for his own people. Lewis supported the claims of locals who held Spanish land grants against a faction of his own people who wanted to nullify all of these claims. As a result he was greatly liked by the old French fur trader elite in St. Louis.[8]

In implementing various policies to achieve his goals and those of the government, Lewis made many enemies and had a stormy couple of years in office prior to his death. Not only did he fight factions led by land grabbers but his own territorial secretary, Frederick Bates, was less than pleased with him. Bates, jealous of Lewis, certainly saw himself as the better man. Although Lewis could often be aloof, abrasive, and build a small slight into a very long and lasting animosity, Bates's hatred for his superior was excessive. Bates took his enmity with Lewis to extremes, writing letters behind the governor's back to undermine his position in the territory. The discord in the governor's own office slowed Meriwether Lewis's goals and hamstrung his policies.[9]

All these aspects of Lewis's governorship are treated in detail in this book. It is hard to say if he had lived past 1809 what might have been different about the story of westward expansion. As a government employee, he was carrying out a larger policy established by the president of the United States, Thomas Jefferson. He was subject to changes in administration, as evidenced by James Madison's presidency beginning in 1809, and to possible removal and discipline if he displeased his superiors in Washington.

Often lost in discussions of Meriwether Lewis's life, because of the controversy surrounding his death, are his accomplishments while in office. Lewis achieved all of the major goals of his administration and laid the groundwork for US hegemony in the trans-Mississippi region. Subsequent governors added no new significant directions or policies to those he had set in place. His methods may have, at times, been unorthodox and imperfectly realized, but he was nevertheless successful, unlike his predecessor, James Wilkinson, in winning over the French inhabitants, in formalizing a treaty with the Osage, in returning the Mandan chief Sheheke-shote to his people, in codifying the laws of the territory, and in solidifying the US presence in the region.[10]

Lewis's most significant failure during this period was his seeming inability to rewrite the expedition journals for publication. It has been referenced as a colossal case of writer's block, as a case of criminal negligence, to allow such an important project to fail. The journal project was indeed important, but Danisi and Jackson present evidence that Lewis was far from idle during the period. As governor he had to juggle his priorities, and service to his country in his official position overshadowed his efforts to add important information to the annals of exploration and science.

Most public perceptions of Meriwether Lewis are colored by reading the available secondary sources, but few people have ever read anything Lewis wrote other than the expedition journals and preparatory letters and invoices for that journey. Thomas Danisi and John Jackson have spent many years in the study of the surviving primary documents written by and about Lewis. They have ferreted out several new sources of information, including those written by supportive friends of Lewis, such as the Samuel Latham Mitchill correspondence and the crucial Mahlon Dickerson diary, both of which reveal far more about Lewis's life than has ever been offered before in a biography. They also introduce some of Lewis's major opponents who tried to thwart his efforts in the Louisiana Territory. Danisi and Jackson have attempted to present a full picture of who Meriwether Lewis was and why his reputation should rest on far more than just his leadership of the 1804–1806 expedition to the Pacific.

If the book is flawed it is in presenting Lewis with few metaphorical warts or blemishes. Lewis was far from perfect as a human being. There were things he was capable of doing, and things that escaped his abilities. By several measures of appreciation Lewis was probably a genius intellectually but was often difficult to get along with, stubborn, and impatient. He alienated many with his rigid class consciousness and sometimes mercurial temper.

There will be many who will disagree with the conclusions made by the authors in this biography, particularly those referenced in their controversial spin on Lewis's death. Yet their research is impeccable, painstaking, and thorough, and there is much here that will be new to even the most dedicated Lewis and Clark scholar.

This book is the result of many long, frustrating years of work, first in painstaking research, then in precise writing, and finally in finding a publisher. All of this effort has only improved the product. I have been privileged to be a part of this process, seeing the work at various stages in its creation. There are those in the community of historians who did not want this book to be published, and I have also been a witness to this. They tried to stop the book in the prepublication stage and insisted on key alterations and deletions during the peer-review process because they disagreed with some of its theories and conclusions. In effect, they wished to censor what you are about to read, for the deletions would have removed what is new and enlightening about this work. Now, happily, Prometheus Books has stepped up to publish this work in its entirety, all of its theories and conclusions intact.

This book is the quintessence of good historical writing, by which the historian examines the available documents and other evidence, presents the information in a lucid and readable style, and offers plausible conclusions based on the evidence for the approval or rejection of the reader. If history and historical writing is condemned to slog along forever in the same well-worn rut, if historians are to be censured or effectively censored by their peers for arriving at different or original conclusions based on evidence, if the reader of history is not to be allowed to reach his or her own conclusions by assessing the persuasiveness of the historian's argument, the profession of being a historian will be diminished immeasurably.

Danisi and Jackson present a new, fresh, and disarmingly different take on the life of Meriwether Lewis. You may not agree with all of its conclusions, but you will never look at Lewis as a historical figure in the same way again once you have read it. For me, that is the essence of good historical writing; take me to new places, show me different scenes, provide new theories and explanations, elevate my consciousness, and inform me anew about the past.

NOTES

1. Examples of historians discounting the later lives of the explorers, either directly or through implication, can be found in Stephen E. Ambrose, *Undaunted Courage: Meriwether Lewis, Thomas Jefferson and the Opening of the American West* (New York: Simon & Schuster, 1996); Richard Dillon, *Meriwether Lewis: A Biography* (New York: Coward-McCann, 1965); and David Lavender, *The Way to the Western Sea* (New York: Harper and Row, 1988). Most get bogged down in telling the story of Lewis's death while glossing over what he did for the last three years of his life.

2. Drew McCoy, "Jefferson and the Empire of Liberty," in *Major Problems in the Early Republic, 1787–1848*, ed. Sean Wilentz, 109–14 (Lexington, MA: D.C. Heath and Company, 1992).

3. Jay Gitlin, "'Avec Bien Du Regret': The Americanization of Creole St. Louis," *Gateway Heritage* 9 (Spring 1989): 2–11; Frederic Louis Billon, *Annals of St. Louis in Its Early Days under the French and Spanish Dominations, 1764–1804* (New York: Arno Press, 1971); Stella Drumm, ed., "Glimpses of the Past: Descriptions of St. Louis," *Missouri Historical Society* 1 (March 1934): 20–30; Charles E. Peterson, "Colonial St. Louis," *Bulletin of the Missouri Historical Society Bulletin* 3 (April 1947): 94–111; (July 1947): 133–49; 4 (October 1947): 11–30.

4. These conclusions are based on a number of sources, including some manuscript letters and information in Jon Kukla, *A Wilderness So Immense* (New York: Knopf, 2003), pp. 284–309, 333–40, as well as letters published in Clarence Edwin Carter, ed., *The Territorial Papers of the United States*, vols. 13 and 14 (Washington, DC: GPO, 1948), hereafter cited as Carter, *TP*; and Donald Jackson, ed., *Letters of the Lewis and Clark Expedition, with Related Documents, 1783–1854* (Urbana: University of Illinois Press, 1962), hereafter cited as Jackson, *LLC*.

5. Unpublished article by Grace Lewis Miller, Grace Lewis Miller Collection, Jefferson National Expansion Memorial Archives; William H. Lyon, "Joseph Charless, Father of Missouri Journalism," *Bulletin of the Missouri Historical Society* 17 (January 1961): 133–45.

6. William E. Foley, "Galleries, Gumbo, and 'La Guignolee,'" *Gateway Heritage* 10 (Summer 1989): 3–17; Stella Drumm, ed., "Glimpses of the Past: The Transfer of Upper Louisiana, the Papers of Amos Stoddard," *Missouri Historical Society* 2 (May/September 1935): 87–91; Frederick A. Hodes, *Beyond the Frontier: A History of St. Louis to 1821* (Tucson: Patrice Press, 2004), p. 212; Stuart Banner, *Legal Systems in Conflict* (Norman: University of Oklahoma Press, 2000), p. 41; LeeAnn Whites, Mary C. Neth, and Gary R. Kremer, eds., *Women in Missouri History* (Columbia: University of Missouri Press, 2004), p. 21.

7. For general background on Jeffersonian Indian policy see James P. Ronda, *Lewis and Clark among the Indians* (Lincoln: University of Nebraska Press, 1984), pp. 4–8, and Anthony F. C. Wallace, "'The Obtaining Lands': Thomas Jefferson and the Native Americans," in *Thomas Jefferson and the Changing West: From Conquest to Conservation*, ed. James P. Ronda (Albuquerque: University of New Mexico Press/St. Louis: Missouri Historical Society Press, 1997). See also Herbert S. Channick, "William Henry Harrison Steals Western Illinois from the Sauk and Fox," *Illinois Heritage* 1 (Winter 1998): 6–9; Kathleen DuVal, "Choosing Enemies: The Prospects for an Anti-American Alliance in the Louisiana Territory," *Arkansas Historical Quarterly* 62 (Autumn 2003): 233–52; Tanis C. Thorne, *The Many Hands of My Relations: French and Indians on the Lower Missouri* (Columbia: University of Missouri Press, 1996); Letter, Thomas Jefferson to William Henry Harrison, February 27, 1803, *Letters of Jefferson*; Indian Speech to Jefferson and Dearborn, January 4, 1806, in *Letters of the Lewis and Clark Expedition*, ed. Donald Jackson, 1: 284–89; Sean Wilentz, "Thomas Jefferson on Indians and Blacks, 1787," in *Major Problems in the Early Republic, 1787–1848*, 122–26 (Lexington, MA: D. C. Heath and Company, 1992).

8. William E. Foley and C. David Rice, *The First Chouteaus: River Barons of Early St. Louis* (Urbana: University of Illinois Press, 1983); William E. Foley and C. David Rice, "Compounding the Risks: International Politics, Wartime Dislocations and Auguste Chouteau's Fur Trading Operations, 1792–1815," *Bulletin of the Missouri Historical Society* 34 (April 1978): 131–39.

9. David B. Gracy II, "Moses Austin and the Development of the Missouri Lead Industry," *Gateway Heritage* 1 (Spring 1981): 42–48; Hodes, *Beyond the Frontier*; Dick Steward, "'With the Scepter of a Tyrant': John Smith T. and the Mineral Wars," *Gateway Heritage* 14 (Fall 1993): 24–37; Thomas M. Marshall, ed., *The Life and Papers of Frederick Bates*, 2 vols. (St. Louis: Missouri Historical Society, 1926), hereafter cited as Marshall, *FB*.

10. *Records of the Office of the Secretary of War*, RG107, SW to ML, July 15, 1809, M221, MS, and ML to SW, August 18, 1809, MS, and Pierre Chouteau Jr. to SW, September 1, 1809, MS (translation), National Archives and Records Administration. Hereafter cited as NARA; *Missouri Gazette*, November 16, 23, 1809.

Preface

Far hence be each accusing thought![1]

This biography is the belated defense of a good man. We hope to correct some of the flawed assumptions and speculations that have taken root from uncritical reliance on the journals of the Lewis and Clark expedition. Fixation on that great adventure has allowed the more complex truth about Meriwether Lewis to wither, a great national hero to become forgotten. In trying to find the truth inside the myth, several theories have been developed that have led to vigorous disputes.

Most of the biographies of Meriwether Lewis flatter his memory, but with reservations. The first was a mere five-thousand-word letter to the editor of the expedition narrative written four years after Lewis's death by the one man who should have best understood him. What Thomas Jefferson wrote in 1813 in response to the request to enliven a dull book has been taken as intimacy scarred over by disappointment that an enlightened protégé died ignominiously. This study hopes to show that what led to Jefferson's assumption of suicide was his failure to fully understand the circumstances. Thomas Jefferson wrote an apology for himself that many have taken as a veiled disappointment in the son he never had.

The following year 1,400 copies of the expedition narrative, mostly based on the daily accounts of William Clark, were published. Captain

Lewis had written sporadically in bursts of often brilliant description. That he had not composed the full report as he went along, or completed it afterward, has been taken as a mark against him by those who hungered for more than what Clark was able to wring out of daily experiences. In 1893 the not entirely careful editor Elliott Coues attempted to enliven the narrative with more material on natural history. This was followed on the hundredth anniversary of the expedition by a fully annotated publication of the journals, edited by the wide-ranging historian Reuben Gold Thwaites. In 1980 Gary Moulton and his staff began the publication of a definitive multivolume updating of the journals and related documents.

In a magnificent collection, *Letters of the Lewis and Clark Expedition, with Related Documents 1783–1854*, Donald Jackson published in 1962 and revised in 1978 an invaluable collection of most of the associated documents. But like the former editors of the journals, he also exercised editorial discretion, which sometimes left out important clues about Lewis.

The book-length biography *Meriwether Lewis of the Lewis and Clark Expedition* had been written by Charles Morrow Wilson in 1934 but was found wanting. John Bakeless followed in 1947 with *Lewis and Clark, Partners in Discovery*. In 1962 the popular novelist Vardis Fisher's *Suicide or Murder* introduced a largely invented death scenario that he knew was already disproven but he wrote it anyhow. The popular historian Richard Dillon noted the above books in his 1965 *Meriwether Lewis: A Biography*. Thirty years later, in 1996, Stephen E. Ambrose astonished the history community by the phenomenal success of his *Undaunted Courage: Meriwether Lewis, Thomas Jefferson, and the Opening of the American West*. Largely reminiscent of Dillon, this was designed to appeal to a broad audience, and did, to the amazement of fellow historians who had been grinding out learned arguments that few beyond academia read. Ambrose set the stage for the flood of material meant to celebrate the bicentennial celebration of the expedition.

When Dillon wrote his Lewis biography in 1965, he found "sixteen works, including juvenile titles, on the two men."[2] At that time, and since, there are also a number of scholarly studies dealing with the explorers and one—sadly—unfinished manuscript by the truly dedicated Grace Lewis Miller. The bicentennial celebration of the Lewis and Clark expedition ended four years of intense promotion with shelves sagging under the weight of books written to renew interest in the men behind the great adventure. Almost all rely on the various editions of the famous journals or on secondary studies derived from them, with little deeper probing into a fuller assessment of Lewis and his life after the expedition.

Meriwether Lewis is most often faulted for not keeping a running journal during the expedition and not completing a narrative book at its end. Anything from Lewis might have been more interesting than William Clark's terse daily accounts. But the officer in charge of a complex operation was not writing for the edification of those celebrating the bicentennial. He had been assigned a specific, difficult job requiring personal initiative and he saw it carried out amazingly well. No matter the after-the-fact invention by those focused on a chummy joint command, senior officer Captain Lewis was ultimately responsible for everything that took place during those three years.

For a proper understanding of the contributions of Meriwether Lewis to the development of the nation, it is necessary to go beyond previously accepted evidence. What the explorer did, or failed to do, *after* the adventure reveals his character and ability to administer the vast territory he defined. At considerable personal cost, he promoted the best interests of the nation during a period when Louisiana was viewed as not quite the bargain it initially appeared. Had tragedy not intervened, might Lewis have become one of the leading members of the famed Virginia dynasties carrying the young country through the formative decades of the new North American century?

Meriwether Lewis was born just as the Americans gathered the determination to separate themselves from a corrupt Europe. At the age of five, just when a boy needed a father, he lost him to the Revolution. During his adolescence his stepfather also died. The price that the son paid toward the creation of the nation was a lifelong responsibility for a widowed mother, his sister and brother, and an inherited second family of half-siblings. He never denied his obligation to mother, family, friend, or country.

Except for the intervention of his neighbor Thomas Jefferson, young Lewis might have lived as just another Virginia planter and rustic gentleman with a few years of frontier military service. Seeing something more in the boy growing up a few miles from Monticello, the architect of independence helped ground him in an appreciation and understanding of natural history. When Jefferson became president he immediately brought his protégé, then a young army officer, into the inner circles of his administration and introduced him to the leading political and scientific men of the nation.

Soon after taking on Captain Lewis as his personal secretary, President Jefferson began preparing him for a more challenging duty. The purchase of the Louisiana Territory finally provided an opportunity to realize a long-standing dream of Jefferson's. For a transcontinental exploration, he wanted a field leader he could trust to do more than record distances and note land-marks. At the beginning of the nineteenth century many of those obliged to pass information across distances were competent correspondents. Their writing was communication, not art, and Mr. Jefferson wanted brilliance. It can only be guessed what the man who had crossed the continent and expe-rienced its wonders might have written, because it was President Jefferson who desperately needed a hand he could trust at the helm of the badly administered Louisiana Territory. By appointing Lewis as governor, the mentor may have sacrificed his protégé.

All too often the sparse record of what developed in Louisiana depends on the words of Governor Lewis's enemies. To gain a better understanding, the authors of this biography have examined the available documents and find that trail is often narrow, biased, or misunderstood. Dependence on the expedition journals has resulted in a one-dimensional image. Roughly two-thirds of previous biographies had depended on the great adventure and only a third were devoted to the life of Lewis. An exhaustive search of archival records has recovered new material and a better understanding of the forces bearing upon Meriwether Lewis after the expedition as he initi-ated the first steps in westward expansion. Original documents have been uncovered and carefully studied in over three hundred reels of microfilm as well as countless papers from national, public, and private collections.

Those who have described the story of the Lewis and Clark expedition have popularized an image that is much a matter of limited perception and not always well-founded interpretation. Because writers have focused pri-marily on the expedition journals and letters, the clarity of what happened —and what happened afterward—has sometimes been clouded by inven-tion that has in some cases passed into accepted understanding. This study tries to adhere to matters as they developed at the time rather than from a later-day overview.

Even his mentor, Jefferson, out of power in 1809 but still interested in the development of the territory, misunderstood what Lewis accomplished as governor of the Louisiana Territory in a brief eighteen months. That was more than his predecessors had done in the past four years. A strong and able governor, Lewis solved difficult problems relating to the proper admin-istration of the justice system, illicit trading, and a looming Indian war along the upper Mississippi. It was not a failure of his overburdened administra-tion but an inescapable lifelong affliction, misunderstood and badly treated, that became the fatal blow. There was no load of burdening debt, nor was there a conspiracy to replace him. When Meriwether Lewis died on the

Natchez Trace returning to Washington in 1809, this biography hopes to show, there was no murder in the wilderness.

NOTES

1. These lines are taken from Alexander Wilson's poem "Particulars of the Death of Captain Lewis," *Port Folio* 7 (January 1812): 38.

2. Richard Dillon, *Meriwether Lewis: A Biography* (Santa Cruz, CA: Western Tanager Press, 1965), p. xvi.

Acknowledgments

The completion of this study owes debts to many institutions and individuals who have provided data and insights. We owe much gratitude to the following Missouri institutions, especially the ones located in St. Louis, which proved to be bastions of archival information: the Missouri Historical Society; Washington University School of Medicine, Bernard Becker Medical Library, Rare Book Department; the Jefferson National Expansion Memorial Library; the Missouri Botanical Library; St. Louis University's Pius Library; Washington University's Olin Library; and the Recorder of Deeds and the Civil Court Archives for the City of St. Louis.

The Missouri Historical Society's archives and library personnel provided years of service, with much thanks to Dennis Northcott, Molly Kodner, and Chris Gordon for their archival expertise; Carol Verble, who procured microfilm from all over the country; Emily Troxell Jaycox, who assisted with maps and localities; and to the library staff, Edna, Jason, and Randy, who fetched countless books and made photocopies with remarkable patience.

The Bernard Becker Medical Library's Rare Book Department provided their extensive holdings on early American and European medicine and is credited with the entire medical aspect of this study, with much thanks to Lilla Vekerdy and Martha Riley, who were pummeled with innumerable requests.

The Jefferson National Expansion Memorial Library, part of the National Park Service, which holds the collection of Grace Lewis Miller, a dedicated historian who was, after research of thirty years, disappointed by her inability to bring her magnificent collection of data to publication. The Miller Collection is a veritable treasure trove of impeccable details.

Doug Holland, the Missouri Botanical Library's director, opened its extensive holdings to our researches. St. Louis University's Pius Library, which holds several microfilm and microfiche collections, and Washington University's Olin Library supplied gargantuan amounts of background material. Mike Everman, the Civil Court archivist for the City of St. Louis, was a stalwart of computer printouts for Lewis and Clark court cases. Patsy Luebbert from the Missouri State Archives we personally thank for enduring fifteen-plus years from two avid scholars, as well as Ken Winn for supporting historical research over the years. And Michael Brodhead, from the National Archives Central Plains region, who helped scour Lewis correspondence on microfilm.

There were other individuals who, in immeasurable ways, broadened the scope of this study. Archivists from the National Archives and Library of Congress in Washington, DC, provided the groundwork to identify pockets of strategic information: Michael P. Musick, Gerard W. Gawalt, Milton O. Gustafson, Wayne Decesar, James Hutson, Brenda Beasley Kepley, Lois South, William Davis, David Wigdor, Richard W. Peuser, and Bradley E. Gernand.

We also thank the following institutions for the loan of microfilm: University of Virginia, Alderman Library of the Lewis, Marks, and Anderson families; New York University Bobst Library's collection of the Gallatin papers; the New York Historical Society for their extensive collections and microfilm resources. In addition, we thank the Museum of the City of New York for allowing the perusal of the Samuel Latham Mitchill papers, the New Jersey Historical Society for permitting the examination of original documents from the Mahlon Dickerson collection, the American Philosophical Society for providing important entry date information of Lewis's Eastern Journal, and the Lewis and Clark Trail Heritage Foundation for their grant in 2004 and for their resourceful scholarly journal, *We Proceeded On*.

Still others we thank: Jane Henley and Bob Doerk for contributions on the Lewis and Meriwether families; Dr. Seth Eisen for his epidemiological expertise; Dr. Daniel Goldberg, a malariologist on the faculty at Washington University School of Medicine in St. Louis, Missouri; historians William Foley and W. Raymond Wood for their scholarly support; Jan Fitzgerald and genealogist Coralee Paul; Jim Williams for pointing the way to Lewis and Clark Masonic literature; and Walter Winchester for allowing the intricate inspection of the Denslow Masonic library once located in Trenton, Missouri, now in Clearwater, Florida.

Finally, we owe much appreciation to Bob Moore from the National Park Service in St. Louis, a Lewis and Clark historian, for reading our first draft and making suggestions on every page of the manuscript, and to Ann Sale Dahl for her scrupulous and helpful editorial suggestions.

Abbreviations

N ote: Abbreviations for many names and sources are used
throughout for brevity.

BSB	Benjamin Smith Barton
FB	Frederick Bates
DB	Daniel Bissell
RB	Russell Bissell
PC	Pierre Chouteau
WC	William Clark
HD	Henry Dearborn
WD	War Department
WE	William Eustis
AG	Albert Gallatin
RG	Record Group—US government designation
WHH	William Henry Harrison
TJ	Thomas Jefferson
ML	Meriwether Lewis
JMA	James Madison
LM	Lucy Marks

CM	Catherine Mitchill
SLM	Samuel Latham Mitchill
JMO	James Monroe
CWP	Charles Willson Peale
MJR	Martha Jefferson Randolph
GR	Gilbert Russell
WS	William Simmons
AS	Amos Stoddard
SW	Secretary of War
JW	James Wilkinson
APS	American Philosophical Society
ASP	*American State Papers*
BFP-MHS	Bates Family Papers
CFC-MHS	Clark Family Collection
FL (Betts and Bear)	*Family Letters of Thomas Jefferson*
GLM	Grace Lewis Miller Collection
JMA-LOC	James Madison Papers, Library of Congress
JNEM	Jefferson National Expansion Memorial Library, St. Louis
JAMA	*Journal of the American Medical Association*
JLCE (Moulton)	*Journals of the Lewis and Clark Expedition*
LLC (Jackson)	*Letters of the Lewis and Clark Expedition*
FB (Marshall)	*Life and Papers of Frederick Bates*
MLC	Meriwether Lewis Collection
MHS	Missouri Historical Society
MCNY	Museum of the City of New York
NARA	National Archives and Records Administration
NARA-CP	National Archives and Records Administration, College Park
NJHS	New Jersey Historical Society
NYHS	New York Historical Society
TP (Carter)	*Territorial Papers of the United States*
TJ-LOC	Thomas Jefferson Papers, Library of Congress

ONE

Prelude to a Great Adventure

The soldier brave of dauntless heart[1]

The presidential election of 1800 had been vicious and toxic. Failing to foresee an impending embarrassment, Thomas Jefferson had already chosen James Madison to be a member of his cabinet council and depended on him to quell party fear of a split vote. But when the college of electors assembled in the muddy new capital in February 1801, it took an embarrassing thirty-six votes before the deadlock between Jefferson and Aaron Burr was finally broken. On February 17, 1801, the House of Representatives chose Thomas Jefferson as the third president of the United States. Next day he wrote to the Revolutionary War veteran Henry Dearborn insisting that he take the job of secretary of war. However, it was mid-May before the president completed his cabinet by replacing Samuel Dexter with Albert Gallatin as secretary of the treasury. The Swiss-born former congressman favored economy and fiscal responsibility in government. The appointment left no doubt that Jefferson intended to remove influential Federalists and replace them with men he could trust to help develop his plans for the nation.[2]

Jefferson was a conversationalist, not an orator. When he was sworn in on March 4 he squeaked through an inaugural address that declared that "we are all republicans . . . we are all federalists . . . a rising nation, spread over a wise and fruitful land . . . advancing rapidly to destinies beyond the reach of mortal eye."[3]

President by the thinnest of margins, Mr. Jefferson had never been west of the Appalachian Mountains, as had few men of his acquaintance. According to the historian Dale Van Every, "He was an easterner who had spent his life in the study, in legislative halls, and in administrative offices. His greatest interests, aside from an intense and all-encompassing scientific curiosity, had been in democratic doctrine, constitutional law, and diplomacy."[4] At a time when the aging heroes of the Revolution were giving way to veterans of the western Indian wars, the president had no military experience and an uncertain appreciation of the profession of arms. And he faced an army swollen out of proportion by Inspector General Alexander Hamilton's knee-jerk reaction to a French threat in 1798 during the Adams administration.

In what might have seemed to be the insignificant appointment of a personal secretary, the fifty-seven-year-old intellectual selected a soldier thirty-one years younger than himself. Past intimacy led the president to believe that the young officer possessed talents that would be very useful for an important role he had in mind. Jefferson approached the recently promoted Capt. Meriwether Lewis because they were well acquainted "from his being of my neighborhood."[5] That was something of an understatement because Jefferson had known Lewis's father and other relatives who were part of the Charlottesville neighborhood around Monticello. From beginnings as tidewater Virginians, over the years those families had followed colonial expansion into the Virginia piedmont. They knew each other well.

The home of William Lewis and Lucy Meriwether, called Locust Hill, was about ten miles west of Monticello. After the birth of a daughter their first son was born on August 18, 1774. That made Meriwether Lewis a child of the new nation, born at the beginning of the Revolution and growing up during the conflict. When his son was just a toddler, William Lewis went off to war. The boy had little to remember of the officer who came home for brief visits to look after the crops and rode off again on a good horse. He had been the third man to sign the Albemarle County declaration of independence from an English king. The boy was just five in mid-November 1779, the last time he saw his father ride away in the rain. Later, a rider came from uncle Nicholas Lewis's home to tell his mother that her husband had gotten soaked trying to cross a swollen stream and had wheezed his life away from pneumonia. Only later did they get to visit the grave.

Locust Hill saw its share of uniformed men during those war years.

Uncle Nicholas Lewis led his regiment against British-instigated Cherokees and was well respected in the community. His mother's brother, uncle Nicholas Meriwether, stepped in to help manage the over a thousand-acre plantation and twenty-four slaves.

In the winter of his father's death there were four thousand British prisoners penned in barracks at the Cart Farm along Ivy Creek. Those were the British prisoners who surrendered near the Saratoga battlefield in upstate New York in 1777. When paroled redcoat officers slipped away and tried to impose their supercilious presence upon Locust Hill, the young widow Lucy Lewis drove them away. The children remembered the tension.

With three children to protect, there was no question that the young widow should remarry. Six months after her husband's death Lucy Lewis married Capt. John Marks, whose health prevented him from further participation in the war. They moved to Winchester when the terrible British cavalry officer Banastre Tarleton raided the country. He failed to seize important rebels like Thomas Jefferson but left Albemarle County razed and shattered.

The war lasted eight years, from 1775 until 1783. After the peace veterans had difficulties settling down. Despite his health, Captain Marks decided to follow his commander, Gen. John Mathews, and established a plantation on the Broad River in Oglethorpe County, Georgia. There his stepson lived on a new frontier with the elbow room a growing boy needs to range the woods and protect the stump-patched fields from varmints. Admirers have concocted stories that he studied and learned to identify the plants and animals he found in those rambles through the post oak and blackjack parklands. But he was just a growing boy, and mastering natural history wasn't the concern of a berry picker and hunter.

When he was thirteen Meriwether was sent back to Albemarle County to be better schooled. Soon he was studying English grammar, Latin, math, a bit of natural science, and was reading geography on his own.[6] Most of what is known about the education and early life of Meriwether Lewis is written in his own hand, in the letters that his mother received and carefully preserved, not as documents to enlighten some future researcher but rather as proofs of their devotion to each other. Due to the wanderings of a boy in pursuit of an education or a son following a military career, the letters that Lucy Marks wrote in return have been lost. But those must have expressed a mother's concern for his health in an unhealthy world, or a widow's concern about a family inheritance that was scattered over four states in vague claims to often unsurveyed lands. Some warrants for land had to do with the father's service during the Revolution. That was a reminder that William Lewis died, not before the enemies' guns, but from the erosion of his health during a life in the field, the same challenging career that her darling son was now also pursuing.

It had been no small thing for each of them when the young boy left the Broad River frontier in spring 1787 to travel north along the Appalachian Mountains, where hostile Indians still ranged.[7] He rode accompanied by someone, a trusted slave perhaps, to the home of his uncle Nicholas Lewis, where he stayed for almost a year while they cast about for a tutor.[8]

It was the practice in a time of few publicly sponsored schools that an education beyond the basics had to be privately arranged and paid. The best scholars in an area were usually ministers who had been educated in England or Europe and taught subjects like grammar, Latin, classic literature, history, and philosophy. After an initial period of uncertainty Lewis began his studies with Parson Mathew Maury, the son of Thomas Jefferson's teacher. In his quest for an education young Lewis later studied with Dr. Charles Everitt and finally the kindly Rev. James Waddell.

Often students would board with their teachers, so studies were an intense, full-time dedication to the disciplines of each subject taken in a concentrated dose before moving on to another. Some boys burned out under the pressure but Meriwether applied himself so diligently that his cousin William D. Meriwether felt he was well enough founded in English grammar that he could read geography on his own and save the tuition. Later, to save money when he studied with Parson Maury, the scholar lived with his uncle Peachy Gilmer.

His younger cousin Peachy Gilmer later described Meriwether as "always remarkable for persevereance, which in the early period of his life seemed nothing more than obstinacy in pursuing the trifles that employ that age; a martial temper, great steadiness of purpose, self-possession, and undaunted courage. His person was stiff and without grace, bow-legged, awkward, formal, and almost without flexibility. His face was comely and by many considered handsome."[9]

The young scholar could afford a good education. Under the transplanted English rules of primogeniture, he, not his mother, inherited the father's estate. A large plantation of almost two thousand acres worked by twenty-four slaves, 147 gallons of whiskey probably distilled on the premises, and £520 in cash was a large responsibility.[10] That made young Meriwether one of those boys who, losing a father at an early age, tries to become his surrogate. The letters that survive demonstrate his concern for his widowed mother, Lucy, but that did not make him a mother's boy.

At eighteen, Meriwether was an adult, perhaps too soon, when he learned from his older sister, Jane Anderson, that their stepfather, Capt. John Marks, had died. Once more a widow, Lucy Marks had written expressing a desire to be nearer to her married daughter and the grandchildren.

When Meriwether responded to that yearning in October 1791, he did not see how he could get away from his schooling for another eighteen months or two years. The letter ended with a curious comment: "It is currently reported here that you are Mrs. Harvey."[11] By the following April he relented and wrote to his mother that he was having a carriage built at Monticello, Jefferson's home, which should be ready by May 12. Lewis brought his widowed mother back to Virginia, settled in at the family estate Locust Hill, and for about a year followed the life of a Virginia planter and young blood.[12]

That was an age that gave scant recognition to childhood and none at all to adolescence. Meriwether became an adult young and had a lot of early life squeezed out of him, replaced with responsibilities he hadn't sought and might in some deep, buried place resent. The other part of his education had not been overlooked. Through the example and advice of his uncle Nicholas Lewis, he learned how to manage his inheritance. That meant riding the fields to ensure that the crops were properly planted, tended, and harvested and that the field hands kept at their work. Those black slaves were under the supervision of an overseer but there was no doubt who was the young master.

How the boy was turning out was noticed by their neighbor. With the special interest of someone who had been through a similar loss of a father at about the same age, Thomas Jefferson had watched the young Meriwether grow into a responsible young man. It is difficult to pinpoint when a mutually shared curiosity about natural science began between Jefferson and Meriwether Lewis. But it ended for the moment when Lewis put on a uniform.

Meriwether was the son of a soldier of the Revolution and the ward of a soldier uncle. Everyone who mattered in his life had worn an officer's epaulette—captains Lewis, Marks, and Uncle Nicholas Lewis. The need for adventure was upon him and when he was twenty Lewis volunteered for a militia company that was being raised to suppress a rebellion by whiskey distillers in western Pennsylvania. Twenty-year-old Lewis was responding to Father Washington's call to put down what was seen as a tax rebellion.

Farmers who had crossed the Appalachian Mountain chain had no easy way of getting their produce to market. Bulky sacks could not be packed across the mountains profitably and floating them down the Ohio and the Mississippi risked grave sickness like yellow fever and malaria.[13] Lacking a convenient market for their crops, frontiersmen had learned to concentrate their wheat, rye, or corn into more portable potables. They had been outraged when the nation specifically taxed what amounted to the only resort of isolated pioneers.

In 1794 a new federal law required the registration of whiskey stills. The eight gallons that a still produced sold for a dollar a gallon. But the tax on them was fifty-six cents. When the notorious land speculator Gen. John Neville tried to fine a local man $250 for failing to register his still, the irate local farmers ran him off and tried to force him to resign his commission. As mobs gathered, shots were exchanged. Maj. James McFarlane led five hundred protestors against the embattled Neville house, where he was shot and killed. Taking this escalation of protest as a test of federal authority, President George Washington ordered the secretary of war to request the governors of four states to raise over twelve thousand militia troops.[14]

No matter that those fellow Virginians across the mountains had no other way of converting their land-locked crops into desperately needed cash, Lewis the young planter joined the local militia. When he rode off on a good plantation horse to sow wild oats with the militia, there was no escaping his responsibilities. He kept his mother reassured about his health, as he did later when he was with the army on the frontier. But he also included allusions in his letters to the high times he and his comrades were having, a suggestion that he believed his mother was no prude and would understand some high jinks. He teased that he might return with "an Insergiant Girl . . . bearing the title of Mrs. Lewis."[15]

The Revolutionary War Gen. Daniel Morgan was a hard man who crushed the tax protest and left a substantial force to police the rebel heartland. Most of the taxation minutemen went home, but Lewis liked the posturing and illusions of field and camp and volunteered to stay on with the occupation force. That was more fun than being a farmer, and he was willing to pay an overseer named Carrell twenty pounds a year to look after his business.[16]

Young Meriwether enjoyed the autumn outing, the amateur display of martial ardor, the good fellowship, "the mountains of beef and oceans of whiskey."[17] Lewis was a Virginia buck on an outing and probably chased away the cold October damp with the local distillation. As winter closed in, the occupying force cut timber for huts on the property of the slain leader of the protest, James McFarlane.

No hint of sympathetic consideration crept into the letters Ensign Lewis wrote home. For him the Whiskey Rebellion was just a lark. He probably drew little distinction between enforcers and the accused and developed a personal relationship during the winter 1794–1795 with the McFarlane brothers; James, John, Andrew, and Lewis were not so much enemies than roistering drinking companions.

There was a moment of tenderness on January 15, 1795, when Capt. Thomas Walker died. Meriwether looked to the necessary arrangements, a walnut post fence around the plot but no gravestone lest unredeemed rebels despoil it. The deceased was the son of Thomas Walker, the founder of Charlottesville and an associate of Mr. Jefferson. Lewis wrote a letter to the captain's father to ease the loss and another on May 23 before leaving the McFarlane farm, confirming that he had planted the six willows that the grieving parent sent to shade the grave.[18]

By then the militiamen knew that last August Gen. Anthony Wayne's legion had defeated the British-instigated tribes at a place called Fallen Timbers in northwestern Ohio. That was an overdue victory after two terrible previous defeats to General Harmar and General St. Clair.

Lewis rationalized his escape from family responsibility in a letter to his mother. His decision to join the Legion of the United States could be explained: "So violently opposed is my governing passion for rambling to the wishes of all my friends that I am led intentionally to err and then have vanity enough to hope for forgiveness. I do not know how to account for the Quixottic disposition of mine . . . than that of having inherited it in right of the Meriwether Family." In other words her "ever sincere tho wandering son" shifted his guilt to his mother's side of the family.[19]

When his discharge loomed, Lewis transferred to the regular army, at the same rank of ensign, on May 1, 1795.[20] Assigned to the Second Sub-Legion, he was at the Greenville headquarters later that year when the defeated tribes agreed to a treaty. That was Lewis's first experience seeing real tribesmen instead of the beggarly basket makers who still hung around the fringes of the planter's Virginia. He didn't understand the long-winded speeches of the placative elders but could not have missed the sullen acceptance of the defeated warriors. In the pomposities of treaty making, the United States ended the forty-year-long war for the Ohio country.

Army life was still fun although Lewis had to endure the war stories of brother officers who had seen real fighting and looked down their noses at whiskey taxers. Too much glory was hard to swallow. On September 24 while in his cups, Ensign Lewis challenged a Lieutenant Elliott.[21] As dueling was against regulations in Wayne's army, on November 6 he was called before a court martial.[22]

After a week of deliberation a sympathetic panel of fellow officers con-cluded that Ensign Lewis was innocent of all charges. However, he was properly chastised and now thought "that the army is a school of debauchery" as well as a proven school of experience and prudence.[23] On November 23 Lewis expected to march northwest and spend the winter in one of the lately built garrisons.

In the time-honored military solution to troubled relationships, Ensign Lewis was transferred to another unit. After two humiliating marches to massacre by the frontier army, Gen. "Mad Anthony" Wayne remade the Legion of the United States into a real fighting unit. Americans were learning to disregard the formalities of European warfare in order to fight Indian irregulars on their own terms. Massed firepower was giving way to better accuracy. That required marksmen who could level down from long distance on an enemy behind a tree. During the recent campaign the Vir-ginian William Clark was assigned to the company of chosen riflemen. That meant he had a talent for picking men with a good eye. Described as "a fine-looking soldierly man," the company commander had an easy frontier mind and was likely to excuse the excesses of a young buck rattling his horns.[24]

The transfer date is unknown but the time line of events points toward the end of November. William Clark later stated that "a few months" before he resigned his army commission in July 1796, Lewis was transferred to his company of chosen riflemen.[25] It was during the next seven months that they became great friends.

In 1795 and 1796, General Wayne's troops suffered from fever. In 1796, 370 soldiers were stricken by an illness that, more than likely, was malaria.[26] On April 6, 1795, Lewis wrote his mother "I have a pretty seveer touch of the dis-order which has been so prevelent among the Troops but have fortunately been restored to my usuall state of health."[27] Again on November 23 Lewis reassured his mother that he had escaped illness.[28] But, if this was an early sign of malaria, it was only the beginning of an affliction that would torture him throughout his life. The recent publication by historian James Holmberg of the William Clark letters reports that Clark was also more sickly than previously believed.[29] Given what Lewis had learned from his mother, a competent herbalist, or from the ill-tempered Dr. Everitt, he was a natural caretaker although there wasn't much that could be done for malaria until an episode had run its course.

In 1796 William Clark resigned his commission, in part to help his older brother George Rogers Clark, whose affairs were a mess. But in that short relationship Lewis and Clark had cemented a lasting friendship and would continue to see and correspond with each other.

A new commander must have taken over the Chosen Rifle Company, but that didn't last long because the Legion of the United States was reorganized. In November 1796, like other soldiers, Lewis was transferred to the First Infantry Regiment. By then the terms of Jay's Treaty with Great Britain were forcing redcoats to surrender the lake posts they had held since the end of the Revolution. The occupation of forts Oswego, Niagara, Detroit, and Michilimackinac fell to the Regiment of Artillerists and Engineers but the infantry remained mobile to deal with problems likely to arise because Jay's Treaty allowed British traders to continue their business with the Indians.

It is possible that Ensign Lewis was assigned to make a reconnaissance in the country but evidence of his activities does not develop until that fall. In October, Lewis accompanied by a dragoon and a horse handler carried dispatches from General Wayne to Pittsburgh, getting lost twice along the way. It is unlikely the ensign could have gone as far as Washington as he was back at Greenville by November 2 when it was acknowledged that he had spent $21.50 of his own funds and was granted a furlough. That would begin after a second trip with dispatches to Detroit, Fort Miami, and Pittsburgh. The ensign was guided by the famous Enos Coon, a former white captive who preferred to live as an Indian.[30] Lewis put Coon up with a Pittsburgh tavern keeper and went on to Washington where his warrant for $21.50 was approved on December 5.[31]

Lewis's furlough was finally approved and he spent Christmas in Charlottesville, where he received orders to remain there on recruitment duty. Ensign Lewis joined the Masonic order on January 28, 1797. He must have been an enthusiastic member and devoted himself to lodge work for on April 3 he had climbed through the orders to receive the degree of Past Master Mason.[32] Lewis went on furlough again and traveled west and south regarding family business on July 24 and wrote from Shelbyville, Kentucky, that he was setting out for Georgia, where the family still held lands and there was business to settle.[33]

Due to the infamous XYZ affair and threat of a war with France, a large military buildup began in 1798. Through that year Ensign Lewis remained posted to recruiting duty close to home in Charlottesville, probably trying to raise men for the company of Capt. Ferdinand Claiborne. Although many new officers were appointed or promoted, it was January 1, 1799, before Lewis made lieutenant.[34] Sent back to Detroit, the young officer was made regimental paymaster, a duty requiring meticulous record keeping. By the first of September 1800, Lewis had the opportunity to travel (mostly in a twenty-one-foot government boat) to places like Wheeling, Limestone, and Fort Washington at Cincinnati or overland to Fort Wayne or Chilli-cothe. Parks Service historian Bob Moore has found no evidence that Lewis visited posts south of the Ohio River that may have fallen into a different military district.[35]

When duty allowed, and sometimes when it didn't, Lewis continued to follow up obligations or opportunities relating to family land holdings. As much as one whole year of his five-year military career was actually spent on leave attending to those private concerns.

Thomas Jefferson, who did not possess a martial mind himself, grasped that his former neighbor Lewis really wasn't cut out to be a military man. Although there was a difference of twenty-six years in their ages, they had opportunities to know each other during the considerable periods that Lewis spent around Charlottesville, on furlough or recruiting duty.[36] It is probable that Lewis found excuses to ride over to Monticello and visit an indulgent mentor. When the great man was away, he had access to Jefferson's extensive library and rode home with volumes in his saddlebags. With just a little gentle guidance he had self-educated himself as a natu-ralist and a man of knowledge, but those were attainments not much in demand in the army.

At some point during that previous relationship, Jefferson and Lewis may have discussed exploration. In spring 1805, as the Corps of Discovery prepared to proceed on up the Missouri River, Lewis noted that he had the "most confident hope of succeading on a voyage which formed a da[r]ling project of mine for the last ten years."[37] As an old man recollecting a painful memory, Jefferson wrote that "Captain Lewis being then stationed at Charlottesville on the recruiting service, warmly sollicited me to obtain for him the execution of that object."[38] If the precise dating is unreliable, a bit too mythic even, there can be little doubt that early on they shared a dream. And that was not necessarily a transcontinental map, or a conve-nient portage between the oceans, but rather the discovery, identification, and proper description of an organic world largely new to science.

On February 23, 1801, the new president, Thomas Jefferson, offered Lieutenant Lewis a duty very different from his previous experience. It was the position as his personal secretary. Jefferson was acquainted with most of the great minds of the nation and promising young men of republican ded-ication. However, the motive behind this unusual offer rested on the pre-vious relationship between two Albemarle County neighbors. Jefferson needed an active young man he could trust.

Within a week of his confirmation as president, Jefferson wrote to Gen.

James Wilkinson at Pittsburgh requesting Lewis's immediate transfer to Washington. Since the mails were not safe from interception Jefferson did not detail his intentions to Wilkinson. Jefferson also wrote the letter to Lewis on the same date. Both letters were enclosed in a packet to Lewis's friend, the Pittsburgh businessman Tarleton Bates.[39] But Wilkinson was not at Pittsburgh and Lewis was somewhere en route from the Michigan country. Bates handed the general's letter to a friend of Wilkinson's and personally delivered the other letter to Lewis when he arrived from Detroit on March 6.[40] Lewis had arrived the night before but by the time he read the president's invitation, the mail had already left. It was four days before Lewis had another opportunity to respond to the president. On March 10 he wrote I "most cordially acquiesce, and with pleasure accept the office."[41]

On March 2, 1801, Lewis had been promoted to captain, which entitled him to command a company.[42] There have been, and still are, officers who believe that there is no more rewarding duty than the care of a company of good men. Although he never enjoyed that challenging authority, a company of the First Infantry Regiment would be carried under his name in the military organization.

Captain Lewis's familiarity with trailing across the wilderness was demonstrated by a requisition for the transport of his baggage and papers to Washington to join the president. He asked the Pittsburgh quartermaster for three pack horses, two pack saddles complete with girths and crupper, four two-foot-long temporary boxes two feet wide and a foot and eight inches deep, with sufficient lash rope.[43] If the ability to throw a hitch was the test, Lewis was already an accomplished frontiersman. It was a good thing he took a spare as one of the horses went lame. It was the first of April when he reached Washington.[44]

The steward of the "President's House" informed the new arrival that he had just missed Mr. Jefferson "by a matter of hours." After waiting for him, Jefferson had finally departed for Monticello to make arrangements for moving his belongings to the presidential mansion in Washington.[45] Expecting that the move would take three weeks he invited Lewis to meet him in Albemarle County.

Having arrived on April Fools' Day, Lewis wasn't quite sure what he was getting into. Although tired from the long journey, Lewis sent a note to Jefferson that he would leave for Monticello in two days and hastily set up his quarters in the president's house.[46] While it is not clear when he actually arrived at Monticello to assist in the packing, Lewis did find time to visit his family. When the president returned to Washington on April 30, his secretary remained in Charlottesville because he signed a power-of-attorney on that date. Lewis legally empowered his younger brother, Reuben Lewis, to "dispose of all or any part of the personal Estate owned by me."[47] That meant that he did not expect to be visiting Locust Hill again for some time.

When Jefferson and Lewis returned to the presidential mansion in Washington they were soon joined by James Madison, his lady, Dolley, and their ten-year-old son. The fellow Virginian was moving to Washington to take up his duty as secretary of state. While searching for a suitable house the family stayed in the mansion for most of the month of May. That must have put a bit of a strain on a rough soldier's manners. The young secretary was a bit taken aback by the exuberant Mrs. Madison. In a country gentleman's rustic expectations, the fair sex was more demure. And then there was their rambunctious boy Payne who clattered about the mansion while the former officer settled into his new duties.[48]

Secretary Lewis brought more than familiarity with the military establishment to the president. While stationed in Detroit, Lewis had been sent on treks through recently pacified Indian country. That had given him an opportunity to pick up on the customs and attitudes of the old French settlers. Although secondhand because he had yet to cross the Mississippi River, Lewis accumulated insights into the habits and activities of Spanish officers. Jefferson was convinced that his secretary held "a knolege of the Western country, of the army & it's situation, might sometimes aid us with informations of interest, which we might not otherwise possess."[49]

One of the first trying tasks was checking off the careers of fellow officers. The anticipated war with France in 1798 had led to the enlargement of the army. After the conflict failed to develop, to Jefferson's Republican mind, the military establishment had become too large. He believed a large army smacked of residual federalism and regarded the army and the navy as potential threats to the nation. Reducing the organization of the overinflated military also included the elimination of officers, and with a bit of selectivity, most of those would be Federalists. During his western duty, particularly as a military paymaster, Lewis had traveled more extensively than most soldiers and was acquainted with a large number of, but far from all, fellow officers.

In June the War Department sent Jefferson a comprehensive list of army officers. As the president's personal secretary, Captain Lewis was set to grade his fellow officers according to their abilities and performance of duty as well as their loyalty to the republican government. That was a heavy responsibility for a young officer required to weigh the future careers of fellow officers. A sensitive man could see that it meant deciding their lives, dreams, hopes. No matter how widely traveled, Meriwether could not have known most of the men he evaluated. He could not rely for advice from other officers because there was only a small guard in Washington and army headquarters was at some distance in Fredericktown, Maryland. Somehow Lewis did it as his duty to the president. His analysis resulted in the retirement of many of the Federalist officers whom Alexander Hamilton had appointed during the buildup.[50] But the judgments were fair and good officers were retained no matter their political convictions.

On the 1797 officer's list after two years service, Lewis had been the lowest of seven ensigns of the First Infantry Regiment. In the reorganization of June 1, 1802, under the Act of March 16, 1802, he became the eighth-ranked captain. Only four officers of the old First that he had known five years before remained. Nineteen others had been swept away by reassignment or elimination, a process in which his hand loomed large.[51]

Although the office of the secretary of war dealt with resignations and discharges directly, it was Lewis who carried the fateful list to the Senate on March 25, 1802. It included the names of those who survived the winnowing and those who would be eliminated. The lesson for the young author was that a military career would be overshadowed by politics.

When he came to the presidency in 1801 Thomas Jefferson had been a widower for nineteen years. Only two of his six children had lived, both girls, upon whom he doted. During the first year of his presidency, Mr. Madison's wife, Dolley, had helped out in the social obligations of the office. During the winter of 1802–1803 it was the president's daughter Mrs. Thomas Mann Randolph Jr. who acted as the "president's lady" on formal occasions. As secretary, Meriwether Lewis was at once a bachelor companion and aide-de-camp to his patron and mentor. It is supposed that a close relationship developed in that big, drafty unfinished hall of a place meant as the presidential mansion.

Jefferson liked to write his own letters. There was the cumbersome polygraph that only a tinkerer like he could have endured in order to write two copies at a time. Or the god-awful wet transfer process used for making the file copies that still torture the reading of those old, blotted pages. Both the president and his assistant were from the Albemarle County schools of composition and grammar. Jefferson had polished his writing style through correspondence with the great thinkers of the world. He had picked up basic French from those years as envoy. Lewis may have picked up a few words or phrases and would learn more dealing with French-speaking Louisianans, but what he understood or could communicate in French was basic.

Two years in the presidential mansion as aide-de-camp or chief of staff was a complete education in Jeffersonian politics. Dinners at the presidential mansion were deliberately informal but still gave Captain Lewis the opportunity to polish his manners and perfect his conversation. Although most dinners were stag affairs, he learned to see a lady properly seated at the table and entertained with small talk, no matter if she was an unintelligible foreign diplomat's wife or someone's charming daughter. When an awkward moment came up, it was his duty to help ease the tension for the president. By those gentle grindings, Meriwether Lewis became a polished gentleman.

Not all of the secretary's distractions were social formalities. Drawn into tidying up a political and personal embarrassment, Lewis had an unpleasant duty of delivering fifty dollars to a Richmond journalist named James Callender. During the vicious exchanges of the 1800 election campaign Callender had written in support of Jefferson. Under the Alien and Sedition Acts he had been fined two hundred dollars and spent nine months in prison for failing to keep his pen and publications under control. In May 1801 he demanded to be reimbursed for the fine and rewarded with a position as postmaster.[52] In buying the extortionist off Lewis endured some very "high-toned" language that included allegations of a scandalous relationship involving the president and a black woman. Whatever the truth of the matter, it was an intimacy that a fellow Virginian and slaveholder could have understood and excused.

Captain Lewis had a foot-slogger's education in the function of government beginning on December 8, 1801, when he carried Mr. Jefferson's first annual message to the Senate and the House of Representatives. During the first session of the Seventh Congress that ran from December 7, 1801, until May 3, 1802, secretary Lewis carried twenty-seven messages from the presidential mansion to the Capitol. As a direct road had not been cut through in 1803 he had to go around by the navy yard to get to Capitol Hill.[53] From December 15 to March 3, 1803, he made more than twenty trips up that muddy detour.[54] Most of the papers he carried had to do with presidential appointments, commissions, consulates, offices of government, the stuff of careers and futures. As secretary he was not required to write every note that the president sent but he was certainly aware of what it took to run a government: good boots.

During those years another observer provided an inside view of what was going on in the presidential mansion. Samuel Latham Mitchill was a New York man of letters and scientific interests who took his seat in the House of Representatives in fall 1801. He was soon invited to those dinners that the president liked to put on, for intellectual stimulation as much as for politicizing members of Congress. As most of the members lived in boardinghouses, there were few refusals to join around an oval table served by a French chef.[55] On January 10, 1802, the company of nine at that table included Mitchill and the president's secretary. Mitchill and Lewis met again a month later and by April 29, Mitchill was referring to the dinner party of "the regulars." Captain Lewis took Mitchill into the president's council chamber to show him Indian artifacts recently found near the Mississippi River. Mitchill found the artisanship impressive.[56] And he would not forget the young officer's interest in the natural sciences.

NOTES

1. Alexander Wilson, "Particulars of the Death of Captain Lewis," *Port Folio* 7 (January 1812): 38.

2. *Index to the Thomas Jefferson Papers*, presidential papers microfilm, series 1 (Washington, DC: Library of Congress, 1976). TJ to JMA, December 19, 1800, Document 18507 and TJ to HD, February 18, 1801, Document 18745, Roll 22; TJ to JMA, March 12, 1801, Document 18921, Roll 23; Table of Federalist and Republican Heads and Office Holders, December 1801, Document 42199, Roll 25; http://memory.loc.gov/ammem/collections/jefferson_papers/ (accessed April 8, 2008).

3. US Congress, Senate, 7th Cong., special sess., March 4, 1801. *American State Papers: Finance, Foreign Relations, Indian Affairs, Military Affairs, Public Lands, Miscellaneous*, 38 vols. (Washington, DC: Gales and Seaton, 1832–1861), Foreign Relations, 1: 56–57, hereafter cited as *ASP*. http://memory.loc.gov/ammem/amlaw/lwsp.html (accessed April 8, 2008).

4. Dale Van Every, *Ark of Empire: The American Frontier 1784–1803* (New York: Arno Press, 1977), pp. 345–46.

5. Donald Jackson, ed., *Letters of Lewis and Clark Expedition with Related Documents, 1783–1854*, 2nd ed., 2 vols. (Urbana: University of Illinois Press, 1978), 1: 1, TJ to JW, February 23, 1801.

6. Details of Meriwether's young life rely on Richard Dillon, *Meriwether Lewis: A Biography* (New York: Coward-McCann, 1965) and the similar material in Stephen Ambrose, *Undaunted Courage: Meriwether Lewis, Thomas Jefferson and the Opening of the American West* (New York: Simon & Schuster, 1996). But Dillon neglected to properly document his sources and Ambrose referenced Dillon.

7. Even more impressive, his younger brother, ten-year-old Reuben, came to visit ML in the fall 1787.

8. ML to LM, May 12, 1787, MLC-MHS.

9. Richard Beale Davis, *Francis Gilmer: Life and Learning in Jefferson's Virginia* (Richmond, VA: Dietz Press, 1939), pp. 360–61; Ambrose, *Undaunted Courage*, pp.

27n26, 475.

10. Dillon says one thousand acres and Ambrose gives no source for this data.

11. ML to LM, October 16, 1791, MLC-MHS.

12. ML to LM, April 19, 1792, MLC-MHS.

13. One of the author's ancestors died on one of those voyages.

14. Harry M. Ward, *The Department of War, 1781–1795* (Pittsburgh: University of Pittsburgh Press, 1962), p. 178.

15. ML to LM, April 6, 1795, MLC-MHS.

16. ML to LM, November 24, 1794, MLC-MHS.

17. ML to LM, October 4, 1794, MLC-MHS.

18. L. Ruth Frick, *Courageous Colter and Companions* (Washington, MO: L. R. Frick, 1997), pp. 303–304.

19. ML to LM, May 22, 1795, MLC-MHS.

20. *Century of Lawmaking for a New Nation: U.S. Congressional Documents and Debates, 1774–1875, Journal of the Executive Proceedings of the Senate of the United States of America*, http://memory.loc.gov/cgi-bin/ampage?collId=llej&fileName =001/llej001.db&recNum=187 (accessed April 8, 2008).

21. Probably Lt. Joseph Elliott, who is mentioned in the orderly book of the Legion of the United States. *The West Point Orderly Books*, United States Military Academy Special Collections Division. *The West Point Orderly Books*, 4 vols. (Columbus: Ohio State Museum, Anthony Wayne Parkway Board, 1954–55); Lee Shepard, ed., *An Old Soldier in Wayne's Army: Journal of Thomas Taylor Underwood* (Cincinnati: Society of Colonial Wars in the State of Ohio, 1945).

22. Eldon Chuinard, "The Court-Martial of Ensign Meriwether Lewis," *We Proceeded On* 8 (November 1982): 14.

23. ML to LM, November 23, 1795, MLC-MHS.

24. SLM to CM, February 18, 1807, Folder 41.321.69, Samuel Mitchill Collection, Museum of the City of New York. At a dinner in Washington Senator Mitchill, who sat between Clark and Jefferson, stated that he "could converse, by turns, with each." Clark was "very conversant with the North American Indians."

25. WC to Nicholas Biddle, August 15, 1811, Jackson, *LLC* 2: 572.

26. Norman Caldwell, "The Frontier Army Officer, 1794–1814," *Mid-America: An Historical Review* 37 (April 1955): 121.

27. ML to LM, April 6, 1795, MLC-MHS.

28. ML to LM, November 23, 1795, MLC-MHS.

29. James Holmberg, ed., *Dear Brother* (New Haven, CT: Yale University Press, 2002), p. 5.

30. Ambrose, *Undaunted Courage*, p. 47.

31. *Records of the Accounting Officers of the Department of the Treasury*, RG217, WS to ML, December 5, 1796, Entry 515, vol. 1, report bk. A, 323, National Archives and Records Administration, College Park, MD. Hereafter cited as NARA-CP.

32. Richard A. Rutyna and Peter C. Stewart, *The History of Freemasonry in Vir-*

ginia (Latham, MD: University Press of America, Inc., 1998), p. 52; Chuinard, "Lewis and Clark, Master Masons," *We Proceeded On* 15 (February 1989): 12–15.

33. ML to LM, July 24, 1797, MLC-MHS.

34. "Century of Lawmaking for a New Nation," http://memory.loc.gov/cgi-bin/ampage?collId=llej&fileName=001/llej001.db&recNum=326 (accessed April 8, 2008); Francis B. Heitman, ed., *Historical Register and Dictionary of the United States Army from Its Organization, September 29, 1789, to March 2, 1902*, 2 vols. (Washington: GPO, 1903). Heitman gives the effective date as March 2, 1799.

35. Ambrose, *Undaunted Courage*, p. 50.

36. RG217, entry 496, vol. 5, letter bk. F, 184, NARA-CP. Lewis's recruitment duty at Charlottesville extended from December 1796 to May 31, 1799.

37. ML, April 7, 1805, in Gary E. Moulton, ed., *The Journals of the Lewis and Clark Expedition*, 3 vols. (Lincoln: University of Nebraska Press, 1983–2001) 4: 10, http://libtextcenter.unl.edu/lewisandclark/index.html (accessed April 8, 2008). Hereafter cited as Moulton, *JLCE*.

38. TJ to Paul Allen, August 18, 1813, Jackson, *LLC* 2: 589.

39. TJ to Tarleton Bates, February 26, 1801, document 18804, roll 22, TJ-LOC.

40. Tarleton Bates to TJ, March 6, 1801, document 18881, roll 23, TJ-LOC.

41. ML to TJ, March 10, 1801, Jackson, *LLC* 1: 3.

42. US Congress, *House Journal*, 6th Congress, 2nd sess., March 2, 1801.

43. Jackson, *LLC* 1: 4n1.

44. ML to TJ, April 5, 1801, document 19134, roll 23, TJ-LOC.

45. TJ to ML, March 31, 1801, document 19106, roll 22, TJ-LOC.

46. ML to TJ, April 10, 1801, document 19159, roll 23, TJ-LOC.

47. ML to Reuben Lewis, April 30, 1801, MSS 9041, 9041-a, "Papers of the Lewis, Anderson, and Marks Families," manuscript, 1771–1908, Special Collections, UVA.

48. TJ to Thomas Mann Randolph, Jr., May 14, 1801, document 19296, roll 23, TJ-LOC; TJ to MJR, May 28, 1801, in Edwin Morris Betts and James Adam Bear Jr., eds., *The Family Letters of Thomas Jefferson* (Columbia: University of Missouri Press), pp. 202–203. Hereafter cited as Betts and Bear, *FL*.

49. TJ to JW, February 23, 1801, Jackson, *LLC* 1: 1.

50. Donald Jackson, "Jefferson, Meriwether Lewis, and the United States Army," *Proceedings of the American Philosophical Society* 124 (April 1980): 91–96.

51. William H. Powell, *List of Officers of the Army of the United States from 1779 to 1900* (1900; repr., Detroit: Gale Research Co., 1967), pp. 38–45.

52. TJ to JMO, May 26, 1801, document 19339 and May 29, 1801, document 19355, roll 23, TJ-LOC.

53. Samuel Latham Mitchill described the location and situation of the president's house: "Thomas Jefferson's mansion is about 1.75 miles from the Capitol. . . . Took a Hackney Coach. The remoteness of Buildings renders it necessary to have many of those vehicles in Washington." Mitchill served in both Houses of Congress 1801–1813. SLM to CM, April 29, 1802, folder 41.321.10, MCNY.

54. US Congress, *House Journal*, 7th Cong., 2nd sess.; 8th Cong., 1st and 2nd sess.; http://memory.loc.gov/ammem/amlaw/lwhj.html (accessed April 8, 2008).

55. Rochonne Abrams, "Meriwether Lewis: Two Years with Jefferson, the Mentor," *Missouri Historical Society Bulletin* 36 (October 1979): 9–10.

56. SLM to CM, January 10, 1802, folder 41.321.36 and April 29, 1802, folder 41.321.10, MCNY.

TWO

Presage of the Garden

To spread the wonders of their tale[1]

There are present parallels to past institutions. The National Aeronautics and Space Administration is essentially a scientific and technical interest, sponsored and funded by the United States and not directly essential to the function of government. This arrangement had an earlier parallel in Thomas Jefferson's personal fascination in what had still to be formalized as "science." He set an example of how disciplines with different interests can be merged together. In many ways the expedition to extend the commerce of the United States would have a distinctly "literary" bent that was beyond its primary mission to find a water route across the continent. In order to better understand that dual obligation it is necessary to grasp the role of the American Philosophical Society.

Defining the unknown continent had always been an American compulsion. But when it came to even as modest an investment as purchasing Peter Pond's 1785 map of the interior, the Continental Congress balked. Getting a copy was left to the persuasive powers of the French expatriate Hector St. Jean de Crevecoeur, who sent it on to his enlightened friends in Paris. Thomas Jefferson undoubtedly saw it there about the same time that he encouraged the fantastic scheme of one of Capt. James Cook's former sailors, John Ledyard, who in 1786 wanted to try crossing North America, west to east, from a Siberian jumping-off place.

Three years later President George Washington and Secretary of War Henry Knox initiated a minimal gesture toward an exploration of the Missouri and Rio Grande rivers that was meant to uncover strategic information. In early 1790 Knox ordered a small military reconnaissance. Lt. John Armstrong only got as far as St. Louis before being stopped, but his findings provided insights into that Spanish-dominated territory. Two years later pressure to know more about the western expanse of the continent increased when news spread that a Boston coastal trader, Capt. Robert Gray, had entered and fixed the longitude and latitude of the mouth of a major western river. He named it for his ship, the *Columbia*.

What government was unable to accomplish, private enterprise might. In January 1793 the learned gentlemen of the American Philosophical Society considered financing a better-supported expedition to the Pacific Ocean. Thomas Jefferson is usually credited with the inspiration to employ the French botanist André Michaux for a transcontinental exploration, but true to his previous interest, it was President Washington who contributed the largest donation to the exploring fund.[2] That fell through in 1793 when the French minister, Edmond Genêt, exposed Michaux as a French agent trying to organize an attack on Spanish possessions.[3]

The American Philosophical Society was a scientific and geographical institution founded in 1743 when Benjamin Franklin visualized an association where individuals could promote useful knowledge, "cultivate the finer Arts, and improve the common Stock of Knowledge." Franklin lamented "that many useful Participants remain uncommunicated, die with the Discoverers, and are lost to Mankind." He believed that the time had come to formalize a society of "Virtuosi or ingenious Men residing in the several Colonies, to be called The American Philosophical Society." The organization should be located in Philadelphia, where the possibility of seven members holding meetings was most likely. The members' professions included a physician, a botanist, a mathematician, a chemist, a mechanic, a geographer, and a general natural philosopher. There was to be a president, a treasurer, and a secretary. The ten members would meet and share their own observations and experiments as well as direct the "constant Correspondence" with all of the members of the society. The subjects of that correspondence included botany, medicine, mining and mineralogy, mathematics, chemistry, mechanics, geography, agriculture, stockbreeding, horticulture, and "all philosophical Experiments that let Light into the Nature of Things, tend to increase the Power of Man over Matter."[4]

Having set up the society in his own hometown, Postmaster Franklin provided an additional stimulus: members did not have to pay postage for society correspondence.[5] In 1768 the society united with another organization and broadened its scope by inviting an international partnership where learning trumped politics "on an immense portion of the globe still unexplored and largely unknown."[6]

The society was an association of learned gentlemen, the thinkers, philosophers, and visionaries of the day who dabbled in a range of scientific interests. The group also included statesmen, doctors, lawyers, and businessmen who wished to be associated with the scientific arm by funding those objectives. But most were only enlightened amateurs when they went beyond their specialty. All too often actual data to support their theories was lacking.

The society operated under the discipline of observational and experimental science and recognized its members through publications, papers read, and prizes awarded. Six committees composed the society's interests: (1) geography, mathematics, natural philosophy, and astronomy, (2) medicine and anatomy, (3) natural history and chemistry, (4) trade and commerce, (5) mechanics and architecture, (6) husbandry and American improvements.[7]

Although the American Revolution slowed the society's course, the relocation of the United States government from New York to Philadelphia ignited a new era of participation and cooperation. In January 1791 the society included two top-ranking government officials, Alexander Hamilton and Edmund Randolph. Two years later John Adams became a member. In January 1797 Thomas Jefferson was elected president of the society.

As secretary of state under George Washington, Jefferson had experienced a bitter dispute with Alexander Hamilton and in August 1793 he vowed to not take any other obligations "which could be utterly against the plan I am proceeding on for my perfect liberation from this place." But foreign events delayed his departure until December 31.[8] By then, he was in a fragile state: his health had broken down and progressively worsened. He later admitted to James Madison and to his daughter Mary that the turmoil had caused a mental breakdown from 1793 to 1797 that made him "unfit for society." At Monticello he saw no one except those who knocked on his door.[9]

Over the next couple of years, Jefferson's correspondence was meager. He explained to his former teacher and legal mentor, George Wythe of Williamsburg, that he was just a quiet farmer. Sometimes Jefferson consulted on matters of mutual interest with his neighbor Col. Nicholas Lewis. They spent time in April 1795 testing out a new contraption that sowed seeds more evenly than the human hand.[10] The colonel's family included a nephew, Meriwether Lewis, who had returned from Georgia two years before in search of an education.

Jefferson confided to Wythe that he was a bit behind on his paperwork and looked to engage a young man from Charlottesville to help him bring that neglected body of material into the order he preferred in all things. Fifteen months into his sabbatical, Jefferson lamented how alone he felt. "I have nobody living with me. . . . I live in my house from an early breakfast to a late dinner . . . often after that till dark."[11] He needed to devote his time to another project like rebuilding Monticello.

During this lonely period he became interested in the inquisitive young Meriwether Lewis. Among the boy's several tutors was Parson Mathew Maury, the son of Jefferson's teacher. It was regrettable that family duties ended the young man's education too soon and he had to devote his energies to being a farm manager. The Whiskey Rebellion in western Pennsylvania gave Lewis an excuse to ride off with other careless young bucks.

But national politics soon imposed upon the scholar in retreat at Monticello. With a mind fixed more on scientific advancement than the political campaign, it was not surprising that Jefferson missed becoming president of the nation by three electoral votes. Although he lost the presidential race to John Adams, on January 6, 1797, Vice President Jefferson was consoled by being elected the new president of the American Philosophical Society. On that wintry day when twenty-five members attended the meeting, Benjamin Smith Barton, Robert Patterson, Charles Willson Peale, and John Vaughan expressed their confidence in Jefferson.[12]

In his first letter as president, Jefferson summarized the essential mission of the society in a bold yet gracious vision that he clearly intended to fulfill.

> The suffrage of a body which comprehends whatever the American World has of distinction in Philosophy & Science in general, is the most flattering incident of my life, and that to which I am the most sensible. My satisfaction would be complete, were it not for the consciousness that is far beyond my titles. I feel no qualification for this distinguished Post, but a sincere zeal for all the Objects of our institution, and an ardent desire to see knowledge so disseminated through the mass of mankind, that it may at length reach the extremes of Society, beggars and kings.[13]

As a longtime member Jefferson felt that the society had been "too much confined in practice to the Natural and Mathematical departments." His objective was to make the society a depository for original manuscripts by the members, "many loose sheets of no use by themselves but of great value when brought into a general depot open to the use of the future historian or literary inquirer."[14] On May 19, Jefferson proposed an audacious plan. "The American Philosophical Society have always considered the antiquity, changes, and present state of their own country as primary objects of their research; and with a view to facilitate such discoveries, a permanent committee has been established."[15]

Appointed head of the committee, Jefferson chose fellow members Judge George Turner of the Northwest Territory, Dr. Caspar Wistar, Dr. Adam Seybert, Charles Willson Peale, commander of the army Gen. James Wilkinson, and Jonathan Williams to assist him. The committee centered on four objectives that, at the heart, became the template of the Lewis and Clark expedition. It would seek out skeletons of ancient creatures, volcanic mounds, plans of ancient fortifications, Indian works of art and descriptions "of whatever is interesting." The society invited researches into the natural history of the earth and expressed a keen interest into the customs, mannerisms, and languages of the Indian nations as well as their migrations.[16] To set an example, six days after being installed as vice president of the United States, Jefferson presented a paper at the APS on the fossilized bones of a mammal, "a quadruped" that he guessed was part of the "never ending circle" of nature.[17]

The undemanding vice presidency gave Jefferson time to steer the society in another direction. While embodying a discipline of curiosity and invention, welcoming contributions of old bones and Indian artifacts from travelers to new places, the organization hadn't promoted the idea of discovery or the idea of paying someone to confirm and authenticate the origin of those artifacts. That idea did not arise until after Jefferson's election.

The society had previously established premiums to "the authors of the best performances, inventions, or improvements, relative to certain specific subjects of useful knowledge."[18] A stipend of fifty to one hundred dollars might be awarded to persons who could aid or improve an existing scientific method. On December 7, 1798, Jefferson's committee began accepting donations from distant places. As an example, James Wilkinson, commander in chief of the Western Army, sent two meteorological journals kept by him when stationed at Detroit and Michilimackinac.[19]

Beyond the hall of science international affairs were intruding. It was taken as a national insult when French envoys demanded a quarter-million-dollar bribe before opening important negotiations. Federalists reacted to the so-called XYZ affair on April 9, 1797, by getting Congress to authorize an army of twelve thousand. To recruit so many new soldiers the army sent officers to their home areas where they had a better chance of inducing enlistments.

Jefferson's protégé Meriwether Lewis had taken a leave of absence from the army in May 1797 to attend to family business in Georgia.[20] He wrote to his mother in July apologizing for the excessive delay and hoping to be soon home to Albemarle County. To escape the recurring "sickly months" in Philadelphia, Jefferson usually returned to Monticello for the summer. It is likely that after the young officer returned, the two neighbors had opportunities to meet.[21]

Prior to his departure for Georgia, Lieutenant Lewis had visited the Charlottesville Masonic establishment, Door to Virtue Lodge No. 44.[22] An association with local gentlemen was a connection to the community that might lead to new recruits. Lewis was still in Charlottesville on October 31 when he became a member of No. 44.[23]

Recruiting possibilities around Charlottesville were promising and in January 1798 Lieutenant Lewis spent the next eighteen months searching for men.[24] During a period of relatively free time that lasted until May 1799, Lewis had plenty of opportunities to see Jefferson. There is no way of knowing what they discussed, but nine months later Jefferson invited Lewis to become his personal secretary.

Lewis modestly expressed his surprise. "I very little expected that I possessed the confidence of Mr. Jefferson in so far as to have produced on his part, a voluntary offer of the office of his private secretary."[25] But Jefferson had been evaluating his young neighbor for years and was well aware of his capabilities. On April 1, 1801, Lewis arrived in Washington and a more intense relationship between the two men began.

After the first session of the Seventh Congress ended on May 3, 1802, President Jefferson returned to Monticello. However, his secretary traveled to Philadelphia to visit a new friend, Mahlon Dickerson. They had met at the president's table and formed an immediate friendship.[26] Among other amusements, on this visit Dickerson and Lewis sat for their portraits in the studio of the artist Charles Saint Mémin. The image of Lewis that the artist caught in a crayon drawing taken from his physiognotrace, a mechanical device for taking a silhouette, was neoclassical and flattering. The artist caught a strong, pleasant profile rising above the fashionable high collar and stock. Their friend William Barton testified to the accuracy. The handsome young man still wore the queue that General Wilkinson had ordered officers to cut last year. Dickerson took Lewis into the highest social circles. Over two weeks they dined several times with Gov. Thomas McKean, Sen.

George Logan, or the United States attorney for the eastern district, Alexander James Dallas. Lewis would have been an active participant in political discussions because of what he had observed working with the president. Romance does not seem to have intruded, as the only feminine contact whom Dickerson recorded in his diary was a Miss Fries.[27]

Lewis had opportunities to meet members of the American Philosophical Society including Dr. Benjamin Smith Barton, Dr. Benjamin Rush, and Andrew Ellicott. In 1797 Dr. Barton brought out a book on the North American Indians, in 1798 a book on the early beginnings of a *materia medica* of the United States and in 1800 a paper on the goiter. A year later his medical treatise on the analogies between yellow fever and the plague was circulated in Philadelphia.[28] In the future these men would continue to exert influence in the scientific community. Rush's *Essays, Literary, Moral, and Philosophical* would come in 1806 and the horticulturalist Bernard McMahon would bring forth the voluminous 648-page *The American Gardener's Calendar* in the same year. Four years later Barton would follow with an updated work on his *materia medica*, the third edition of a 120-page tome covering various aspects of botanical remedies.[29]

The kingpin of scientific publishing was New York Rep. Samuel Latham Mitchill. Since 1797 Mitchill had edited a journal titled the *Medical Repository*. This mix of news, reviews, and articles amounted to a cornucopia of medical, geographical, astronomical, political, and botanical enlightenment. Mitchill met the president's secretary during the preceding session of Congress but was presently at his home in New York.

While he was in Philadelphia Lewis may have heard more discussion about a book that Dr. Caspar Wistar had mentioned to Jefferson on January 8. This was the London publication of Alexander Mackenzie's *Voyages from Montreal, on the River St. Lawrence, through the Continent of North America, to the Frozen and Pacific Oceans, in the Years 1789 and 1793*. After his social month in Philadelphia Lewis returned to Albemarle County to attend family business and be available to the president at Monticello. Mackenzie's *Voyages* was a title that Thomas Jefferson was unable to resist. But it was not until June 21 that he got around to ordering a copy from a New York book dealer, at the same time that he also ordered London cartographer Aaron Arrowsmith's latest map of North America. Those purchases could not have been delivered to Monticello until sometime in August. As Donald Jackson pointed out, fellow American Philosophical Society member Benjamin Smith Barton visited Jefferson from August 10 to 25 without mentioning in his diary any discussion with his host about Mackenzie's exploration.[30]

A great deal more has been made of this book than the actual content justifies. Mackenzie's book was a typical fur trade travel journal sandwiched between a history of the Canadian business and fifteen concluding pages certain to raise the hackles of a man who had written the Declaration of Independence. Ignoring the interior boundary of 49.37 north latitude drawn at the peace ending the American Revolution, this presumptive fur trader wanted it reset at 45 degrees north from the Atlantic to the Pacific. Britain's "right to claim is equal to that to the north of it." When the Columbia River was considered as the line of communication from the Pacific, Mackenzie seemed to back off to 48 degrees north, which was still enough territory to complete "the entire command of the fur trade of North America."[31]

The book was an indisputable record of the first transcontinental crossing and the elimination of the old myth of a northwest passage by water. When he wrote it, the contest was between several British interests and Mackenzie was trying to gain favor from the government for his faction. But a careful reader could easily see that Mackenzie had failed to find a practicable outlet to the Pacific Ocean for the fur trade of the greater northwest. His crossing in the latitudes where British competitors had to operate was actually a disappointment. As far as business was concerned, it was a barren return. A sophisticated reader like Jefferson surely recognized that the book had been edited and polished for public consumption by a ghost-writer who plagiarized information from other sources. There is no doubt that Jefferson and Lewis read the international implication with considerable interest and discussed it before they returned to the capital. But after mid-November there were graver issues to consider.

In early 1802 Jefferson had learned from "a variety of channels . . . that the [secret] retro-cession of Louisiana from Spain to France had been agreed upon."[32] By November 25 he knew that the reaction of outraged Spanish officials at New Orleans was the closure of the port to all outgoing ocean vessels. That was in direct conflict with the 1795 treaty of San Lorenzo between Spain and the United States allowing Americans the right of deposit, export, and import without paying a Spanish tariff.[33] A breach of the treaty could set off a war. Alexander Hamilton and other militant Federalists were in favor of just seizing New Orleans. If the United States didn't act, it was likely that Great Britain would.

On his way to the second session of Congress on December 6, 1802, Dr. Samuel Latham Mitchill took the time to stop in Philadelphia to attend a lecture by Dr. Rush on "the facilities of the mind" and by Dr. Wistar on "osteology." Two days later when he dined with the president, Mitchill surely shared those interesting topics as table conversation. But as an editor as well as a doctor, he was not particularly impressed by the president's message to Congress on the fifteenth, which he wrote to his wife was "full of peace and plenty," not entirely in keeping with recent developments.[34]

Two days later John Randolph of Virginia, who was no friend of the president, raised the question of free navigation of the Mississippi River by asking the president to lay out all the papers of the Department of State relative to Spanish violation of the existing treaty of friendship between the two countries. Jefferson provided that information on the twenty-second with a caution about protecting the interests of the citizens by not publicly exposing too much. Confidential material continued to be sent over to Congress at the end of the year. Then in early January 1803 President Jefferson sent James Monroe to France to cooperate with the United States minister Robert Livingston in an attempt to purchase New Orleans.

That may seem a poor time to be considering an exploration through Louisiana. The idea actually began before December 2 when Carlos Martinez de Yrujo, the Spanish *encargado de negocios*, reported to the foreign minister in Madrid.

> The President asked me the other day in a frank and confident tone, if our Court would take it badly, that the Congress decree the formation of a group of travelers, who would form a small caravan and go and explore the course of the Missouri River in which they would nominally have the objective of investigating everything which might contribute to the progress of commerce; but that in reality would have no other view than the advancement of geography . . . its object would not be other than to observe the territories which are found between the 40 and 60 [degrees] from the mouth of the Missouri to the Pacific Ocean, and unite the discoveries that these men would make with those which the celebrated Makensi made in 1793.[35]

A Spanish officer had precipitated what might very well turn into a war. If the United States didn't move quickly to resolve the issue, England might try to take possession of what was now, secretly, French territory. The claim of the United States to the primary discovery of the Columbia River had to be upheld. Jefferson could not have been interested only in what he described to the Spanish minister as a literary adventure, purely in the interests of science. Although scientific exploration was a longtime interest of the president, what the nation required at this critical moment was a military reconnaissance.

There was a historical precedent dating back to the Washington administration in 1790 when the president and the secretary of war made a failed attempt to explore the Missouri River and "any of the navigable streams that run into the Great North River which empties itself into the gulf of Mexico."[36] A few years later when Jefferson tried to get a French botanist to explore the Missouri under the auspices of the American Philosophical Society, what happened was very close to what was now being considered. Unfortunately, André Michaux had turned out to be a secret agent of France and that had embarrassed the sponsor but now Jefferson was ready to try something curiously similar and secretive.

Although he sidled around it in his message of the fifteenth, the president had already approached the Spanish minister about exploration of the Missouri River and had his secretary work up a cost estimate. There was a question whether the Constitution provided for stimulating or funding what was put forward as scientific advancement. Disclosing a military objective was inadvisable but on Secretary of State Madison's suggestion, Jefferson disguised his intentions by asking Congress to fund an expedition that would extend the commerce of the nation.

Although he was commander in chief during this crisis, Jefferson was also still an amateur scientist. Because exploration was something that Jefferson had tried to lead the APS into funding ten years before, anything discovered beyond the narrow geographical mission of the expedition would be forwarded to the society in Philadelphia. As several members had mastered the business of publishing their own work, the knowledge gained on the expedition could be easily disseminated to the public.

Jefferson was already corresponding with a naturalist friend about the possibilities of information on population, natural history, and other subjects including the extinct mammoth or *Megatherium*, a giant slothlike creature about the size of an elephant. He characteristically called those exchanges "Philosophical transactions."[37] Later Jefferson noted: "Capt. Lewis was now become my private Secretary, and on the first mention of the subject he renewed his solicitations to be the person employed."[38] The proposed expedition would have two very different purposes. Besides exploring the Missouri to its headwaters and finding a direct water route to the Pacific Ocean, the expedition would also collect specimens and data on natural history for an institution of private gentlemen.

That combination of purposes, public and private, was in fact the expression of Thomas Jefferson's personal fascination with science. In his defense, it should be remembered that the merging of public and private interests was nothing new. In this case, the expedition was going anyway and it would be a more complete usage of public funds to get the most out of it. And that meant that Captain Lewis would also have to think of himself as a field scientist, gathering the information that Jefferson previously hoped an expert like Michaux might have collected.

President Jefferson wrote three messages to Congress on January 18, 1803. Two were short notes, the second transmitting a report from the secretary of war about the trading houses and Indian relations. After Captain Lewis read them to that body, they were duly entered into the congressional journals. The third message was a four-page-long letter headed "confidential" that was laid on the table for the Senate executive committee. The first part of this was an enlarged restatement of the Indian matters. But two-thirds of the way through the president segued into considerations about western commerce and the potential of the Missouri River as a transcontinental connection. This might be explored by an "intelligent officer and ten or twelve chosen men . . . for two thousand and five hundred dollars . . . for the purpose of extending the external commerce of the U.S."[39]

Mr. Jefferson finally explained what he had in mind. The interests of commerce placed the principal object within the constitutional powers and care of Congress, and that it should incidentally advance the geographical knowledge of our own continent cannot but be an additional gratification. The nation claiming the territory, regarding this as a literary pursuit "would not be disposed to view it with jealousy."[40]

As early as last November Jefferson had discussed that proposal with Secretary of the Treasury Gallatin but did not include it in his December 15 annual message. Anticipating a negative reaction, Secretary of State Madison suggested hanging the proposal on the hook of extending commerce. A month later when Jefferson shared the proposal with the Senate executive committee he cautioned secrecy. But time was running out and something had to be done before the session ended. If an expedition was not approved now, it would be another year before it could be started.

At three o'clock on January 31, 1803, the galleries were cleared and the House of Representatives remained behind closed doors for an hour before adjourning. Although constrained from telling his wife what happened, Representative Mitchill could not resist.

> Perhaps I might let you know something about this *Political Secret*, was I not restrained by my own decision because I have just set down after making a Speech against taking off the Injunction of Secrecy. You must however not imagine any thing about it, nor pretend to suppose that a

secret expedition is meditated up the river Missouri to its source, thence across the Northern Andes and down the Western water-courses to the Pacific Ocean, and that the reason of keeping it secret is that the English and Spaniards may not find it out and frustrate it.[41]

It was not surprising that when the purchase was arranged, some pertinent documents relating to that bold stroke would be printed in the *Repository*. Readers were exposed to discoveries made by two Spanish explorers and detailed aspects about the upper Missouri River. As an example, the journal of James MacKay's Spanish expedition up the Missouri River wound up at the American Philosophical Society and was published in Mitchill's *Repository*.[42] The journal as well as MacKay's corresponding map became part of the packet of background material that was carried on the expedition.

Much of the secrecy during December had to do with the potential purchase of the port of New Orleans, which would resolve the threat to the interior nation of being cut off from world access. On January 12, 1803, two million dollars had been set aside for that purchase. As the nation was dealing with France about this purchase, it really didn't matter if Spain might be offended by an exploration.

On the same date that Representative Mitchill revealed the secret to his wife, the Spanish minister in Washington, Marques de Casa Yrujo, was penning a letter to his superior Don Pedro Cevallos that the Senate was considering the project but that fear of offending "one of the European nations" might keep them from proceeding.

The proposal remained under the lock of secrecy until February 26 when the House was cleared and the secrecy prohibition removed. Those in attendance included Samuel L. Mitchill of New York, David Meriwether of Georgia, and William Eustis of Massachusetts, but there is no way of knowing how they voted. On that day the Committee for Enrolled Bills presented three to the president for his approval. There was "An Act for making further provision for the expenses attending the intercourse between the United States and foreign nations; an Act for continuing in law an Act for establishing trading houses with the Indian tribes; and lastly, an Act for extending the external commerce of the United States." Two days later a message was received from the president by his secretary, Mr. Lewis, notifying that Mr. Jefferson had approved and immediately signed those acts on the twenty-sixth.[43] But two days previously, Jefferson had already written to the French naturalist Bernard Lacépède that the United States was sending a small exploring expedition to the source of the Missouri and whatever river was near it that ran into the Pacific Ocean.[44]

There was no doubt who would head this expedition. Jefferson had been grooming Captain Lewis for the role of a field naturalist for several years, perhaps since he had known him as a boy.[45] Whether Jefferson began nurturing Lewis as a field scientist as early as the Michaux fiasco or later when the young officer spent a good deal of time in the vicinity of his great library, it is evident that the farmer from Monticello had fostered Lewis's interest in the natural sciences. Mentoring had brought a ready pupil along to the point where he was the perfect choice to lead an exploring expedition. What Meriwether hadn't already absorbed could be filled in by a crash course from his fellows at the APS.[46] Jefferson confidently sent Lewis to those members of the APS as the scientific-minded person who would lead an expedition into the western wilderness. He confirmed that Lewis was "brave, prudent, habituated to the woods, & familiar with Indian manners & character. He is not regularly educated, but . . . possesses a great mass of accurate observation on all subjects of nature which present themselves here, & will therefore readily select those only in his new route which shall be new."[47]

Jefferson wrote letters to five of the most highly trained and knowledgeable men at the APS endorsing Lewis as the leader and chief information gatherer. On February 26 Jefferson wrote to Andrew Ellicott about instruments and training in celestial navigation for Captain Lewis. Other letters went out in the next few days to Benjamin Smith Barton, Caspar Wistar, and Benjamin Rush, as well as applications for English and French passports. The Spanish were not consulted.

Lewis was supposed to arrive for instruction by the second week in March 1803 and leave in June.[48] During those three months he was expected to obtain a decisive grasp of the necessary disciplines. That was a tall order but he already had a sound base of knowledge and could draw upon a basic foundation he had been acquiring for several years. The instruction he would now receive should complement that prior understanding. He finished his training as a field scientist when he returned to Philadelphia.

Given the background of scientific understanding within the membership of the APS, it was no surprise that certain members were interested in a plan for western exploration that might yield new scientific insights. Having burned its fingers on the Michaux intrigue, the organization had waited a decade until its president, Mr. Jefferson, was in a position to bring the government into scientific inquiry. Now the learned society would share in completing the scientific education of Meriwether Lewis.

Although it is difficult to pinpoint when a mutually shared curiosity about natural science began between Thomas Jefferson and Meriwether Lewis, the explorer later confirmed it was when he noted in a journal that he had the "most confident hope of succeading on a voyage which formed a da[r]ling project of mine for the last ten years."[49] And that was not necessarily a transcontinental military map or a convenient portage between the oceans. Rather he would discover, identify, and properly describe a world largely new to science.

NOTES

1. Alexander Wilson, "Particulars of the Death of Capt. Lewis," *Port Folio* 7 (January 1812): 39.

2. The first mention about this expedition to the Pacific Ocean was discussed in mid-1792. George Washington wrote Jefferson on January 22, 1793, that if the American Philosophical Society could not foot the bill, he would "readily add my mite to the mean for encouraging Mr. Michaud's undertaking." Jackson, *LLC* 2: 667.

3. Landon Y. Jones, *William Clark and the Shaping of the West* (New York: Hill and Wang, 2004), p. 91.

4. Carl Van Doren, "The Beginnings of the American Philosophical Society," *Proceedings of the American Philosophical Society* 87 (July 1943): 277, 279, 280.

5. Ibid., p. 280. Sending letters in that day was expensive; a five-page letter cost ten dollars' postage (equivalent to 1943 values) while a one-page letter from New York to Philadelphia amounted to seventy-five cents.

6. Gilbert Chinard, "The American Philosophical Society and the World of Science," *Proceedings of the American Philosophical Society* 87 (July 1943): 1, 7.

7. Edward C. Carter II, *One Grand Pursuit: A Brief History of the American Philosophical Society's First 250 Years, 1743–1993* (Philadelphia: American Philosophical Society, 1993), p. 6. Members were encouraged to donate their own manuscripts and maps, which today account for some of the library's holdings.

8. TJ to Edmund Randolph, August 5, 1793, document 15649 and TJ to Richard Dobson, August 30, 1793, document 15823, roll 19, TJ-LOC.

9. TJ to JMA, April 27, 1795, document 16842, roll 20, TJ-LOC; TJ to Mary Jefferson Eppes, March 3, 1802, Betts and Bear, *FL*, p. 219.

10. TJ to John Taylor, April 13, 1795, document 16835, roll 20, TJ-LOC.

11. TJ to George Wythe, April 18, 1795, document 16840, TJ-LOC. No mention is made of the young man's name in subsequent letters.

12. Henry Phillips Jr., "Early Proceedings of the American Philosophical Society . . . from the Manuscript Minutes of Its Meetings from 1774 to 1838," *Proceedings of the American Philosophical Society* 22 (1884): 246.

13. Gilbert Chinard, "Jefferson and the American Philosophical Society," *Proceedings of the American Philosophical Society* 87 (July 1943): 267.

14. Ibid., p. 270.

15. Ibid.

16. Ibid.

17. Phillips, "Early Proceedings," pp. 250, 252–53.

18. *Early American Imprints*, first series, *1639–1800* (New York, Readex Microprint, 1955–1969), no. 35106.

19. Phillips, "Early Proceedings," p. 274.

20. ML to Nicholas Johnson, May 2, 1797, MLC-MHS.

21. TJ to Mary Jefferson Eppes, July 4, 1800, Betts and Bear, *FL*, p. 189. Jefferson wrote in July 1800, "Mrs. Monroe is now in our neighborhood to continue during the sickly months." A yellow fever epidemic had also tortured Philadelphia in 1793 and 1798. For background see John Harvey Powell, *Bring Out Your Dead* (Philadelphia: University of Pennsylvania Press, 1949).

22. William Mosely Brown, *Freemasonry in Staunton, Virginia* (Staunton, VA: McClure Printing Co., 1949), p. 46. ML visited the lodge on May 30.

23. Masonic scholars Ray Denslow and William Mosely Brown differ on the date of Lewis's admittance. Brown cites the minutes of October 31, 1797: "On the motion of Brother William Chambers and seconded by Brother David Parry . . . Brother Meriwether Lewis . . . is admitted a member of this lodge. On the petition of Meriwether Lewis; it is ordered that a Diploma be granted from this lodge, on his complying with the By laws (i.e. paying five shillings)."

24. Jefferson corroborated this in his remark, "Capt. Lewis being then stationed at Charlottesville on the recruiting service."

25. ML to John Thornton Gilmer, June 18, 1801, MLC-MHS.

26. Mahlon Dickerson to Silas Dickerson, April 21, 1802, and May 1, 1803, Dickerson Papers, box 3, New Jersey Historical Society.

27. Mahlon Dickerson Diary, May 19, 1802, Jackson, *LLC* 2: 678–79.

28. Francis W. Pennell, "Benjamin Smith Barton as Naturalist," *Proceedings of the American Philosophical Society* 86 (September 1942): 113.

29. Charles Evans, *American Bibliography*, 2nd series (New York: Peter Smith, 1941), document 268; Ralph R. Shaw and Richard H. Shoemaker, *American Bibliography: A Preliminary Checklist for 1806* (New York: Scarecrow Press, 1961), documents 10771, 11306, and 19478.

30. Donald Jackson, *Thomas Jefferson and the Rocky Mountains: Exploring the West from Monticello* (repr., Norman: University of Oklahoma Press, 2002), pp. 121–24.

31. Alexander Mackenzie, *Voyages from Montreal on the River St. Laurence through the Continent of North America to the Frozen and Pacific Oceans in the Years 1789 and 1793 with a Preliminary Account of the Rise, Progress and Present State of the Fur Trade of That Country* (1801; facsimile repr., Readex Microprint, 1966), pp. 397, 411.

32. *Records of the US Senate*, RG46, Robert Livingston to Rufus King, December 30, 1801, M1403, roll 4, frame 0613, NARA.

33. Jerry W. Knudson, "Newspaper Reaction to the Louisiana Purchase," *Missouri Historical Review* 63 (January 1969): 188. Also known as the Pinckney Treaty of 1795.

34. SLM to CM, December 6, 1802, folder 41.321.26 and December 8, 1802, folder 41.321.8 and December 15, 1802, folder 41.321.53, MCNY.

35. Carlos Martinez de Yrujo to Pedro Cevallos, December 2, 1802, Jackson, *LLC* 1: 4.

36. Henry Knox to Josiah Harmar, December 20, 1789, Jackson, *LLC* 2: 661. New information reveals how the secretary of war obtained the map of the Missouri River: Thomas C. Danisi and W. Raymond Wood, "James MacKay: International Explorer," *Missouri Historical Review* 102 (April 2008): 157.

37. TJ to Bernard Lacépède, February 24, 1803, Jackson, *LLC* 1: 15–16.

38. TJ to Paul Allen, August 18, 1813, Jackson, *LLC* 2: 589.

39. US Congress, *House Journal*, 7th Cong., 2nd sess., January 18, 1803; US Congress, *Senate Journal*, 7th Cong., 2nd sess., January 18, 1803; Jefferson's Message to Congress, January 18, 1803, Jackson, *LLC* 1: 13. A copy exists in the president's hand and the document was also recorded in the *Senate Executive Journal*.

40. Ibid. That sidled around the recent Spanish objections because Jefferson knew that Louisiana had been secretly returned to France.

41. SLM to CM, January 31, 1803, folder 41.321.265, MCNY.

42. Thomas C. Danisi and W. Raymond Wood, "Lewis and Clark's Route Map: James MacKay's Map of the Missouri River," *Western Historical Quarterly* 35 (Spring 2004); JW to HD, June 13, 1805, Jackson, *LLC* 2: 689; Samuel L. Mitchill, ed., *Medical Repository*, 12 vols. (New York: 1804–1812), 4: 27–36.

43. US Congress, *House Journal*, 7th Cong., 2nd sess., February 26, 1803.

44. TJ to Bernard Lacépède, February 24, 1803, Jackson, *LLC* 1: 15–16.

45. TJ to Paul Allen, August 18, 1813, Jackson, *LLC* 2: 589. Years later, Jefferson recalled that he met Meriwether Lewis while a Lewis carriage was being built at Monticello and they talked about a proposed expedition. Jefferson wrote that Lewis volunteered to lead it and was not dissuaded when Jefferson said that it would be a two-man expedition. Jefferson may have misremembered as he resided in Philadelphia as secretary of state in 1792–1793, and the only time that he visited Monticello was from mid-July to October 1, 1792 (roll 16, TJ-LOC). That was the time when Lewis was away in Georgia to retrieve his mother.

46. American Philosophical Society abbreviated as APS.

47. TJ to Benjamin Rush, February 28, 1803, Jackson, *LLC* 1: 18–19.

48. Lewis delivered messages to Congress until the session ended. US Congress, *House Journal*, 7th Cong., 2nd sess., March 3, 1803.

49. ML, April 7, 1805, Moulton, *JLCE* 4: 10.

THREE

Organizing a Western Journey

First of his country to explore[1]

Forty years after inheriting Louisiana from France, Spain secretly retroceded the vast, poorly utilized, increasingly expensive holding of Louisiana to Napoleon Bonaparte. In early 1802 President Jefferson had learned that the exchange had actually been agreed upon and took steps to exploit an opportunity to acquire New Orleans and the adjoining extent of West Florida.[2] Something unexpected developed for the United States' negotiating team when France offered to let them have the entire territory, a third of the continent, without waging a war or causing bloodshed. When the deal was completed on April 30, 1803, the French minister commented, "You have made a noble bargain for yourselves, and I suppose you will make the most of it."[3] Because it took from a month to six weeks for confirmation to arrive, the president would be unaware of this development until early summer.

When Jefferson asked Congress to fund an expedition to explore the Missouri River, he may have thought to improve American Capt. Robert Gray's discovery claim to the Columbia River. The challenge was finding a transcontinental connection between the Columbia and Missouri river systems.[4] In his confidential message to Congress asking for funding, President Jefferson suggested the potential for the expansion of commerce. But as far as he knew at the end of 1802, the trade of the Missouri River was the prerogative of Spain. Jefferson's message implied that the United States meant to take a more active role in pursuing business relations with the largely unknown tribes of Indians beyond the Mississippi. To realize that goal, he thought that an intelligent officer with ten or twelve chosen men "fit for the enterprize . . . might explore the whole line, even to the Western ocean."[5] They could hold conferences with Indians on the subject of mutual trade, although that would be taking place in the territory of another nation.

As soon as the proposal was approved, Jefferson informed his friends in the American Philosophical Society that Capt. Meriwether Lewis was designated to lead the expedition and would soon be coming to Philadelphia for additional scientific instruction. Lewis did not rush off immediately, however, and continued to deliver the president's messages to Congress until the last session at six p.m. on March 3, 1803.

Twelve days later Captain Lewis departed Washington to go to the federal arsenal at Harper's Ferry and arranged for fifteen of the latest rifles. Another object of his visit was having the mechanics build the iron frame for a collapsible, portable boat. As it turned out, the complexity of the project required his personal supervision and took up far too much time. Ignoring that there were experienced boat builders and boatyards around Pittsburgh, the captain sent a letter to Rep. William Dickson at Nashville asking him to arrange the construction of a keelboat and light wooden canoe according to the enclosed description. But as it would turn out, no boats were at Nashville.

Lewis also communicated with other army officers for the men he would need. At some point he exchanged letters with John Conner, a notable Delaware fellow traveler, then living on the White River. Like the guide Enos Coon, whom Lewis knew during his travels carrying military dispatches, Conner preferred to live as an Indian and the captain may have known him by reputation. Lewis also requested that Conner bring along two of his tribal associates.

Both Lewis and the president expected the business at Harper's Ferry would take a week but it took almost a month. After stopping at army headquarters in Fredericktown, Maryland, Captain Lewis went on to Lancaster, Pennsylvania, where Andrew Ellicott gave him a two-and-a-half-week course in how to make celestial observations. Anyone who has attempted to learn celestial navigation without a calculator knows that it takes more than a week to absorb, and Lewis did not arrive in Philadelphia until about May 8.[6] Jefferson had already prompted Robert Patterson and doctors Caspar Wistar, Benjamin Rush, and Benjamin Smith Barton to suggest any additions to the developing plan confidentially.[7]

Upon his arrival in Philadelphia, Lewis immediately began instruction with the nexus of academic, geographical, philosophical, botanical, and medical thought associated with the APS. His tutors held the highest standard in their respective fields. Lewis met with Benjamin Smith Barton, who taught him natural history. As Lewis would be traveling to an unfamiliar area, he received help in going over the innumerable species of plants already known so he had an idea of how to recognize a new species. Robert Patterson, professor of mathematics, added to what he had learned from Ellicott about navigation and the computation of longitude by means of lunar observations. Dr. Benjamin Rush, the foremost medical doctor of his day, instructed him in the treatment of the sick and ways to prevent illness. Rush later gave Lewis a substantial list of questions concerning the Indians of Upper Louisiana—diseases, remedies, and a host of other inquiries ranging from eating and sleeping habits to religious ceremonies. After those short courses in nineteenth-century scientific understanding, Lewis, the field observer, was ready to be sent on his way. Of course the eager young man could not have absorbed a complete education in several disciplines in such a short time. A great deal depended upon what he already knew. After working for six weeks the scholar's head was spinning with hastily crammed facts and not always practical suggestions. He planned to return to Washington on the sixth or seventh of June but appears to have still been in Philadelphia as late as the eleventh.

Fearing that arrangements were losing momentum, Jefferson had returned to Washington to make himself available to his protégé. Working in the mansion they discussed the problems of fielding a transcontinental exploration, what to take, what not to take. A tinkerer like Jefferson could not have resisted those interesting little details like carrying powder in lead canisters that could be melted down when empty to mold balls. They went over every available map and traveler's description and sent off for more.

Despite what has been made of Alexander Mackenzie's ghostwritten narrative as an incentive, both men already understood the British threat to United States commerce. Lewis needed a reliable hunter/interpreter but Jefferson feared that John Conner, the experienced trader Lewis was considering, was too closely associated with the British traders who were still operating in the United States under the provisions of Jay's Treaty in competition with the government trade factories.[8]

Lewis's prior service on a recently pacified Indian frontier was nothing compared to what the captain would meet on the Missouri River. The two planners also discussed someone to second Lewis. Two years before, not long after starting as secretary, Captain Lewis wrote to his former company commander and friend, William Clark, asking him to look into some land in Ohio that belonged to his half brother John Marks.[9] Clark arrived in Washington in August 1801 to appear in US district court concerning his brother George Rogers Clark's fifteen-year-old lawsuit.[10] Their meeting is interesting because it took place not long after Lewis finished evaluating the military officers. It is possible that Lewis might have introduced his friend to the president.[11] From what William was doing to salvage the standing of his elder brother, it was apparent that he was a man of solid character and responsibility who was willing to share his understanding of western developments.

During 1801–1802 Lewis and Clark corresponded in the style of an ongoing friendship while other communications were sent through official channels. In 1802 Jefferson was interested in a post that George Rogers Clark had built at the mouth of the Ohio River, commanding the Mississippi almost a quarter of a century before. Secretary of War Dearborn forwarded the inquiry to William Clark but it was George Rogers who replied on December 12, writing that his younger brother "is well qualified almost for any business. If it should be in your power to confur on him any post of Honor and profit, in this Countrey in which we live, it will exceedingly gratify me."[12] The letter arrived in Washington about the time that Jefferson sent his message to Congress asking for an appropriation for the expedition.

Lewis wrote to Clark on May 17, 1803, asking him to extend hospitality to "an old and intimate friend," a Mr. Gelston of New York, who was bound for New Orleans and would probably stop at Clarksville. A month later Lewis apologized to Clark for taking so long to have completed district court papers relating to Clark's 1801 visit.[13]

With the tiny budget of $2,500 that had been authorized, the expedition began as a small command of ten men and one officer. However, it was already becoming apparent that the expedition had expanded in size and scope. Grasping that more than the authorized ten soldiers might be required, Jefferson authorized Lewis to engage any other men that "I may think useful in promoting the objects or success of this expedition." The mission was perilous and the president insisted that Lewis "err on the side of your safety, and to bring back your party safe even if it be with less information."[14] Beginning to be described as "double manned," the expedition now possessed the ingredients to be a success.[15]

On June 19, Lewis wrote to Clark again, a remarkable letter that began with information to Clark about court papers dealing with a private matter. Then he embarked on an entirely new subject. "From the long and uninterupted friendship and confidence which has subsisted between us I feel no hesitation in making to you the following communication under the fulest impression that it will be held by you inviolably secret untill I see you, or you shall hear from me again." Thus Lewis asked Clark to join him.[16] As Lewis prepared to leave Washington he was unsure if Clark would accept his offer. In the event that he declined, Lewis was provided with a blank commission for a lieutenant or ensign that could be filled in later to appoint his second-in-command.[17]

Lewis's previous field experience had been as a young subaltern when there was a company commander making the important decisions. Now he was the captain who had to deal with that responsibility himself. Organizational genius, not quite, but Lewis was remarkable in working out what would be necessary to maintain men for an uncertain period of time beyond resupply.

Anyone who crammed in necessities for weekend camping or an extended pack trip in the mountains can appreciate the remarkable record of items that Meriwether Lewis assembled and packed for shipment to St. Louis. The final count lists at least 179 items, many in multiples to provide fifteen outfits for individuals. The medicine chest contained fifty items of chemicals, compounds, and instruments.

He had to move a ton and a half of goods from Philadelphia to Pittsburgh. At some point, Lewis had given up the idea of having boats built at Nashville and reassigned the job to a Pittsburgh area builder. Keelboats built in the Pittsburgh vicinity were mostly drifted downstream to New Orleans, where some might even be rigged for sailing and sent to sea.[18]

Frontier defense and political formalities should have been enough to occupy the president and the secretary of war. But another element was added when the exploring expedition was to be funded and supported by the War Department. That required forewarning the scattered western military establishment. As Captain Lewis prepared to leave Washington the War Department sent letters to military personnel informing them to expect a special military expedition to explore the Missouri River. Stationed at the Carlisle, Pennsylvania, recruiting rendezvous, Lt. William A. Murray was ordered to assist Meriwether Lewis in selecting "eight of the best and most sober of your party for immediate command to Pittsburgh." The man who best qualified would be made a lance corporal to command the party to Pittsburgh where they would report to Lt. Moses Hooke, the assistant military agent.[19]

Farther west, captains Daniel Bissell of Fort Massac, Russell Bissell, and Amos Stoddard of Kaskaskia were also instructed "to afford Capt. Meriwether Lewis all the aid in your power in selecting and engaging men to accompany him on an expedition to the Westward." Additional men might be required and commandeered from their companies. It was suggested that the men who wished to join the expedition must exhibit a "character of sobriety, integrity and other necessary qualifications," which would render them suitable for such service. Dearborn emphasized that Bissell and Stoddard should furnish Lewis with one sergeant and "eight good men who understand rowing a boat," who would then take Lewis as far up the Missouri as they could go before the winter season froze the river.[20]

Mr. Jefferson's idea of observing the glorious Fourth of July involved listening to a band of Italian musicians serenading everyone at the Executive Mansion. Presumably there was some punch as the celebration included the announcement of the purchase of Louisiana. The next day Lewis left Washington and three days later wrote Jefferson from Harper's Ferry reciting problems getting the outfit transported. The iron boat frame was beginning to be a costly mistake. Meriwether realized that time was wasted seeing it built that might have been better spent in Philadelphia with his tutors. Those days had not been entirely devoted to instruction and advice as he also had to shop for the expedition equipment. As those purchases began to accumulate he also realized that building the boats in Nashville wouldn't work. The correspondence correcting that miscalculation and the orders to have the boat built near Pittsburgh are missing. How that was handled—a new builder selected, plans forwarded, a price agreed upon—represented a misstep that embarrassed the otherwise well-executed organization of the expedition.

Lewis planned to continue through Charles Town, Frankfort, Uniontown, and Redstone Old Fort to Pittsburgh. As that route took him by a place he had known during the Whiskey Rebellion, Lewis may have renewed his acquaintance with the McFarlane family.

At Pittsburgh by July 15 Lewis received his mail. Colonel Cushing, the head of the Adjutant General's Office, wrote Lewis on July 9 encouraging "That your expedition may be pleasant . . . and advantageous to our Country; and when its toils and dangers are over . . . you may enjoy many years of happiness, prosperity and honor."[21]

Back in February Jefferson had written his French naturalist friend Bernard Lacépède that they were sending a small exploring expedition to the source of the Missouri and whatever nearby river drained to the Pacific. Receiving the letter through the courtesy of James Monroe, Lacépède replied on May 18 about what he took as a glorious contribution to science. Jefferson wrote Lewis on July 14 adding an excerpt from Lacépède's letter specifically describing British naval officer William Broughton's examination of a hundred miles inland from the mouth of the Columbia River. From there the party saw and named Mount Hood. Lacépède guessed that mountain was a "dependence," or an appendage of the Stoney Mountains. Then there must be a short passage, Jefferson concluded, and "easy communication by rivers, canals & short portages between N. York for example & the city that could be built at the mouth of the Columbia . . . what a route for the commerce of Europe, Asia & America."[22]

Meriwether received Jefferson's letter at Pittsburgh on July 22 and immediately replied with an astonishing equanimity, revealing nothing of how he should have felt upon being charged with a continental quest. The captain modestly started his response with trivial details about a forgotten dirk and bridle or the delay about the completion of the boat being built up the Monongahela River. By then goods had arrived from Harper's Ferry.

Lewis resisted an egotistical response to Jefferson because the information that Lacépède mentioned was old stuff between them. Mr. Jefferson could afford to get excited; after all he had just bought half a continent and had a glimpse of the future. They had known about the cession of Louisiana before Lewis left Washington but the Lacépède letter gave the expedition greater national and international significance.

Lewis had still not received an answer from Clark when he wrote to Jefferson on July 26. Anxious to find a second-in-command, he opened the subject with Lt. Moses Hooke, who agreed to go with him.[23] By the time the secretary of war approved Hooke's reassignment on August 3, Lewis had received Clark's first letter. The mail had reached Clark and on July 17 he replied that he would "cheerfully join you in an official Charactor."[24]

Gratified that Clark would accompany him, Lewis wrote words that could only come from a close friend: "I could neither hope, wish, or expect from a union with any man on earth, more perfect support or further aid in the discharge of the several duties of my mission, than that, which I am confident I shall derive from being associated with yourself."[25]

When Jefferson finally received the confirmation he wrote Dearborn, "I have the pleasure to inform you that William Clark accepts with great glee the office of going with Capt. Lewis up the Missouri." And Dearborn happily responded, "Mr. W. Clark having consented to accompany Capt. Lewis is highly interesting, 'N adds very much to the ballance of chances in favour of ultimate success."[26] Having the two chiefs approval lent further support to the Lewis command.

Although the contract called for completion by July 20, the keelboat was still unfinished when Lewis arrived in Pittsburgh. The boat builder kept pushing back delivery until getting it done boiled down to keeping a crew of boat builders sober. When that delay combined with the lowering water in the Ohio, Lewis realized that the schedule was slipping away from him.

While waiting for the boat, it is supposed that Lewis bought a large black Newfoundland breed dog for twenty dollars. The problem of getting on the river must have been on his mind as he named the dog Seaman. After a torturing month the boat was finally complete. Having lost the opportunity for an earlier departure to avoid low river levels, he now had to ship part of the outfit overland.

Lewis left Pittsburgh on August 31, 1803, with a pilot and ten men of which seven were soldiers apparently detached from the command of Lt. William A. Murray and "three young men on trial they having proposed to go with me throughout the voyage."[27] That was late in the year and the water in the Ohio was low. On the first day, Lewis found that all of the men, including himself, had to get out of the boat and lift and push it over shallows. By nightfall, they had traveled ten miles and were "much fatigued." After giving the men whiskey Lewis retired at 8:00 p.m., convinced that the laden keelboat had to be lightened.

Working the awkward boat down through the low water of the Ohio River was so exhausting that Lewis stopped keeping a daily journal on September 18. He wrote a letter to William Clark on September 28 and another to President Jefferson on October 3, both dated at Cincinnati and bracketing the week he spent there resting his men.[28]

The long letter to the president concerned Jefferson's fascination with ancient bones. Dr. William Goforth had been excavating at the Big Bone Lick about seventeen miles away. It is uncertain whether Lewis went to see the site but he spent a good deal of time with the doctor examining and describing a find to the scientific-minded Mr. Jefferson.

The doctor's son-in-law, former lieutenant John Armstrong, had been the first officer assigned to explore the Missouri River back in 1790. During a week in a place where there wasn't all that much to do, the two veterans recalled the previous mission, no longer a secret as the acquisition of Spanish Louisiana had mooted any lingering resentment. Surely Armstrong shared what he had learned thirteen years ago, maybe got out a copy of his now outdated memorandum to give the young explorer an early insight into the experience and veracity of the men he would be meeting in St. Louis. They must have laughed that the price for exploring the Missouri had grown from Armstrong's modest "one hundred and ten dollars and thirty-nine ninetieths of a Dollar" to the rather munificent $2,500 that Congress had approved.[29]

The voyage down the Ohio to Clarksville took until October 15. When Lewis finally arrived and connected with Clark, the expedition began in earnest. After eleven days gathering supplies, hiring men, and enlisting soldiers for what was designated as the "Corps of Volunteers for Northwestern Discovery" the two officers continued on.[30] On November 18, Lewis and Clark left the Ohio River and headed upstream on the Mississippi River, reaching the first major river town, Kaskaskia, on November 29. They were falling behind schedule because they lacked the men who could move the boat against a strong current. For the next nine days, the captains busied themselves with selecting recruits from the companies of captains Bissell and Stoddard.

At Kaskaskia Lewis learned that the Spanish lieutenant governor in St. Louis would not allow them to proceed up the Missouri until he had clearance from his superiors in New Orleans. Lewis would have to meet Carlos Dehault Delassus and try to convince him otherwise. But the Spanish officer only spoke French and Lewis had to ride on to Cahokia, the next town, to find an interpreter while Clark brought the boats on.

Something of the feeling of the moment was expressed in a letter from a gentleman in Kaskaskia to his friend in Philadelphia. On December 8 he wrote,

> Captains Lewis and Clark (commissioners appointed by the President to ascertain the source of the Mississippi, &c.) arrived here six day since, and this day set out again proceeding on their voyage up the Mississippi. They appear to be gentlemen well qualified for the enterprize, and in good health and spirits and seem disposed to brave every difficulty. But from information however, from high authority, I am persuaded the Spanish government will not at this moment permit them to enter the Missouri river—Thus situated they will be under the necessity of remaining below its mouth until the existing differences are adjusted between the United States and that nation.[31]

Some of those old villages on the Illinois shore had been established in the late seventeenth century. The inhabitants had a long history in trade, using the Mississippi River corridor from Prairie du Chien in the north to New Orleans at the mouth. But across the river Spanish authorities were apprehensive about the threat posed by an increasing American population. Those traders or trappers were not allowed on the Missouri River, where the authorization of monopoly trading licenses gave Spanish citizens an advantage. Ominously, now the American Captain Lewis appeared in Cahokia looking for someone to help forward an exploration of that river.

When Lewis arrived in Cahokia he met Nicholas Jarrot, a Cahokia merchant who offered a part of his land for the short-term residence of the corps.[32] The other interpreter was John Hay, a transplanted Frenchman with an English name. When Captain Lewis crossed the river to St. Louis on December 7 both men accompanied him to present his passport papers to Lieutenant Governor Delassus.

The documents the captain presented confirmed that the corps intended to ascend the Missouri River on a route that would take them to the Pacific Ocean. Passports were signed by British and French ministers but there was no authorization from the Spanish minister.[33] Because Delassus had not been officially informed of the sale of Louisiana, he became suspicious and, in a last opportunity to exercise an official prerogative, refused to allow the expedition to depart until he had official permission from his superiors in New Orleans. It would be the next spring before he could expect to have an answer.

Delassus was a provincial officer stationed far from the seats of Spanish authority in New Orleans, Washington, or Spain. His superiors had not shared their apprehension of a growing United States threat to the interior provinces. The "observations" of the secret Agent Thirteen, setting a scenario for what was expected to develop after the transfer of Louisiana to the United States, had yet to be written.[34]

In hindsight, it is equally appalling how little Jefferson and his cabinet knew about Louisiana from old maps and geographical concepts that owed as much to past imagination as present fact. It is doubtful that James Monroe or Robert Livingston paid much attention to any maps when they saw the opportunity of Napoleon's unexpected offer. There was a vague grasp of almost mythic history, of La Salle or Cadillac, the French and Indian wars, the collapse of New France, and the greed of a British regime that wanted its North American colonies to bear the financial burden of imperial conquest. Even as enlightened as he was, Jefferson had only a slight understanding of that shadowy past.

Lewis was in fact the president's special agent overseeing a political process like nothing the nation had previously addressed. Lewis had no authority to enter into duties officially delegated to the perfectly competent Capt. Amos Stoddard, who was authorized to receive the transfer of the territory and act as interim governor. But no one doubted that Lewis's previous close relationship with Mr. Jefferson had not ended when he took on the expedition.

St. Louis received the forerunner of the new order with condescending hospitality. From December 1803 until the end of February 1804, Meriwether Lewis was the only American officer on the west side of the Mississippi above New Orleans. His poise, restraint, and projection of a promising future made the first impression on those concerned new citizens. The representative of the United States strode up the hill into town in an expression of single-handed, personal diplomacy.

Although Delassus's decision was an official setback, Lewis and Clark were actually too late to ascend the Missouri River. The plans made last April for a small party had been too optimistic.[35] The purchases that Lewis made in the east were for a complement of ten or twelve men, with a safety margin of fifteen. After the ascent of the Mississippi from the mouth of the Ohio it was apparent that more men would be needed to stem the powerful Missouri River. When Clark took the corps to Wood Creek he was considering around forty prospective boatmen. The increased number of men meant that additional supplies would be necessary. With the winter season already upon them, it would have been foolish to move on to a distant camp in an inhospitable country.

After his initial interview with Lieutenant Governor Delassus, a dispirited Lewis trudged down to the riverbank to meet William Clark, who was sailing past St. Louis "under stripes and colours." Clark wrote that "hundreds came to the bank to view us."[36] In the crowd Clark surely recognized some of his old acquaintances from previous visits to the west shore of the Mississippi.[37]

Lewis properly returned to the United States' side at Cahokia to complete his reports on developments while Clark sailed on to find an excellent site for a winter camp about eighteen miles north of St. Louis, up a little river opposite the mouth of the Missouri. The experienced woodsman noted that the country around the camp afforded good hunting with "innoumerable quantiss. of fowls of every discription."[38] The corps immediately began construction of huts to shelter them during the winter.

Meanwhile Lewis needed to consult with the only two reputable cartographers in Upper Louisiana. Antoine Soulard was the Spanish surveyor general. James MacKay's experiences as a middle river trader had produced a partial map of the Missouri River. Both the Cahokia interpreter John Hay and Indiana Territorial Governor William Henry Harrison had old inaccurate copies of that map but MacKay might be able to provide a more reliable map of the first fifteen hundred miles of their journey.

While Clark readied what came to be called Camp River Dubois, or Americanized to Wood Creek, Lewis returned to St. Louis to begin compiling answers to Jefferson's list of queries about Louisiana.[39] For the basic geography Lewis interviewed Surveyor General Soulard, who had drawn a map, "Ydea Topografica," of North America eight years earlier. Two years later Soulard and MacKay had collaborated in a complete revision of that map.[40]

But would Soulard, a Spanish officer, answer Lewis's questions concerning the census and quantity of land already granted? That was privileged governmental information. So was the number of immigrants from the United States within the last year, the proportion of slaves to whites, population of free whites, quantity of ungranted lands claimed by persons, species of rights accorded to the inhabitants to hold their lands, the wealth of the inhabitants, the position and extent of the settlements, the state of agriculture.

When Lewis interviewed Soulard he was pleased that the surveyor general appeared friendly and was giving "unqualifyed assurance of his willingness to serve me." But the man also exhibited "extreme trepidation" with some of the questions, leading Lewis to conclude that "the eye of despotic power" was always upon the poor fellow. To ease the concern Lewis tried to tell Soulard that US citizens had the liberty to give information to strangers. Soulard replied that the policy of his government forbade it. However, when Lewis asked about the population, Soulard did give him that information in round numbers. At least that was an opening and prompted the democratically minded Lewis to write later that the inhabitants "move more as tho' the *fear of the Commandant*, than *that of god*, was before their eyes." When the United States took possession of Louisiana, Lewis felt that the inhabitants would come forward and volunteer information. But for the time being, "every thing must be obtained by stealth."[41]

Delassus hospitably invited Lewis to dine but remained wary of his intentions. Several points expressed by Lewis did not ring true with Delassus. One was the number of men to accompany the expedition, "which truly cannot be less [than twenty-five] so as to be able to be somewhat secure among the nations and cannot be larger because of the difficulty of the provisions in such an expedition."[42] That was a lot of strange soldiers to turn loose on the river.

In these early developments Captain Lewis was more than a field officer organizing an exploration.[43] Still thinking of him as an aide, Jefferson required Lewis to run errands and attend to distracting details; although it was beyond his primary responsibility, the officer was also collecting information on Louisiana for the president. While waiting to leave, Lewis could also observe and report on any unexpected consequences of the purchase.

Initially the expedition was conceived as river mapping with some scientific benefits on the side. With the purchase of the entire unknown territory of Louisiana the mission had been expanded to a primary goal of finding a water route between the Missouri River and the Pacific Ocean for the purposes of commerce.[44] It was suddenly possible to link United States territory to its discovery claim to the Columbia River. Whether that represented Jefferson's vision of a transcontinental nation or was the consequence of an unexpected development has been the subject of endless speculation. It is possible that on long evenings before a fireplace in the presidential mansion, Thomas Jefferson had shared his thoughts with his young protégé, but documentary proofs are lacking and this can only suppose that Captain Lewis was caught up in a snowballing situation.

From what Lewis was able to extract from his initial social encounters in St. Louis, financial trouble west of the Mississippi River had been developing for a decade. Spain had found that expanse too expensive to maintain. The territorial politics of the past half century had been devoted to preventing the British from gaining a foothold. But the Spanish were increasingly concerned about what the Americans next door might do.

There was a starry-eyed notion that the purchase of the Louisiana Territory was a monumental bargain that doubled the size of the nation in a deftly financed deal and was expected to expand the commerce of the nation. But the republic was not just getting a new land. It had inherited the people who lived there. The old part of that population were Indians, French-speaking Indian traders and Missouri River boatmen. The new element was American immigrants whom Spain had induced to come and settle, on the promise of lands as a barrier to the appearance of more of their kind. They were not a faction where patriotism for the United States glowed very brightly.

The people had existing claims to land provided by the Spanish administration. Lewis soon sensed that those inhabitants were already concerned how the new regime would respect their property rights. In that cashless society, personal fortunes were mostly tied up in skins and pelts, stashes of lead, or claims to lands made under the Spanish authority. With the transfer hanging over it, paper agreements didn't mean much to a community that had no idea how the United States would honor grants made under the Spanish administration. They would not have been pleased to know that holdings would have to be identified and surveyed before the nation could begin selling unclaimed tracts to produce revenue.

Captains Lewis and Stoddard were soon aware that land speculation was surfacing. Already there were rumors from apparently reliable citizens of Indiana Territory that something was amiss, that the departing Spanish governor had issued fraudulent certificates that established suspect claims. The administration needed to know that and Lewis encouraged Stoddard to submit it to Washington as soon as possible.[45]

Although the Indian trade was expected to become a huge revenue producer, if what his new friends told Lewis was true, the actual expectations were bleak. Sending trading outfits up the Missouri to bypass jealous customers was risky business that had not proved very profitable. When the traders tried to increase production by introducing trapping instead of leaving that task to the Indians, they risked offending the tribes.

After inheriting an $83 million deficit from the Washington and Adams administrations, the Jefferson administration added $15 million more. How could Secretary of the Treasury Albert Gallatin hope to incorporate the territorial purchase price into a busted budget? Did Lewis dare communicate that discouraging observation to Jefferson?

Captain Lewis considered the southern approaches to Louisiana, and how that related to the old Spanish colony of Santa Fe. Before leaving Cincinnati he had written the president that he was thinking of making a horseback exploration during the winter "up the Canceze River and towards Santafee." After reading that on November 16, Jefferson responded in no uncertain terms, "One thing however we are decided in: that you must not undertake the winter excursion which you propose in yours of Oct. 3. Such an excursion will be more dangerous than the main expedition up the Missouri . . . and hazard our main object."[46] Jefferson could not have the captain of his dream expedition gallivanting off on risky adventures.

While he absorbed that emphatic instruction, there were practical matters that needed attention. Until he met Clark on the lower Ohio, Lewis had complete responsibility for the organization and equipping of the expedition. After trying out the nine recruits from Carlisle and Pittsburgh he found most of those men wanting. Only John Colter and young George Shannon appear to have been enlisted before more likely men were found at Maysville, Kentucky. Lewis wrote to Clark on December 17 explaining that George Drouillard, the expert hunter they engaged at Fort Massac, had returned from South West Point in Tennessee with recruits who did not possess the necessary qualifications for an extended service. For the rest they raided the companies of captains Bissell and Stoddard at Kaskaskia. A lot would depend on whether Clark could get them into shape before it was time to leave in the spring. Stoddard's soldiers would only go as far up the

Missouri as their assistance was necessary and would be sent back as soon as possible because Stoddard was going to need all the men available to him. As understandable as that was, Meriwether could not let it interfere with his primary mission.

It was obvious that there was a division of responsibilities between the joint leaders.[47] Despite interpretations by historians about the co-command between Lewis and Clark, there was a division of responsibilities. By super-intending the soldiers and assuming responsibility for daily operations, including writing a daily journal, Clark left Lewis free to deal with more complex issues.

In his expedition design, Lewis recognized his own limitations from the very first. In Clark he had found a solid man who would see to daily opera-tions. It was no insult to Clark that he was as steady as Lewis was im-pressionable. Lewis knew that he was not temperamentally suited to the supervision of the men. Not much could go off course when the route was confined to the channel of the river. Instead of plodding along some muddy rut he would be better employed observing and absorbing a broader experi-ence, ranging afar to absorb the essence of what was being encountered.

It would be spring before Delassus assured Lewis that there were not objections to permitting the expedition to ascend the Missouri. Meantime, they needed James MacKay's updated map in order to understand what they faced. While Lewis distracted Delassus in St. Louis, it was up to Clark to take the initiative.

Camp River Dubois was almost across from the mouth of the Missouri river, eighteen miles from St. Louis and about thirty miles from St. André, where MacKay lived. It began snowing on December 29 and continued intermittently through the New Year until January 4, when the temperature in "a warm corner" of Clark's hut read twenty degrees. The following day, the ice-filled, ever treacherous Mississippi was perilous for any boat. It was said that "such vast quantities of ice float down the part that is not frozen, that, to attempt to go down it in any thing but a small canoe, would be rushing into the jaws of death."[48]

Perilous or not, Clark was determined to have an accurate map. Without informing Lewis or Stoddard, he dispatched Private Joseph Fields up the Missouri to locate James MacKay and invite him to Camp River Dubois. Fields had to travel "30 miles up" the river to where MacKay was commandant of the St. André district.[49]

Clark's journal entry for January 10, 1804, shows that the meeting was intentionally kept secret. While Lewis had assured Delassus that the Corps of Discovery would wait until the spring to begin the expedition, Clark was already getting things going. He ordered Fields to find MacKay and bring him to camp regardless of the short-term illegality. Fields went under the cover of the wintry conditions and if he was apprehended as a trespasser, it was only a matter of a few months before the transfer of the country would moot that technicality.

But would the St. André commandant accept the invitation? Anything he did would also be illegal as he would be leaving the country without a passport.[50] Exposing a classified government document like his official map of the Missouri River could result in a charge of trafficking and cost him his command.[51]

Fortunately MacKay had heard in September that the United States had bought Louisiana. Realizing that he would soon be out of a job, he had already written a Kentucky congressman that he intended to become a US citizen, even if that deprived him of his office and salary.[52] By handing over a map important to the American party, MacKay would demonstrate his new allegiance.

Fields probably departed on January 7, the same day that Clark began to sketch a map of the Missouri River "for the purpose of correcting from the information which I may get of the countrey to the NW."[53] Fields found MacKay on the morning of the ninth as he was witnessing the signing of a warranty deed at St. André. Later in the day, MacKay went to Marais des Lairds, which was close to Portage des Sioux, a thin strip of land above and just a bit north of Camp River Dubois. After surveying some out lots on the morning of January 10, MacKay set out to go to Camp River Dubois.[54]

Clark was watching from Camp River Dubois as Private Fields crossed the Mississippi at midday "between sheets of floating ice with some risque." Suspicious that Fields had taken so long to return, Clark questioned him about the trip and was told that "the ice run so thick on the Missouri" that it had been impossible for him to cross. Clark feared Fields had remained "so long" on the Missouri that he had been recognized by the inhabitants. But Fields assured him "that the people is greatly in favor of the Americans" and sometime after 1 p.m. James MacKay arrived at the camp.[55]

Due to the winter weather, the afternoon arrival and the fact that they needed time to discuss the intricacies of a map written in French that covered fifteen hundred miles of the river, MacKay stayed overnight and possibly longer.

Clark's journal entries for the next two days were short. He continued to complain of being ill due to a severe "Ducking" on the ninth and the persistent illness that had tortured him for the last two months. It was well into January before Clark began making detailed calculations based on the distances from Camp River Dubois to the Mandan nation, from the Mandans to the Rocky Mountains, and from those mountains to the Pacific Ocean. His calculations filled several pages.[56]

With the final piece in place Clark drafted a new map that was based on previous maps made by MacKay and Soulard, and from information gleaned from the Chouteau brothers and various other traders. The map covered the area from St. Louis to the Pacific Ocean showing the possible routes. Jefferson received it in July from Pierre Chouteau, who conducted the Osage delegation to Washington.[57]

For the most part, Meriwether remained in Cahokia or St. Louis while William ran the camp and trained the soldiers. There was a period in February into early March when Clark became too sick to continue under those harsh conditions. He had to return to St. Louis and recover his health. Captain Lewis took over the camp and journal keeping, which recorded a series of minor problems as the soldiers tried out their commander. A serious problem developed in March when Lewis had to go to St. Louis for a week and returned to find that several men had balked at orders from Sergeant Ordway; "mortified and disappointed at the disorderly conduct," Lewis wrote a detachment order that confined the four men to the compound for ten days.[58] Could that be taken as a difference in command presence?

Meantime, Clark had made an error in character evaluation when he arranged for the entrepreneur Manuel Lisa to contract a crew of French hands to move a laden pirogue up the Missouri. As the time for departure neared, for whatever reason Lisa failed to meet that obligation. Lewis turned to the very accommodating Auguste Chouteau, who came up with eight boatmen beholden to him. After double-damning Lisa, Captain Lewis had a better grasp of the competitive underside of the St. Louis mercantile community.[59]

As the winter eased, Captain Stoddard prepared for his arrival in St. Louis to complete the transfer. National honor made it necessary to make a good first impression. On February 18, Stoddard wrote Delassus to arrange a meeting and begin preparations for the transfer. After taking time to have it translated from English, Delassus answered Stoddard on February 20 and invited him to his home.[60]

In the seven months since Stoddard's arrival at Kaskaskia, he had seen St. Louis many times—from a boat on the Mississippi. On a freezing February day Stoddard finally met the man who had stopped Captain Lewis from ascending the Missouri River. When Stoddard pulled his boat ashore two miles below St. Louis, a troop of volunteer horsemen met and escorted him to the government house where a large group of citizens had assembled.[61] Lieutenant Governor Delassus welcomed Stoddard as the commissioner of the French Republic. When Stoddard noted that the Spanish flag was still flying, Delassus assured him that he was ready to deliver the province.

That evening many of the townspeople enjoyed "a most Sumpcious Dinner, & a large Compy" and celebration.[62] But during the day the weather turned very cold and the Mississippi was blocked with ice. The boats bringing Stoddard's soldiers were forced ashore six miles below on the east bank of the Mississippi River.[63] While the bigwigs toasted each other, the soldiers shivered.

The following morning Stoddard made a formal demand for Louisiana. March 9 was set as the date for the ceremony and after a day to demon-strate French dominion, Louisiana would be transferred to the United States postponing the transfer for almost two weeks. Stoddard blamed the delay on Delassus's illness and the ice on the Mississippi.[64] During the interval the Spanish officer gave Stoddard a list of individuals who merited attention and commendation for past good behavior.[65]

At 12:45 in the afternoon of March 9, Delassus delivered the province. He praised the inhabitants, "thirty-six years . . . the fidelity and the Courage with which you have defended this Flag will never be forgotten: and in my capacity as commissioner, I sincerely wish you, all happiness and prosperity."[66] Various military protocols followed as the flag of the garrison was moved to the public square before the government house where the Spanish troops paraded. When the Spanish flag was lowered and the French banner run up, there was a discharge of a cannon. After this Stoddard received the keys to the fort and an exchange of papers took place.[67]

The following day, March 10, 1804, Upper Louisiana became the prop-erty of the United States. Captain Stoddard's company marched through the town to the garrison, raised the American flag, and fired a "federal salute."[68] Stoddard's oration welcoming the inhabitants into the United States centered on liberty and democracy.[69] He "felt all the delicacy of such a task," and that "every sentence seemed to contain a compromitment of myself and the Government."[70]

"[P]ressed by many zealous friends to our Government to publish a cir-cular address to the people," Stoddard later apologized to his superiors because "I had no precedent to guide me in the draft, I hope its defects will be excused."[71] The quiet ceremony had "excited the sensibilities of many people, the ceremonies of investiture drew tears from the eyes of all—but they were not tears of regret."[72]

Stoddard immediately plunged into a daunting load of administrative obligations but Lewis and Clark took time to attend social functions and interview the inhabitants. They also toured some nearby districts and took short trips up the Missouri River with Pierre Chouteau and Charles Gratiot.[73] In accordance with Pierre Chouteau's generous hospitality, they made "the house of this gentleman" our home while his brother-in-law Charles Gratiot graciously made horses available to them.[74]

It was a letter from the secretary of war that spoiled Meriwether's digestion. He expected that Clark would be appointed a captain, which would put them on an almost equal command footing. But the appointment was only for the low rank of a second lieutenant.[75] The army that Lewis had harrowed for the president had become sensitive to promotions that jumped the officers' list and Congress was not going to let the president override that rigid formality.[76] Lewis had overstepped his bounds when he promised Clark a captaincy and all he could do at this late moment was assure Clark "by G—d," that his compensation "shall be equal to my own."[77] What they would do on the expedition was pretend to hold a joint command, as the behavior and morale of the men was more important than a title in a governmental ledger.

Much was at stake. Stemming the Missouri River was going to be very different than a float on the beautiful Ohio. There were no settlements to rely on. And just forty miles up the Missouri, the banks teemed with drastically different Indians. What the expedition lacked in river skills was made up in arms, military expertise, and twenty-five handpicked men "capable of bearing bodily fatigue in a pretty considerable degree."[78] They had selected and trained an elite corps and now it was time to test them on the great river.

NOTES

1. Alexander Wilson, "Particulars of the Death of Captain Lewis," *Port Folio* 7 (January 1812): 38.

2. A recent treatment of the circumstances can be found in Jon Kukla, *A Wilderness So Immense* (New York: Alfred A. Knopf, 2003).

3. Jerry W. Knudson, "Newspaper Reaction to the Louisiana Purchase," *Missouri Historical Review* 63 (January 1969): 203, 184.

4. Bernard DeVoto, "An Inference regarding the Expedition of Lewis and Clark," *Proceedings of the American Philosophical Society* 99 (August 1955): 188.

5. Jefferson's message to Congress, January 18, 1803, Jackson, *LLC* 1: 12–13.

6. Henry Muhlenberg, the well-known botanist and friend of Mahlon Dickerson, also lived in Lancaster. Dickerson (1770–1853) was adjutant general of Pennsylvania, governor and senator from New Jersey, and from 1834 to 1838 the secretary of the navy. Dickerson wrote in his diary in 1807 that he "went botanizing" with Dr. Muhlenberg on several occasions. Mahlon Dickerson, Diary 1801–1809, July 21–23, 1807, Dickerson Papers, NJHS.

7. TJ to Robert Patterson, March 2, 1803, Caspar Wistar and Benjamin Rush, February 28, 1803, BSB, February 27, 1803, Jackson, *LLC* 1: 16–21.

8. Established during the Washington administration the Indian Trade Factory system was an attempt to deal fairly with the tribes through government-sponsored and supervised stores. For background see Paul Francis Prucha, *American Indian Policy in the Formative Years, the Indian Trade and Intercourse Acts, 1790–1834* (Cambridge, MA: Harvard University Press, 1962).

9. ML to WC, June 27, 1801, Jackson, *LLC* 1: 101n3. These lands on Brush Creek were probably in the Virginia Military Tract next to the initial seven ranges.

10. *Jackson*, LLC 1: 57 and 2: 738; WC to John T. Mason, July 5, 1801 (photocopy), and John Armstrong to WC, August 3, 1801 (photocopy), reference file, Clark Family Collection-MHS; James Holmberg, ed., *Dear Brother: Letters of William Clark to Jonathan Clark* (New Haven, CT: Yale University Press, 2002), p. 30.

11. That would have been interesting as it was during Jefferson's not entirely effective watch as governor of Virginia that George Rogers Clark's debt problems were allowed to pile up.

12. George Rogers Clark to TJ, December 12, 1802; Landon Y. Jones, *William Clark and the Shaping of the West* (New York: Hill and Wang, 2004), p. 111.

13. ML to WC, May 17, 1803, Jackson, *LLC* 2: 738, and ML to WC, June 19, 1803, Jackson, *LLC* 1: 57. Jackson states that Lewis in May had still not made up his mind to invite Clark on the expedition. It was only after Lewis returned to Washington that the expedition plans had been enlarged upon—and then made sense to invite Clark, his preferred choice.

14. Jefferson's instructions to ML, June 20, 1803, Jackson, *LLC* 1: 64.

15. TJ to ML, November 16, 1803, Jackson, *LLC* 1: 137.

16. ML to WC, June 19, 1803, Jackson, *LLC* 1: 57–60. Lewis's invitation to Clark detailed the size and scope of the planned enterprise in at least five pages. He concluded his remarks with "Thus my friend you have so far as leasure will at this time permit me to give it you, a summary view of the plan, the means and objects of this expedition. If therefore there is anything under those circumstances, in this enterprise, which would induce you to participate with me in its fatigues, it's dangers and it's honors, believe me there is no man on earth with whom I should feel equal pleasure in sharing them as with yourself."

17. War Department, July 2, 1803, Jackson, *LLC* 1: 104.

18. George Thurston, *Pittsburgh As It Is* (Pittsburgh: W. S. Haven, 1857), pp. 67–69.

19. Thomas H. Cushing to William A. Murray, June 20, 1803, Jackson, *LLC* 1: 67.

20. HD to RB, AS, and DB, July 2, 1803; HD to RB and AS, July 2, 1803, Jackson, *LLC* 1: 103–104.

21. Thomas H. Cushing to ML, July 9, 1803, Jackson, *LLC* 1: 107.

22. TJ to ML, July 15, 1803, Jackson, *LLC* 1: 109–10.

23. ML to TJ, July 26, 1803, Jackson, *LLC* 1: 113.

24. WC to ML, Clarksville, July 18, 1803, Jackson, *LLC* 1: 110. Clark also sent letters to Lewis and Jefferson on July 24 informing them of his decision. WC to ML, Louisville, July 24 and WC to TJ, Clarksville, July 24, 1803, Jackson, *LLC* 1: 112–13.

25. ML to WC, Pittsburgh, August 3, 1803, Jackson, *LLC* 1: 115.

26. TJ to HD, August 13, 1803, document 23157 and HD to TJ, August 28, 1803, document 23219, roll 28, TJ-LOC.

27. ML, August 31, 1803, Moulton, *JLCE* 2: 1 and note 3. The editor suggests that George Shannon and John Colter may have joined by then.

28. ML to WC, September 28 and ML to TJ, October 3, 1803, Jackson, *LLC* 1: 124–31.

29. John Armstrong, "Memorandum," box 2, folder 6, collection M0006, Indiana Historical Society.

30. Six soldiers enlisted included John Colter on the fifteenth, George Gibson, George Shannon and John Shields on the nineteenth, and William Bratton and Nathaniel Pryor on the twentieth. Most gave their birthplaces as Virginia while Gibson and Shannon were from Pennsylvania.

31. *Philadelphia Daily Advertiser*, January 7, 1804, p. 3. Very likely the informant was William Morrison, whose Philadelphia connection was his uncle Guy Bryant.

32. ML to TJ, December 19, 1803, Jackson, *LLC* 1: 145. This arrangement has been disputed.

33. Carlos Dehault Delassus to Juan Manuel de Salcedo and the Marques de Casa Calvo, St. Louis, December 9, 1803, Jackson, *LLC* 1: 142.

34. "Reflections on Louisiana" was incorrectly attributed to the Spanish officer Vincente Folch in James A. Robertson, *Louisiana under the Rule of Spain, France and the United States, 1785–1807* (Cleveland: Arthur H. Clark Company, 1911), p. 343. It was later identified from the hand of Gen. James Wilkinson, commanding general of the United States Army.

35. Holmberg, *Dear Brother*, p. 76.

36. Ibid., p. 61.

37. WC had previously visited St. Louis in summer 1797, meeting François Valle, the commandant at Ste. Genevieve, Lt. Gov. Zenon Trudeau, and the Chouteau brothers. Jones, *William Clark*, pp. 95–97.

38. Holmberg, *Dear Brother*, p. 62.

39. Donald Hastings Jr., "It's Name Is 'Camp River Dubois,'" *Lewis and Clark Society of America*, special ed. (January 2003): 3.

40. Danisi and Wood, "Lewis and Clark's Route Map," p. 59.

41. ML to TJ, December 28, 1803, Jackson, *LLC* 1: 151.

42. Carlos Dehault Delassus to Juan Manuel de Salcedo and the Marques de Casa Calvo, St. Louis, December 9, 1803, Jackson, *LLC* 1: 143.

43. ML to WC, June 19, 1803, Jackson, *LLC* 1: 57. "The object of this Act as understood by its framers was to give the sanction of the government to exploreing the interior of the continent of North America, or that part of it bordering on the Missourie & Columbia Rivers."

44. Jefferson's instructions to ML, June 20, 1803, Jackson, *LLC* 1: 61.

45. *ASP, Public Lands* 1: 193–94; Carter, *TP* 7: 168.

46. ML to TJ, October 3 and TJ to ML, November 16, 1803, Jackson, *LLC* 1: 131, 137.

47. Gary E. Moulton, "The Missing Journals of Meriwether Lewis," *Montana: Magazine of Western History* 35 (Summer 1985): 28–39; Jones, *William Clark*, pp. 125–26.

48. *ASP, Miscellaneous* 2: 94.

49. WC, January 10, 1804, Moulton, *JLCE* 2: 154.

50. The Spanish authority required that its inhabitants obtain passports to travel from one district to another. US Supreme Court, *Guitard v. Stoddard*, 16 Howard 494 (1853), p. 502; http://supreme.justia.com/us/57/494/case.html (accessed April 8, 2008).

51. ML to TJ, December 28, 1803, Jackson, *LLC* 1: 149–50.

52. James MacKay to John Fowler, September 24, 1803, document 4166-67, Breckinridge Papers, LOC.

53. Ernest Staples Osgood, ed., *The Field Notes of Captain William Clark, 1803–1805* (New Haven, CT: Yale University Press, 1964), p. 16.

54. Danisi and Wood, "Lewis and Clark's Route Map," p. 71.

55. WC, January 10, 1804, Moulton, *JLCE* 2: 154.

56. Osgood, *The Field Notes of William Clark*, pp. 14, 16, 19–23.

57. Jackson, "A New Lewis and Clark Map," pp. 119–26.

58. Detachment Orders, March 3, 1804; Moulton, *JLCE* 2: 178.

59. ML to WC, May 6, 1804, Jackson, *LLC* 1: 180.

60. AS to Charles Dehault Delassus, Kaskaskia, February 18, 1804, and Charles Dehault Delassus to AS, February 20, 1804, Amos Stoddard Papers, MHS.

61. AS to William Claiborne and JW, March 26, 1804, Amos Stoddard Papers, MHS.

62. Holmberg, *Dear Brother*, pp. 76–77; "Transfer of Upper Louisiana," p. 113, MHS.

63. "Transfer of Upper Louisiana," pp. 95–96.

64. AS to HD, March 10, 1804, Amos Stoddard Papers, MHS; "Transfer of Upper Louisiana."

65. Frederic L. Billon, *Annals of St. Louis in its Early Days* (St. Louis: 1886), pp. 364–71.

66. "Transfer of Upper Louisiana," p. 86.

67. AS to Claiborne and JW, March 26, 1804, Amos Stoddard Papers, MHS.

68. Ibid.

69. Hibbert, "Major Amos Stoddard." Stoddard delivered several Masonic orations. *Early American Imprints*, first series, no. 36370-71.

70. "Transfer of Upper Louisiana," pp. 95–96. An old word meaning commitment and compromise.

71. Ibid.

72. Ibid., p. 97.

73. Osgood, *The Field Notes of William Clark*, p. 27.

74. WC to William Croghan, May 2, 1804, Jackson, *LLC* 1: 178; WC, December 22, 1803, Moulton, JLCE, 2: 139.

75. HD to ML, March 26, and ML to WC, May 6, 1804; 172 and 179 and WC to Nicholas Biddle, August 15, 1811, Jackson, *LLC* 2: 572.

76. The Corps of Engineers, to which Clark hoped to gain an appointment, allowed for two captains, two first lieutenants, and two second lieutenants. *Records of the US House of Representatives*, RG233, HD to the House of Representatives, December 1803, M1268, roll 12, frame 0326, p. 136, NARA. Clark was commissioned a second of artillery.

77. TJ to HD, August 13, 1803, document 23157, roll 28, TJ-LOC.

78. ML to WC, June 19, 1803, Jackson, *LLC* 1: 58.

FOUR

Trouble in the Expedition's Blood

The chief belov'd, the comrade dear[1]

As time for the departure of the expedition neared, Captain Lewis had remained in St. Louis helping Pierre Chouteau ready a delegation of Osage Indians for a trip to Washington. At the last minute Auguste Chouteau had procured eight *engagés* to accompany the expedition as far as the Mandan/Hidatsa villages, about fifteen hundred miles up the Missouri, and sent them on to Clark at Camp River Dubois. When Lewis left St. Louis for St. Charles on May 20 he was accompanied by those who had been associated with him and Clark over the past five months. The entourage of military officers included Captain Amos Stoddard and lieutenants Milford and Worrell. The civilians were Auguste Chouteau, Charles Gratiot, doctors Seth and Jeremiah Millington, and a dozen or more of the inhabitants of St. Louis. After a heavy rain forced them to take shelter, the party did not arrive across the river from St. Charles until the early evening. While there are no notes about the conversations Lewis might have had with the party, it must have been an exciting ride.

Clark had assembled the crew at Camp River Dubois and set out for St. Charles on the fourteenth. That had given him an opportunity to make some adjustments in how the keelboat was loaded and where the men were best stationed. When the two captains were reunited they hired two inter-

86

preters, enlisting them as privates in the army. François Labiche was an Omaha mixed-blood who would prove to be invaluable as a French-to-English interpreter. Although he had one eye and was nearsighted, another Omaha mixed-blood, Pierre Cruzette, was skilled in the sign language and was an excellent boat pilot.[2]

Captain Lewis was about to ascend to his destiny on the strength and dedication of those he had drawn into this adventure. Not all that much has survived about them. The seven soldiers who started with him from Pittsburgh were released to go to an unkindly fate at Fort Adams on the fever-ridden lower Mississippi. The date of the enlistment of the brothers Joseph and Reuben Fields and Charles Floyd shows that they were paid beginning from the first of August. John Colter was enlisted on October 15, a day after Lewis arrived at Clarksville. George Gibson, George Shannon, and John Shields were taken on the nineteenth and Nathaniel Pryor on the twentieth. Going on to Fort Massac the two captains had engaged George Drouillard, the noted local army express carrier, to go to South West Point, Tennessee, and bring back the recruits whom Capt. John Campbell was slow in sending. The other members of the Corps of Discovery Clark recorded in various confusing rosters had been drawn from the companies of captains Russell Bissell and Amos Stoddard.[3]

It was midafternoon on May 21 when the Lewis and Clark expedition set out from St. Charles. As Lewis noted, "the men posses great resolution and they are in the best health and spirits."[4] The cheers of the St. Louis delegation died away as the boats moved slowly into the current. Stoddard described the flotilla as "a boat of 18 oars attended by two large pirogues all of which were deeply laden and well-manned."[5] Several of the engaged boatmen were experienced enough to have other opinions and likely saw the top-heavy, narrow of beam, round-bottomed keelboat as a poor craft for this unrelenting river. With the soldiers manfully pulling their oars to the pace set for them by Labiche and Cruzette as *avaunts* (bowmen), the Monongahela ark plowed upstream. One of the pirogues was rowed by soldiers with another French bowman, François Rivet, to break them in. The other pirogue had a French crew.

It was soon apparent that this was not the relatively placid Ohio or the broad, surging Mississippi. The spring freshet was sluicing between no end of impediments. What the expedition needed was an experienced *gouvernail* (steersman) to read the water, foresee building sandbars or caving river-banks, and seek out the less aggressive current. Instead of someone who could read the Missouri, there were two amateurs in command and inexperienced non-coms at the helm. They were learning what most real river men like Cruzette, Labiche, or Rivet already knew.

Three days out they nearly lost the boat when a moving sandbar ran under it, the tow rope parted, and the round-bottomed thing nearly capsized. Shifting the crew to one side to keep it righted may have been the only solution but it was still bad boatmanship. The next day when they interviewed the experienced trader Regis Loisel, he must have wondered how far those amateurs would get. Loisel was returning from a winter at his Cedar Island trading post near the Teton Sioux. The trader left his clerk François Antoine Tabeau and a number of hunters among the Cheyenne and Arikara Indians. After giving the two captains "a good Deel of information" Loisel wrote letters that the corps could carry back to Tabeau or maybe to his former partner Hugh Heney. The Sioux interpreter Pierre Dorion was following Loisel with two *cajeaux* loaded with the returns from fur trading. Before the Americans went on Loisel may have authorized them to enlist Dorion if he was inclined. He could turn over his duties as a steersman to a returning soldier.

A couple of weeks later Stoddard received a report that the expedition was proceeding fifteen miles a day, something of a feat for traveling upstream so heavily laden.[6] After that the communications slowed to rumors and finally stopped as the flotilla sailed into a communications dead zone.

In the most recent editing of the journals of the Lewis and Clark expedition, editor Gary Moulton and his associates at the University of Nebraska Press describe in thirteen volumes the twenty-seven-month journey. Because that wealth of glowing detail and accurate notes has been mined in many other books, it will not be repeated here.[7] But there is an innocence in what the two captains and the other journalists recorded. Although the trip up the Missouri was a first experience for the captains and the men, they were actually traveling the seasonal waterway of an Indian trade route that had been used for the past fourteen years. There are other journals or recollections of several traders also recording the middle passage of the Missouri River, sometimes in close detail but mostly just noting the familiar landmarks, tribal encounters, and disasters. For this part of the journey, rather than discovery, the corps was trailing the customary mercantile life of the middle river.

That in no way detracts from the upstream efforts of the Corps of Discovery, which had as its mission accurately mapping and recording the details of this newly important river—at times a trying new experience for the two not entirely experienced officers. For the soldiers sweating under the late spring sun, every inch gained was hard work as they bucked a current that came down from the fountains of the continent. Most traders used the spring freshet to ride downstream and waited until it had passed before returning with new outfits.

The soldier-boatmen had to row, tow, and pole over fifteen hundred uncompromising miles. Their labor may have been more difficult because a debilitating malaria parasite lay dormant in their livers. When those tiny devils periodically responded to whatever tide or time determined a reawakening, a soldier had to keep pulling his oar or be branded a slacker by his fellows. Nor was it encouraging to see their leaders laid low, even delirious, by an affliction only known as "the ague." In the view of the medical historian Eldon D. Chuinard, it was likely that every member of the Corps of Discovery who set out from Camp River Dubois in the spring of 1804 was "infected with chronic malaria."[8] Those chills and fevers were not well understood and no one could escape them.[9]

Nineteenth-century medicine was in its infancy. It is difficult for modern Americans whose concerns are about health insurance, Medicare, or Medicaid to grasp a time when illness and convalescence consumed a major portion of one's life. The several studies that have examined the medical aspects of the Lewis and Clark expedition usually keep clear of reporting the illnesses that traveled with its members. Although the expedition's medical chest fulfilled the military requirements of that time, the box lacked a single aspirin, a sterile needle, or an effective treatment for malaria.

Many in America suffered from a scourge most only knew as the ague. Malaria was democratic and public figures like Thomas Jefferson, James Madison, and William Clark were included among the almost universal sufferers. Although they did not know the cause, they were all too familiar with the pattern of behavior that occurred or recurred during the warmer months of the year. That was the time that President Jefferson described as the "sickly season" while refusing to admit he also suffered.[10] So did other diseases like yellow fever or typhoid fever, but the ague recurred throughout the year, covertly, disguising itself so well that it was not fully understood until the last decade of the nineteenth century.[11]

Before Lewis left for St. Louis, an outbreak had been raging in Washington and Philadelphia.[12] In late August the wife of Secretary of War Dearborn "and Mr. Wingate have for ten days past been laid up by intermitting fevers."[13] Captain Lewis found no escape as he traveled down the Ohio. There was a place where he noticed that mistletoe began appearing on trees and he recognized from past experience that location was the

Meriwether Lewis, November 13 and 14, 1803, Eastern Journal, APS. Courtesy of Thomas Danisi.

Nov 13th left Massac this evening about five oclock—descended about three miles and encamped on the S.E. shore raind very hard in the eving and I was siezed with a violent ague which continued about four hours and as is usual was succeeded by a feever which however fortunately abated in some measure by Sunrise the next morning,

Nov 14th set out by light at sun rise I took a doze of Rush's pills which operated extremely well and I found myself much to my satisfaction interely clear of fever by the evening- passed Wilkinson ville about 12 Oclock opposite to which is the first a great chain of rocks stretching in an oblique manner across the Oho

As Meriwether Lewis traveled down the Ohio River, he stopped writing from September 18 until November 11, when he began misdating the entries, which he corrected two weeks later. Curiously, he left most of the thirteenth blank, perhaps planning to fill in additional comments later. He only wrote seven lines at the bottom of that page describing his weakening health, which was carried over to the next page. What this facsimile reveals is the state of mind of a sufferer who appears to have endured and dismissed recurring malarial attacks prior to the present episode. Somehow he also managed to organize and lead an expedition into an unknown as exotic as a trip to the moon. Here is graphic proof of the condition of his health at this critical moment and of his determination to continue the mission.

beginning of the fever zone. "The fever and ague and bilious fevers commence their baneful oppression and continue through the whole course of the river with increasing violence as you approach its mouth."[14] Lewis knew malaria, a disease that he had acquired early in life, would be inescapable; he had seen it and nursed others who were stricken with it.

During the layover in Cincinnati, Lewis apparently remained healthy. Not long after the two officers met at Louisville, Clark was also taken violently ill. He was still so sick when they reached Cape Girardeau that he didn't leave the boat. Other studies have passed this off as a recurring bowel problem. But there is a similarity to malarial symptoms that Clark seemed to have shaken off at Kaskaskia. Not long after leaving the Ohio and turning up the Mississippi toward Kaskaskia, Lewis became violently ill. Previous suffering had taught him what to expect and he wrote on November 13 "raind very hard in the eving and I was siezed with a violent ague which continued for about four hours and as is usual was succeeded by a feever which however fortunately abated in some measure by sunrise the next morning."

It never occurred to anyone that mosquitoes were carriers of that dreaded disease. Most of the soldiers whom the two captains enlisted along the way had been serving in the malaria hot zone and it is not unreasonable to suppose they had not escaped infection that was in some way related to the mosquito breeding season.

If mosquitoes were the vector for malaria, less than a month into the expedition, Lewis and Clark began noting those bothersome insects. More than ninety statements were made throughout the journals detailing how mosquitoes plagued the expedition.[15] Tribes along the middle river had probably been exposed through prior contacts with infected traders.

The following year, when tribal delegates were being assembled to visit President Jefferson, Osage Indian agent Pierre Chouteau wrote several letters detailing his observations of sick Indians in St. Louis. Upon their arrival in St. Louis, they became very ill—some even died. Chouteau claimed that these Indians were ill because they had never been introduced to civilization.[16] But the Indians could have become infected before they reached St. Louis because the Missouri River in the warmer months was infested with swarms of mosquitoes.

As the keelboat plowed on against the unrelenting current, Clark kept the daily journal and Lewis worked up notes on their scientific observations. They wrote in small, four-by-seven-inch notebooks, bound at the top, using quill pens in tight, small hands to conserve precious paper. No printed version has ever captured the intimacy of those little books written in brown ink.[17] When tribesmen came into council with the strangers, the two captains had to remember what they heard through the string of interpretation. Later in their quarters on the boat or around a campfire on shore, at a comfortable distance from the chattering men's messes, they wrote their notes.

Early in his career Lewis had known the defeated Indians who were forced to agree to the Greenville treaty. Those were peoples of the woodlands and cane breaks who had been sullenly retreating from the advancing frontier for many years. Now, as the expedition passed up the Missouri River, he was entering the world of the western plainsmen, the indeterminate ranges of the wandering peoples who hunted buffalo and lived in skin tents. Their values, experiences, and expectations were different from what a United States officer had encountered before.[18]

To understand the river tribes Lewis and Clark relied on their prior experience. A critical reading of the journals suggests that the two captains imposed early nineteenth-century preconceptions into the data they recorded. Due to the difficulties of communication, even when they had experienced interpreters available to them, what they thought they heard was subject to misunderstanding as it passed through several imperfect translations. At times they may have been deliberately misled by a tribal spokesman inflating his people's or his personal importance at the expense of neighbors or enemies.

During those meetings a large body of data was accumulating. Not all of that appears in Clark's daily journal because Lewis was also recording his observations and discoveries in natural history in other ways, a pocket notebook perhaps, or in separate notes that have since been lost where he jotted down figures on population, territorial ranges, or intertribal relations. Those were later formalized during the winter at Fort Mandan.

Officers in the field usually had enough paperwork completing reports and bringing accounts into order. During the Fort Mandan winter captains Lewis and Clark had the additional duty of describing what had developed along the way. That was no small task to accomplish in rough, close quarters lacking basic furniture or writing facilities, in a room so cold that ink froze in the inkwell.

Lewis and Clark made an estimate of the many tribes that the nation had "inherited" with the Louisiana Territory in a compilation of the native peoples living west of the Mississippi, information they had gathered directly from the tribes they had encountered or heard as hearsay from a number of sources. The two fledgling ethnographers worked out a chart of fifty-five tribes or bands that they organized into nineteen categories. The document made sense on the large sheet of paper that Clark pasted together. Amateur and imperfect in many ways, it was the best study done so far, predating the academic discipline of ethnohistory by many years. The corps was still far from home, wintering on the Pacific shore, when the second session of the Eighth Congress published that data. Reducing the large sheet to the restricted size of a printed page required breaking it up into separate lists that confused the data and lessened its impact.[19]

The mapping that Clark did at Fort Mandan was another matter. Although the primary mission required the production of an accurate map of the Missouri River, Clark was concerned about where they were going as much as he was about where they had been. He based his map on a template drawn in Washington provided to Lewis before he left, adding details from what had been learned from Indian traders who had preceded them. But that mostly ended at the Mandan/Hidatsa villages. For what lay beyond, the captains interviewed responsible tribesmen whose geographical concepts were direct and simple. Clark drew a speculative map that was a composite of existing information from travelers who knew the upper Missouri and its major tributary, the Yellowstone, from direct experience. Of course there were mistakes between what his informants tried to get across and what Clark perceived. Some of those errors would persist in the cartographic record for years to come.

Lewis and Clark also milked geographic clues from the British clerks who brought trading outfits overland to the Mandan villages from the Assiniboine River in British territory. At that time François-Antoine Larocque and Charles McKenzie had not been far beyond the villages of their customers. Another contact was Loisel's erstwhile partner Hugh Heney, who was now working for the North West Company. After showing up with proprietor Charles Chaboillez's prompt response to a letter from the Americans, Heney was more forthcoming than his fellow clerks. He provided a sketch map of the region between the Mississippi and the Missouri where British traders had dominated Spanish territory for years. Perceiving that Heney's loyalties were flexible, the Americans began thinking that he might be a likely candidate to represent the United States in this forsaken part of the world.

The data that Lewis and Clark collected kept them at the writing desk for much of the horrendous northern winter. In the spring those lists, reports, descriptions, analyses, and maps were carefully packed and labeled to be shipped back downstream with the returning keelboat and its crew.

That was all that the United States would hear of them until the expedition reappeared.

After bundling up the reports and letters they had written and sending them back, Lewis and Clark prepared to go on. When the Corps of Discovery departed from Fort Mandan, it was stripped to a lean, efficient crew. Captain Lewis was jubilant that they would be the first civilized men in the wilderness.

> as this state of mind in which we are, generally gives the colouring to events, when the immagination is suffered to wander into futurity, the picture which now presented itself to me was a most pleasing one, entertaing as I do, the most confident hope of succeading in a voyage which had formed a darling project for the last ten years, I could but esteem this moment of my departure as among the most happy of my life.[20]

The corps traveled through what some have described as a sexual paradise. But the behavior of the two captains during the expedition is opaque. While the leaders were obliged to set a good example, journal entries show that the men were dallying with willing Indian women and paying the price of infection. To counter the consequences, Lewis or Clark had to employ one of those four penis syringes in the medicine chest. Those brass instruments injected a concoction of mercury, which was the accepted medical treatment of the time. The intimacy of that doctoring may have discouraged their opportunities for future dalliances.[21]

Treatment may have also extended to the interpreter Charbonneau's woman. Sacagawea, who accompanied the expedition from the Hidatsa villages, was suffering from a complaint as the expedition approached the Great Falls in mid-June 1805. After dosing her for three days with various concoctions, on the sixteenth "Doctor Lewis" recorded his treatment:

> I found that two dozes of barks and opium which I had given her since my arrival had produced an alteration in her pulse for the better; they were now much fuller and more regular. I caused her to drink the mineral water altogether. wen I first came down I found that her pulse were scarcely perceptible, very quick frequently irregular and attended with strong nervous symptoms, that of the twitching of the fingers and leaders of the arm; now the pulse had become regular much fuller and a gentle perspiration had taken place; the nervous symptoms have also in a great measure abated, and she feels herself much freer from pain. she complains principally of the lower region of the abdomen, I therefore continued the cataplasms of barks and laudanum.[22]

According to a theory presented by Dr. Eldon D. Chuinard in his book *Only One Man Died*, it is possible that she was "suffering from chronic pelvic inflammatory disease due to gonorrheal infection. Some of her symptoms, such as twitching of the fingers and arms, could have been due to loss of minerals resulting from the captains' bleeding her."[23]

There has been a recent attempt to pin a venereal infection on Lewis precisely dating to two days in August 1805 when the Corps of Discovery watched the Shoshones dancing. This tortured reasoning and its conclusions have been generally dismissed. The speculation misses the obvious fact that the two captains had passed through the disease-ridden tribes of the middle Missouri and Mandan/Hidatsa the previous year, and spent a winter among the Mandan without infection.[24]

An incident of malaria was recorded at the Three Forks of the Missouri on July 27. William Clark was unwell with a high fever, chills, and fatigue. Lewis dosed the bilious condition with his usual remedy, five of Dr. Rush's mercury-loaded pills, but when Clark was still sick on the twenty-ninth, Lewis "prevailed on him to take the barks," which meant an unpleasant decoction of Peruvian bark or cinchona containing a natural but minute source of quinine.[25] The expedition lay over for three days to allow Clark to recover.

Sickness paralyzed the expedition after they struggled over the difficult Lolo Pass and descended into Nez Perce territory. Instead of colts, the party began eating dried salmon, berries, and cakes of camas roots. The fish or the cakes may have contained bacteria to which the Nez Perce were immune. But the exhausted and starved corpsmen were not and many of them became violently sick with acute diarrhea and vomiting. Lewis was virtually immobilized with dysentery. Although the condition did not appear to require purgatives, the well-meaning Clark in the usual practice of nineteenth-century medicine dispensed Rush's pills, emetics, and salts.[26]

After spending the winter at the mouth of the Columbia River, the Corps of Discovery headed home during the summer 1806. When the expedition split up in western Montana, Clark followed the Yellowstone River back to the Missouri and Lewis took the road over the mountains that the Salish usually followed in going to hunt buffalo near the Great Falls. Exploring north to determine how far boundary claims might be pushed, his little party of four ran into eight rambling young Indians. Lewis took them to be the dreaded Minnetarie of Fort de Prairie (Atsina, or plains Gros Ventre) but they in fact were Piikani Blackfeet.

After camping together overnight the Indians made an attempt to disarm or unhorse the strangers. In the resulting melee, one Piikani was stabbed to death and Lewis shot another in the stomach with his pistol. The headlong retreat of the Americans meant that Lewis would never know that the fugitive he shot recovered, or that the Piikani held no hard feelings for an unfortunate encounter.[27] He believed that he had killed the boy.

Upon returning to the Mandan/Hidatsa villages the two captains heard that one of the North West Company clerks they met the previous year had paralleled their westward voyage by traveling with Crows on the Yellowstone. Larocque had reached a point beyond the Big Horn River. Just before the corps returned, two proprietors of the North West Company visited the Hidatsa and accompanied them to a peace council with the neighboring Cheyenne. Those intrusions into United States territory clearly ignored the warnings Lewis had given to the British clerks to avoid trying to influence tribes under United States jurisdiction. But when the American flotilla passed the Mandan/Hidatsa villages in August, there was no way of predicting, or inhibiting, another intrusion. When Lewis and Clark reported from Fort Mandan in 1805, Clark estimated that it would take seven hundred soldiers to secure Louisiana from foreign incursion.[28] Lewis continued down the Missouri convinced that confirming the republic's authority on the upper river was going to be a major problem.

As they descended the Missouri the returning corps met several groups of traders and boatmen returning to accustomed wintering places near the middle river tribes. Obviously the United States administration had not discouraged the Indian trade. Upon reaching St. Louis Lewis was gratified to learn that the governor of the territory had taken action to limit British intrusion on the upper Mississippi. Before leaving for military duties in the south, Gen. James Wilkinson sent an expedition to the head of the Mississippi. Lt. Zebulon Pike had warned off British traders in the north and was now on the southern plains.[29]

The returning Corps of Discovery was unaware of the Spanish reaction to what was seen as a threatening new neighbor. As they neared the end of their journey, the two captains met a former brother-in-arms, past captain of artillery John McClallen. The recently resigned officer was taking an assortment of goods suitable for the New Mexican market to Santa Fe. Clark and the other journalists described McClallen's outfit in their journals but it would be almost a year before Lewis commented on this risky test of international relations.[30]

After stopping overnight at Cantonment Belle Fontaine, on September 23 the members of the Lewis and Clark expedition stepped out of the boats on the St. Louis riverbank.[31] Their long voyage of discovery was over. For weeks they had been talking about coming home, taking a luxurious hot bath, having a real shave, buying new clothes, and receiving their pay.

The date of their arrival is confirmed by a letter that the wealthy St. Louis resident John Mullanphy wrote on September 23, 1806. Mullanphy recognized a scoop and his short, excited note was rushed across the Mississippi in time to catch a rider headed east. Mullanphy's bold stroke was effective as his letter was published in the *Palladium*, a Frankfort, Kentucky, newspaper, on October 4.[32] An extract of a letter dated St. Louis, September 23, 1806, said:

> Concerning the safe arrival of Messrs. Lewis and Clark, who went 2 years and 4 months ago to explore the Missouri, to be anxiously wished for by every one, I have the pleasure to mention, that they arrived here about one hour ago, in good health, with the loss of one man who died. They visited the Pacific Ocean, which they left on the 27th of March last. They would have been here about the 1st of August, but for the detention they met with from the snow and frost in crossing mountains on which are eternal snows. Their journal will no doubt be not only importantly interesting to us all, but a fortune for the worthy and laudable adventurers. When they arrive, 3 cheers were fired. They really have the appearance of Robinson Crusoes, dressed entirely in buckskins. We shall know all very soon, I have no particulars yet, JOHN MULLANPHY[33]
>
> P. S. They left St. Charles, May 20th 1804, and returned there Sept. 21st, 1806.
>
> J. M.[34]

On September 21, while still in the boat, Lewis had started a draft of a letter to President Jefferson, which he later restarted. Lewis dated the fair copy on the day of their arrival. The president's former secretary knew that the second session of Congress would begin in December. Because his first letter to Jefferson was crucial, he sent word to Cahokia postmaster, John Hay, to hold the mail. But the expedition letters represented a large typesetting challenge and the first actual letters from the explorers would not appear until a few weeks later.

Working with Clark, Lewis also drafted a publicity release in the form of a letter, written by Clark to his brother Jonathan in Louisville, who would probably release it to the nearest newspaper. On the night of their arrival, while Meriwether polished the letter to his mentor, Clark penned a fair copy to his "Dear Brother."[35] The next day he added a short personal note confirming the intention behind it: "I have not time to write more as the post is waiting at the dore." Then as a postscript Clark added, "*Note* please to have my letter to you of yester published if you think proper." As the only newspaper in Louisville was irregular, Jonathan Clark saw the letter carried to Frankfort, where it was published in the *Palladium* on October 9 and in the *Western World* on the eleventh.[36]

That long and detailed letter described a momentous journey filled with hardship, wonder, bravery, and starvation. It would herald a new beginning of their story and spark a world of repetitive literature for decades to come. After finishing the letters, the two officers simply went to bed. Next morning the post carrier crossed the river on the first leg of their spreading fame.

The St. Louis welcome began two nights later at the huge party staged at Christy's tavern. Lewis and Clark heard seventeen expansive toasts proposed followed by an eighteenth after the reeling captains retired for the night.[37] If they blushed at the grand toasts and praise, a four-month outdoor tan concealed it. They were all heroes, they were all going to be famous.

Perhaps a bit more than they could have imagined. Five days after the post departed, Lewis wrote another letter that is only addressed to an unidentified "Dear Sir." It would be almost a week and a half before the "Dear Brother" letter reached Frankfort, but on October 7, the Cahokia postmaster opened and read the "Dear Sir" letter. It was more than John Hay could resist and a week later he made a copy and sent it with a covering note to his old friends in the British fur trade. Enemies of the nation would have a pretty complete description of the discoveries of the corps before it was in the hands of the president.[38]

In his description of "the most practicable Route which existed across the continent by way of the Missesouris & Columbia Rivers," Lewis was confident this track presented immense advantages to the fur trade:

> as all the Furs collected in 9/10 of the valuable Fur Country of America may be conveyed to the Mouth of the Columbia & shipped from thence for the East Indies by the 1st of August in each year, & will of course reach Canton earlier than the Furs which are annually exported from Montreal reach Britain.[39]

His letter essentially described a plan that the North West Company of Montreal already had under way and would be extremely interesting to the trader who would conduct it.

By the first week of October, Lewis and Clark began discharging their

men and doling out pay. They had to write a considerable number of discharges praising the service and dedication of each man as well as bonds
upon themselves certifying that a corpsman would receive "for his services
on that expedition a compensation to Lands equal to that granted by the
said States to a Soldier of the Revolutionary Army." The last section of each
man's discharge paper read:

> I with cherfulnefs declare that the ample support which he gave me under
> every difficulty. the manly firmness which he evinced on every occation
> and the fortitude with which he bore the fatigues and painfull sufferings
> incident to that long Voyage entitles him to my highest confidence and
> sincere thanks. while it eminently recommends him to the consideration
> and respect of his fellow citizens—[40]

Although he had sent Private John Newman back to St. Louis because
of bad behavior, Lewis was feeling generous when he learned that Newman
had been "extremely serviceable as a hunter on the voyage to St. Louis and
that the boat on several occasions owed her safety . . . to his personal exertions."[41] The discharges were completed by October 10, the same date that
William Clark wrote to the secretary of war with the terse statement, "The
enclosed commission haveing answered the purpose for which it was
intended, I take the liberty of returning it to you."[42]

Paying off the soldiers had a nice ring but it is questionable if much
specie actually changed hands. Cash was short in St. Louis and only a hundred dollars was mentioned by Lewis.[43] The former corpsmen apparently
received bills drawn upon the War Department, which they took to
someone like a merchant and endorsed to him, receiving the probably dis-
counted value in store credit or chits.

After the men of the corps received their pay and the promise of land
grants according to their service, some would be going back to their companies and others were only too glad to leave the army. On the twenty-ninth
Joseph Whitehouse received the land bond that he conveyed to George
Drouillard in exchange for $280. The document was completed in the pres-
ence of Sergeant Ordway and the St. Louis attorney William C. Carr. John
Collins, who gave his home as Frederick County, Maryland, did the same.
Others like Silas Goodrich, William Werner, and Jean Baptiste LePage also
assigned their land warrants to Sergeant Ordway as soon as they received
them. But by March 3, 1807, eight others, including Goodrich, would petition Congress for the land grants to be laid off in Louisiana or Indiana, where
they intended to settle and commence new lives.

After the paperwork was completed the close companions for the past two and a half years took leave of each other and went their separate ways. Those who stayed in Louisiana seem curiously ignored. A scan of the index to the territorial papers does not show their names appearing with other citizens, not on the petitions that were circulating to recommend replacements for an unpopular governor, not, with the exception of Fraser, in the calls to resist separatist activities. In some cases they can be traced in lesser public documents, but several men of the Corps of Discovery just slipped away. Others can be followed in the records of the early beaver hunting expeditions.

For Captain Lewis, the expedition had been more than a formative experience that allowed him to prove to himself what he could do in a demanding situation. That didn't quite prove that he was a leader of men in the "once more into the breach" tradition, but it showed that he was fully capable of organizing and orchestrating a complex expedition. The highly technical demands of modern space exploration require the cooperative efforts of tens of thousands of engineers and administrators. Faced with a similar demanding challenge, Meriwether Lewis had done it on his own.

NOTES

1. Alexander Wilson, "Particulars of the Death of Capt. Lewis," *Port Folio* 7 (January 1812): 38.

2. Members of the Expedition, Moulton, *JLCE* 2: appendix A; Stephen Ambrose, *Undaunted Courage* (New York: Simon & Schuster, 1996), p. 386.

3. William Simmons, the accountant for the War Department, noted these names. Recruits in 1803: Charles Floyd, Nathaniel Pryor, William Bratton, John Colter, Reuben Fields, Joseph Fields, George Gibson, George Shannon, and John Shields. Recruits in 1804: Cruzette, François Labiche, and John B. Lepage. Reenlistments in 1805: John Ordway, Patrick Gass, John Collins, Hugh McNeal, John Potts, John B. Thompson, Richard Windsor, Peter Wizer, and Alexander Willard. Bounties for recruits paid to Robert Frazer: Silas Goodrich and Thomas P. Howard. Richard Warfington was a corporal in Capt. John Campbell's company and John Newman, a private in Daniel Bissell's company. Pvt. Moses B. Reed was from Lewis's original detachment. A Meriwether Smith was paid $67 and released May 20, 1804. Among the boatmen hired at St. Louis these were the ones whom the War Department accounted for: Charles Hebert paid at Ricara Village, October 11, 1804; Baptist Deschamp and Charles Pennin (Peter Pinaut?) paid May 28, 1805; B. Lajueness, E. Malboeuf, and François Rivet on July 28, 1805. Other soldiers and interpreters: Richard Warfington was paid August 4, 1805, and John Newman, August 20, 1805. John Ordway paid $112 for a horse, saddle, bridle, and employ-

ment in the public service from St. Louis to Washington under the direction of Capt. Meriwether Lewis. Ordway paid an additional $49 assisting Meriwether Lewis and the Mandan Indians and pack horses from October 11 to January 19, 1807. François Labiche, assistant interpreter and pack horseman employed by Captain Lewis, $23.80 from October 21 to January 20, 1807. Peter Provenchere employed as interpreter by Mr. Chouteau, paid $121 from October 10 to February 9, 1807. René Jusseaume paid $94.44 as Indian interpreter to the Mandan to January 19, 1807. Simmons described York as Clark's black waiter. RG217, entry 366, vol. 12, letterbook N, pp. 6965–67, 6611; vol. 11, letterbook M, pp. 6307–6509; vol. 10, letterbook L, pp. 5891–5928; entry 515, vol. 5, report book E, pp. 25, 142, 149, 150, NARA-CP.

4. ML, May 20, 1804; Moulton, *JLCE* 2: 241.

5. AS to HD, June 3, 1804, Amos Stoddard Collection, MHS.

6. Ibid. The information likely came with the soldier who exchanged with Dorion.

7. The governor-appointed Washington Lewis and Clark Trail Committee, the Washington State chapter of the Lewis and Clark Trail Heritage Foundation, and the Washington State Library have produced a bibliography that encompasses two hundred of the most significant books published about the Lewis and Clark expedition.

8. Eldon Chuinard, *Only One Man Died: The Medical Aspects of the Lewis and Clark Expedition* (Glendale, CA: A. H. Clark, 1980), p. 175n.

9. When Lewis and Clark met with James Aird on September 3, 1806, Clark wrote, "this gentleman received both Capt Lewis and my self with every mark of friendship. He was himself at the time with a chill of the agu on him which he has had for several days." Moulton, *JLCE* 7: 346.

10. TJ to Joseph Priestley, June 19, 1802, document 21355, roll 26, and TJ to William Dunbar, September 21, 1803, document 23322, roll 29, TJ-LOC.

11. L. J. Bruce Chwatt, "Ague as Malaria," *Journal of Tropical Medicine and Hygiene* 79 (August 1976): 168–78. From the Italian, malaria means "bad air" and gained prominence after the 1880s when it changed its meaning from an "aeriform poison," or miasma to the disease itself. Margaret Humphreys, *Malaria, Poverty, Race, and Public Health in the United States* (Baltimore: Johns Hopkins University Press, 2001), p. 46.

12. Samuel L. Mitchill, "Malignant Fever in Philadelphia, 1803," *Medical Repository* 7 (1804): 144–49.

13. HD to TJ, August 28, 1803, document 23219, roll 28, TJ-LOC.

14. ML, September 14, 1803, Moulton, *JLCE* 2: 81.

15. Robert R. Hunt, "The Blood Meal: Mosquitoes and Agues on the Lewis and Clark Expedition, Part 1," *We Proceeded On* 18 (May 1992): 7.

16. PC to WHH, May 31 and June 12, 1805, and PC to SW, October 1, 1805, Pierre Chouteau letterbook, pp. 58–61, 71–74, MHS.

17. A facsimile of the first three journals has been published by the APS.

18. For background see James P. Ronda, *Lewis and Clark among the Indians* (Lincoln: University of Nebraska Press, 1984).

19. *ASP, Indian Affairs* 1: 705–43.

20. ML, April 7, 1805; Moulton, *JLCE* 4: 10–11.

21. A number of journal entries confirm the condition of the men but attempts to exploit the sexual conduct of the two officers is wholly speculative.

22. ML, June 16, 1805; Moulton, *JLCE* 4: 302n1.

23. Chuinard, *Only One Man Died*, pp. 287–89.

24. Reimert T. Ravenholt, "Triumph Then Despair: The Tragic Death of Meriwether Lewis," *Epidemiology* 5 (May 1994): 377. A more recent publication, Thomas P. Lowry, *Venereal Disease and the Lewis and Clark Expedition* (Lincoln: University of Nebraska Press, 2004) has not been consulted. Lewis's description of Indian women's hygiene is a vigorous refusal to mingle with them. "I think its most disgusting thing I ever beheld is these dirty naked wenches." His knowledge of the effects of venereal disease was abundantly described throughout the journals: "once this disorder is contracted it . . . always ends up in decepitude, [decrepitude] death, premature old age." ML, March 19 and January 27, 1806, Moulton, *JLCE* 6:239–40, 436.

25. ML, July 27, 29, 30, 1805, Ordway, July 27, 28, 30, 1805; Moulton, *JLCE* 4: 254 and 436–38, 5: 11.

26. Had this been the venereal disease Ravenholt guessed, Clark would have resorted to the usual treatment.

27. All versions of the journals repeat the incident but there is evidence from another trustworthy documentary source that the circumstances were different. John C. Jackson, "The Fight on Two Medicine River," *We Proceeded On* 32 (February 2006): 14–23.

28. Clark's estimate of the military forces necessary to secure the Missouri held that a captain's command totaling fifty-four was necessary to protect the mouth of the Yellowstone from British traders and ensure peace between the tribes. A lieutenant and thirty-nine men were enough to guard the Great Falls. In all he laid out thirteen places that should require a military presence. WC, 1804–1805; Moulton, *JLCE* 3:479–80, 491n1.

29. Elliott Coues, ed., *The Expeditions of Zebulon Montgomery Pike*, 2 vols. (facsimile repr., New York: Dover Publications, Inc., 1987); Donald Jackson, ed., *The Journals of Zebulon Montgomery Pike with Letters and Related Documents*, 2 vols. (Norman: University of Oklahoma Press, 1966).

30. A compilation of previous studies dealing with the enigmatic Captain McClallen is in Harry M. Majors, "John McClellan in the Montana Rockies 1807: The First American after Lewis and Clark," *Northwest Discovery: Journal of Northwest History and Natural History* 2 (November/December 1981): 554–630.

31. WC wrote in the journal that they rose early the morning of September 23 and "took the Chief to the publick store & furnished him with Some clothes." ML authorized $65.55 for goods furnished to a Mandan chief, two squaws, and three chil-

dren at Belle Fontaine factory. RG217, Peter Hagner to ML, November 15, 1806, entry 515, vol. 5, report book E and vol. 11, letterbook M, p. 6508, NARA-CP.

32. The *Palladium* letter may have contained more data as another version printed in New York on October 31 is quite different. "From a Kentucky paper of Oct. 4, Highly Interesting Intelligence, St. Louis, Sept. 23, 1806 Captains Lewis and Clark are just arrived, all in very good health. They left the Pacific Ocean the 23d of March last—they wintered there—they arrived there in the last November; there were some American vessels there just before their arrival. They had to pack one hundred and sixty miles from the head of the Missouri to Columbia River. One of the hands, an intelligent man, tells me the Indians are as numerous on the Columbia, as white are in any part of the United States. They brought but one family of Indians, of the Mandan nation. They have brought several curiosities with them from the Ocean. The Indians are represented as being very peaceable. The winter was very mild on the Pacific. I am yours, &c."

33. Reprinted in the *Connecticut Herald*, November 4, 1806, p. 3.

34. *American Citizen (NY)*, October 31, 1806, p. 3.

35. Rightly called the most important letters of the expedition, these are: ML to TJ, September 21, 23, 1806; WC to George Rogers Clark, September 23, 1806; ML draft of the WC letter, September 24, 1806, Jackson, *LLC* 1: 317–35. Further discussion of the sequence is treated in James Holmberg, ed., *Dear Brother: Letters of William Clark to Jonathan Clark* (New Haven, CT: Yale University Press, 2002), pp. 101–107.

36. Lewis's draft of the Clark letter, September 24, 1806, Jackson, *LLC* 1: 330; Holmberg, *Dear Brother*, pp. 115–18.

37. James P. Ronda, "St. Louis Welcomes the Lewis and Clark Expedition," *We Proceeded On* 13 (February 1987): 19–20.

38. ML to an unknown correspondent, October 14, 1806, Jackson, *LLC* 1:335–43. John Hay may also have read the much stronger opinions expressed in the report to the president on how to oppose, undermine actually, the British competition in the north.

39. Ibid., 1: 337.

40. William Bratton's discharge, October 10, 1806, Jackson, *LLC* 1: 347–48. While Jackson had published only one of those discharges, a second example confirms that Lewis and Clark duplicated the document for the other men. James Holmberg, "Lost and Found: Discharge Papers of John Shields," *We Proceeded On* 30 (February 2004): 37.

41. ML to HD, January 15, 1807, Jackson, *LLC* 1: 365.

42. WC would have been unaware that he had been promoted to first lieutenant vice (replacing) First Lieutenant John B. Walbach promoted Vice Captain John McClallen resigned. McClallen was the Santa Fe trader they met a few days before.

43. ML borrowed four hundred dollars to see the Indians to Washington and two hundred dollars for his own return.

FIVE

A Field Scientist and the American Philosophical Society

The learned, on Europe's distant lands[1]

The duties that President Jefferson outlined for Lewis when he left Washington encompassed a wide range of scholarly inquiry. Jefferson's charge to explore the "Missouri & whatever river, heading with that, leads into the Western ocean" and "obtaining a correct map of the Missouri" was a mission that any competent army officer could have led.[2] As it turned out, the expedition produced imperfect results; a misleading map of the Southwest and only half of a practical portage between the Missouri and the Columbia rivers.

If that was all Jefferson was seeking, Lewis might have been more useful by remaining his secretary. But the enlightened amateur scientist expanded that mission. As president of the American Philosophical Society, Jefferson imposed his personal agenda for an additional scientific mission.[3] He managed to weave it into the publicly sponsored framework of the military expedition. Lewis had been preselected to fulfill Jefferson's long-standing dream. "Capt. Lewis is brave, prudent, habituated to the woods, & familiar with Indian manners & character. He is not regularly educated, but he possesses a great mass of accurate observation on all subjects of nature which present themselves here."[4] To make sure this was properly recorded, Jefferson required Lewis and others to keep journals.

Almost the entire experience of the expedition has been culled from those little notebooks, mostly written by William Clark. Historians and less-informed writers complain that Lewis should have written more. But at the beginning of the journey, the two officers decided that Clark would keep the record of daily events, leaving Lewis free to concentrate on a variety of other subjects. The notes Lewis kept during the expedition demonstrated his ability as a field scientist and the contribution he was making to nineteenth-century science.

Those notes account for nearly all of the missing journal entries that critics would have him writing.[5] A critic of neglected opportunities, Paul Russell Cutright selected "three lengthy unexplained hiatuses" in the journals: May 13, 1804, to April 7, 1805; August 27, 1805, to December 31, 1805; and August 13, 1806, to September 24, 1806; and in 1984 Cutright added another hiatus that he amended by remarking that a bullet in Lewis's left thigh "is only one of the four with a ready explanation." After being wounded and despite finding writing difficult, he wrote a plant description, not in the journal but in a botanical notebook.[6]

To ensure success for that challenging responsibility Jefferson drew in the top five members of the American Philosophical Society. Andrew Ellicott, Robert Patterson, Caspar Wistar, Dr. Benjamin Rush, and Dr. Benjamin Smith Barton were eminent scholars in specialized fields who helped augment Lewis's basic understanding.

Previous accounts have failed to question how Lewis could have learned such an astonishing amount of scientific knowledge in a ridiculously short time. That short course included the complex fields of botany, mineralogy, zoology, astronomy, meteorology, as well as some basic training in medicine. That concentrated prepping was only effective because Lewis already possessed a broad knowledge that would not have been expected in a military officer or the president's secretary. Long before he was sent to Philadelphia to take that crash course, Lewis had funded his knowledge. As Jefferson put it, Lewis "has been for some time qualifying himself."[7] The amateur scientist of Monticello had fostered that in a willing disciple. They knew each other as searching minds.

The help that Lewis received from members of the society, in a very short period of time, complemented and expanded his prior studies and turned him into a competent field scientist. That was confirmed when, not counting Jefferson, thirteen members elected Lewis to the American Philosophical Society. When John Vaughan issued a certificate of his election on November 21, 1803, it was sent to Jefferson because Lewis was already on his way.[8] As a more able member than most of the Philadelphia literati, he would travel to places certain to produce discoveries.[9]

That was an exciting prospect as nineteenth-century science was mostly a contemplative pursuit. At the time, natural science was composed of three kingdoms: mineral, animal, and vegetable. Although there were worlds to be discovered there was not that much real data to provide comparisons or the technology for experimentation. Most members of the APS had libraries but not laboratories. Basic principles were still being worked out at a time when reference material was sparse and often elemental.[10]

For instance, according to the 1803 understanding of botany there were several stages of practical scientific inquiry. A nurseryman could start a plant from seed and tend its growth. When a plant flowered, a botanist classified it according to the century-old system developed by the botanist Carl Linneaus. Finally, a horticulturist could recommend it for a garden or an herbalist could test its medicinal qualities. Sometimes the seed was so original that it became part of a select herbarium.[11]

Before leaving St. Louis on the expedition, Lewis boxed a shipment of mineral specimens that Pierre Chouteau delivered to Jefferson in July. The box contained silver, lead, and "an elegant specimen of Rock Chrystal . . . from Mexico," which Jefferson sent to the APS member Charles Willson Peale in May 1805.[12]

As the keelboat and pirogues labored up the Missouri River, Lewis got out of the boat and tramped along the muddy shore collecting exciting new botanical discoveries. While Clark supervised the little flotilla and recorded mundane daily developments, Captain Lewis ranged afield filling in the scientific information that was an invaluable by-product of the narrow mission of mapping. A list sent back from Fort Mandan in the spring of 1805 records thirty days when Lewis was out finding interesting plants along the middle Missouri. The list does not include the days he hiked and found nothing of interest to a botanist or mineralogist. The solitary hiker across the bluffs and into the ravines had to recognize and eliminate known plants as well as find new ones.

Finding and collecting new specimens of plants, mammals, birds, and reptiles was rigorous fieldwork. The daily boat journals overlook the physical exertion that Lewis put into collecting on foot, the only way it could have been done. Lewis's hands-on effort gathered specimens that learned men would welcome, analyze, and describe in the most extensive new information on the natural history of North America.[13]

Lewis and Clark alternated days on shore or riding on the boat. Clark dutifully maintained the daily journal although what he noticed afield were often the observations of a frontier meat hunter. The days on the boat when Lewis wrote nothing were probably spent sorting, analyzing, and preserving specimens. Like a modern laboratory scientist he needed time to absorb what he had found and formulate conclusions in his mind. Later, during the winter camp there would be time to compile that data. He had no obligation to answer the yet-to-be-made demands of later writers to provide material for their speculations.

During the winter 1804–1805 at Fort Mandan, Lewis and Clark spent a good deal of time over their writing desks developing lists of what had been collected. Meriwether attached labels to the plant specimens. Everything produced during the trip up the Missouri was carefully boxed and sent back down the river and to Washington for President Jefferson. Traveling fast on the freshet the keelboat arrived in St. Louis on May 22.[14]

The collection suffered its first degradation at St. Charles when several gentlemen came on board whom Corporal Warfington, the boat commander, felt unable to deflect. One of them, William Joseph Clark, came to St. Louis the previous November to sell beaver skins. He happened to be dining with Colonel Meigs, Edward Hempstead, Dr. Renaud, two Frenchmen, and a Mr. Baum. Clark wrote:

> [J]ust as we rose from dinner news came that Capt. Lewises Barge which had been Exploring the Mesoori was just Landed. I went on board and Saw a great many Curiosities Such as mocisons Buffaloe Robes Goat Skins Birds and a prairai Dog and the Chief of the Recarreau Indians who was a Very Large fat man Very much pitted with the Small Pox. I smoked with him as a Brother.[15]

Along the way the keelboat party had scooped up a number of Indians who would be sent to visit the president. After some dispute over authority, it was decided to hold the visiting tribesmen in St. Louis to avoid the oppressive heat and risk of disease during the terrible summer traveling season.

After Warfington was released to return to his company, he traveled by way of Vincennes and Louisville carrying the fair copies of the material rewritten at Fort Mandan. On May 27 Indiana Territory governor William Henry Harrison read a letter from Clark but his failure to forward the dispatches immediately might have delayed them as long as two weeks. The packet included Clark's uncorrected journal, which was being sent with an apology for the unpolished form to the president and the secretary of war. In a time when the fastest pace was that of a loping horse, it was ironic that

President Jefferson read the first news of the expedition's return about June 25 in a Kentucky newspaper, and spent the next two weeks impatiently waiting to see what Captain Lewis had accomplished.[16]

As he passed through Louisville, Warfington left a box of rough field notes and Missouri River maps with Clark's brother Jonathan.[17] Meanwhile Captain Stoddard, assisted by a crew that included two of the former corpsmen, took the expedition keelboat on to Fort Massac.[18] On June 13 General Wilkinson, who was descending the Ohio, wrote that he had not seen the dispatches from the expedition but had had conversations with Captain Stoddard.[19] Stoddard went to Fort Massac to intercept the general and get a jump on his rival for authority, Maj. James Bruff. Stoddard filled Wilkinson in on matters in St. Louis and the general began planning what he would do when he took over as governor of the territory. About the same time, Pierre Chouteau started the boxed specimens down the Mississippi to New Orleans, where Governor Claiborne would arrange their shipment east.[20]

Congress and other government functionaries had already departed the capital to avoid the sickly season. The president was ready to return to Monticello but was delayed by the slow-moving postal rider.[21] It was the fourteenth of July when he finally received the letters and dispatches from Fort Mandan.[22]

The reports and descriptions of the Missouri River, its tribes, flora, and fauna represented a wealth of intensely interesting new material.[23] It was something that the sponsor of the expedition could not leave unread for the next three months—nor unpublicized.

Jefferson released his letter from Lewis to the *United States Gazette*, which published it on July 19. Versions were picked up and reprinted in the *Pittsfield Sun* and *New York Commercial Advertiser*.[24] Given the limitations on communications of the time, Jefferson created a wave of publicity that would keep up interest in the expedition.

After a quick once-over of the dispatches from Fort Mandan, Jefferson sent the twenty-nine detailed map sheets of the Missouri River to Secretary of War Dearborn, who would arrange for the Washington City surveyor Nicholas King to reduce them to a manageable scale. Then Jefferson bundled up the rest of the letters, reports, and descriptions to study during the summer.[25]

Monticello was not the sanctuary that Jefferson longed for. Matters of national significance were inescapable, public or private obligations traveled with him, letters from petitioners and adherents, a vicious note from some religious crackpot accusing him of being godless, even notification of his election to the Washington City school board. Delivered in bunches by the mail rider, those letters were answered personally with short, always courteous notes. The farmer also had his fields and the Bedford estate to oversee. Visitors took up a generous host's precious time.[26]

Somehow the enlightened amateur scientist and dedicated tinkerer made time to spread out two large documents that came back from Fort Mandan. He bent over the large map drawn by Clark that filled in the description of the Missouri and speculated about the country beyond Fort Mandan. It had been drawn from descriptions by Indians who had traveled west as far as the divide between waters flowing to the Atlantic and those to the Pacific. Showing the Yellowstone almost connecting with streams flowing to Spanish possessions surely proved the theory of a continental fountain of waters. The map was backed up by Lewis's descriptive "Summary view of the River and Creeks."[27] Another large document that tried Jefferson's aching back had been made from seven pages of paper pasted together into an awkward twenty-nine-by-thirty-five-inch sheet. This charted the data on the western tribes that Lewis and Clark compiled from many sources, including their own observations; today we would call it a spreadsheet.[28]

The "Estimate of Eastern Indians" now resides in the archives of the APS.[29] Across the top were placed nineteen questions about Indians, with ruled columns drawn to the bottom of the page. Along the left side were listed fifty tribes or bands whose accustomed territories extended from the Great Lakes westward to the continental divide and south from the Canadian plains to north Texas. Where additional information was available, the two captains filled in the line opposite the tribe.[30]

As an overview of the Indian world, there was nothing like it but Jefferson must have found that data disappointing. Instead of finding a place to resettle the dispossessed tribes east of the Mississippi and begin their conversion into productive yeoman farmers, the spreadsheet revealed that there were many more Indians living in the West. Those hunters might not be receptive to refugees.

In August Jefferson was informed that specimens from Fort Mandan, shipped through New Orleans, had arrived.[31] There was no government facility to receive materials of a scientific nature and Etienne le Maire, the "maître d'hôtel" for the presidential mansion, was dealing with them as best he could. Those precious specimens could not be ignored.[32]

That was in keeping with the letter Lewis had written on April 7 authorizing the president to forward the specimens to the APS and share other data with a select few of his cabinet. Lewis was not being presumptuous in sending the president specific instructions. They were a team of a kind. Jefferson recognized that Lewis knew enough for field collection but he was not sufficiently proficient in the scientific terminology of several disciplines. If that required expert guidance, the specimens might as well be made available to them now.

Three weeks before he intended to return to Washington, Jefferson wrote to Dr. Samuel Mitchill concerning Lewis's wishes and indicating that he was willing to have the collection forwarded to the society at Philadelphia "from whom we are to hope to learn their contents."[33] "These have been forwarded with a view of their being presented to the Philosophical society of Philadelphia in order that they may under their direction be examined or analyzed."[34]

The specimens were still in Washington on October 4 when the sponsor of scientific exploration finally looked over the collection, selected a few things for his Indian hall, and sent the rest on to the APS. But he admitted to Charles Willson Peale that the packages had been opened, several times for airing, and the contents confused. Those were being sent to Peale to sort out.[35] The society response was recorded in the minutes of November 15, 1805:

A box of plants, earths, and minerals, from Capt. Meriwether Lewis, per Jefferson, who wishes the seeds sent to Mr. Wm. Hamilton; Vaughan and Sybert to examine the earths and minerals; resolution requesting Mr. Hamilton to plant the seeds and report the results with description and specimens.[36]

Lewis not only gathered new plants and specimens of rocks, but he also sent back living birds, a prairie dog, the stuffed skins of a male and female antelope with their skeletons, a weasel, three squirrels from the Rocky Mountains, the skeleton of a coyote, a bobcat skin, horns of the mountain ram, antlers of the black-tailed deer, and many more. Lewis also settled an ongoing debate about the existence of a mountain goat. Ten years later George Or gave full credit to Lewis for collecting the genuine specimen that was then on exhibit.[37]

The prairie dog was still living a year later.[38] That dry statement misses the moment when Lewis found that he had wandered into the raw dirt and mounds of a prairie dog town and realized that he was surrounded by little, stiff-backed sentinels at attention but cautiously keeping close to their burrows. Not that they feared a man. The big sky above was the home of their enemies, the hawks. It's anybody's guess how long it took to capture one, build a roomy cage, feed it, care for it, and treat it as a pet before sending it eastward.[39]

In the distribution of the live specimens, Peale's Natural History Museum got the famous magpie and the APS a lizard. On December 20 the society received another shipment and Vaughan cataloged donations including insects and two small animals that were referred to Dr. Benjamin Smith Barton, the leading authority of entomology.[40] In late 1805 Dr. Barton announced the discoveries in his *Philadelphia Medical and Physical Journal*: "Among the animals which have been lately observed in the Missouri-country, by Mr. Lewis are the following: Hare, Marmot, Stoat, Squirrel."[41]

Barton saved the best for last. Lewis had also collected a number of plants watered by the Missouri and its branches that were "new, or very rare." Preparations were already being made for a lecture at the society, which would conclude that "These specimens will serve as a beginning of a Flora Missourica."[42]

That collection proved what Captain Lewis had been doing. Leaving the daily expedition journals to Clark, he kept several others containing specific observations and data related to botany, zoology, and meteorological and astronomical observations.[43] Maintained by date, some had long passages describing the anatomy of a plant or detailing rock formations or the incredibly minute calculations of the sun and moon. When Lewis found something particularly interesting he wrote at length about it. This calculated reticence has since become a criticism of Lewis based on the desire of students of the expedition for more material to fulfill their expectations. The disappointment of a fandom he could not have imagined was not Lewis's obligation. As captain of the expedition he had assigned keeping of a daily record to Clark and, except when unusual developments might justify adding something, he saw no reason to generate repetitious entries. On the other hand, Clark sometimes recopied Lewis's better written pieces into his record book, perhaps to improve his writing skills.

Jefferson was willing to see the specimens forwarded without seeing them himself, but the extensive summary of the rivers and creeks or the estimate of the eastern Indians, both impressive documents, and the map were considered government property. Lewis and Clark were specific about the disposal of the letters and documents, particularly Clark's uncorrected field journal.

> Capt. Clark dose not wish this journal exposed in it's present state, but has no objection, that one or more copies of it be made by some confidential person under your direction, correcting it's gramatical errors &c. Indeed it is the wish of both of us, that two copies should be made, if convenient, and retained untill our return; in this state there is no objection to your

submitting them for the perusal of the heads of the departments, or such others as you may think proper. *A copy of this journal will assist me in compiling my own for publication after my return.*[44]

Lewis clearly indicated that he intended to write a book about the expedition and the documents forwarded to Jefferson were the raw material he would use. Samuel Latham Mitchill also explained that Lewis and Clark were "expected to publish a narrative of their journey and discoveries." Mitchill could not have come up with that idea without a conversation with Thomas Jefferson.[45]

When the Ninth Congress assembled on December 3, the president sent a long message laying out the problems facing the nation. He noted increasingly difficult foreign relations, the fatal impact of epidemics, and the latest on Indian territorial cessions. But all he said about the exploration was "A state of our progress in exploring the principal rivers of the country, and the information respecting them hitherto obtained will be communicated as soon as we shall receive some further relations which we have reason shortly to expect."[46]

The president was waiting for reports from an expedition to the Southwest that he had started. Before the Corps of Discovery left St. Louis, Jefferson had warned Lewis that he was trying to get Congress to approve funds for several other explorations. Encouraged by correspondence with the Natchez scientist William Dunbar and the Natchitoches Indian agent John Sibley, he hoped that a survey of the Red River might uncover a water route to Santa Fe. Dunbar was joined by a Philadelphia chemist and mineralogist, George Hunter, but they allowed their expedition to be deflected to an unimpressive examination of the Ouachita tributary of the Red River.[47]

It was February 19, 1806, before Jefferson's secretary, Isaac Coles, delivered a fuller statement to Congress that was accompanied by documents. That body heard the reading of the president's message and took a day to consider the printing of two hundred copies of the president's message and the documents for the use of the Senate. By then Nicholas King had also completed four copies of Clark's speculative map of the West, one for the War Department, one for State, another for Congress, and presumably one for the president.[48]

The reports of the Lewis and Clark expedition, and the Dunbar-Hunter expedition and writing of John Sibley, shared a congressional publication. The publication included an edited version of the April 7, 1805, letter from Lewis. Jefferson had taken out those sentences having to do with instructions on how the records were to be handled or copied. Although it was proper to leave out unnecessary details, the omission also covered the fact that Jefferson was exposing the material to a larger audience than Lewis might have planned. The publication of Lewis's summations on geography, Indians, and natural history introduced the first findings of Lewis and Clark to the world eight months before the two captains returned.

What Lewis had written during the winter of 1804–1805 was probably meant as the beginning of a more complete work. It can be argued that data on geography and Indians had been collected at government expense and the chief executive had the right to publish it under the title, "Communicating the Discoveries Made in Exploring the Missouri, Red River and Washita by Captains Lewis and Clark, Doctor Sibley and Mr. Dunbar with a Statistical Account of the Countries Adjacent." Two hundred copies of the three-hundred-page document were printed in the city of Washington by A. & G. Way, Printers.[49] The publication was also serialized in the *National Intelligencer* in October and November 1806.[50]

Editor Mitchill was always up to date. The *Medical Repository* for January 1806 published a review of the Lewis and Clark map and in the next issue the president's message was reviewed.[51] A year later Richard Phillips of London would bring out a 116-page hardbound version of the federal document for the edification of a British audience.[52]

The first year of the operations and discoveries of the Corps of Discovery and the scientific evidence they had collected were already published and widely circulated before the expedition returned. Beyond proving the value of the federal investment, that exposure may have been an innocent expression of Jefferson's enthusiasm. Jefferson had not hesitated to draw attention to largely scientific benefits collected at government expense. The *Medical Repository* spoke to the specific scientific community, and reviews and knock-off editions filtered down to a mildly interested general public. As a public relations tactic, that kept up interest until the explorers returned.

In September 1806 the successful crossing of the continent by a United States expedition was an achievement that even disinterested citizens could appreciate. It was high adventure in the best tradition and the returning heroes were feted and feasted. The APS's stake in the expedition was less glamorous. In a time when most laymen considered science as something of an oddity, enlightened idealists tended to herd like musk oxen beleaguered by wolves. Since the death of Benjamin Franklin, the enlightened amateur Mr. Jefferson had been the most enthusiastic supporter of the society and of exploration.

The American body must have felt in genteel competition with the respected British Royal Society. A patriotic correspondent chided Jefferson for intending to send geographical information to the London cartographer Aaron Arrowsmith. The writer considered that privileged information that untrustworthy rival governments might use against the nation.

The critic had a point because more than science was involved. Among the miscellaneous documents that came back from Fort Mandan was Clark's estimate of the military force necessary to protect the Indian trade and keep the "Savages" at peace with the United States and each other. That proposed a total of seven hundred officers and men in twelve postings mostly concerned protecting the northern border from British intrusion. Louisiana was becoming a potentially expensive proposition.

Thomas Jefferson, the amateur sponsor of discoveries, had no way of knowing that the North West Company of Montreal, in which Mackenzie was interested, was already planning to extend its trade across the northern Rocky Mountains onto the Pacific slope. Their astronomer and surveyor, David Thompson, was being considered to expand operations to the Pacific.

By mid-February 1806 when the "intelligence" contributions of the expedition were being published, the delayed Indian delegation from the West arrived.[53] After hearing the president's address the Indians toured New York and Philadelphia. The painter William Dunlap and editor Mitchill came from Philadelphia to observe and interview the Arikara chief whom Lewis and Clark had sent down in spring 1805. They knew him as the *Ankedoucharo* (village chief) and spoke to him through his interpreter, Joseph Gravelines.[54] Mitchill had already seen one of the four copies of the map and jotted down enough notes to explain it to his subscribers. Mitchill's review also showed how deeply the men of science associated with the APS were inspired by the wealth of data that their fellow member Lewis had contributed to their understanding. Mitchill compared details with the drawings that the visiting Osage Indians made in chalk on the floor, and particularly admired the large map on a buffalo robe made by the Arikara. He took it as proof "of the proficiency made by these children of nature, in the physical geography of the western country." The map ended up in the president's house.

> here I saw an Indian curiousity—It is a *map done by the Missouri natives, on a fine dressed Buffaloe skin* . . . it is of the same whitish on buff colour on this soft and clean hide which is as large as that of an Ox. There is a delineation by an Aboriginal hand of the vast River Platte & Missouri, and of the Principal streams, mountains, villages and minerals, lying between those prodi-

gious water-courses. Among these remarkable things are marked four mines of Platina, several of copper, and a volcano. It is really a pleasing proof of the Geographical Knowledge of these self-educated people. It was a short time ago sent to Mr. Jefferson by Gov. Wilkinson of Louisiana.[55]

NOTES

1. Alexander Wilson, "Particulars of the Death of Capt. Lewis," *Port Folio* 7 (January 1812): 39.

2. TJ to Benjamin Rush, February 28, 1803, and TJ to Robert Patterson, November 16, 1805, Jackson, *LLC* 1: 18 and 270.

3. TJ was president of the APS from January 6, 1797 to February 1815. Gilbert Chinard, "Jefferson and the American Philosophical Society," p. 267; TJ to John Vaughan, February 8, 1815, document 36136, roll 47, TJ-LOC.

4. TJ to Benjamin Rush, February 28, 1803, Jackson, *LLC* 1: 18.

5. Paul Russell Cutright, "Meriwether Lewis: Zoologist," *Oregon Historical Quarterly* 69 (March 1968): 5; Paul Russell Cutright, "The Journal of Captain Meriwether Lewis," *We Proceeded On* 10 (February 1984): 8–10.

6. Over the years the concept of those "hiatuses" have been unchallenged as fact, and allowed to negatively impact Lewis's real role on the expedition. WC has been characterized as the dedicated journalist and ML as a laggard. In fact, he was busy making observations on natural history.

7. TJ to Robert Patterson, March 2, 1803, Jackson, *LLC* 1: 18.

8. John Vaughan to TJ, November 21, 1803, document 23559, roll 29, TJ-LOC; Henry Phillips, "Early Proceedings," pp. 342–43.

9. Jefferson regarded some APS members as "brother literati of Philadelphia." TJ to Benjamin Smith Barton, December 21, 1806, document 28613, roll 37, TJ-LOC.

10. Silvio Bedini, *Jefferson and Science* (Raleigh: University of North Carolina Press, 2002); Simeon J. Crowther and Marion Fawcett, *Science & Medicine to 1870: Pamphlets in the American Philosophical Society Library*, Library Publications No. 1 (Philadelphia: American Philosophical Society, 1968); *Early American Imprints*, First series, no. 35106; Edward C. Carter II, *Most Flattering Incident of My Life: Essays Celebrating the Bicentennial of Thomas Jefferson's American Philosophical Society's Leadership, 1797–1814* (Philadelphia: American Philosophical Society, 1997).

11. Today, the Academy of Natural Sciences of Philadelphia holds the Lewis and Clark Herbarium. Containing 222 sheets of pressed plants, the herbarium is a working scientific collection "which has attained the status of a national icon for its association with the famous explorers." Earl E. Spamer and Richard M. McCourt, "The Lewis and Clark Herbarium of the Academy of Natural Sciences," *Notulae Naturae* 475 (December 2002): 1; Moulton, *JLCE* 12: Herbarium of the Lewis and Clark Expedition.

12. ML to TJ, May 18, 1804, Jackson, *LLC* 1: 192; TJ to CWP, May 5, 1805, document 26015, roll 33, TJ-LOC.

13. Governor Wilkinson sent additional items with AS, who led the Indian delegation to Washington. TJ wrote BSB on December 22, 1805, "Under another cover I send you drawings & specimens of the seed, cotton, & leaf of the cotton tree of the Western Country . . . to these I must add . . . from the journals of Lewis and Clark that the boughs of the tree are the sole food of the horses up the Missouri during winter." TJ to BSB, document 27042, roll 34, TJ-LOC; Carter, *TP* 13: 265 and 317.

14. PC to WHH, May 22, 1805, Jackson, *LLC* 1: 242.

15. "Diary of William Joseph Clark," *Register of the Kentucky State Historical Society* 25 (January 1927): 200, Monday, May 20, 1805.

16. TJ to WE, June 25, 1805, Jackson, *LLC* 1: 249. An account appeared in the *National Intelligencer and Washington Advertiser* on July 17, 1805.

17. Warfington continued to spread news of the expedition as he returned to South West Point. On June 18 the Lexington *Kentucky Gazette* published the account of one of the men who returned with the express and stories from letters from others of the party.

18. JW to HD, June 15, 1805; Carter, *TP* 13: 135.

19. JW to HD, June 13, 1805, Jackson, *LLC* 2: 688.

20. PC to William Claiborne, June 15, 1805, and William Claiborne to TJ, July 6, 1805, Jackson, *LLC* 1: 248 and 250.

21. TJ to HD, July 14, 1805, Jackson, *LLC* 1: 251; TJ to William Jarvis, July 6, 1805, document 26326, roll 34, TJ-LOC; TJ to Anne Cary Randolph, July 6, 1805, Betts and Bear, *FL*, p. 275.

22. TJ to William Claiborne, July 14, 1805, Jackson, *LLC* 1: 252.

23. From June 1805 until mid-1806, Jefferson wrote numerous letters to colleagues about Lewis's discoveries. When the shipments arrived in Philadelphia, APS members wrote to Jefferson with intriguing responses. Moulton's introduction in the herbarium gives a general view but one must read these letters to feel Jefferson's excitement toward Lewis. Moulton, *JLCE* 12.

24. *United States Gazette* (Pennsylvania), July 19, 1805, p. 2; *Pittsfield Sun* (Massachusetts), August 1805, p. 1; *New York Commercial Advertiser*, July 22, 1805.

25. TJ to HD, July 14, 1805, Jackson, *LLC* 1: 252; AG to TJ, July 15, 1805, document 26379, roll 34, TJ-LOC.

26. William Martin to TJ, July 14, 1805, document 26374 and William Bentley to TJ, July 18, 1805, document 26388 and John Gardiner to TJ, July 22, 1805, document 26401 and Polly Logwood to TJ, August 28, 1805, document 26583, roll 34, TJ-LOC.

27. Moulton, *JLCE* 3: 336–69. Theorists believed that all the streams of the West began from one height of land.

28. *ASP, Indian Affairs* 1: 705–43; TJ to Andrew Ellicott, October 25, 1805, document 26777, roll 34, TJ-LOC.

29. Moulton, *JLCE* 3: 386–450.

30. James P. Ronda, "Lewis & Clark and Enlightened Ethnography," In *Westering Companions: Essays on the Lewis and Clark Expedition* (Great Falls, MT: Lewis and Clark Trail Heritage Foundation, Inc., 1990), p. 62.

31. Robert Purviance to JMA, August 12, 1805, document 26501 and HD to TJ, August 15, 1805, document 26521, roll 34, TJ-LOC.

32. Ibid., TJ to Etienne le Maire, August 17, 1805, document 26533 and TJ to HD, August 22, 1805, document 26556, TJ-LOC.

33. TJ to SLM, September 8, 1805, Jackson, *LLC* 1: 258.

34. Ibid., 1: 231–36. (The original handwritten letter can be found in the TJ-LOC, document 25876-80, roll 33.) Edited copies are also found.

35. TJ to CWP, October 6, 9, 21, 1805, Jackson, *LLC* 1: 260–61, 263–64.

36. Phillips, "Early Proceedings," p. 379.

37. Henry Setzer, "Zoological Contributions of the Lewis and Clark Expedition," *Journal of the Washington Academy of Sciences* 44 (November 1954): 356–57; Paul Russell Cutright, *Lewis and Clark: Pioneering Naturalists* (Urbana: University of Illinois Press, 1969), p. 390.

38. A bemused Dolley Madison commented that ML had mistaken a squirrel for a dog. Anna Payne Cutts to Dolley Payne Todd Madison and Mary Coles Payne, September 1, 1805, document DPM0102, Dolley Madison Digital Edition, http://rotunda.upress.virginia.edu:8080/dmde/ (accessed April 8, 2008).

39. September 7, 12, 1804; Moulton, *JLCE* 2: 52–53, 67.

40. Cutright, *Lewis and Clark*, p. 380; Francis W. Pennell, "Benjamin Smith Barton as Naturalist," p. 113; Phillips, "Early Proceedings," p. 380.

41. Benjamin Smith Barton, "Facts and Observations: Natural History, Zoology," *Philadelphia Medical and Physical Journal* 2 (1805): 159; BSB to TJ, November 17, 1805, Jackson, *LLC* 1: 271.

42. Barton, "Facts and Observations," p. 176.

43. In the Fort Mandan Miscellany, the editors identify these as Codex O, the treatise on the Missouri River geography, Codex R containing botanical material, and Codex Q dealing with zoological observations. Moulton, *JLCE* 3: 333–34.

44. ML to TJ, April 7, 1805, Jackson, *LLC* 1: 231–32 (emphasis in italics is ours); William Claiborne to TJ, July 6, 1805, document 26347 and Robert Purviance to JMA, August 12, 1805, document 26501, roll 34, TJ-LOC. Purviance stated that the entire shipment had arrived in separate lots.

45. Phillips, "Early Proceedings," p. 188; Samuel Mitchill, "Lewis's Map of the Parts of North America," *Medical Repository* 3 (1806): 316.

46. US Congress, Senate, 8th Cong., 2nd sess., December 3, 1805.

47. In the attention erroneously given to attempts to intercept the Corps of Discovery, it is generally overlooked what those concerned Spanish officers might have made of a United States exploration, headed by a mineralogist, that appeared to be looking for a route to the New Mexican silver mines.

48. RG217, entry 515, report book E, vol. 5, p. 25, NARA-CP. King was paid

$159. Samuel Mitchill described this map, ". . . soon there will be sent to Congress a better Map of Louisiana than ever appeared, compiled under the eye of Mr. Jefferson and Mr. Dearborn from the communication of Capts. Lewis and Clark and other manuscript maps & documents of travellers." SLM to CM, February 10, 1806, folder 41.321.435, MCNY.

49. *Early American Imprints*, Second series, no. 11633.

50. Dan Flores, "Editor's Introduction," in *Southern Counterpart to Lewis & Clark: The Freeman & Curtis Expedition of 1806* (Norman: University of Oklahoma Press, 2002), p. 45.

51. Mitchill, "Lewis's Map," pp. 315–18; Samuel Latham Mitchill, "Review: Message from the President of the United States Communicating Discoveries Made in Exploring the Missouri," *Medical Repository* 4 (1807): 165–74.

52. Joseph Sabin, *A Dictionary of Books Relating to America*, 29 vols. (Amsterdam: 1961), 9–10: 311 (Sabin 40826).

53. The delegation included twenty-one individuals from ten Indian nations and two interpreters. TJ to Benjamin Smith Barton, January 11, 1806, document 27223, roll 35, TJ-LOC; John C. Ewers, "Chiefs from the Missouri and Mississippi and Peale's Silhouettes of 1806," *Smithsonian Journal of History* 1 (Spring 1966): 11–12.

54. SLM to CM, January 2, 1806, folder 41.321.422, MCNY; "Remarks on the Speech Attributed to an Indian Chief," *Early American Imprints*, Second series, no. 9927.

55. SLM to CM, January 29, 1806, folder 41.312.430 and February 19, 1806, folder 41.321.440, MCNY; Mitchill, "Lewis's Map," p. 318.

SIX

Return to St. Louis

Subdu'd by boldness, and amazed[1]

F or Meriwether Lewis, it was like coming back from a trip to the moon. As much as he appreciated a hero's welcome, for the moment the explorer was satisfied to put his legs under a real desk, and, sitting on a pillow to ease his recently healed wound, to write again. His mind brimmed with what he had seen: spectacular places, promising fields, rich resources, and powerful rivers. There were new plants and unusual animals to describe. To make those scientific findings more than mere curiosities, he had to properly describe them—in a book that cried to be written.

The daily journals were fine as private records but needed to be edited and expanded into a readable narrative. Much of the material about western Indians had already been put together at Fort Mandan and sent back to Mr. Jefferson. Now he wished that he had done something similar during the dreadful winter of 1805–1806 that was spent at Fort Clatsop on the Pacific Coast. He faced the necessity of summarizing a year and a half of additional scientific observations.

Lewis was already feeling pressure to get started because Pvt. Robert Fraser had approached him about publishing his personal journal by subscription. As there was no press in St. Louis, anything immediate wasn't likely; Fraser had to write out his prospectus in longhand. He may even have had the surveyor Antoine Soulard working on a map although that couldn't possibly equal what Clark had produced from accurate observations.[2] Because Lewis saw himself as the most qualified scientist on the expedition, he needed to complete his work before scurrilous books appeared.

The government-sponsored expedition required a comprehensive report and Clark's maps. Lewis wasn't sure what Mr. Jefferson expected of him. The letters that he had written to his mentor were personal descriptions meant to satisfy a kindred scientific mind. Undoubtedly Jefferson expected him to enlarge upon those outlines in something suitable for presentation, perhaps even publication by the American Philosophical Society.

As Lewis completed the lingering details of the expedition he was still operating under the president's letter of credit. By the end of the second week, he wrote government drafts to the merchants Wilkinson & Price, Hunt & Hankinson, and Falconer & Comegys. There was a bill of exchange for $91.50 to the tavern keepers Calvin Adams and William Christy who put on the big celebration two days after the expedition returned.[3] Settling store accounts, auctioning off the surplus gear, or carrying out other details of closing down the expedition provided opportunities to hear about the present state of the Louisiana Territory and what had transpired while they were gone.

The small, muddy St. Louis village they had left twenty-seven months ago had been an empty stage. Now it was crowded with a cast of characters who meant to alter it to their personal script. The grand toasts they offered to welcome the returning explorers said more about expectations than it did about the heroes.

Beyond the excitement and celebration of their return, the town was bubbling with old gossip and present hearsay. Opinions on the unsatisfactory conduct of the government were slipped in between the toasts or over the counter as the officers settled their debts. The two captains had an earful from self-interested individuals who recognized that they would soon be reporting to the president. Peddling something discreditable about others was not exactly what a hero in his moment of glory wanted to take with him to Washington, but Lewis was still the eyes and ears of the president.

Even as they were being feted, Lewis and Clark were appalled by the shambles that St. Louis had become. The extension of United States authority had passed from a well-meaning captain of artillery to a recently promoted major, James Bruff, who had an oversized opinion of himself. As far as Indiana Territory governor William Henry Harrison's administration went, Upper Louisiana enjoyed indifferent neglect. Gov. James Wilkinson had tried to move too fast and then was called away to military duties. At the present Upper Louisiana was being run by the territorial secretary Joseph Browne, who was thought to be very close to former vice president Aaron Burr.

The complexities Lewis noted before leaving had multiplied in the past two years. Upper Louisiana was simmering with discontent over trade restrictions and the problems of getting land grants or claims authenticated. It would have helped Lewis to understand what had taken place if he had been able to talk to a trustworthy friend. After finishing his duty as interim civil commandant, Captain Stoddard shepherded an Indian delegation to Washington and was assigned to a new post. Lewis remembered that factions had started to appear when Stoddard conducted the transfer. Now he learned that from the beginning poor Stoddard had been undercut and duped. As civil administrator he tried to deal with the apprehensions of the old inhabitants and the raw greed of new opportunists who meant to cut up another pie as lucrative as the Indian land cessions east of the Mississippi. Instead of befuddled tribesmen, this time they meant to dispossess the French who held prior Spanish land grants. Stoddard had unwittingly been drawn into disputes over valuable lead mines. After Major Bruff took over as military commandant, it was evident that authority was not going to work.

The initial responsibility of constructing a government had fallen to William Henry Harrison, governor of the adjacent Indiana Territory. But Harrison had been a distant, disinterested administrator who did not appear in St. Louis until October 1804 when he came to make civil appointments and establish courts. As an example of this casual approach, Edward Hempstead, a Connecticut lawyer visiting Vincennes, had been left with the appointment of deputy attorney general.[4]

The administration in Washington also made long-distance appointments: four district commandants, a postmaster, territorial court judges, clerks, justices of the peace, and a sheriff.[5] Patronage was a republican prerogative but most of the administrative appointments, no matter what origin, went to men who were ambitious to gain lucrative roles in a territory in flux. It should have been no surprise that power struggles developed between those aggressive newcomers. As the president's secretary, Lewis had seen enough of Washington's political underbelly to recognize the simmering discontent in Upper Louisiana. He pitied the man who would have to resolve it.

In early 1805 President Jefferson had gone to the top of the military hierarchy by sending General of the Army Gen. James Wilkinson to take command as governor and as superintendent of Indians.[6] But those who thought that military commandants would ease the transition from an authoritative Spanish administration to the blessings of republican government were disappointed. The general brought his habit of command against the ambitions of self-interested federal appointees, land speculators, and power brokers. Upon his arrival in July 1805 Wilkinson immediately formed a pessimistic opinion of the current political climate in St. Louis:

> Two or three Pettifoggers, two or three Renegadoes and the Same number of impatient Natives, left to the free exercise of their wits, were more than Sufficient to embroil this Community, which I found raging with personal animosities in all quarters, excepting the District of St. Charles, where Colonel Meigs by his Temperate firmness, his good sense and impartiality had acquired universal confidence and preserved the Strictest harmony.[7]

Lewis was gratified to learn that the general had immediately moved to inhibit the intrusion of British traders. He limited trade licenses to US citizens and required that boats hauling trade outfits up the Missouri be manned by local boatmen. That hadn't worked out as well as hoped; the returning corps met the British trader James Aird, who got around the governor's decree on a technicality.

Marking out the territory like a pissing wolf, the general also launched reconnaissance in all directions to explore and show the flag. Zebulon Pike took a boat party up the Mississippi, where he warned off British traders, wintered, and returned in spring 1806. Pike had been immediately directed on another mysterious mission upon the southwestern plains. George Peter had been sent to locate a place for a military post meant to bring the bothersome Osage Indians to heel. James Wilkinson, the general's son, had been sent in late fall 1805 to establish a temporary military post at the mouth of the Platte River. The general's actions paralleled what Lewis and Clark had recommended from Fort Mandan. In addition to these public expeditions, the general also sponsored two private adventures south and north with his own funds.[8]

Previously experienced in fighting and dealing with Indians, Wilkinson should have been well qualified to administer the new territory. Unfortunately the St. Louis community immediately polarized into pro- and anti-Wilkinson factions. When he tried to assert government authority over the lead lands, the resulting uproar forced him to rescind his order. Wilkinson's opponents were capable of outrageous charges and outright lies, the same political abuse Lewis had seen heaped on President Jefferson. If sympathy meant anything in that cesspool, Governor Wilkinson had inherited an impossible job.

As the commanding general of the army, Wilkinson left St. Louis on August 16 to deal with Spanish activities on the lower Mississippi frontier. As far as Lewis could see, Wilkinson's actions as governor had been generally positive. His problems came when he tried to control the rampant greed for land. The cabal ranged against the governor included the insufferable

Ste. Genevieve commandant Seth Hunt, Judge Lucas, or the young lawyer William C. Carr, who found any excuse to disparage the administration, even trying to make a case for treason.[9]

After being away for almost three years, Lewis and Clark were unaware of momentous developments. The New York lawyer Aaron Burr had been vice president when Lewis carried Jefferson's messages to the Hill. After his campaign for governor of New York failed, Burr killed Alexander Hamilton in a duel over those bitter politics. Lately Mr. Burr appeared to be involved in a filibuster directed against Spanish possessions. Ever seeking a crack in Wilkinson's armor, his enemies linked that to the three expeditions that he started toward the Southwest: the first under the command of his son, the second under Lieutenant Pike with young Wilkinson as his second, and that curious private trading venture to Santa Fe by past Capt. John McClallen.

When Wilkinson departed in mid-August to address a military problem with the Spanish on the lower Mississippi, the territorial government was in disarray and most citizens expected that he would not be returning. As a loyal soldier Lewis was taken aback when Maj. James Bruff came to him with a catalog of complaints about the general.[10] After being disciplined for disrespect, Bruff claimed that the general and Burr were acting in concert about something traitorous. He intended to remain in St. Louis until mid-November "to counteract and appose their attempts, and pull down their standard."[11]

Campaigns were already under way to project Wilkinson's replacement. The old inhabitants supported Secretary Browne, but he was too closely associated with Aaron Burr. Another faction promoted the St. Louis district commandant Samuel Hammond, a former congressman. Those in St. Charles would have liked to see their commandant Return Jonathan Meigs as governor.

During October while the two captains were finishing up the business of the expedition, rumors about Burr and his plans were still circulating in St. Louis. Part of that cloud cleared before Lewis and Clark departed when the town learned that a compromise had been arranged with the Spanish. After ensuring that there would be no war, the general then arrested Burr on the lower Mississippi. Already the vicious local cabal was howling that General Wilkinson had betrayed his fellow conspirator.

No matter the imposed politics, Spanish or American, St. Louis was a mercantile town. Exploration yarns went only so far before the conversation came around to what really mattered: the Indian trade, skins, hides, peltry. Because commercial houses in Philadelphia or Baltimore supplied the goods used to make up trading outfits, their western associates had obligations to meet. Most local merchants appreciated that Governor Wilkinson had done a bold thing putting the British traders at arms length. But until there were effective controls in Upper Louisiana, most of the prime beaver of the upper Mississippi and Missouri rivers would continue to flow through Prairie du Chien and Michilimackinac to Montreal exporters.

No one spent much time in St. Louis without recognizing the standing and influence of the Chouteau family. Their grand houses stood along First Street until 1805 when Pierre's house burned to the ground.[12] When Lewis and Clark were organizing the expedition the half brothers Auguste and Pierre Chouteau had been very accommodating. Auguste Chouteau was the St. Louis business functionary of the family and Pierre was their connection to the Indians. In the absence of Captain Stoddard, Chouteau's brother-in-law Charles Gratiot acted as Lewis's agent. Because of his long-standing relationship with the Osage, the most powerful tribe south of the Missouri River, Pierre Chouteau had been charged with conducting a delegation of those Indians to Washington. After they arrived on July 11, 1804, President Jefferson and Secretary of the Treasury Albert Gallatin were disappointed with the results. Their expectation of a treaty and a cession of a large tract of Osage land had not been accomplished.[13]

In seeking information for the president, Lewis turned to the Chouteaus and by mid-October he had the latest on the regional Indian situation. Commissioned Osage Indian agent Pierre Chouteau returned to St. Louis authorized to do what was necessary to begin turning those hunters into yeoman farmers.[14]

In November Pierre Chouteau had compiled a report showing the amounts that the Spanish previously paid for diplomatic Indian gifts. He estimated that the annual compensation of merchandise for the Indian trade on the Missouri amounted to $35,000 to the Grand Osage, $8,000 to the Little Osage, Kansa $8,000, Ottos $8,000, Missouris $4,000, Panis $5,000, Republique $4,000, Loups $3,000, Mahas $10,000, Poncas $1,500, Sioux $1,500, Mandan $2,500, Ricaras $2,000—$92,500 in total.[15] No surprise that Pierre's future as a federal agent began to dim in the eyes of a budget-minded administration. Congress only authorized $500 for military and Indian expenditures in the Louisiana Territory.

When a band of Iowa Indians arrived in St. Louis, on Lewis's invitation, Chouteau had to send them back because he had no specific orders from the president. Although the burning of his house had been a serious blow to his assets, leaving him strapped for cash, the federal agent appeased the disappointed tribesmen with gifts at his own expense. When the government failed to promptly reimburse him for the Indian gifts he had advanced, Chouteau was getting desperate.

Government parsimony could very well result in Indian attacks on frontier settlers. After suggesting that more Indians be invited to visit the president, Pierre Chouteau left for the Osage country in August and reappeared in mid-October with six Osage chiefs.[16] Lewis and Clark had returned to St. Louis by then, which meant that Chouteau could accompany them and the Mandan entourage.[17]

The Jefferson administration needed to find a way to make the new country pay for itself. To justify the purchase, the Louisiana Territory had to become a revenue producer instead of a burden on the treasury. Beyond the Indian trade the best opportunity lay in the mineral wealth of the new territory. Miners were in the habit of finding lead close to the surface without being concerned about the ownership, taking mineral from government property subject to leasing and glad to have a handy place to deliver the ore for smelting.

In the Ste. Genevieve District the transplanted Yankee Moses Austin was to lead what the Chouteau brothers were to the Osage. After immigrating in 1797 and renouncing his US citizenship, he obtained a Spanish grant of 6,300 acres for the largest lead reserves near Ste. Genevieve. Before leaving on the expedition Lewis had recommended that Stoddard get Austin to write a dissertation on the lead mines. What Stoddard forwarded so enthused the president that it was included in his November message to Congress.[18]

But there were those who complained that this insufferable Yankee had the Ste. Genevieve lead mines sewed up with his efficient smelter and could set prices as he chose. St. Louis storekeepers complained that beyond an occasional shovel or pick there wasn't much market for them in the lead mines. When Governor Wilkinson began enforcing federal rights to lead lands that upset the system and set off another feud.

Stoddard also sent a devastating report detailing potential frauds in old land titles, which propelled Washington to suspend land rights.[19] All Spanish land titles would be held by the American government until Secretary of the Treasury Albert Gallatin appointed a three-man Board of Land Commissioners who would take testimony on the merits of each claimant's title and make recommendations.[20] There was no doubt that the land titles of old settlers were in disarray. The majority of the French could not speak or read English and nothing had been done to explain the problems to them. On top of that, new settlers were arriving daily and squatting on public land.

In a new churning economy, the previous reliance on bartering wasn't working. Many of the old inhabitants needed to sell parts of their holdings in order to obtain cash money. Due to the cost, many claims had never been surveyed or even properly described. Now they were being told that their titles were seriously deficient and incomplete. Those old inhabitants believed that the new infrastructure of Upper Louisiana had been designed to disassociate them from their land. All they could do was form committees to address their grievances to Congress.

During the third week of October, just as Lewis and Clark were finalizing their business in St. Louis, a heated argument erupted between the judges of the territory regarding deficient surveys. Some contained errors in the form of erasures. Postmaster Rufus Easton decided that "Captains Lewis & Clark" would be "faithful messengers of their state and condition" and on October 19 had them "personally inspect" the survey books that were found in an unbound state, very different than those kept in a US surveyor's office.[21] Easton hoped that Lewis and Clark would inform President Jefferson about the situation and encourage him to make a decision. Like it or not Meriwether Lewis, the explorer and naturalist, was being sucked into Upper Louisiana politics.

When Lewis and Clark departed St. Louis at the end of October, five of the top administrative posts had been vacated: governor, recorder of land titles, attorney general, one territorial judge, and one land board commissioner. Mr. Burr's associate Territorial Secretary Joseph Browne was running the government and petitions were being circulated for his successor.

Captain Lewis had absorbed the major problems trying Upper Louisiana. Whether President Jefferson would welcome those insights was yet to be seen. At least they would come from a trusted source.

NOTES

1. Alexander Wilson, "Particulars of the Death of Capt. Lewis," *Port Folio* 7 (January 1812): 39.

2. Fraser's pursuit of the two captains with information about the Burrites in St. Louis was not entirely altruistic, as by December 13, 1806, and January 6, 1807, Fraser ran ads in the Philadelphia *Aurora* that surely interested members of the APS. They were still anticipating debriefing fellow member Captain Lewis. Soulard had journeyed up the Missouri and had drawn several upper Missouri maps for James MacKay and the Spanish government. Mitchill, "Descriptive Observations on Certain Parts of the Country in Louisiana," *Medical Repository* 3 (1806): 309.

3. ML to HD, October 12, 1806, Jackson, *LLC* 1: 349, fn.; ML to SW, 1806, RG107, M222, roll 2, frame 0657, NARA. Donald Jackson misprinted the amount that Lewis paid Christy as $19.50 (Jackson, *LLC* 1: 349 n., October 17, bill of exchange, no. 111).

4. William E. Foley, "Edward Hempstead," in *Dictionary of Missouri Biography* (Columbia: University of Missouri Press, 1999), p. 391.

5. Carter, *TP* 13: 40, 54–68.

6. Ibid., 13: 95.

7. Ibid., JW to SW, July 27, 1805, 13: 164–65.

8. JW to HD, June 13, 1805, Jackson, *LLC* 2: 690.

9. JW to SW, December 31, 1805, Jackson, *LLC* 1: 368–70.

10. According to Bruff, "I also made a communication to Captain Lewis immediately after his return and related the conversations between Judge Easton and myself." *Annals of the Congress of the United States, 1789–1824*, 42 vols. (Washington: Gales & Seaton, 1834–1836), appendix, p. 620. *Annals of Congress*, "Trial of Aaron Burr," http://memory.loc.gov/cgi bin/ampage?collId=llac&fileName =017/llac017.db&recNum=306 (accessed April 8, 2008).

11. Ibid., appendix, pp. 599–600, 621. Bruff had been writing letters to friends in Washington since the first of the year. WC was present in 1807 when Bruff carried his complaints to the secretary of war. Later, with some encouragement from Burr's lawyer, Bruff volunteered to try to discredit Wilkinson at the Richmond trial and Lewis may have seen him there.

12. PC to TJ, March 30, 1805, Pierre Chouteau letterbook, pp. 25–26, MHS. "On the 15 March my house burned to the ground—in the space of one hour twenty-five years of unremitting work lost."

13. TJ to AG, July 12, 1804, document 24594 and TJ to William Dunbar, July 17, 1804, document 24620, roll 30, TJ to HD, October 20, 1804, document 25028, roll 31, TJ-LOC; *Records of the Adjutant General's Office*, RG94, AGO to SW, July 11, 1804, M565, roll 2, frame 0076, NARA.

14. Commission of Pierre Chouteau as Indian agent, July 17, 1804; Carter, *TP* 13: 33. Chouteau would hold that agency for more than a decade. The president was unaware that the Osage had promised a large tract of their land to the Chouteaus for their efforts in assisting them. That could not be considered federal land until the tribes ceded it, but according to the Northwest Ordinance, neither could it be handed over to private individuals.

15. PC to SW, November 19, 1804, Pierre Chouteau letterbook, p. 17, MHS.

16. Ibid., pp. 60–63.

17. Three delegations had preceded this one: the first led by Pierre Chouteau in the spring of 1804, another shepherded by Captain Stoddard in October 1805, and the last one in November 1805 led by Eli Clemson. His deputation comprised the Arikara chief who died in Washington, the Missouri Indians, and their interpreters. Indian agent James Colbert brought a delegation of Chickasaw, Creek, and Chippewa Indians and met Clemson in St. Louis, where they all headed to Washington (RG217, entry 366, vol. 11, letterbook M, pp. 6230–31, 6451, NARA-CP).

18. ASP, *Public Lands* 1: 188–91.

19. Ibid., p. 193.

20. Carter, *TP* 13: 122, 124.

21. Rufus Easton to TJ, December 1, 1806; Carter, *TP* 14: 45. Easton became the first postmaster of St. Louis (Jo Tice Bloom, *Dictionary of Missouri Biography*, p. 271).

SEVEN

Welcome and Unwelcome Rewards

His was the peril, glory, pride[1]

L ewis and Clark rode away from the old fur trade center of St. Louis, a town excited by what they had reported. Anticipating major changes in the Indian trade, Congress had already hired factors, agents, and interpreters to operate new government trading establishments.[2] At the Cantonment Belle Fontaine Indian trade factory located eighteen miles north of St. Louis, the assistant factor George Sibley, a factor being the designation of the individual in charge of the government-run works, wrote a glowing letter about the expectations:

> [W]e shall see floating down the Missouri, valuable cargoes of East-India Merchandise; I need Say no more, this bare hint will be Sufficient for you to build on for weeks & months. I cannot predict what effect these things will have on my Fortunes tho' certain it is they will have a very material one.[3]

About October 21, Lewis and Clark, Clark's servant York, Sergeant Ordway, and the interpreter François Labiche left St. Louis, accompanied by Osage Indian agent Pierre Chouteau and the Mandan and Osage delegations. Prominent among those was Sheheke-shote (or chief Big White Coyote) and his family who had been brought down from the Mandan villages. Having already shepherded a previous Indian delegation, Chouteau thought the trip to Washington should take about forty days.[4] Their route through Vincennes and to the falls of the Ohio took nine or ten days. From there they proceeded to Clark's home and rested for a few days. At the home of Jonathan Clark in Louisville on November 9, they were treated to a banquet, ball, and bonfires.

They were not exactly traveling unnoticed. News accounts had raced ahead of them in the Frankfort, Kentucky, *Palladium* of October 9, the *New York Commercial Advertiser* of October 30, the *New York Evening Post* of November 4, and the *Connecticut Herald* of November 4, 1806.

Four days later at Frankfort, they went their separate ways. Chouteau went directly to Washington with the Indians, interpreters, and non-coms. Clark and York headed to Fincastle, Virginia, to visit the Hancock family and see if their daughter Julia Hancock was a marriage prospect. And Lewis rode to Charlottesville to see his mother and family before going on to Washington.[5]

It was December 13 when Lewis arrived at his home in Albemarle County to embrace his mother and family. But loving intimacy soon had to yield to public approval. The community staged another banquet at the Stone Tavern in Charlottesville where there were laudatory speeches and modest responses from the returned hero. After spending Christmas Day with his family Lewis departed for Washington that evening. He finally reached Washington late in the evening of December 28 and found a warm welcome at the presidential mansion.[6]

It had been October 26 when President Jefferson received the letter Lewis dated September 23 at St. Louis. He read it with "unspeakable joy." So much time had passed without hearing about the expedition that it "had begun to be felt awfully."[7]

President Jefferson wanted to see everything. Lewis produced a new map, somewhat revised from the Fort Mandan version, that described the country west of the mountains. After descending the Yellowstone, Clark had added the tributaries flowing into that river. The revised map was large but it really wasn't necessary for the chief executive, no matter how excited, to crawl around on the floor to examine it.[8]

Although forewarned about the difficulties of an overland portage between the Missouri and the Columbia, Jefferson was pleased that Lewis had found a good road from the Great Falls for half of the distance. But the trail over the mountains where the expedition endured two trying passages was impracticable—a major disappointment.

It was disappointing that Clark encountered no Indians descending the Yellowstone and Lewis's foray from the Great Falls only met eight thought-to-have-been Minnetaries. Chouteau and the Indian delegation finally arrived on December 20 but the president waited until Lewis was present to welcome them.[9] In a burst of enthusiasm Jefferson took them to the theater that evening. Getting into the spirit of the occasion, several of the visitors went up on the stage to dance during the intermission.[10] Samuel Mitchill met Lewis on December 30:

> Capt. Lewis has reached this place after the performance of a journey across the Continent of North America, quite across to the Pacific Ocean, and back again . . . he proceeded westward, and crossing the Northern Andes, near some of the sources of the Missouri, travelled before the Vigorous Weather set in, as far as the Ocean, near the mouth of the Columbia River. Here he remained during the inclement part of 1805-6; and as soon as the spring was far enough advanced for marching, he started for home. And here, he is once in good health & spirits. I feel rejoiced on his own account, an account of Geography & Natural History; and on account of the Character and Honour of Country that this expedition has been successfully performed.[11]

Another celebration took place on New Year's Day when the citizens traditionally came to pay their respects to the president and get a glimpse of the colorfully dressed Indian entourage. Mitchill paid his compliments to Mr. Jefferson at the president's house on the Palatine Hills, Mitchell's way of referring to the unfinished presidential mansion:

> While I was looking round and meditating what to do with myself, the Miss Johnsons . . . expressed a desire to be escorted to the side of the room where the newly arrived Indians were. I at once became their pioneer and showed them the King and Queen of the Mandanes, who with a child of theirs, have come from a journey of about 1600 miles down the Missouri to see their great Father the President. His majests were gaily dressed in a regimental coat, &, but his Consort was wrapped in a blanket, and had not the smallest ornament about her. She resembled exceedingly one of our Long Island squaws. [Mitchill was a resident of Long Island, New York.] There was also another Mandane woman there, who was wife to a Canadian White man, that acted as interpreter [René Jusseaume]. She had two children with her. We also looked at the five Osages and the one Delaware warriors of whom I wrote you before.[12]

The big Washington testimonial banquet at Stelle's Hotel was put off in the hopes that Clark would arrive.[13] Finally on January 14, 1807, it was attended by the citizens of Washington, several officers of government, members of Congress, and strangers of distinction including Pierre Chouteau, the French translator Pierre Provenchere, the Mandan chief Sheheke-shote, and his personal interpreter René Jusseaume.[14] The newspaper the *Sun* reported:

> Capt. Lewis was received with the liveliest demonstrations of regard. Every one present seemed to be deeply impressed with a sentiment of gratitude, mingled with an elevation of mind, on setting down, at the festive board, with this favorite of fortune, who has thus successfully surmounted the numerous and imminent perils of a tour of nearly four years, through regions previously unexplored by civilized man.[15]

The list of laudatory toasts included two directed to the Mandan visitor Sheheke-shote.

The Red People of America would live "Under an enlightened policy gaining by steady steps the comforts of the civilized, without losing the virtues of the savage state," which would be followed by the somewhat ominous "The Council Fire—May it long continue to diffuse a warmth, without consuming those who surround it." The toasts ended with the recognition of agriculture that might have recalled Lewis's former position as the capital district's corresponding secretary to the National Board of Agriculture, or more likely Jefferson's intention to convert wandering people like these to yeoman farmers.[16] After an evening at a well-spread table with toasts interspersed with appropriate songs and instrumental music, Captain Lewis rose next morning to address the compensation due to the members of the expedition.

At the autumn opening of Congress President Jefferson had briefly detailed the findings of the Corps of Discovery without getting into the spiraling costs. He recommended additional compensation to show "that Messrs. Lewis and Clarke, and their brave companions, have, by this arduous service, deserved well of their country."[17]

Then Jefferson had other matters on his mind. Throughout October the president had received warnings of a conspiracy in the West. On November 27 he had issued a proclamation that an unlawful military expedition against the Spanish dominions of Mexico was under way and warned all persons to "withdraw without delay." So most of the president's message to Congress on December 2 concerned the resolution of the confrontation with Spanish forces on the Sabine River where General Wilkinson had found an acceptable compromise.

But the general also confirmed a matter of grave consequence. It appeared that former vice president Burr was threatening to sunder the nation at the Allegheny Ridge or, that failing, maybe along the Mississippi. He had twenty thousand dollars to buy boats and hire mercenaries, so what the conspirators were capable of executing was a threat that could not be ignored. In exposing Burr, General Wilkinson appeared to be standing firm on the side of the administration.

Captain Lewis now added what he had observed in St. Louis, not only about a conspiracy but also about the deplorable state of the territory. At this moment that place was in the hands of the territorial secretary Joseph Browne, who was closely connected to the traitorous Mr. Burr. That information added to something that was already under discussion, the appointment of a new governor for Louisiana.

While Lewis and Clark were exploring the extent of Louisiana, the Jefferson administration was grappling with how to make that vast territory carry its own weight. There seemed to be potential in natural resources like lead or the fur trade. But land couldn't be sold until it was properly identified and surveyed, and lead mines couldn't be leased or commercial relations with Indians developed until a fractious community was brought into line. For the last three years Jefferson had been trying to establish a territorial government and formulate some basic laws.[18]

After the initial temporary appointments General Wilkinson had seemed to be the man for the job. But sending an authoritarian into a power struggle only resulted in an ugly, contentious mess made even worse when the general was called away to other military responsibilities.[19] Wilkinson had written to his close friend Sen. Samuel Smith of Maryland that he expected to be replaced. In urging the president to appoint someone whose conduct would not be "insulting to you," Smith suggested that a successor should be "a Gentleman. . . . One who has not been in Louisiana or has in any manner participated in the misunderstandings that have happened there."[20] Jefferson replied that "not a single fact has appeared to doubt that I have made a fitter appointment than Genl. Wilkinson." It was unfortunate that ordering him to the lower Mississippi to deal with a Spanish threat left the Louisiana Territory in the hands of Burr's former brother-in-law.[21]

Jefferson and his cabinet began discussing the appointment of a reliable governor for the Louisiana Territory in October. Although James Monroe's enemies described him as "indecisive . . . has no opinion on any subject" and a mediocre lawyer, the diplomat would have been a good choice because he was an old friend and proven diplomat who could take direction without a fuss.[22]

Jefferson tried to appoint Monroe in 1804, but he was still involved in overseas matters and the compromise had been General Wilkinson. When the president looked to Monroe again in May 1806, the diplomat was still otherwise engaged. Hoping that Monroe would be able to take the job, Jefferson left the position open to the end of August, then September, and to the last week of October.[23] His concern for the welfare of Louisiana was of desperation when he wrote to Samuel Smith:

> ... nothing can be more inveterate than the discord at St. Louis. If it were lawful to remove every officer that has been appointed, I believe, it the only step which could cure the service: but the tenure of office not permitting this in every case, would still keep in one at least of the bitterest partisans in that place as well as ... the feuds among our own adventurers who have emigrated thither have made a most unfavorable impression on the natives as to the character of our government.[24]

At the eleventh hour, Jefferson and his cabinet had to come up with an alternative. After receiving the first letters from Captain Lewis, the president saw him in a new light. From the newspapers, it was apparent that a national hero was emerging. Treasury Secretary Gallatin also supported the idea of appointing a governor with no former ties with anyone connected to the Louisiana Territory when he wrote Jefferson on October 25, 1806.

> I do not know the news of the last mail, the fortunate arrival of Capts. Lewis at St. Louis excepted. If you select him for Governor, ought not provision to be made for the contingency of his leaving that place for Washington before the arrival of a commission? and does not that render the appointment of a Secretary who may govern in the interim still more important?[25]

The template for the new administration of the Louisiana Territory was clear. The president needed a man he could trust in that cesspool of opportunists and uncertain citizens, particularly if the Burr business turned hot. What could be better than implanting a new national hero to govern a country he knew better than anyone? Having Captain Lewis resign his commission and return to St. Louis as governor was a brilliant stroke that should erase grievances and restore confidence.

Perhaps Thomas Jefferson meant well, but he was driven by political demands. How and when Meriwether Lewis was made aware of that dubious "honor" is uncertain. The appointment could not have been planned before he left to lead the expedition and no correspondence survives to indicate that he was forewarned later. The surprised explorer and field naturalist must have wondered what qualified him for political office.

How would an inexperienced administrator be expected to bring that fractious territory to order? And he needed time to complete a literate chron-
icle of the expedition.

By January 1807 Captain Lewis knew he would have to return to the
political cesspool of St. Louis and try to govern a fragmented community. He
knew from personal experience that the territory stretched as far as the Rocky
Mountains and was sandwiched between Spanish influence on the south and
west and British pressure on the north. Lewis must have realized what the
appointment as governor of the Louisiana Territory really meant. Already
saddled with competing priorities, he would be preoccupied with disputes
between stubborn self-seeking men who could not see beyond their own
noses. If he balked or protested that he had too much to do just realizing the
product of the last three years of his field work, it did not matter Jefferson had
no recourse but to pawn his prized pupil to salvage that territorial mess.

Recognizing that Lewis would be tied up with final tasks including the narrative, Gallatin urged Jefferson to find a new secretary for the Louisiana Territory who might govern in the interim. They did not have to look far. At the end
of December that man dropped in their laps. Between October and December
was time enough for Gallatin to suggest that a treasury officer in Detroit might
find it convenient to be in Washington. Frederick Bates was already familiar
with territorial politics, land claims, post roads, and business affairs when he was
considered for the number two position in the Louisiana Territory.[26]

Frederick Bates had gone to Detroit in 1798 to open a mercantile store.
After four years he was losing money and accepted a job as deputy postmaster. A Detroit official named Samuel Tupper praised Bates's attributes.

> Mr. Bates is a young gentleman who is descended from a respectable family
> in Virginia where he received an academic education. . . . In his manners he
> is modest & unassuming, but firm and decided in his opinions. He is stu-
> dious, temperate, and industrious and his moral character stands unim-
> peached. His attachment to republican measures is unquestionable . . .[27]

Recommendations like that helped Bates serve in a number of civil
capacities: receiver of public monies, land commissioner, and judge in the
Detroit, Huron, and Erie districts. Those appointments were under the
jurisdiction of the State and Treasury departments, and Bates frequently
corresponded with James Madison and Albert Gallatin.

In early January 1806 Tarleton Bates had been killed in a duel. Frederick received word of the death a few months later, temporarily closed his
office, and departed Detroit in November to go to Pittsburgh and attend to

his brother's affairs. From there he went on to Washington to make a lengthy report on the Michigan land grants. So Bates was conveniently in the Capitol on February 4, 1807, when he was offered two jobs: territorial secretary and recorder of land titles for the Louisiana Territory.[28]

One of his younger brothers later suggested that Frederick was pressed into service for Upper Louisiana "and transferred against his will" to St. Louis. Bates wrote from Washington on February 9 that he was resigning from the various posts in Detroit and modestly hinted of dissatisfaction in the new positions: "Circumstances which I knew not how to control prevented my immediate return" to Detroit. Two weeks later the Senate approved his appointments and he was soon on the road west to act as interim governor until Lewis arrived, just as Gallatin had suggested last October.[29]

Obviously there had been serious discussions about the appointment and what would be required of Bates. Those included the president, Captain Lewis, William Clark, and Frederick Bates himself. Everyone understood that Captain Lewis would be tied up in Washington settling the expedition accounts and final report. And he would have to travel to Philadelphia to arrange the publication of a narrative written for a broader audience as well as for the scientific community. That would take time, several months perhaps, and in the meantime the territorial secretary would be required to perform duties beyond the requirements of his office. Jefferson realized that he was sending a man inexperienced in the complexities of frontier government to deal with the mess that Lewis had reported. But there was no way to avoid it.

Lewis was also aware of the awkward way that his political life was beginning, one foot in government, the other still in science. That may have been an excuse for a curious slip of his pen in introducing *Fleming* Bates to Auguste Chouteau. When Lewis wrote to Chouteau on February 11, it was to confirm that he had carried the concerns of the French citizens of Louisiana about land matters to President Jefferson. He warned Chouteau that it would take time before those could be acted upon. The letter also conveyed a curious request.

> I shall probably come on to St. Louis in the early course of the next fall, for the purpose of residing among you; in such an event I should wish timely to procure a house by rent or otherwise for my accommadation, and I have fixed my eye on that of Mr. Gratiot, provided we can come on terms which may be mutually agreeable. I would prefer renting or leasing to purchase; in either case the enclosure of the garden must be rendered secure, and the steps & floor of the piazza repaired by the 1st October next—I

would thank you to request Mr. Gratiot to write me on this subject and to state his terms distinctly as to price, payment &c, in order that I may know whether my resources will enable me to meet them or not, or whether it will be necessary that I should make some other provision for my accommodation.[30]

Does this suggest that Lewis had seriously considered returning to St. Louis before he left in the fall 1806? As an army officer on active duty, he could not predict where he might be assigned. The concern for repairs, and particularly enclosing a garden, indicate that he may have considered resigning his commission and moving his mother and family there. But his sense of duty prevailed.

On February 28 the Senate received the following appointment, which was confirmed two days later:

THOMAS JEFFERSON, President of the United States of America, To all who shall see these presents, Greeting:

Know Ye, That reposing special Trust and Confidence in the Patriotism, Integrity and Abilities of MERIWETHER LEWIS, of Virginia, I have nominated, and by and with the advice and consent of the Senate do appoint him Governor in and over the Territory of Louisiana; and do authorize and empower him to execute and fulfil the duties of that office according to Law; and to Have and to Hold the said office with all the powers, privileges and emoluments to the same of right appertaining for the term of three years from the day of the date hereof, unless the President of the United States for the time being should be pleased sooner to revoke and determine this Commission.

In Testimony whereof, I have caused these Letters to be made patent, and the Seal of the United States to be hereunto affixed. Given under my hand at the City of Washington, the third day of March in the year of our Lord one thousand Eight hundred and Seven; and of the Independence of the U States of America, the Thirty first.

Th. Jefferson
By the President, James Madison Secretary of State.[31]

There were still problems about rewarding Clark. Lewis had not forgiven the administration for failing to give his friend the equal rank of captain and forcing them into false pretenses during the expedition. Now the president and the secretary of war tried to make amends by a tactic that had already failed for them in another appointment. They tried to promote

Clark to the post of lieutenant colonel of the First Infantry Regiment. Jumping the officer's list had already been tried previously for the commandant of St. Louis but other officers who were patiently waiting for advancement howled in protest. Once again Congress balked and the explorer would have to be satisfied with the less prestigious rank of brigadier general of the Louisiana militia.[32]

Captain Lewis had promptly delivered a roster of the men that included their rank and his remarks on their respective merits and services:

> With rispect to all those persons whose names are entered on this roll, I feel a peculiar pleasure in declaring, that the Ample support which they gave me under every difficulty; the manly firmness which they evinced on every necessary occasion; and the patience and fortitude with which they submitted to, and bore, the fatigues and painful sufferings incident to my late tour to the Pacific Ocean, entitles them to my warmest approbation and thanks; nor will I suppress the expression of a hope, that the recollection of services thus faithfully performed will meet a just reward in an ample remuneration on the part of our Government.[33]

The secretary of war transmitted the list of the officers, noncommissioned officers, and privates who formed the party. He believed that the expedition met "with a degree of boldness, perseverance, and judgment, and success, that has rarely, if ever, occurred, in this or any other country." Dearborn recommended that all the men receive double pay and a grant to the expedition members of 320 acres that they could locate on any surveyed lands now for sale in the United States. Captain Lewis would receive 1,500 acres and Clark, 1,000 acres. That didn't satisfy Lewis, who proposed to Dearborn "that no distinction of rank so noticed as to make a difference in the quantity of land granted to each," and he preferred "an equal division" of the quantity granted.[34]

Congress had moved slowly to reward the heroes. After being read two times "the bill was ordered to be presented to a committee of the whole House."[35] More weeks passed with congressmen deliberating on the various types of compensation. Finally, on February 20, 1807, the House resumed discussing that the land warrants could be either located or received at the land offices in payment at the rate of two dollars an acre.[36]

Gratitude was fleeting. The delay and discussion were indications that not every representative of the people was starry-eyed about the completion of an expensive adventure. Others failed to see how the exploration actually benefited the nation as they had been told. The House soundly rejected that idea. "It was contended that double pay was a liberal compensation, and that this grant was extravagant and beyond all former precedent." Representative Lyon believed that the double pay amounted to more than sixty thousand dollars and coupled with the land grant could exceed that sum three or four times. He believed that the companions of Lewis and Clark "might go over all the Western country and locate their warrants on the best land, in 160 acre lots." After considerable debate, a motion was made to recommit the bill.[37] On February 28 the time to adjourn was approaching as the House deliberated late into evening. A bill was passed bestowing double pay and a grant of 320 acres located in the Louisiana Territory at the rate of two dollars an acre.[38] Both Lewis and Clark received 1,600 acres each, an equitable officer's compensation. Sent to the Senate for confirmation, the bill passed on March 3, 1807.[39] Other matters concerning the expedition were still pending.

It was necessary to get the Mandan chief Sheheke-shote and his family back to their people and avoid a repetition of the problems surrounding the death of the Arikara chief who had died before he could be returned.[40] Clark immediately left for St. Louis to oversee that and settle the compensation of the expectant corpsmen. But going over the specimens and making better descriptions would take time that Lewis had to steal from other duties; he couldn't turn that over to anyone else.

A final report had to be written and published. Lewis knew William Clark well enough to dismiss him as a coauthor. Apologies about his writing style accompanied Clark's field journal that had been sent back in spring 1805. When they reached St. Louis the previous September, Lewis had to write a model for Clark's letter to his "Dear Brother" because it would likely end up being published somewhere.[41]

An undeniable sense of mutual respect between them had worked very well in the field where Clark was the active and effective leader of the men, and Lewis, the actual commander, concentrated on the collection, identification, and cataloging of scientific data. That included meetings with Indians when Clark was more effective in close encounters.

Knowing Clark, Lewis had a friend's acceptance of his limitations. Solid, stolid, direct action was not what the writing of a scientific masterpiece demanded. The narrative of the expedition needed brilliance and dynamic descriptions of discoveries. It would not be enough to just correct and polish up the raw journals, and line them up for readers to plod through. Seeing what needed to be done, Lewis wanted time to sit down at a desk and let his mind work. He could pen pages of beautiful words to enlighten and enlarge the vision for those who would never have the opportunity to see it for themselves. Instead, his mentor had made the concentration he needed to write difficult by loading him with the task of being governor of Louisiana.

Meanwhile, Lewis remained in Washington completing several obligations. He had to commit all of his expedition expenditures to paper and the treasury accountant at the War Department, William Simmons, had a reputation of being manic in the pursuit of details. The expenditures were complex and it took time to locate and tabulate the innumerable ledger items. The total cost had risen.[42]

Sometime in late 1802 or early 1803 Lewis had given Jefferson an estimate of what he thought the expedition would cost. On a single piece of paper he had laid out eleven headings totaling $2,500. Four years later, under a myriad of headings, the expedition costs exceeded $38,000.[43] A final accounting could not be made because receipts had still not arrived, some vouchers had not come in for payment, and others had not been credited. Perfectly legitimate government expenses were wrung out of the costs by a bookkeeper who could not understand what it meant to operate in the field. Every time that the accountant demanded another scrap of information, Lewis had to shuffle through his less-than-tidy records.

That time-consuming paperwork intruded upon the other matters Lewis was trying to get out of the way—much more pressing than answering an accountant's demands.[44] There were some items that Simmons felt Lewis should pay personally. It would be the end of July before all the questions were finally resolved and the paperwork submitted to Secretary of War Dearborn on August 5. Due to the lack of some receipts, the accounting left Lewis responsible for a large sum of money.[45]

While Governor Lewis dealt with matters that any petty bureaucrat might handle just as well, the masterpiece of exploration and scientific discovery was being set aside. When Lewis finally got away to Philadelphia, he went under an already impossible deadline. Going there was hindered by another development that reduced the governments of the United States and Louisiana to bedridden invalids.

March in the presidential mansion was a difficult time as Congress tried to end the session before the threat of sickness descended on the capital. On the eleventh Lewis wrote Clark that after being previously in pain he had taken "some pills last night," felt better and had "no doubt of recovering my health in a few days."[46] By mid-month those in the presidential mansion were suffering from an ailment that may have been a respiratory infection, the flu, or a coincidental recurrence of ague (malaria). Whatever it was brought the president low too, and he mentioned that Lewis, also a sufferer, was nursing Jefferson's son-in-law, Thomas Mann Randolph.[47]

In February 1807 Jefferson was distracted by the emotional condition of his son-in-law, who had become estranged and moved from the presidential mansion to a Washington boardinghouse. Randolph was an unimpressive congressman who had previously threatened suicide. It was feared that he might be drifting down that dark road again. When Lewis helped nurse him, it would have been at the boardinghouse and a lesson (forecast, perhaps) of how the ague could drive a man to the edge.[48] Later Lewis paid a bill for a mulatto woman who had been hired to nurse Mrs. Madison.[49] At the end of March the president tried to abandon the capital but was not able to get away until April.

They had received a gift that never stops giving from the *Anopheles* mosquitoes that bred in the surrounding swamps and stagnant ponds or in the rain barrels of the unfinished Capitol.[50] Needing blood to nourish their eggs, the females of the species in a diabolical exchange left the unwilling donor with a microscopic guest. A step above the amoeba on the scale of development, *Plasmodia* protozoa parasites invaded the human liver and hatched in the blood, causing enlargement of the spleen and liver, severe anemia, delusions, chills, fevers, delirium, and even death.

A primary attack could last from one to two months depending upon the parasitic species, but those who suffered probably couldn't remember when they were first afflicted because the torture recurred and was untreatable. Most of those who suffered for years had no idea what caused the intermittent fevers that might last for hours once a day, or every third or fourth day for a period of weeks. Those intermittent *paroxysms* came in states of cold, hot and sweating, or fits. The ague hurt. Four years before the wave of illness at the presidential mansion, a learned graduate of medicine noticed that his patients experienced great anxiety "at the height of the fit, as to feel like an intolerance of life itself."[51]

Even the enlightened president of the nation did not grasp what was dragging them down.[52] Exercise was Thomas Jefferson's answer because "idleness begets ennui, ennui the hypochondria, and that a diseased body."[53] He doctored himself as though he were a mechanism with temperamental plumbing: if clogged, feed it a purging compound; if too fast to discharge, administer a constricting compound; if slow, bleed off the offending substance.[54] "Thus, fulness of the stomach we can relieve by emetics; diseases of the bowels, by purgatives; inflammatory cases, by bleeding; intermittents by the Peruvian bark; syphilis, by mercury; and watchfulness [insomnia] by opium; &c."[55] Bathing his feet in cold water every morning to prevent respiratory disease may not have prevented a cold but it got Jefferson started on dealing with the problems of the nation.[56]

It was not encouraging that Jefferson lacked confidence in American medicine, whose practitioners he thought were worse than ignorant.[57] Its study should be reserved to Europeans, who at least ran schools that were beginning to penetrate the mysteries of the human body, he observed.[58] The "hypocondriac affections" that he later wrote about referred to a disease known as *hypochondriasis*, a complex physical condition.[59]

One of the most admired American doctors, Benjamin Rush, believed in bloodletting even to the point of fainting. His obstetrical technique included bleeding thirty ounces at the onset of labor coupled with the administration of laxatives. He attributed the yellow fever epidemic of 1793 to coffee rotting in the warehouses.[60]

The presidential mansion was no worse off for having an explorer to treat the ailing. Meriwether Lewis must have been infected with malaria since his youth, maybe even in the crib, as the young of that terrible time were as susceptible as grownups. Both he and Clark suffered from the ague when they served in the northwest army and Lewis recognized the place on the Ohio River near the mouth of the Kanawa where the fevers began. Clark had recurring bouts of something that has been passed off as an intestinal condition, but hypochondriasis could hit a man as hard in the gut as in the spirit.[61]

The famous figures were not alone. For Americans at the turn of the nineteenth century, malaria was pandemic. The literature of the time is full of clues to suffering or sufferers. Military posts often had so many sick that it was difficult to come up with enough men to mount the guard. Officers refused assignments to the lower Mississippi because that could be a death sentence. Congressmen retreated from Washington from July to September due to their "utter repugnance . . . to be here in the sickly months."[62] What is missing from the historical record are those illiterate, anonymous backwoods families who suffered and died in obscurity.

As long as there were others around who were infected, and mosquitoes to bite them, there was no defense. Abatement of the insect breeding season did not mean escape because the parasite lurked in the liver. It was not a matter of hot or cold climate, as malaria was described as far north as the New England states or the Canadian province of Ontario. Had anyone understood what was causing the invasion, they might have imagined relief when the mosquito cycle of life closed. But too many were infected and next year the whining little demons would siphon parasites from their infected bodies and inject them into another bloodstream.

Jefferson was evasive but Lewis knew those symptoms all too well. His body resorted to chills and fevers to throw the ague off and his blood boiled as it tried to kill it. Agonizing headaches denied the pen.[63] Dark thoughts crowded reason. Randolph was down and Lewis tried to nurse him.[64] Jefferson fled hoping to regain his strength at Monticello. Although Lewis was anxious to leave for Philadelphia, they were still in the mansion on April 5.

Recovering from another soul-blasting episode of the ague was hard enough, but Meriwether was burdened by the focus-splitting duality of what he needed to do. He was both a governor and a naturalist. Somehow before addressing the responsibilities of that troubled office, he had to distribute the specimens that were the scientific returns of the expedition to those who would help him properly describe and evaluate them while arranging their assistance in compiling the volume dealing with natural history. Beyond that challenge he also had to find the time to compose an inspired narrative of the great adventure. In order to realize a reward, Clark and he would then have to become booksellers.

The next leg of his continental journey took him away from the presidential mansion on April 6. According to the account book that he began keeping, the sagging rider took until the ninth to get only as far as Baltimore. After spending several days there recovering his strength, Meriwether Lewis finally reached Philadelphia on April 14, 1807.

NOTES

1. Alexander Wilson, "Particulars of the Death of Capt. Lewis," *Port Folio* 7 (January 1812): 38.

2. John Sibley to HD, October 8, 1803, RG94, M661, roll 7, frame 0261, NARA.

3. George Sibley to Samuel H. Sibley, October 25, 1806, Sibley Papers, Lindenwood Collection Transcripts, MHS.

4. Jay H. Buckley, *William Clark: Indian Diplomat* (Norman: University of Oklahoma Press, 2008), p. 55; PC to HD, October 21, 1806, Pierre Chouteau letterbook, pp. 107–108, MHS.

5. James Holmberg, ed., *Dear Brother: Letters of William Clark to Jonathan Clark* (New Haven, CT: Yale University Press, 2002), p. 122n1.

6. SLM to CM, December 30, 1806, folder 41.321.464, MCNY.

7. TJ to ML, October 26, 1806, Jackson, *LLC* 1: 350–51.

8. Stephen Ambrose dramatized Jefferson's perusal of the map (*Undaunted Courage* [New York: Simon & Schuster, 1996], p. 411). TJ had received the large Fort Mandan map about July 13, 1805, and wrote, "I have left Lewis's large map with a servant to be carried to your office tomorrow morning. it is the 29 half sheets which contained very accurately his survey of the river & no more. Mr. King being with me this morning I gave them to him to be reduced to a scale of 20 miles to the inch for engraving" (TJ to HD, July 14, 1805, Jackson, *LLC* 1: 252).

9. SLM to CM, December 21, 1806, folder 41.321.458, MCNY. "The Osages . . . arrived here. Last evening I saw them. They are tall and whitish like the rest whom we have seen."

10. Ambrose, *Undaunted Courage*, p. 410.

11. SLM to CM, December 30, 1806, folder 41.321.464, MCNY.

12. SLM to CM, January 1, 1807, folder 41.321.74, MCNY.

13. *National Intelligencer*, January 9, 1807.

14. The *New-York Gazette & Daily Advertiser* printed a report of the dinner on January 22.

15. *Sun (Washington, DC)*, February 7, 1807, p. 4.

16. Ibid; *Republican Watch-Tower (Washington, DC)*, March 9, 1803, p. 2.

17. US Congress, *House Journal*, 9th Cong., 2nd sess., December 2, 1806.

18. Carter, *TP* 13: 40–41, 73, 92–96, 97–98, 383, 420–21.

19. While the House of Representatives approved Wilkinson's appointment, it was not without a fight. Some members "condemned the union in one individual of both military and civil authority as repugnant to the Constitution." Carter, *TP* 13: 504, fn6.

20. Samuel Smith to TJ, May 4, 1806, document 28159, reel 35, and August 8, 1806, document 28158, reel 36, TJ-LOC.

21. JW to Samuel Smith, March 29, 1806, and Samuel Smith to TJ, April 28, 1806, Carter, *TP* 13: 466, 502–504.

22. Ron Chernow, *Alexander Hamilton* (New York: Penguin, 2004), p. 542.

23. TJ to JMO, January 8, 1804, document 23766-72, reel 29, and TJ to JMO, May 4, 1806, document 27777-78, reel 35, TJ-LOC. Monroe was not interested in a governorship, as is evident in his replies of March 15, 1804, and July 8, 1806. See letters 179 and 190, TJ and JMO correspondence, Gawalt, Manuscript Division, LOC.

24. TJ to Samuel Smith, October 15, 1806, document 28352, roll 36, TJ-LOC.

25. AG to TJ, October 25, 1806, document 28381, TJ-LOC.

26. In November 1806, Bates departed Detroit for Washington to make a report on French and English land grants (Marshall, *FB* 1: 17–18). It was a fortuitous time to arrive in Washington when he was needed most by the president.

27. *General Records of the Department of State*, RG59, Samuel Tupper to TJ, March 15, 1804, M418, roll 1, frame 0736, NARA.

28. Marshall, *FB* 1: 8–11, 14, 17–18, 91; Carter, *TP* 14: 117.

29. Edward Bates, "Letter Giving Sketch of Frederick Bates," *Michigan Pioneer Collections* 8 (1907): 563; FB to TJ, February 9, 1807, RG59, M418, frame 0744, NARA; Elvert M. Davis, *The Bates Boys on the Western Waters* (Asheville, NC: Inland Press, 1960), p. 115.

30. ML to Auguste Chouteau, February 11, 1807, Frederick L. Billon Papers, MHS.

31. US Congress, *Senate Executive Journal*, 9th Cong. 2nd sess., February 28, 1807, in Carter, *TP* 14: 107n; http://memory.loc.gov/ammem/amlaw/lwej.html (accessed April 8, 2008).

32. Everett S. Brown, *William Plumer's Memorandum of Proceedings in the United*

States Senate 1803–1807 (New York: Da Capo Press, 1969), pp. 633, 637; HD to TJ, February 24, 1807, and TJ to the Senate, February 28, 1807, Jackson, *LLC* 1: 375–76; Dumas Malone, *Jefferson and His Time*, 6 vols. (Boston: Little, Brown, 1948–1981), 5: 226, fn32.

33. US Congress, *House Journal*, 9th Cong., 2nd sess., January 2, 1807; ML to HD, January 15, 1807, Jackson, *LLC* 1: 369.

34. HD to Willis Alston, January 14, 1807, Jackson, *LLC* 1: 363.

35. *Annals of Congress*, House, January 23, 1807, p. 42.

36. The Act Compensating Lewis and Clark, March 3, 1807, Jackson, *LLC* 2: 377. A land warrant was an authorization to receive a quantity of public land at an unspecified location. Warrants could be transferred for a higher price than the government guaranteed.

37. *Annals of Congress*, 9th Cong., 2nd sess., February 20, 1807, pp. 591–92.

38. The Act Compensating Lewis and Clark, March 3, 1807, and Messrs. Lewis & Clark's Donations Lands, March 6, 1807, Jackson, *LLC* 2: 377, 380.

39. US Congress, *Senate Journal*, 9th Cong., 2nd sess., March 3, 1807.

40. *Records of the Bureau of Indian Affairs*, RG75, JW to SW, April 9, 1806, M15, roll 2, frame 0090, p. 191, NARA.

41. Lewis's draft of the Clark letter, September 24, 1806, Jackson, *LLC* 1: 330–35.

42. RG217, entry 353, vol. 4, ledger D, p. 1989, NARA-CP.

43. Lewis's Estimate of Expenses, 1803, and Financials of the Expedition, August 5, 1807, Jackson, *LLC* 1: 8–9 and 2: 419–28.

44. By the time the accounts were completed, Simmons had devoted hundreds of ledger pages to Lewis's expedition. RG217, Selected Volumes from the Accountant of the War Department, microfilm roll 14, #85, MHS.

45. Eventually, Simmons submitted paperwork to start the process of a federal lawsuit against Lewis. A sum of $8,800 could not be reconciled. RG217, entry 353, vol. 4, ledger D, p. 1991, NARA-CP. The suit was terminated upon Lewis's death.

46. ML to WC, March 11, 1807, Jackson, *LLC* 2: 385.

47. TJ to MJR, March 2, 6, 9, 11, 12, 13, 16, 20, 23, 27, and 30, and April 2, 5, Betts and Bear, *FL*, pp. 297–306.

48. Fawn M. Brodie, *Thomas Jefferson: An Intimate History* (New York: W. W. Norton, 1974), pp. 394–96.

49. There is a curious note in Lewis's account book dated May 13, a payment to Amy of six dollars for a mulatto woman for nursing Mrs. Madison.

50. SLM to CM, March 17, 1802, folder 41.321.48, MCNY. "It does not seem to be healthy here. . . . The Season for Agues has not arrived, or it is probable we should see many cases of that disorder . . . there is a wide tract of low and marshy land between the River Potomack and Pennsylvania and New Jersey Avenues. In Autumn intermittents prevail over the Region. The circulation of the water is very slow & sluggish. . . . There seems to be something unwholesome in the fogs & damps which overhang situations on the east sides of the Rivers."

51. *Early American Imprints*, Second series, no. 3692, p. 39.

52. It is probable that Jefferson held to the notion that intermittent fever and bilious fever were separate disorders. He also believed that the northern region was less apt to sickness than the southern. "We have in that state a college (Wm. & Mary) just well enough endowed to draw out the miserable existence to which a miserable constitution has doomed it. It is moreover eccentric in its position, exposed to bilious diseases as all the lower country is, & therefore abandoned by the public care, as that part of the country itself is in a considerable degree by its inhabitants. We wish to establish in the upper & healthier country, & more centrally for the state, an University on a plan so broad & liberal & *modern*, as to be worth patronizing with the public support, and be a temptation to the youth of other states to come." TJ to Joseph Priestley, January 18, 1800, document 18142-44, roll 22, TJ-LOC.

53. TJ to Martha Jefferson, March 28, 1787, Betts and Bear, *FL*, p. 34.

54. Taken loosely from James Bordley and A. Harvey, *Two Centuries of American Medicine, 1774–1976* (Philadelphia: W. B. Saunders Company, 1976), p. 34.

55. TJ to Caspar Wistar, June 21, 1807, document 29558, roll 38, TJ-LOC. Transcribed document on LOC Web site.

56. TJ to Vine Utley, March 21, 1819, document 38339, roll 51, TJ-LOC.

57. TJ to William Green Mumford, June 18, 1799, document 18037-39, roll 21, TJ-LOC. Letter is partly illegible; for transcription, see Merrill D. Peterson, *Thomas Jefferson—Writings* (New York: Library of America, 1984), p. 1065.

58. TJ to Caspar Wistar, June 21, 1807, document 29558, TJ-LOC.

59. Stanley W. Jackson, *Melancholia and Depression* (New Haven, CT: Yale University Press, 1986), p. 274; Esther Fisher-Homberger, "Hypochondriasis of the Eighteenth Century—Neurosis of the Present Century," *Bulletin of the History of Medicine* 46 (July/August 1972): 391.

60. Bordley and Harvey, *Two Centuries of American Medicine*, p. 35; A. W. Woodruff, "Benjamin Rush, His Work on Yellow Fever and His British Connections," *American Journal of Tropical Medicine & Hygiene* 26, supp. (September 1977): 1056.

61. ML to TJ, September 14, 1803, Moulton, *JLCE* 2: 81; Daniel Drake, "Report on the Diseases of Cincinnati in the Spring of 1828 . . . for Ague and Fever," *Western Journal of the Medical and Physical Sciences* 2 (1828–1829): 219.

62. TJ to JMO, October 26, 1806, document 28385, roll 36, TJ-LOC. While Congress let out in March so that its members could return home and attend to their personal business, the summer months in Washington were dreaded by the clerks who worked for the secretaries.

63. From mid-March to the beginning of April when he departed Washington bound for Monticello, Jefferson was debilitated and wrote, "I am writing under a severe indisposition of periodical headache, with scarcely command enough of my mind to know what I write." TJ to JMO, March 21, 1807, document 29195-6, roll 38, TJ-LOC.

64. TJ to MJR, March 6, 1807, Betts and Bear, *FL*, p. 298.

EIGHT

The Seeds of a Masterpiece

Their country opts to view at last[1]

I t was December 28, 1806, before the architect of exploration saw Captain Lewis comfortably settled in the presidential mansion. Despite official and social distractions, the explorer was eager to meet various members of the American Philosophical Society. Jefferson wrote two members that "I am happy at the same time to greet them on the safe return of a valuable member of our fraternity from a journey of uncommon length & peril. He will ere long be with them, & present them with the additions he brings to our knolege of the geography & natural history of our country, from the Missisipi to the Pacific."[2]

That soon had the learned community chattering. Despite the press of presidential business and the cloud of Burr's activities, Jefferson found time to gratify his scientific friends who were clamoring for a chance at the specimens. He wrote that Lewis had brought back a considerable amount of seeds that needed to be distributed to those best prepared to work with them.[3]

Given the assistance members of the society had provided during the organization of the expedition, Lewis hoped that they would assist him in the preparation of a narrative of the expedition. Fortunately, one of the first major figures that he had met as Jefferson's secretary was a scientist editor. Samuel Latham Mitchill had been a foremost supporter of the expedition.

As a member of the House Committee on Commerce and Manufactures, on March 8, 1804, he had delivered a report to the House that encouraged a broader application for what began as a mapping project.[4]

The expedition was already under way up the Missouri when Representative Mitchill restated the mission of captains Lewis and Clark as "attempting a passage to the western shore of the South Sea." He had gone on to state:

> It is highly desirable that this elusive region should be visited, in some parts at least, by intelligent men. Important additions might thereby be made to the science of geography. Various materials might thence be derived to augment our knowledge of natural history. The Government would thence acquire correct information of the situation, extent and worth of its own dominions, and individuals of research and curiosity would receive ample gratification as to the works of art and productions of nature which exist in those boundless tracts.[5]

In many ways that was a more inspiring statement of the mission of the Corps of Discovery than Jefferson's. And it came from a scientific-minded public man with an editor's sense to foresee that this would be the first great story of the new century. No surprise then that Mitchill spoke with Lewis within the first two days of his return to Washington and set up a dinner meeting with him the following week.[6] As soon as he was with Lewis, Mitchill raised the question of the burning plains of the Missouri that he had seen pictured on the Arikara chief's buffalo skin map.[7] Lewis assured him that a strata of coal burning underground produced that kind of slag or pumice.[8] There had to be a book.[9]

Expectations were running high. The *National Intelligencer* was already anticipating a publication that "would not merely gratify literary curiosity, but open views of great and immediate objects of national unity." That did not necessarily mean the private journals of the two officers, which were all that Lewis had at the moment to edify the president. Those were as rough as Clark's expedition journal sent back from Fort Mandan in spring 1805. What the press, and perhaps the public, expected was something similar to the well-written reports sent by Lewis at the same time.

Lewis was shocked to find that his reports from Fort Mandan had already been published.[10] In February 1806 Congress had authorized the publication of two hundred copies of this first report but that amounted to roughly a third of the book that Lewis intended to write.[11] If not enough, duplicate editions of the entire congressional document appeared in 1806 in New York and Natchez, and a year later in London.[12] Pirated editions began cropping up in New York, Philadelphia, London, and Germany a few years later, which essentially stole and perhaps bastardized the field work accomplished as far as Fort Mandan.[13] In writing from Fort Mandan, Lewis had been careful to explain that he intended to publish his own work in a major narrative. But the president jumped the gun when he was pressed to show some results of the expedition.

His appetite for new discoveries unsatisfied, Mitchill had taken Lewis away from his host by inviting him to dine with him at his Washington lodgings. The physician, lawyer, scientist, and professor of chemistry admired the astronomical and other scientific attainments of a guest still recovering his table manners after two and a half years in the rude wilderness. It was not meant as flattery when Mitchill admitted that a scientist could only look upon Lewis "as a man returned from another planet."[14] And that was high praise from a public man whom Jefferson called "the congressional dictionary" and others looked to for advice.[15] Mitchill's literary and scientific attainments were widely recognized and his guest felt honored to exchange ideas with a remarkable man. "His knowledge of the physical sciences, his varied and intimate acquaintance with classical literature, both ancient and modern, his attainments in history and political science, his practical acquaintance with public affairs, and his remarkable familiarity with the common and useful arts, caused him to be looked upon as a fountain of learning always ready to pour forth abundant streams of knowledge to every thirsty applicant." As a witty friend once said of him, "'Tap the doctor at any time, he will flow.'"[16]

That was what Lewis hoped to do because he needed advice on how to begin. His dinner companion was the founder and editor of the *Medical Repository*, the leading scientific journal of the nation. In a review of the first reports and maps sent back from Fort Mandan, Mitchill added that he would refrain from publishing the map before the explorers returned. "They may be expected to publish a narrative of their journey and discoveries. And it is expected these new facts in geography will form a part, and a most valuable one too, of their book of travels in the west."[17] This amounted to an announcement to the scientific community that the explorer would produce a full description of the scientific accomplishments.[18]

Indeed, that was a large order. Could Lewis write a book? Because Jefferson liked to compose his own letters, the president's secretary had been more of an aide-de-camp than a copyist. Now he had to complete a narrative of the expedition that would recount the experience, recapture a sense of the adventure, and recover a feeling of the natural world that they had passed through like innocents in a garden. That was a daunting challenge even a practiced man of letters might have taken months or years to complete. But Lewis, the only man who could do the glorious subject justice, would have only a couple of months to write it.

During the first year of the expedition, the Fort Mandan shipment had returned about sixty plants. As the expedition proceeded up the Missouri River, Lewis collected more. Preserving the botanical specimens took a good deal of careful preparation. The practice of botanical pressing began with fresh plants, full of moisture, that required fastidious attention until fully dry. Those were laid out on absorbent paper and exposed to the sun, then pressed and the process repeated. Once dried the plants were fitted with identification tags and stored in watertight containers.[19] Lewis had managed to do that while riding in a small pirogue or during layovers on land.[20]

Some were almost lost during a canoe upset going up the river. Near the White Bear Islands he made an underground deposit for the plants he found between Fort Mandan and the Great Falls, trusting that precious body of fieldwork to a hole in the ground.[21]

As Lewis told those gathered around him at a reception, when he returned to the cache next spring he found that the rains had flooded the hole and destroyed some articles, including "all my specimens of plants" except for two twigs, which bear the date of that period. His papers and a chart of the Missouri, though damp, had escaped complete ruin.[22] Then he was prevented from replacing the spoiled collection as the boats descended the Missouri because he had been incapacitated by a hunting accident that left him unable to walk. So there were only a few specimens from the most northern reach of the expedition.[23]

Ironically, Jefferson had instructed Lewis not to collect any material that was already known and be "guarded, by exact observation of the vegetables and animals of his own country, against losing time in the description of objects already possessed." Still, returning with more than two hundred new plant specimens, not counting animals, was proof that Lewis had taken Jefferson's wishes to heart.[24]

Six days after the president informed Congress of the expedition's return, he assured fellow society member Caspar Wistar that a map of their route would probably be engraved and sent to the APS as soon as Lewis arrived.[25] On December 21 he wrote Charles Willson Peale that the captain was expected to bring much in the lines of botany and natural history.[26] He had a letter from a mutual friend on behalf of the botanist Henry Muhlenberg asking for seeds of rare plants from the expedition. On the twenty-sixth he had a similar request from the Philadelphia gardener Bernard McMahon.[27] McMahon and William Hamilton were horticulturists well prepared to deal with them.[28]

Just seeing the collected specimens put in the proper hands to be scientifically analyzed and described would cut into the short time that Meriwether Lewis would have before taking over his duties as governor of the Louisiana Territory. Illustrations would need to be commissioned, drawings made of the dried plants to enliven their description, and scenes of geographical features sketched. There were lists of native tribes to enlarge upon. Lewis faced the responsibility of describing over half of the continent to a public still wondering what had been acquired. That meant that the book, books as it turned out, had to be more than mere information. They had to be convincing on an emotional level. Could he do it?

Evidence suggests that the journals of Lewis and Clark were separate functions. Clark handled the writing of the daily journals while Lewis attended to the scientific obligations of collecting and preparing dozens of assorted specimens. Although not a competent speller, Clark's daily record demonstrated his ability as a solid journalist. But he was no poet. That distinction went to Lewis, whose use of imagery and poetic license shines in his writing.

Lewis understood how to wrap words around a meaning, that "colouring to events" that some have criticized. His description of the departure from Fort Mandan revealed a deeply felt creativity.[29] As the continent climbed higher and unnamed mountains rose on every horizon, the rambling naturalist climbed out of the deep channel of the river in his daily search for specimens—and was inspired. "While I viewed these mountains I felt a great pleasure in finding myself so near the head of the heretofore conceived boundless Missouri." But the realist knew that they would have to find a way through those precipitous mountains, which "in some measure counterbalanced the joy."[30]

Mitchill would stay his pen, allow a scoop to pass, and give Lewis time to prepare his manuscript. The explorer would need to write, see that his specimens were properly described and drawings prepared. Revisions and amendments would require time.[31] But Samuel Mitchill, perhaps as no other, understood what a major work could mean to the career of the young naturalist. In a letter to his wife he described an amazing collection of artifacts that Lewis brought with him from the expedition.

I went to the President's House to see the specimens of Natural history brought by Capt. Lewis from Louisiana, and his Map of the regions he has visited between the Mississippi and the Pacific. He has several non-descript animals, among which are five species of quail, partridges and grous that are probably new to naturalists, three or four sorts of squirrels besides those which are found in the Atlantic regions; and a white-coated quadruped of a character somewhat between the *Sheep* and Goat, having both hair and wool for a fleece. . . . He has brought with him the seeds of many plants . . . his Map of those parts of North America is the most instructive of his bounties. It gives an enlarged and Comprehensive view River Missouri, and of the vast streams. . . . Of these the Platte alone is larger than the Mississippi. . . . The Waters are more precipitous on the other side of the Rocky Mountains. Their descent is too Great to render them navigable by boats even in their passage downward. . . . This journey has not only enlarged our knowledge of Natural History and Geography but dispensed to our men of monied enterprize a view and hitherto unexplored Country for Beaver skins and the fur-trade.[32]

Based on Lewis's accounts, Mitchill also described the Rocky Mountains, the rivers beyond those mountains, the natives of those rivers, and bartering otter and beaver pelts with blue beads. Mitchill ended his letter lauding Lewis's accomplishments and praising the immensity of Lewis's discoveries.[33]

While Mitchill wrote his thoughts to his wife, Patrick Gass was readying his journal for publication. Both the experienced editor and Lewis were appalled when they learned that the former corpsman Gass had fallen in with a Pittsburgh bookseller who meant to bring out a fast, first version of the trip. That could only be a cheap paraphrase of the great adventure, one that pandered to public curiosity. And perhaps bleed off the popular market. The precipitous publication of Sergeant Gass's journal was an outrage that Mitchill never forgot, mentioning it many years later in his "Discourse on Thomas Jefferson, More Especially as a Promoter of Natural and Physical Science."[34]

For the explorer with so much to say, the shock of losing the potential audience for his projected book was devastating. While still in St. Louis, he had given Private Robert Frazer permission to publish his private journal. Now Gass was also planning to cash in on his notes. Lewis wrote an ungracious letter and allowed it to be published in the *National Intelligencer* of March 18. He had a literary property to protect and tried to discredit competitive publications. The letter was followed by an early version of the prospectus of "Lewis and Clark's Tour to the Pacific Ocean through the Interior of the Continent of North America" and was followed by the editorial insertion, "Editors of Public Prints in the United States, disposed to aid the publication of this work, are requested to give the foregoing a few insertions."[35] And in some unstated way that reaction may have reflected a deeper frustration over what Jefferson had done in appropriating and publishing the Fort Mandan material.

The prospectus vendetta would be all for naught. The letter by Lewis probably deserved the nasty response that David McKeehan published in the *Pittsburgh Gazette* of April 7. According to him the Gass journal would be off the press by the end of June. Copies were actually ready for distribution by July 7, 1807, and the public snatched it up. Editions soon appeared everywhere, even in London.[36] Mr. Jefferson was not pleased.

Although the returning explorer, the national hero, was flattered by public acclaim, the natural scientist was still unrecognized. The scientific aspects of the three-year expedition demanded close attention and Lewis was the only man in Washington who understood what completing the full story could mean. And he needed to get to Philadelphia where he would be in contact with those who would help write and publish the book.

That was going to take time, because Lewis intended to do more than merely publish the raw field journals. He intended to produce a synthesis of the journals coupled with precise descriptions of the natural history specimens that he had collected, a comprehensive description rather than a mere adventure book as the Gass and Frazer books promised to be.

Going to Philadelphia continued to be delayed as some in the presidential mansion began showing signs of sickness by the end of February. On March 11 Lewis was still sick and taking pills. Despite that, three days later when he wrote the letter panning the Gass publication, Lewis had already worked out a rough version of the book prospectus that was published in the *National Intelligencer*. Lewis also sent a copy to the Philadelphia printer John Conrad & Company for an estimate. It was another two weeks, however, before Lewis could leave the illness-ridden presidential mansion. Jefferson attributed the delay to Lewis's nursing of the president's son-in-law, Thomas Mann Randolph, but admitted to his daughter that "we are but a collection of invalids."[37] Randolph's malarial symptoms had shown up in February and the rest of the presidential household were also sufferers through March.[38]

Lewis was trying to address matters to do with Louisiana and it was President Jefferson who attended to the forwarding of seeds to Bernard McMahon on the twentieth and to McMahon and William Hamilton on the twenty-second. When McMahon received those seeds he was so appreciative that he planned to provide Governor Lewis with a collection of culinary and ornamental plant seeds that could be introduced to St. Louis when he went there.[39]

It is unlikely that Lewis escaped a recurrence of his own illness and must still have been weak when he finally left Washington, arriving in Philadelphia on April 14; three days later he attended a meeting of the APS. It must have been one of the highlights of his career to be recognized by learned men who shared his interests. What accolades and praises were accorded to Lewis at that meeting we will never know, but the discoveries on the expedition were numerous. Philadelphia would hear more about the expedition when Lewis attended two more of the society's monthly meetings on June 17 and July 17. The minutes of the June 17 meeting mentioned Lewis: "Specimens of Natural History from the cabinet lent to Capt. Lewis. Mr. Peale, by permission withdrew his paper on the Antelope, because Capt. Lewis would publish a fuller description in his book."[40] Lewis could, of course, describe the antelope, an oddity at that time ranging along the Missouri, specimens of which had been included in the Fort Mandan shipment.

These events leave little doubt that Lewis's intentions were scientific but there were practical matters to address first. He had already outlined his intentions for a book or books with the printer John Conrad.[41] From what must have been a rudimentary description, Conrad worked out an estimate of the cost. By the beginning of April, Conrad came up with a total cost of $4,500 and a revised proof of the prospectus.[42] The prospectus described a narrative of the voyage in the first volume and a second volume devoted to geography, Indians, and the fur trade embellished with a number of plates. A third volume would be confined exclusively to scientific research, principally in natural history under the heads of "Botany, Mineralogy, and Zoology . . . including a Comparative View of Twenty-three Vocabularies of Distinct Indian Languages."[43] Adventure, Indians, and science, and of course, the great map of North America. That was a large order and the still-weak Lewis faced a monumental task.

Germane to any publication should be Lewis's natural history journals. In order to convert the raw data from those botanical or zoological notebooks, Lewis would have to write descriptions in order to broaden the nature and scope of the publication. But difficulties had developed when Jefferson admitted that through some unfortunate mishandling, the first specimens from Fort Mandan had been separated from the labels.[44] Others had been lost, some apparently callously discarded.

How well was Lewis prepared to deal with the natural history volume described in the prospectus? He had accomplished a remarkable job as a field naturalist, collecting and sending back a wealth of specimens that experts would be studying for years to come. But at the writing desk was where the collection had to be realized in a way that would impress the small, close scientific community.

There were examples in those notebooks that showed he could do it. In one of the botanical codices he capably brought dull stuff to life:

> I met with a singular plant today in blume of which I preserved a specemine, The second set of stamens are very minute are also four and placed within and opposite to the petals, these are scarcely persceptable while the 1st are large and conspicuous . . . the fillaments are capillary equal, very short, white and smooth. the anthers are four, oblong, beaked, erect, cohering at the base, membranous.

Two pages long, this particular description employed thirty technical terms of the one hundred and fifty that he regularly used throughout his notebooks.[45]

The codices reveal how well Lewis followed the agenda that members of the APS helped him develop. They had taught him the systematic discipline that he employed for several scientific fields. That he excelled in those pursuits is evident throughout the field notes. Lewis brought back more than two hundred species of plants, new minerals, and descriptions of animals. Converting the raw data in those worn notebooks meant devoting himself to analysis and description. But when it came time to realize that body of raw material, difficulties began crowding in. What the APS had not prepared him for was professional jealousy.

Bernard McMahon, John Vaughan, Charles Willson Peale, Caspar Wistar, Benjamin Smith Barton, and others had written to Jefferson congratulating him on the return of the Corps of Discovery. Wistar wrote that the society experienced "the most anxious solicitude and the greatest curiosity as to their discoveries."[46] Jefferson responded to Barton that Lewis would bring much new information to the "lines of botany and natural history." He believed that Lewis would ask Barton and "brother literati of Philadelphia" for help.[47] When Lewis returned to Philadelphia, in addition to the above, he met with Dr. Benjamin Rush and the mathematician Robert Patterson, also members of the APS who helped organize the expedition.

But gardeners and seed growers were closer to the soil than botanists. Lewis needed to consult with those whose occupation was centered on plants. He had grasped that if a unique plant had been lost in transit, a backup could be grown from the seeds that he had collected.[48] Lewis's association with the seed men dated back to his arrival in Lancaster, Pennsylvania, in April 1803 to receive training in navigation. The schooling was expected to last about ten or twelve days. Because Lewis did not depart until about May 7, it has been speculated that he was slow to learn the use of the sextant and chronometer.[49] But new evidence suggests that Lewis spent time with longtime society member and botanist Henry Muhlenberg, who also lived in Lancaster.[50] Curiously, Muhlenberg's interest in obtaining seeds was not very successful; as late as November 1809 he had only received six different seeds that had turned out to be valuable plants.[51]

Bernard McMahon, the Philadelphia botanist and gardener, had previously received corn and gourd seeds from the Fort Mandan collection and grew them successfully during the summer of 1806. McMahon wrote Jefferson on December 26, 1806, hoping to procure "some seeds of the indigenous plants of the western parts of America, if you received such from Capt. Lewis on his return." Jefferson immediately replied that Lewis brought a considerable number of seeds and he had recommended that Lewis take them to William Hamilton and McMahon.[52]

The list of seeds that came back with the explorers included: a flesh-colored flower, wild parsnip, wild plumb, peas common to the Columbian plain, flowers from Clark's River, sunflower, shallon cherry, honeysuckle, black currant, purple currant, yellow currant, Arikara currant, red currant, service berry, Rocky Mountain cherry, eggplant, wild flax, and species of tobacco.[53] The expedition had not neglected collecting after leaving Fort Mandan.

As soon as the news of the return of the expedition began circulating in the East, the seed sellers and gardeners became restless. Spring was coming on and they were anxious to plant several of the expedition findings. Jefferson sent McMahon a batch that had been destined for his Monticello garden, admitting that he was too preoccupied by other matters to do them justice. He wanted McMahon to commit the seeds "earlier to the ground," because he assumed that Lewis would be delayed.[54]

By the third week of March 1806 spring was approaching and Jefferson, in accordance with Lewis's wishes, sent McMahon another packet of seeds. Jefferson was convinced that these seeds were "the fruits of the expedition." That made McMahon and Hamilton "the depositories of these public treasures."[55]

Lewis also made a point of connecting with the horticulturist William Hamilton. On March 26, 1804, Lewis had sent "some slips" from the Osage plum and apple to Jefferson requesting they be forwarded to Hamilton.[56] At an estate known as the Woodlands, Hamilton cooperated with other gardeners and botanists in the cultivation of plants; such a connection implied a working laboratory for Lewis's botanical specimens, which allowed Lewis to send unique seeds to eager associates who would know best how to cultivate them. Mitchill was delighted with some of the specimens that Lewis displayed at a dinner engagement: "He has brought with him the seeds of many plants; and showed me several presses of dried plants in fine preservation. These make an instructive herbarium of the Regions to which he passed."[57]

Living plants instead of dried specimens could then be shared with the scientific community through a partnership that established the Lewis and Clark herbarium as well as the initial development of a "Flora Missourica," begun with the Fort Mandan shipment of two separate bundles of dried plants.[58] A growing garden was insurance, and to further ensure propagation Lewis sent duplicate seeds to Muhlenberg.[59] That was why McMahon had been so eager to meet with Lewis and show him what had been accomplished. But when Jefferson responded to McMahon's December letter, he indicated that Lewis would be delayed for some time, an obligation that eventually pushed back the departure for three months.

Jefferson wrote that Lewis had brought significant discoveries to his attention and remarked that "he was the fittest person in the world for such an expedition."[60] McMahon replied on March 27, stating that he had never seen "seeds in a better state of preservation."[61] That meant that a seedsman and nurseryman recognized Lewis's proficiency as a naturalist and could write directly to him instead of going through Jefferson.

Dr. Benjamin Smith Barton was the leading American botanist of the time. According to Jefferson's wishes, he was supposed to work on the botanical descriptions and edit the scientific volume. But the arrangement that Lewis had painstakingly worked out with Barton had gone awry. When Barton received the sixty plants from the Fort Mandan shipment, he lost thirty of them. This was an oversight that no real scientist would have allowed. It has been suggested that he discarded plants that were the same or too close to known plants, but that is also irresponsible because the data on the places and times they were taken was also valuable information.[62]

Lewis lost two important botanical caches in the field, but how could Barton lose them in his tiny home? When Lewis arrived in Philadelphia, he and Barton began with a good relationship. But at some later point the explorer and the eminent society member had words. "There were some differences between him and me," wrote Barton, "originating wholly in the illiberal and jealous conduct of some of my enemies here, unto laboured, not without some effect, to exorte uneasiness in his mind, as to my friendship for him."[63]

No matter how well Jefferson regarded Barton, the choice was a mistake considering what Lewis had to accomplish. Absentminded, overworked, underpaid, and, worse yet, Barton seemed to treat his professional career as a hobby. He was indeed overloaded but no one else could fill the void. Perhaps there was an irony in the friendly inscription that Lewis wrote in Barton's copy of Antoine du Pratz's *History of Louisiana* on May 9: ". . . it has since been conveyed by me to the Pacific Ocean through the interior of North America, on my late tour thither and is now returned to it's proprietor by his Friend and Obt. Servt."[64]

Was Barton more interested in publishing his own work? Or was he afraid that Lewis would eclipse him? Muhlenberg later wrote that "Barton speaks rather too hard of Lewis's Discoveries. . . . We may expect a valuable acquisition to natural history and to botany in particular not with standing the rigid censure of Doctor Barton."[65] Lewis did what many would have done under such circumstances—he excluded Barton and agreed to find someone else to make the drawings of the botanical specimens.

McMahon mentioned that his associate Hamilton had employed an immigrant gardener named Frederick Pursh.[66] After working for Hamilton until sometime in 1805, Pursh switched his services to Barton as a part-time curator and collector. Then in November 1806, after Pursh had a disagreement over wages with Barton, McMahon hired him.[67] Now McMahon suggested that Lewis employ Pursh instead of relying on Barton.

The botanical specimens that Lewis collected had been living, three dimensional plants. Now they were dried, flat things that a botanical illustrator could only hope to enliven. It was up to Lewis to breathe new life into them by carefully guiding an artist and describing them with his own words. His challenge was to give new plants to a nation hungry, helping its citizens understand what they had inherited in Louisiana.

There must have been a moment when Lewis gently folded back the specimen paper revealing an almost intact plant. Some of the leaves were beginning to lose their color and crumble. He recalled how this plant had bloomed all round him under the prairie sun, a field of bright color in the gently breathing grass. He had found it on the top of a bluff. Far below in the curving river there had been bars crowded with driftwood on the upstream end. In his enthusiasm to walk and suck in this curious, thirsty world he had gotten ahead of the crawling boats. In the distance they looked like water bugs. Kneeling, he had cupped this rare thing in his palm, studied the leaves to see their shape and form, counted the branching. He thought hard to find a place where it fitted in the catalog of known plants, and deciding it was something new, gently loosened the soil around the roots and folded it into a creased page torn from his notebook.

Regardless of what Barton thought, APS members continued to inquire about the publication of Lewis and Clark's travels. Muhlenberg's letters stated the inquiry clearly: "Have you heard whether Capt., now Gov. Lewis is soon to publish his noble work?"[68]

McMahon had been getting restless too. He led the way with raising Lewis's new discoveries, which Muhlenberg described. "Mr. McMahon goes on very briskly with his botanical garden and much may be expected from his great industry. He has given me the same information respecting Mr. Lewis's work. Mr. Pursh undertook the description of the plants and I think finished it with the drawings."[69] McMahon and Muhlenberg knew the value of the plants since they had taken such a keen interest in them. Even though Muhlenberg states he only received six seeds from Lewis, they were all unique and he did not want to circulate that fact. "I will not publish anything about them until his work has been published."[70] Everyone did not feel the same way.

Also included with the most recent shipment was the start of the Lewis and Clark herbarium, more than two hundred plants strong, many unheard of at that time. Society members praised Lewis's expertise in picking ones that were new. McMahon, the avid collector diligent about raising Lewis's plants, harvested a variety of currants and gooseberries. He stated that Lewis had brought twenty "new species" of plants and five or six new "genera." Jefferson, who corresponded with McMahon, spoke about the Mandan corn and pea that he was growing, "remarkable for its beautiful blossom and leaf." Muhlenberg was ecstatic over the seeds Lewis sent him and in 1809 believed that they would "all prove to be valuable plants. A very fine Ribe has flowered this year . . . with yellow flowers . . . so a new garlick. Next year I hope to see the rest."[71]

When McMahon recommended his own employee, Frederick Pursh, to Lewis, he described him as being "better acquainted with plants . . . than any man I ever conversed with on the subject."[72] But after taking about a year to finish the work for Lewis, Pursh would sit around doing almost nothing until McMahon farmed him out to a botanist in New York. When Pursh left for New York, Lewis still owed him money.[73] So did Barton. Pursh took Lewis's botanical specimens to London.

By 1809 McMahon worried that Lewis's discoveries could fall into the wrong hands. He feared that "they should make their way into the hands of any Botanist, either in America, or Europe, who might rob Mr. Lewis of the right he had to first describe and name his own discoveries, in his intended publication." McMahon strongly believed that the botanical theft was imminent. While he had not parted with any of the plants from seeds, he had "strong reasons to believe that this opportunity was coveted by [blank] which made me still more careful of the plants."[74]

While McMahon would not suggest the identity of the perpetrator, the only candidate was Pursh. "The original specimens are all in my hands, but Mr. Pursh had taken his drawings and descriptions with him" when he left for New York. Pursh took more than the papers with him, because specimens from Lewis's collection ended up in the collection of A. B. Lambert, vice president of the Linnean Society in London.[75]

After working as a gardener in New York, Pursh would return to England. A botanist could see that Pursh possessed exciting and new material. He was hired by Lambert. It is possible that Pursh may have even taken the plants from Barton's home that were later thought lost. He had. Whatever the circumstances would be—theft, desire to be compensated—it is to Pursh's credit that he attributed Lewis with the discoveries that were published in his 1813 botanical book, *Flora Americae Septentrionalis*.[76]

As a mineralogist Lewis had gotten off on the wrong foot when he corrected editor Mitchill about the source of pumice found floating in the lower Missouri. Mitchill had previously published an article speculating about a volcano that the Arikara chief had indicated on his map:

> In a late conversation I had with him he gave me a description of the burning plains up the Missouri . . . which produce such intense heat as to form lava, slag, and pumice-stone by the same process that forms those volcanic substances in the burning mountains of other countries. The piece of Missouri pumice . . . is from one of these burning plains . . . the minerals called volcanic are not necessarily the production of volcanoes, but of plains burning underground. Such are the curious processes of Nature, and so wonderfully diversified are her works![77]

Lewis was disappointed when he learned the disposition of the collection of sixty-seven mineral specimens that had been sent back from Fort Mandan. Rough handling had crumbled some of the earths and most had lost their labels before being listed in the APS's donation book by the committee of librarians John Vaughan and Dr. Adam Seybert. They hadn't been able to make much of them and Seybert finally gave up trying to arrange them.[78]

Most historical attention has focused on the correspondence concerning the specimens sent back from Fort Mandan in 1805. However, four years later Charles Willson Peale made a list of exploration items then in his museum, which included a number of tribal artifacts from the Columbia with attention to the roots and foods eaten by the western tribes. Some of the animals sent back previously had been reconstructed, but both shipments suffered from poor attention during the trip by ship. Some were beyond Peale's salvage abilities.

Meriwether was very pleased when the prospectus was published in the Philadelphia *Aurora* on June 16, 1807. By way of celebration, that morning he and his friend Mahlon Dickerson accompanied a party to Peale's museum to see a stuffed monkey and other exhibits. Some of the displays were specimens that he had sent back from Fort Mandan.[79]

A later list of the donations presented by Gov. Meriwether Lewis and Gen. William Clark was specific:

Part of the articles collected by Messrs. Lewis and Clark, viz. a complete dress of the Soux Indians, chiefly composed of crows skins, singularly ornamented, one of the leggings belonging to this, is ornamented with stripes, indicating the number of scalps taken by the wearer. Hat, made by a Clatsop woman, near the Pacific Ocean.—Leggings worn by the Pallotepallers, residing on Lewis's river, west of the rocky mountain. Cap, such as are worn by the women on the plains of Columbia. A curious Indian pot, found in digging a well, at the Great Saline, near Ste. Genevieve, about 17 feet below the surface of the earth—a large buffaloe mantle, worn by the Soux Indians—a smaller one, worn by the Crow Indians—two very handsome tobacco pouches, made of otter skins, ornamented with porcupine quills, &c. of the Soux tribe. Another from the Ioways—do. From the Foxes—a handsome belt, from the Winnebagoes. A great variety of wampum, some of which indicating peace or war—the choice of either— desire of retaliation for injuries received—a desire of accommodation, &c. Tobacco pouch, of otter skin, sent to the party by the Socks. Moccosins, worn by the Ottoes. A piece of white buffaloe's skin, from the Missouri. A great quantity of arrows from the different tribes of Soux. A handsome Soux garter. Two ornaments, worn round the neck, by the natives of the plains of Columbia. Amulets taken from the shields of the Blackfoot nation of Indians, and others, presented to the party by themselves. Roots, such as are eaten by the inhabitants of Columbia Plains, and some bread made with them. The first items were received by Peale on the 24th of June 1806 from Neeslaneparkcooh, the great chief of the Pottopallers, as an emblem of the poverty of his nation, which he described in a very pathetic manner. A bag made of grass, by the Pishquilpahs on the Columbia river; another used as a water cup, of the same materials. A cap of the same. A Spanish dollar, received from the Pallotepaller's, a nation inhabiting Lewis's river, who had never previously seen white men. Stone spear points, from the natives inhabiting the rocky mountain.[80]

Peale had mounted and drawn the mountain quail and Lewis's wood-pecker, as well as painting a portrait of their collector. As he informed a friend, the artist had completed the portrait of Lewis by early May 1807. During the sitting he had heard a good deal about the expedition and drawn some conclusions.

> Govr. Lewis (late Captain on an expedition up the Missouri) he is the first Person who has crossed to the Pacific Ocean. McKinsey [Mackenzie] only went to a River which ran into the South Sea. But M[ess]rs. Lewis and Clark have actually visited the sea shore, and I have animals brought from the sea coast, also some parts of the dress &c of the Natives of the Columbia River, [and] have some animals totally unknown before the pre-sentation to Naturalists, which we are now mounting to put into the Museum. The drawings for Governor Lewis's Journal I mean to draw myself to be engraved for the work. It is a work that seems to excite much attention, & will I hope have a great sale & give considerable profit to this bold adventurer.[81]

Peale had completed three drawings by June 6 so they must have been avail-able for inspection. Lewis had gone on to other duties when Peale finished the wax figure of the explorer wearing the Shoshone chief's shawl or "tippet" made of 140 ermine skins. The hero was holding a calumet or cer-emonial pipe, and there was an appropriate label emphasizing the inten-tions of the United States toward its wards. At that time Peale was still mounting the head and horns of a bighorn sheep intended for Jefferson's home museum.[82]

Lewis's contribution included descriptions of about fifty birds. At some point during the time in Philadelphia, Lewis became acquainted with fellow society member Alexander Wilson. The itinerant young ornithologist pro-fessed to have applied to President Jefferson to accompany the expedition as a volunteer naturalist but nothing had come of it. Wilson was trying to get his book of bird illustrations published and was fascinated with Lewis's woodpecker and Clark's nutcracker in Peale's museum.[83] Because they shared a mutual publishing problem, and he liked the poetic fellow, Lewis had authorized Wilson to make use of the ornithological specimens brought back from the expedition. "It was the request and particular wish of Capt. Lewis, made to me in person, that I should make some drawings of such of the feathered tribes as had been preserved, and were new."[84]

In early June most of the items Jefferson sent by water from Washington to Monticello had been lost; only moose and elk horns had been saved. On the twenty-seventh Lewis responded that "it seems peculiarly unfortunate that those as least which had passed the continent of America and their exposure to so many casualties and wrisks should have met such destiny in their passage through a small portion only of the Chesapeak."[85]

The next day Dickerson and Lewis were visiting Governor Thomas McKean of Pennsylvania when they heard the news that a British warship had attacked and captured the American frigate *Chesapeake* off the Virginia capes. If there was a war as a result of the incident, Lewis realized that he should be at his duty station as governor of Louisiana, which was vulnerable to attack by British-allied Indians. But it was another three weeks before Dickerson and he walked around Philadelphia's central square for the last time.[86]

NOTES

1. Alexander Wilson, "Particulars of the Death of Capt. Lewis, *Port Folio* 7 (January 1812): 39.
2. TJ to Jonathan Williams and CWP, January 12, 1807, Jackson, *LLC* 1: 360–61.
3. TJ to Bernard McMahon, January 6, 1807, Jackson, *LLC* 1: 356.
4. US Congress, *House Journal*, 8th Cong. 1st sess., March 8, 1804; Alan David Aberbach, *In Search of an American Identity: Samuel Latham Mitchill, Jeffersonian Nationalist* (New York: Peter Lang, 1988), p. 74n45.
5. *ASP, Miscellaneous* 1: 390–91.
6. SLM to CM, December 30, 1806, folder 41.321.464, MCNY.
7. February 19, 1806, folder 41.321.440, MCNY.
8. SLM to CM, January 7, 1807, folder 41.321.75, MCNY.
9. Mitchill wrote to Col. Jonathan Williams, December 31, 1806, "I have just had a conversation with Capt. Lewis, who has just returned from his journey to the Pacific Ocean. He is a very interesting Traveller, and will in due time furnish us with a Book & Map of his Adventures and Discoveries" (US Military Philosophical Society Papers 2: 40, NYHS).
10. *United States Gazette (PA)*, July 19, 1805, p. 2; *New-York Commercial Advertiser*, July 22, 1805, p. 3; *American Citizen (NY)*, July 22, 1805, p. 2; *Bridgeport Herald (CT)*, August 1, 1805, p. 1; *Eastern Argus (ME)*, August 2, 1805, p. 2; *Pittsfield Sun (MA)*, August 3, 1805, p. 1.
11. US Congress, *Senate Journal*, 9th Cong., 1st sess., February 20, 1806; *ASP, Indian Affairs* 1: 705–43.
12. *Early American Imprints*, Second series, nos. 10326, 11632; Sabin 40826.
13. *The Travels of Capts. Lewis and Clarke* (London: Printed for Longman,

Hurst, Rees, and Orme, 1809); *Early American Imprints*, Second series, nos. 18775, 23216, 28817.

14. Samuel L. Mitchill, *Discourse on Thomas Jefferson, more especially as a Promoter of Natural & Physical Science* (New York: G&C Carvill, 1826), p. 28.

15. "Dr. Mitchill's Letters from Washington, 1801–1813," *Harper's* 58, April 1879, p. 740.

16. Ibid.

17. Samuel Latham Mitchill, ed., *Medical Repository*, 12 vols. (New York: 1804–1812), 3: 315–16.

18. Rodney True, "Some Neglected Botanical Results of the Lewis and Clark Expedition," *Proceedings of the American Philosophical Society* 67 (1928): 3.

19. Paul Russell Cutright, *Lewis and Clark: Pioneering Naturalists* (Urbana: University of Illinois Press, 1969), p. 312.

20. Lewis's botanical excursions are too numerous to mention. For insight into his forays, see Susan H. Munger, *Common to this Country: Botanical Discoveries of Lewis & Clark* (New York: Artisan, 2003).

21. Moulton, *JLCE* 8: 107.

22. Ibid.

23. Velva E. Rudd, "Botanical Contributions of the Lewis and Clark Expedition," *Journal of the Washington Academy of Sciences* 44 (November 1954): 354.

24. Susan Delano McKelvey, *Botanical Exploration of the Trans-Mississippi West, 1790–1850* (Corvallis: Oregon State University Press, 1991), pp. 71–82.

25. TJ to Caspar Wistar, December 8, 1806, document 28542, roll 37, TJ-LOC.

26. TJ to Charles Willson Peale, December 21, 1806, document 28611, TJ-LOC.

27. Michael Leib to TJ, December 22, 1806, Jackson, *LLC* 1: 353–54.

28. TJ to Bernard McMahon and TJ to William Hamilton, Jackson, *LLC* 2: 388–90.

29. His biographer Richard Dillon wrote, "For two other characteristics Lewis should be remembered. His grace with the English language was considerable. The meaning of the 'literary pursuit' which he headed was, indeed a politico-commercial-scientific expedition but the narrative and description of our national epic of exploration are worthy of rescue from the national ignorance caused by the veiled paraphrase and transmutations of Messrs. Biddle and Allen in editing Lewis's journals for publication." Richard Dillon, *Meriwether Lewis: A Biography* (Santa Cruz, CA: Western Tanager Press, 1965), p. xviii.

30. Paul Russell Cutright, "Meriwether Lewis's 'Colouring of Events,'" *We Proceeded On* 11 (February 1985): 11–12.

31. Dr. Paul Cutright presented a convincing argument for "Meriwether Lewis's coloring of events" through his analysis of selected passages from the journals. Those show that given time to order his thoughts Lewis could have written a compelling, literate narrative. Robert A. Saindon, ed., *Explorations: Into the World of Lewis & Clark: Essays from the Pages of* We Proceeded On, *the Quarterly Journal*

of the *Lewis and Clark Trail Heritage Foundation*, 3 vols. (Great Falls, MT: Lewis and Clark Trail Heritage Foundation, 2003), 3: 1049–68.

32. SLM to CM, January 12, 1807, folder 41.321.62 and January 16, 1807, 41.321.103, MCNY.

33. SLM to CM, January 16, 1807, folder 41.321.103, MCNY.

34. Mitchill, *Discourse*, p. 29.

35. ML to the Public, March 14, 1807, Jackson, *LLC* 2: 385–86, n. At least one paper, the *Public Advertiser*, obliged by reprinting the prospectus in the March 25, 1807, edition.

36. Patrick Gass Prospectus, March 23, and David McKeehan to ML, April 7, 1807, Jackson, *LLC* 2: 390, 399–408n2.

37. TJ to MJR, March 16, 1807, Betts and Bear, *FL*, p. 302.

38. Ibid., pp. 297–306.

39. TJ to Bernard McMahon, March 20, 22, 1807; TJ to William Hamilton, March 22, 1807, Jackson, *LLC* 2: 388–91, 398.

40. Henry Phillips Jr., "Early Proceedings of the American Philosophical Society . . . from the Manuscript Minutes of Its Meetings from 1774 to 1838," *Proceedings of the American Philosophical Society* 22 (1884): 396–98.

41. The authors speculate that had those lost letters survived, they could have explained more than a plan for a book; they would have detailed the dream.

42. Conrad's Estimate of Publishing Costs, April 1807, Jackson, *LLC* 2: 392–94.

43. Conrad Prospectus, April 1, 1807, Jackson, *LLC* 2: 394–97.

44. Actually the disruption of the carefully packed specimens began when the keelboat reached St. Charles. "Diary of William Joseph Clark," May 20, 1805, p. 200; TJ to John Vaughan, January 14, 1806, document 27242, roll 36, TJ-LOC.

45. Paul Russell Cutright, "Meriwether Lewis: Botanist," *Oregon Historical Quarterly* 69 (June 1968): 151.

46. Caspar Wistar to TJ, December 5, 1806, document 28530, roll 37, TJ-LOC.

47. TJ to BSB, December 21, 1806, Jackson, *LLC* 2: 694.

48. Paul Russell Cutright, Stephen Ambrose, Dayton Duncan, Earle Spamer, and Richard McCourt have pointed out that Lewis had been distressed beyond words when losing two invaluable caches of plants on the expedition. Lewis hadn't expressed or written any emotional response because he had retained the seeds and could recover lost ground.

49. Stephen Ambrose, *Undaunted Courage* (New York: Simon & Schuster, 1996), p. 87.

50. Muhlenberg was a friend of Mahlon Dickerson and according to Dickerson's diary in 1807 they "went botanizing" together on several occasions. Mahlon Dickerson's Diary, July 21, 23, 1807, 1801–1809 Diary, Dickerson Papers, NJHS.

51. Michael Leib to TJ, December 22, 1806, Jackson, *LLC* 1: 354n1.

52. TJ to Bernard McMahon, January 6, 1807, Jackson, *LLC* 1: 356.

53. Ibid., p. 357n1. For an interesting discussion of tribal tobacco usage see the

chapter "Smoke," in Jack Nisbet, *Visible Bones: Journeys across Time in the Opening of the Missouri Fur Trade* (Norman: University of Oklahoma Press, 1963).

54. TJ to Bernard McMahon, March 20, 1807, Jackson, *LLC* 2: 388–89.

55. TJ to Bernard McMahon, March 22, 1807, Jackson, *LLC* 2: 390.

56. ML to TJ, March 26, 1804, Jackson, *LLC* 1: 170

57. SLM to CM, January 16, 1807, folder 41.321.103, MCNY.

58. Benjamin Smith Barton, "Facts and Observations: Natural History, Zoology," *Philadelphia Medical and Physical Journal* 2 (1805): 176; Velva E. Rudd, "Botanical Contributions of the Lewis and Clark Expedition," *Journal of the Washington Academy of Sciences* 44 (November 1954): 355.

59. James A. Mears, "Some Sources of the Herbarium of Henry Muhlenberg," *Proceedings of the American Philosophical Society* 122 (June 1978): 164; Joseph Ewan, "Frederick Pursh, 1774–1820, and His Botanical Associates," *Proceedings of the American Philosophical Society* 96 (October 1952): 612.

60. TJ to William Hamilton, 22 March 1807, Jackson, *LLC* 2: 389.

61. Bernard McMahon to TJ, March 27, 1807, Jackson, *LLC* 2: 391.

62. Earle E. Spamer and Richard M. McCourt, "The Lewis and Clark Herbarium of the Academy of Natural Sciences." *Notulae Naturae* 475 (December 2002): 8, 10–11.

63. BSB to TJ, October 16, 1810, document 34010, roll 44, TJ-LOC.

64. ML to BSB, May 9, 1807, Jackson, *LLC* 2: 695.

65. Henry Muhlenberg to Stephen Elliott, November 8, 1809, Stephen Elliott Correspondence, typescripts in the Academy of Natural Sciences.

66. Munger, *Common to this Country*, pp. 605–608.

67. Joseph Ewan, *Introduction to the Facsimile Reprint of Frederick Pursh's Flora Americae Septentrionalis (1814)* (Braunschweig, Germany: J. Cramer, 1979), p. 41; Bernard McMahon to TJ, December 24, 1809, Jackson, *LLC* 2: 485.

68. Henry Muhlenberg to Stephen Elliott, June 16, 1809, Stephen Elliott Correspondence.

69. Ibid., November 8, 1809.

70. Ibid.

71. TJ to Bernard McMahon, July 6, 1808, Jackson, *LLC* 2: 441–42; Henry Muhlenberg to Stephen Elliott, June 16, 1809, Stephen Elliott Correspondence.

72. Bernard McMahon to TJ, April 5, 1807, Jackson, *LLC* 2: 398.

73. A. Scott Earle and James L. Reveal, *Lewis and Clark's Green World* (Helena, MT: Farcountry Press, 2003), pp. 218–19; Bernard McMahon to TJ, January 17, 1809, and TJ to Bernard McMahon, January 13, 1810, Jackson, *LLC* 2: 446, 488–89.

74. Bernard McMahon to ML, April 5, 1807, and to TJ, December 24, 1809, Jackson, *LLC* 2: 398, 485.

75. Thomas Meehan, "The Plants of the Lewis and Clark's Expedition across the Continent, 1804–1806," *Proceedings of the American Philosophical Society* 50 (January–March 1898): 13.

76. Moulton, *JLCE* 12: 3–4. The date of publication was 1814 but the APS received two advanced copies of the printed book in December 1813.

77. SLM to CM, January 7, 1807, folder 41.321.75, MCNY. This letter was printed in "Dr. Mitchill's Letters from Washington: 1801–1813," p. 750.

78. ML to TJ, April 5, 1807, and TJ to David Robinson, August 26, 1805, Jackson, *LLC* 1: 239–40n258.

79. Dickerson's Diary, June 16, 1807, Jackson, *LLC* 2: 682. Lewis paid the *Unites States Gazette*, a Philadelphia newspaper, to print the Prospectus ad forty-four times from June 25 to October 17, 1807.

80. *American Watchman* (Delaware), "Late Additions and Donations to Peale's Museum," March 10, 1810, p. 3. The copy printed in Jackson, *LLC* 2: 476–79 is different. The name for the Nez Perce (Pallotepallers) is confusing. Alvin M. Josephy, *The Nez Perce Indians and the Opening of the Northwest* (New Haven, CT: Yale University Press, 1965), p. 649n30 discusses ten variations on the correct spelling.

81. CWP to John Hawkins, May 5, 1807, Jackson, *LLC* 2: 410–11.

82. CWP to TJ, January 29, 1808, Jackson, *LLC* 2: 439–40.

83. Charles William Janson, *The Stranger in America* (London: J. Cundee, 1807), p. 193. Peale was also the recipient of many of the skeletons and preserved hides that Lewis and Clark sent back. The stuffed exhibits for the museum included the "long clawed grisly bear" from the Missouri River and several birds.

84. Munger, *Common to this Country*, p. 100; Clark Hunter, ed., *The Life and Letters of Alexander Wilson* (Philadelphia: American Philosophical Society, 1983), p. 100.

85. ML to TJ, June 27, 1807, Jackson, *LLC* 2: 418.

86. Dickerson's Diary, June 20, 1807, Jackson, *LLC* 2: 684.

NINE

Lewis in Love

Affections's steps shall linger here[1]

L ike lonesome sailors on the sea, Lewis and Clark coursing the Missouri on their return must have had moments when their banter came around to marriage. Confident that they would soon be established in the eyes of the nation, they were thinking of trading in the state of bachelorhood for more stable lives. How to accomplish that was uncertain, for they were products of a time somewhere between a mannered colonial past and a footloose future that had cut them off from the social attachments of a settled community.

The names the two captains laid on the mouths of the rivers they passed weren't that imaginative, certainly not romantic, until Clark attached the name of "the Selebrated" Marthy (Martha Fontaine) to a river. She was an eighteen-year-old Louisville beauty and neighbor of his brother Jonathan. The romantic mood wasn't catching, as a month later when Meriwether took his turn at naming, all he could come up with was his cousin-once-removed Maria Wood. She was Uncle Nicholas Lewis's granddaughter whose parents must have brought her down to Charlottesville occasionally to visit Colonel Nick and Captain Molly, as his wife was familiarly known, at their home "The Farm" near town. But the girl was only thirteen when he last saw her before leaving on the expedition. The naming

168

of Maria's River must have been more sentimental than romantic, although the notation in the journal was that "the hue of the water of this turbulent and troubled stream but illy comport with the pure celestial virtues and amiable qualifications of that lovely fair one."[2]

Maria's River was one of the first significant places where the Corps of Discovery made a major geographical decision. They had to decide which was the main river and which a tributary. After that sentimental expression the expedition went on up the Missouri naming Smith's River for the secretary of the navy, the Dearborn for the secretary of war, and the Jefferson, Madison, and Gallatin to complete the cabinet.[3]

When they returned from the expedition, Lewis and Clark were essentially strangers to society beyond their immediate families. Both men were determined to locate and court potential brides. It is difficult to imagine that William Clark had been dwelling on the possibility of Julia Hancock as a wife. She had been a child of nine when he first saw her five years before and must be around fifteen now.[4] But when they started east Clark went to Fincastle, Virginia, to visit his friend William Preston, it was a bit of luck that he was just in time to attend a double wedding at Colonel Hancock's home. Fifteen-year-old Julia was glowing as girls do at such ceremonies, and the thirty-seven-year-old Clark was smitten.[5] Perhaps she caught the bridal bouquet.

When they were together again in Washington, Clark confided his intentions about Miss Hancock to Lewis. His determination remained strong through the next two months when the explorers had ample opportunities to meet and assess what there was of Washington femininity at the dinners and balls they attended. After receiving the cash to pay the men and their land warrants, Clark headed west by way of Fincastle to press his suit. Two days after he left, Lewis sent a letter after him. "I must subjoin a wish that you would make your disertations on the subject of _____ [marriage] to Miss _____ [Hancock] as short as is consonate with your amorous desires, for god's sake do not whisper any attachment to Miss _____ or I am undone. ——"[6]

A few days later the letter caught up with Clark at Fincastle and he coltishly responded, "I have made an attack most vigorously, we have come to terms, and a delivery is to be made first of January." Turning to Lewis's expectations, Clark continued:

> My F.[riend] your choice is one I highly approve, but should the thing not take to your wish I have discovered a most lovly girl Butiful rich possessing those accomplishments with is calculated to make a man hapy—inferior to you—but to few others the Daughter of C— His politicks is in opposi-

tion to yours. I understand the father of my —— is also a Fed which I did not know untill the other day. I took him to be a good plain republican.[7]

Quaintly evasive, those exchanges leave no doubt that the two returned explorers were on the make and shopping for brides in a not entirely romantic way. But Lewis was not so fortunate as Clark in searching for a marriage prospect. Although eligible young ladies must have flattered him with their attention at social functions, duty came first. He became tied up in the details of closing down the expedition, accepting the appointment as governor of the Louisiana Territory, and getting to Philadelphia to start the process of writing a book about the experience.

Penetrating the social behavior of fashionable young bachelors during the federal era is challenging. The surviving documents reflect the formal conventions of that time and do not provide a true picture of how young people actually conducted themselves. Most personal letters suggest that love was as much an ideal as an emotion. As far as the famous dinners were concerned, Mr. Jefferson had set an informal example for his secretary because "pell mell" was his preference for going to the table, although that miffed those accustomed to formality. There must have been occasions when the handsome young secretary had opportunities to offer his arm to unattached young ladies and practice his charm at the table. Or did the expansive social arbiter Dolley Madison, all in fun, come up with wickedly sly dining table suggestions sure to redden Lewis's complexion. Unfortunately, most of Jefferson's famous dinners were gentlemen's gatherings. There were few unattached women in the raw, muddy capital where many congressmen from distant places lived in boardinghouses.

Lewis arrived in Philadelphia, a place of established decorum, just before the spring blossoms brightened the brick streets. His best connection toward finding a bride suitable to be the governor's lady was his friend Mahlon Dickerson. They had met at Jefferson's table in April 1802 and liked each other from the first. A month later Lewis accompanied Dickerson to Wilmington, Delaware, where they spent a fun week together.[8] They spent more time when Lewis returned the next year to organize the expedition. Dickerson's diary shows that Captain Lewis mixed social life with the scientific mentoring and the names of Miss Patterson and Miss Nicholas suggest that the bachelors were doing more than taking walks around the park. Dinner parties and polite visits to the homes of friends were opportunities to meet young ladies, but Lewis was about to undertake an exploration and in no position to come to an understanding with a likely lady.[9]

He was a good-looking young man as the later silhouette portrait by Charles Saint Mémin shows. But that caught him in profile, and the three-quarter view by Peale is less flattering. Lewis was a good dresser, maybe a bit fastidious even, which the buckskin imagery has missed. Being a bit bowlegged was no detriment to a masculine image. That was the parentheses around the term "horseman" and Lewis had spent as much time in the saddle as a modern commuter wastes in traffic jams. If he could, he rode the best horse available, preferably one of those plantation trotters bred to refine a comfortable animal for inspecting the crops. But he had no problems with the half-wild ponies that the hiking explorers gratefully traded from western Indian breeders who were developing distinctively marked herds on the Columbia plain. Captain Lewis's ride after the Minnetarie (Piikani Blackfeet) confrontation was a remarkable demonstration of endurance. That was a story to impress young ladies.

In his sometimes outrageous novel *Burr*, Gore Vidal casts the life of gentlemen in those times in a more earthly light. As he gained a broader social experience in Philadelphia experience, Lewis realized that the raw and muddy capital was a socially uninspiring place. Most of the associations were with temporary congressmen, politicians, or government clerks living in boardinghouses. No wonder a man like Mitchill wrote daily letters to his wife in New York. As the president's aide Lewis had helped resolve some indiscretions and never committed a word about it to paper. Dickerson's diary is archly discreet. As a gentleman lawyer he was not inclined to record visits to low houses in a city dedicated to brotherly love. Although they wrote like bedazzled adolescents, Dickerson and Lewis were mature men whose masculine needs were real. Social conventions were a restraint, as was the fear of venereal infection.

When the trees began to bud in April 1807 Lewis was quite enjoying himself with his friend Dickerson.[10] During the three months he spent in Philadelphia, Dickerson's record paid closer attention to the ladies they found excuses to visit, and sometimes revisit. Those comments may reflect his friend's interest in finding a suitable mate before he had to go to distant Louisiana.

But the misses Patterson and Nicholas did not resurface again in the diary, which suggests that the eligible young ladies had not stayed unattached for the past three years. During a hot June and July, Dickerson and Lewis visited a number of homes that may have sheltered eligible daughters. On June 15 they spent a pleasant evening "chez Dr. Bache" and arranged next day to escort Mrs. Bache and others to see the stuffed monkey in

Peale's museum. That was the perfect opportunity to show off the accomplishments of the hero of exploration and science whose portrait and specimens were also on display. Having Mrs. Bache and the sisters, Mrs. Sergeant and Mrs. Waters, as friends brought respectable married ladies into the hunt.[11] Perhaps they concerned themselves with finding a suitable object for the attention of the attractive hero.

Captain Lewis was a man of substance with valuable properties strung around the country. He was the governor of a new territory whose political prospects were on the rise. His manners had been learned in the house of the sophisticated Thomas Jefferson and his laurels won among the respected scientists of Philadelphia. He was the reigning national hero whose exploits exploring a vast wilderness could be read in prestigious newspapers. And he was a handsome, well-cut bachelor who danced well at the balls he attended. But something didn't click.

Mr. Lewis was a Virginian and one must assume, a Jeffersonian republican. Daughters might be thrilled by his southern manners but parents observed that his future lay in a frontier French town of uncertain respectability. That was a concern for the wife shopper, too. A governor's lady would be meeting rustic strangers, dirty-linen Frenchmen, Spanish scoundrels, and even Indians. That required someone who was more than a giddy girl.

Ever discrete, as the time when Lewis would have to leave approached, Dickerson noted that "my Friend Capt. L. in trouble."[12] Donald Jackson interpreted that to "the attention he [Lewis] was lavishing on Philadelphia women."[13] But when he left Philadelphia, the only prospect that he carried in his mind was the intriguingly unidentified Miss E— B—y, to whom he might have been introduced by their mutual friend Richard Rush, the son of Dr. Benjamin Rush.[14] At that time Rush was a twenty-seven-year-old bachelor, still two years away from his own marriage.

But it was four months before Lewis opened much light on his experiences. He was back in Albemarle County on November 3 when he wrote to Dickerson to arrange for John Mark's education as "we both know young men are sometimes in want of such a friend." Lewis then returned to romance:

> . . . So much for business, now for the *girls*.
> My little affair with Miss A—n R—ph has had neither beginning nor end on her part; pr. Contra, on my own, it has had both. The fact is, that on enquiry I found that she was previously engaged, and therefore dismissed every idea of prosecuting my pretentions in that quarter, and am now a *perfect widower with rispect to love*. Thus floating on the *surface of occasion*, I feel

all that restlessness, that inquietude, that certain indiscribable something common to old bachelors, which I cannot avoid thinking my dear fellow, proceeds, from that *void in our hearts*, which might, or ought to be better filled. Whence it comes I know not, but certain it is, that I never felt less like a heroe than at the present moment. What may be my next adventure god knows, but on this I am determined, *to get a wife.*

Do let me hear from you as frequently as you can, and when you have no subject of more importance talk about *the girls.* You see already from certain innate workings of the sperit, the changes which have taken place in my dispositions, and that I am now so much unlike my former self, that I speak of those bewitching gipsies as *a secondary consideration.*[15]

It was a letter between intimates but a little strained coming from a thirty-three-year-old man. It was more like what a moonstruck adolescent might have written. Lewis could not have been that innocent. But he was muddling around in unfamiliar areas, stuck between the stilted practices of the past century and the frontier new.

Historian Donald Jackson suggested that the puzzling A—n R—ph was not the married daughter of Dr. Benjamin Rush.[16] Contemporary historian Kathryn Moore has recently concluded that the initials were for Anne Cary Randolph, Jefferson's granddaughter.[17] Lewis knew her mother from times when she acted as the president's hostess and he had recently nursed her father, Thomas Mann Randolph, through a severe bout of malaria. The family lived at Edgehill, a few miles east of Monticello.

But the Jefferson family letters do not indicate that Lewis had an opportunity to meet the fifteen-year-old girl when he returned from the expedition. Jefferson did not mention Lewis in the regular correspondence he kept up with his botanically interested granddaughter. Nor does she. The lack of a response might have been the reason for Lewis's dismissive comment.

Still, it is possible that Lewis read her letters to Randolph while he was caring for him, or penned reassuring words on the father's behalf. In April 1807 when Lewis was trying to get away to Philadelphia, sixteen-year-old Anne Randolph was planting seeds of flowering prairie peas that the explorer had sent to Jefferson.[18] Those later bloomed in one of the oval beds at Monticello, although a romance did not.

The references that Lewis made about his disappointed overtures did not entirely mask shyness. Meantime, Lewis may have met the sixteen-year-old Letitia Breckenridge or her younger sister, Elizabeth. That introduction could have been made during a visit with his friend William Preston in Botetourt County or perhaps he called on her when he was in Richmond observing the Burr trial.[19] But in the November letter to Dickerson, Lewis revealed that his heart was still in Philadelphia. Lewis was bewitched.

Sometime after November 23 Lewis and his younger brother, Reuben, rode south to visit Clark's prospective father-in-law Colonel Hancock, and presumably pass judgment on the bride. When they arrived the two bachelors were treated to the presence of two charming ladies. But it was his brother, Reuben, who was bowled over by the Misses Breckenridge. He could not resist writing a letter of sibling banter to his half sister Mary Marks about their brother's brief encounter with the ravishing Letitia Breckenridge. Although both of the Lewis men were taken by the display of form, features, and beauty, the lady in question was evasive. After a couple of days she left on the excuse of meeting her father and returning to Richmond.[20]

The woman hunter's dilemma was a matter of gossip as far west as Vincennes, Indiana, where the merchant and army contractor George Wallace wrote to Territorial Secretary Bates on December 2. "What is the matter with yr. Governor? he is rather backward (I suspect) in pressing his suit with a handsome Vergn girl—that keeps him—he gave me a hint last spring of his intentions when at Phild." Feeling oppressed by his responsibilities, Bates added that to the resentment he was building toward the much-delayed governor.[21]

Governor Lewis arrived in St. Louis in March 1808 and addressed himself to the business of the Louisiana Territory. On May 29 he wrote to Clark, chiding him on his marriage and lack of gallantry toward the bride. Lewis confided his embarrassment for not finding a suitable partner "when it is recollected what a musty, fusty, rusty old bachelor I am." But Clark was doing something to resolve his friend's marital dilemma and Lewis was responsive. "I trust you do not mean merely to tantalize us by the promise you have made of bringing with you some of your Neices."[22]

That was the "beautiful and accomplished" Ann Clark Anderson, whose fame among the St. Louis bachelors has lasted in the literature throughout the years. The eighteen-year-old vision created such a stir among the young bucks that one wit suggested a town meeting so she could be disposed of to a suitor by lot. Miss Anderson had agreed to accompany the new bride from Louisville and ease her entry into a new life on the frontier. Both ladies suffered terribly from mosquitoes during the voyage down the Ohio River and up the Mississippi. Her discomfort may have dampened any encouragement to Dr. Richard Brown of Louisville, who may have accompanied the party in hopes of getting something started with Ann, but he turned back at the mouth of the Cumberland when she proved unresponsive.[23]

It is possible that Clark agreed to bring Ann along in order to expose his niece to his best friend. Certainly they had the opportunity to get to know each other well, crammed together in the four-room Campbell house on the corner of South Main and Spruce streets.[24]

A few weeks after the Clarks arrived, Lewis sat down and replied to a letter that William Preston had written him from Nashville, apparently announcing that Letitia Breckenridge had married a Richmond man on the second of June.

> How wretchedly you married men arrange the subjects of which you treat ... you have gained that which I have yet to obtain, *a wif*; pardon me therefore for beginning where you left off ... before you came to the point. then *she is off*, passed—off the hooks, I mean in a matrimonial point of view; be it so, the die is cast, may god be with her and her's, and the favored angels of heaven guard her bliss both here and hereafter, is the sincere prayer of her very sincere friend to whom she has left the noble consolation of scratching his head and biting his nails, with ample leisure to ruminate on the chapter of accedents in matters of love and the folly of castle-building. well, I find it an amusing study notwithstanding admirably calculated to kill time, and when I find myself without imployment I will begin again ...

But he couldn't leave it at that and continued with comments on the good character of the successful suitor who would be . . .

> sluming away life with his fair one in the fassionable rounds of a large City. such is the life she has celected and in it's pursuit I [word missing here] which she may meet all the pleasures of which it is susceptable. I consider Miss E— B— a charming girl, but such was my passion for her sister, that my soul revolts at the idea of attempting to make her my wife, and shall not consequently travel that road in quest of matrimony. so much for *love*, now in order I shall take up *friendship* . . .[25]

Meriwether referred to Letitia's younger sister, Elizabeth, who was only fourteen.

With Lewis mooning over what seems to have been more of an imaginary than an actual courtship, it is not all surprising that nothing developed with Miss Anderson. Ann was certainly flattered by the attention she got from most of the eligible men of the town and Lewis seemed always a step behind in his romances.

While Clark was away building Fort Osage, it was up to Lewis to look after the pregnant Julia and her companion Ann, who Clark called Nancy. By October Nancy had enough of St. Louis and was ready to return home to Louisville. But it was another month before a suitable party assembled that she could safely accompany. There is no indication that Lewis was all that disappointed. The complex business of the territory demanded his complete attention.[26]

Prairie fires may have been burning within six miles of town but the romantic spark had gone out in Lewis. On November 9 he had to settle for the brotherhood of fellow Masons when celebrating the opening of the first St. Louis Masonic lodge.[27] Lewis led the procession and, as Clark pointed out, was installed as master of the institution.[28]

NOTES

1. Alexander Wilson, "Particulars of the Death of Capt. Lewis," *Port Folio* (January 1812): 40.

2. Maria Wood was the daughter of Lewis's cousin Mildred Lewis and her husband, David Wood. The family lived on a modest holding on Webb's Mountain along Buck Mountain Creek. For their generous assistance with this identification the authors would like to thank Jane Henley and Bob Doerk.

3. Maria Wood married James Clarkson in 1809 and the family moved to Kanawha County in what is now West Virginia.

4. Landon Y. Jones, *William Clark and the Shaping of the West* (New York: Hill and Wang, 2004), p. 142. Jones puts to rest the myth that Clark had named a western river for her as he likely added it to his map later, after they were married.

5. Ibid., p. 155.

6. ML to WC, March 13, 1807, CFC-MHS.

7. ML to the Public, March 14, 1807, Jackson, *LLC* 2: 386. Might WC have referred to a daughter of Dabney Carr?

8. Mahlon Dickerson to Silas Dickerson, April 21, 1802, and May 1, 1803, Mahlon and Silas Dickerson Bound Letters, box 3, Dickerson Papers, NJHS.

9. Mahlon Dickerson Diary, May 12, 17, 22, and 31, 1803, Jackson, *LLC* 2: 679.

10. Mahlon Dickerson Diary, 1801–1809, Dickerson Papers, NJHS. Mahlon writes on Wednesday, April 15, "Met with my friend Capt. Meriwether Lewis."

11. Mahlon Dickerson Diary, June 16, 1807, Jackson, *LLC* 2: 682.

12. Jackson, *LLC* 2: 683.

13. Ibid. Lewis may have become ill during that time because previous diary entries made by Dickerson state he too is unwell. In his letter to Dickerson on November 3 Lewis remarks that his health is much improved since seeing him.

Donald Jackson omitted printing the April and May 1807 entries of the Dickerson Diary, 1801–1809, Dickerson Papers, NJHS.

14. ML to Mahlon Dickerson, November 3, 1807, Jackson, *LLC* 2: 720 and notes. Rush was educated as a lawyer at Princeton and was a cultured young man on his way to a distinguished public career.

15. Ibid.

16. Actually Jackson had a miscopy and the original reads "A—n R—ph." Meriwether Lewis to Mahlon Dickerson, November 3, 1807, Statesman Collection, MG31, box 2, folder 38, NJHS. The file for this letter is labeled Lewis Meriwether.

17. Kathyrn Moore, "The Lost Years of Meriwether Lewis," *Journal of the West* 42 (Summer 2003): 58–68. We concur.

18. TJ to MJR, June 1, 1807, Betts and Bear, *FL*, pp. 306–307.

19. James R. Bentley, "Two Letters of Meriwether Lewis to Major William Preston," *Filson Club History Quarterly* 44 (April 1970): 174n8.

20. Reuben Lewis to Mary G. Marks, November 29, 1807, MLC-MHS.

21. George Wallace to FB, December 2, 1807, BFP-MHS.

22. ML to WC, May 29, 1808, CFC-MHS. Despite the intimacies between friends it is interesting that most of this letter was copied in another's hand, most likely Isham Lewis, who visited Meriwether in St. Louis (Carter, *TP* 14: 221).

23. Taken broadly from James Holmberg, ed., *Dear Brother* (New Haven, CT: Yale University Press), pp. 131–38.

24. Grace Lewis, "The First Home of Governor Lewis in Louisiana Territory," *Missouri Historical Society Bulletin* 4 (July 1958): 358.

25. Bentley, "Two Letters of Meriwether Lewis to Major William Preston," pp. 171–72.

26. WC to John O'Fallon, November 22, 1808, John O'Fallon Collection, MHS.

27. *Early American Imprints*, Second series, no. 16954. MHS has a hard copy.

28. Holmberg, *Dear Brother*, p. 161.

TEN

The Shadow of Aaron Burr

And Fame on tip-toe ready stands[1]

W hen former captain Lewis returned to Washington in late July 1807, the president and the cabinet had left for the summer. The cost of the expedition had grown to fifteen times the initial estimate and Lewis was answerable for the whole undertaking.[2] Although Lewis touched base with Treasury Secretary Gallatin and Secretary of War Dearborn when they passed through Philadelphia on the way to their homes, the subject of the outstanding expedition bills was apparently not discussed. All of the bills of the expedition had been charged against the War Department, so Lewis wasn't all that eager to deal with the accountant William Simmons in a sweltering annex. For the former captain, now governor of the Louisiana Territory, dealing with that War Department bean counter was like a sliver festering under his fingernail, something that nags no matter how one tries to ignore it.

Simmons didn't miss anything. In his Report Book E, the accountant noted that Sergeant Ordway was paid $112 on January 9, 1807, for his assistance in conducting the Mandan Indian delegation and their pack horses from St. Louis to Washington. The interpreter for the Mandan chief, René Jusseaume, received $50.06, and a half breed named "Francis Labuiche" got $23.50 for trailing along as assistant interpreter and pack horseman.[3] To a tight-fisted bookkeeper with an implied mandate for economy from the treasury secretary, that looked like the kind of extravagance he was supposed to discourage. But exchanges between Lewis and Clark after they received their appointments show that they were still concerned that a soldier like Private Warner had not abused the trust they placed in him.[4]

The accounting entries for the Lewis and Clark expedition span hundreds of pages and are listed in several record, account, and ledger books.[5] When the long list of expenditures was presented, most were approved based on the evidence that Lewis had in hand. But some were still being questioned and Lewis went away from the meeting with Simmons feeling uneasy. How could he vouch for a government horse, purchased for a handful of blue beads, that was later eaten? Simmons seemed unable to grasp what it was like to operate in the wilderness, months away from authorizing an expenditure. Simmons's understanding stopped at the bottom line of that long column of figures. But his objections to the lack of documentation could leave Lewis personally responsible for thousands of dollars of bills that he could not authenticate.

Passing through Baltimore in late July, Lewis could have been in touch with Sen. Samuel Smith, who was General Wilkinson's supporter in Congress. The general was now in Richmond waiting to testify at the treason trial of Mr. Burr. Governor Lewis might want to question him about the experience of the previous administration of Louisiana.

At the beginning of his role as territorial secretary and interim governor, Frederick Bates had bombarded Lewis with letters and reports on almost every detail. While Meriwether was in Philadelphia distracted by arrangements for publishing the book, most of Bates's letters went to the War Department and had not been forwarded. Lewis read them when he was in Washington and took time to address some of the problems Bates reported.

In answer to Bates's letter of May 18, Lewis suggested that he should cooperate with Governor Harrison for the return of some Osage prisoners taken by the Sacs. "As a matter of general policy it appears to me that it would be well to mention to Mr. Bates, Genl Clark and Gov. Harrison on the subject of recovering those prisoners, that nothing should be given to the individuals possessing them for their delivery and that it would be better to give double the amount to the chiefs of some of their more powerfull neighbors to compel their delivery than to redeem them by purchase from their owners."[6] Lewis was determined that kidnapping was not to be rewarded. In August Bates wrote again, prodding Lewis by asking when he intended to assume his duties in St. Louis.

There were also letters from Clark to the War Department that required a response. A newly discovered memo suggests that Gov. Lewis was trying to deal with his duty from long distance.[7] It was headed, "Observations with remarks of M. Lewis on the several subjects embraced by the inclosed communications which were referred to him by the Secretary of War." After reading Clark's letters of May 15 and June 1, the governor favored ordering a horse-powered mill in Kentucky to be forwarded to Chouteau for the use of the Osage.[8] That included hiring a "discreet" blacksmith named Joseph Lambert to be employed for at least two years to repair arms and implements of husbandry.[9] The prices in peltry that the smith could charge the Indians were carefully specified: $1.25 for a beaver, $2 for a buckskin, $1 for a doeskin. As the very useful Pierre Dorion had been ordered to reside with the Tetons, he should be paid his past salary.[10]

The unpleasant business with Simmons seemed to be completed by August. With that trying chore out of the way, Lewis went on to Albemarle County for a reunion with his family and to Monticello to report to Jefferson on how things had gone toward publishing the books.

Lewis told Jefferson in Philadelphia that he began the monumental task of projecting a plan and writing the narration of the expedition. In most cases the reception and assistance he had been given by his former scientific mentors was generous and they had agreed to help in the description of the scientific returns. But that important work was frustrating because it now had to be done under a publishing deadline. Instead of the leisure to order his thoughts and exercise his pen, Lewis had to get it started before he left to take over the government of Louisiana Territory. Somehow, the reward for completing a successful exploration had been turned against him.

Jefferson had been confident that matters were going well since mid-May when his present secretary, Isaac Coles, returned from Philadelphia.[11] But from the moment of their meeting and Lewis's recitation of progress, everything between the two men was overshadowed by two developments that threatened the nation.

Governor Lewis was in Philadelphia when he heard of the British attack on the unprepared *Chesapeake*. Like others, he was incensed at the outrageous act but there were larger potential consequences. He had to consider how the potential of a war with Britain might affect his yet-to-be-assumed government of Louisiana Territory. When he joined Jefferson in midsummer, he found the president trying to get the nation prepared for a war while trying to avoid it by diplomatic means. Reluctantly facing what might become a war, Jefferson called a special session of Congress, but that could not convene until October.

Thomas Jefferson kept many of the letters he received and answered during the months of July and August 1807. Those show that Monticello was not a haven from the ongoing responsibilities of the presidency. Preparations for a war loomed in the exchanges with his scattered cabinet as they prepared to raise an army of a hundred thousand if the British tried to attack Norfolk or snatch New Orleans. Offers were coming in from militia officers or patriotic citizens offering to serve.[12] One of those passed on from the War Department was a letter from Louisiana Territory Secretary Bates asking if he was authorized to accept the services of a company of volunteers organized at the lead mines.[13]

On August 8 Jefferson forwarded the offer for the founding of the *Mine a Breton* military school to Lewis.

> . . . as you are now proceeding to take upon you the government of the territory, I pray that you will be the bearer of my thanks to them for this offer, and to add the pleasure it gives me to receive further their assurances that they will cordially co-operate in the restoration of that harmony in the territory so essential to it's happiness & so much desired by me.[14]

The last part of the acceptance indicated that Jefferson was very much aware of the situation in St. Louis, in good part based on what Lewis had told him from personal observation and from what was developing at the Aaron Burr trial in Richmond.

Both the president and the governor were appalled by the actions of a man whom they knew personally and the enormity of what he apparently attempted. When Lewis and Clark returned to St. Louis in September 1806, they heard rumors and read newspaper speculations that former vice president Aaron Burr was up to something of dangerous consequence. Rumors had been circulating that he was making plans to break off the western country at the chain of the Allegheny Mountains, or that he was gathering a force to attack Spanish possessions.[15] Some said that Burr was in cahoots with General Wilkinson.[16]

The explorers were still on the road to Washington at the end of November with this ominous news when President Jefferson issued a proclamation, based on information received from General Wilkinson, warning the nation that Burr and his followers planned to seize the port of New Orleans as a base for launching an attack upon Vera Cruz and, ultimately, Mexico City.

In October, General Wilkinson exposed the plot to the president and then apprehended Burr. But a Mississippi Territory grand jury refused to indict Burr and turned him loose to circulate about the West in disguise, until he was recaptured in Alabama. When Lewis arrived in Washington at the end of December, he learned that Mr. Jefferson, distracted by those developments, had only devoted a few sentences in his annual message to Congress about the successful return of the Corps of Discovery. Another message to Congress on January 22, 1807, was a long description of the plot that diverted congressional attention from the compensation and rewards for the Corps of Discovery.

A month later when the president nominated Lewis to be governor of Louisiana, that post appeared to have become a critical element of the unfolding story. The former corpsman Robert Frazer, whom Lewis had favored with permission to publish his private journal of the expedition, brought a report directly to Jefferson that Burr's associates had been intercepted trying to reinforce an expedition that was descending the Ohio. Some of the participants were prominent men in St. Louis; one, Robert Wescott, was the son-in-law of Territorial Secretary Joseph Browne.[17] The new appointee to that office, Frederick Bates, would not arrive to relieve Browne before the end of March. That meant that in addition to dealing with the vicious factions that previously embarrassed Governor Wilkinson, Lewis would have to stifle residual separatist sentiments.

By March 26 the conspirator had been brought to the United States Circuit Court at Richmond, where he appeared before Chief Justice John Marshall. On April Fool's Day, Marshall decided that there was insufficient evidence of treason but a charge could be made for high crimes and misdemeanors. But a trial scheduled to open on May 22 didn't allow much time for the prosecution to gather evidence from distant places.

In May while Lewis was busy in Philadelphia with the details of the expedition, Burr and a battery of lawyers were defending against charges that had been brought by President Jefferson. Marshall narrowed the charge by holding that proof of treason required an overt act. Burr's lawyers demanded that Jefferson furnish confidential documents in his possession and that he testify in person. On June 13 the president refused, citing principle of executive privilege that Chief Justice John Marshall did not pursue.

General Wilkinson, the main witness against Burr, arrived on June 15 and by June 24 the grand jury had indicted Burr for high crimes and misdemeanors. Despite speculations that General Wilkinson was involved with Burr, the general had acted promptly by having Burr arrested on the lower Mississippi and tried for treason in a Mississippi territorial court.

That trial was still going on when Lewis rejoined Jefferson. Sometime in August Lewis saw the president at Monticello, expecting it to be the last visit before he departed for St. Louis. He found Jefferson distracted by the trial of former vice president Aaron Burr. In less than a month after legal proceedings began at Richmond, the grand jury had produced a subpoena requiring the president to testify, especially about the confidential letter he had received from General Wilkinson outlining a treasonable plot. Jefferson refused to expose the executive office to questioning and having refused the subpoena, the president couldn't go to Richmond as an observer. At the very least he had to appear aloof from the legal proceedings some were already calling a persecution of Mr. Burr. But if the federal prosecution was faltering, Jefferson had to know why. The Lewis family home at Locust Hill was just ten miles down the Ivy Road from Monticello. Because it was unnecessary to write letters when he could ride over and speak with the president in person, the record of those exchanges are missing.

Jefferson had never gotten away from the habit of using Meriwether for those little chores that gentlemen performed to accommodate each other. But the Richmond proceedings were something bigger, and near the end of August Lewis went to Richmond as Jefferson's eyes.

Thomas Jefferson preferred resolving international problems by negotiation, but he was being pushed by Congress to raise an army of thousands and to build a fleet. In that day the Pentagon-like establishment walked in the two silver-heeled boots of General Wilkinson. There were no staffs of military planners devising strategies or excuses for failures. The commanding general was it. What might Wilkinson do with a hundred-thousand-man army? Was he really as close to Burr as the lawyers insinuated? The president and the secretary of war had to be sure that their only general was not thinking of himself as another Bonaparte.

Was General Wilkinson as bad as Burr's lawyers painted him? Governor Lewis did not ride to Richmond to be entertained by the closing days of a failed justice system, nor to gain insights on how to deal with ungovernable Louisiana. As he had done as the president's secretary when judging the officers of the army, now Lewis had to evaluate the character and intentions of the commanding general and report them to Jefferson.

There was more to the general than a gilt-encrusted bag of wind. In an age of dueling there were Wilkinson loyalists who might invent an excuse for a challenge to anyone impugning their hero. An assessment did not need to be put to paper when it was spoken between old friends. The only suggestion of the opinion that Lewis may have brought back from Richmond is that the president and secretary of war continued to rely on

Wilkinson. The general was sent back to New Orleans to try to hold a fever-decimated army together and to resist a potential British invasion.[18]

No matter how poor a showing General Wilkinson made as the star witness against Burr, Jefferson had no other general to defend New Orleans should the British decide to snatch it from the United States. If the British decided to invade from the north via the upper Mississippi, the governor of the Louisiana Territory represented one of the first lines of defense. Coordination was necessary.

On the first of September the jury found that the treason charge had not been proved and a second trial began to try Burr of the misdemeanor of trying to attack a nation at peace with the United States. Staying as an observer until mid-September, Meriwether returned to report to Jefferson that the defense strategy had been to disparage General Wilkinson with rascals in the audience calling him a "finished scoundrel" or an "admirable trumpeter."[19] But Wilkinson was tough and it would take more than ridicule, criticism, and censure for the general to abandon his position.

As well as being APS members, Lewis and Wilkinson shared an interest in western exploration.[20] As governor, Wilkinson sent junior officers to the upper Mississippi and into the Osage country. When his son, Lt. James Wilkinson, tried to establish a military presence at the mouth of the Platte River, Kansa Indian hostility had turned him back. Undeterred, the general sent Lt. Zebulon Pike on an ill-defined but carefully conceived excursion toward the Southwest. On June 22, 1807, President Jefferson had reminded Secretary of War Dearborn that the United States had sent the civilian surveyor Thomas Freeman with orders to explore the Red River from the mouth. Lieutenant Pike would follow the Red from its source downward.[21] Unfortunately, Pike got on the Rio Norte (Rio Grande) by mistake and had been apprehended. Spanish forces had also stopped Freeman from proceeding.[22] Those expeditions detracted to some degree from the accomplishments of the Corps of Discovery and may represent a lessening interest in the publication of a book. General Wilkinson, the sponsor of three expeditions, was still in Richmond on September 15 when he wrote Jefferson that he had intended to send Pike's report of the Southwest expedition with Governor Lewis but had been too preoccupied to do it.[23] The implication is that Lewis was brought up-to-date on the Pike exploration by the man who knew the motivation behind it.

When Lewis saw Jefferson again at Monticello in mid-September, that would be their last meeting. It was a two- or three-day ride from Charlottesville to Richmond and Lewis was back there again on October 8 when he asked United States Attorney William Wirt to negotiate payment of the second quarterly installment of his salary as governor.[24] By then the president had returned to Washington to prepare for the opening of the special session of Congress to address the *Chesapeake* problem.

Between the legal proceedings Meriwether also had opportunities to question his predecessor as governor about the political and material complexities of administrating the Louisiana Territory.[25] General Wilkinson gave him an earful because he had just been dealing with the accusations of former major James Bruff, who brought his personal grudge into the trial. Lewis could believe that. Not long after the expedition returned to St. Louis, Bruff had treated the explorer to a list of complaints against the general. Clark had been in the secretary of war's office when Bruff spewed more insinuations to justify his resignation. According to the general there were other snakes in the grass like Judge Easton and that cabal of St. Louis opportunists. They would oppose any administration that interfered with their schemes.[26] Only a dedicated martyr would look forward to assuming the government of Louisiana.

Lewis must have felt that he was already spread too thin. But the two biographies of Meriwether Lewis by Dillon and Ambrose have concluded that not much happened for him during the summer 1807. Speculations that Lewis wasted that time drinking or looking for a wife are unlikely because his mother, Lucy Marks, would not have allowed her son, at the apex of his career, to waste himself carousing or chasing girls. After all he was also an absentee farmer who had to attend to personal matters. It is not a great step to recognize that Lewis expected to be gone for some time and spent many days looking after neglected family matters and seeing to the futures of his brother, Reuben, and half brother, John Marks.[27]

If a master of intrigue like Wilkinson had been unable to manage those political opportunists, what could Lewis expect to accomplish? That prospect may have caused him to concentrate on how to deal with the responsibility. As he began working a scenario to address it, he was still signing himself Captain Lewis.

Fans of the expedition journals have neglected the observations that Lewis wrote while at Locust Hill. Before actually taking over the government of the Louisiana Territory, he wrote what amounted to a recapitulation of his observations as an explorer, a reflection on what had developed since, and a plan on how to proceed. The observations demonstrated Lewis's grasp of the situation and what he needed to do. One of the most important documents written by Meriwether Lewis, this long consideration of past Spanish failures and current British threats to the United States' relationship with the new Indian tribes it had inherited has been overlooked and misinterpreted.

This remarkable document represents what Meriwether Lewis had learned during the exploration or observed and evaluated before and after, as that now applied to his government of the Louisiana Territory. The original has been lost but the not entirely informed editors of the expedition narrative had the study, and not knowing what to do with it, probably inserted the usual editorial polishing-up and tucked it into the end of the book. That version was republished in the Thwaites and Coues versions of the journals, and in the *Letters of Lewis and Clark* by Donald Jackson.

Jackson surmises that the "Observations and Reflections" were intended for the edification of the secretary of war because "He used it as part of a later letter to Dearborn, then got further mileage from it by giving it to his friend and protégé Joseph Charless, editor of the *[Missouri] Gazette*."[28] However, much that Lewis discussed would have been of considerable interest to the recently appointed superintendent of the Indian trade, or to Congress, which could remake the laws if it could be led to understand the situation. But it was really a plan of action.

The "Observations" represent a recognition of how the United States was going to have to deal with the acquisition of Louisiana and its inhabitants. After getting past the fear of the forbidding forests and mountains and learning how to deal with woodland Indians, Americans faced a new challenge in the West. On the expedition, Lewis learned that the familiar forests gave way to open plains where seminomadic native peoples were already sophisticated in the ways of commerce. Those hunters were likely to be protective of their natural resources in furs and peltry. Lewis needed to convince the leaders of the nation that gaining that vast expanse had radically changed how they would have to deal with independent Indians. He took the time to carefully work out in detail what was meant to educate . . . someone. In that way, the paper represented the practical, political returns of the expedition.

The Indian problem could not be separated from an extended and defenseless frontier or from the benefits that should accrue to the United States from the possession of Louisiana. Lewis looked ahead to "the future expenditure of blood and treasure, which may be involved in the defence of this country." He analyzed the failures of the previous Spanish government in their dealings with the tribes and the evils that flowed from those measures "as well to the Indians as the whites." He meant to profit from those errors and apply more correct measures in his government.

British intrusion into the Indian trade had since grown to the possibility of actual war. If military forces were unavailable for frontier defense then commerce might provide a barrier to foreign exploitation. Lewis knew that traders from Prairie du Chien entered Louisiana by way of the Des Moines or Minnesota rivers. Northern traders infiltrated the upper Missouri from the Red or Assiniboine rivers. Those operations employed a credit/debt system that kept tribal customers dependent and under their influence.

Lewis saw the fur trade and the Indian trade factory system as a tie with the tribes. It was also a future industry. If British merchants were prohibited from trading in Upper Louisiana, American merchants could use their profitable trade to successfully compete with powerful British operations.

As Lewis meticulously laid down details on how to regulate exchanges between American traders, Indians, and intrusive British traders, what he wrote reveals as much about the character of the author as it does about the situation he was analyzing. The "Observations" are a thought-out plan of action by a man who could approach a difficult problem with careful, almost detached preparation before plunging into hasty action as had his predecessors. One of the most important documents written by Meriwether Lewis, it is a revealing insight into his mind. And his courage, as he must have realized that he faced a complex situation and might be getting into something over his head.[29]

NOTES

1. Alexander Wilson, "Particulars of the Death of Capt. Lewis," *Port Folio* 7 (January 1812): 39.

2. GLM, box 39, folder 13, p. 16, JNEM.

3. Selected volumes from the accountant of the War Department, microfilm roll 14, #85, MHS.

4. WC to ML, March 15, 1807, Jackson, *LLC* 2: 387–88.

5. For a sample, see Jackson, *LLC* 2: 419–31.

6. Marshall, *FB* 1: 114–19.

7. Memorandum on state militia quotas, July 18, 1807, document 29758, roll 38, TJ-LOC. A list of quotas of militia required from each state as part of the hundred-thousand-man army does not include the Louisiana Territory.

8. ML to SW, 1807, RG107, S1807, M222, roll 2, frame 0952, NARA.

9. SW to WC, August 17, 1807, RG75, M15, roll 2, p. 328, NARA.

10. ML to SW, 1807, RG107, S1807, M222, roll 2, frame 0952, NARA.

11. TJ to Thomas Mann Randolph, May 24, 1807, Jackson, *LLC* 2: 696.

12. These concerns run through the Jefferson Papers for July and August.

13. FB to HD, June 22, 1807, Marshall, *FB* 1: 148–49n86. Bates had responded promptly to the February 24 act of Congress authorizing the president to accept volunteer companies not to exceed thirty thousand men.

14. TJ to ML, August 8, 1807, Carter, *TP* 14: 139.

15. Letters written to TJ detailing movements of the conspirators: January 10; February 10; March 5, 28, 29; and July 14, 1808, rolls 35–36, TJ-LOC. After the provocateurs were together in Lexington, the federal district attorney for Kentucky, Joe Daviess, called for a grand jury to investigate the possibility that they meant to break up the nation.

16. For early analysis of the situation in St. Louis, see Clarence E. Carter, "The Burr-Wilkinson Intrigue in St. Louis," *Missouri Historical Society Bulletin* 10 (July 1954): 447–64.

17. Robert Frazer to TJ, April 16, 1807, document 29312, roll 38, TJ-LOC.

18. JW to HD, December 13, 1807, RG107, W413, M22, roll 3, NARA.

19. Attributed to Washington Irving, who was an observer at the trial.

20. Henry Phillips Jr., "Early Proceedings of the American Philosophical Society . . . from the Manuscript Minutes of Its Meetings from 1774 to 1838," *Proceedings of the American Philosophical Society* 22 (1884): 266.

21. Dan L. Flores, "Editor's Introduction," in *Southern Counterpart to Lewis & Clark: The Freeman & Curtis Expedition of 1806* (Norman: University of Oklahoma Press, 2002).

22. TJ to HD, June 22, 1807, document 29561, roll 38, TJ-LOC.

23. JW to TJ, September 15, 1807, document 30145, roll 39, TJ-LOC. Compare this with the assassination theory promoted by David Leon Chandler, *The Jefferson Conspiracies: A President's Role in the Assassination of Meriwether Lewis* (New York: William Morrow and Company, Inc., 1994), p. 322, and repeated by Frederick J. Fausz and Michael A. Gavin, "The Death of Meriwether Lewis: An Unsolved Mystery," *Gateway Heritage* 24 (Fall 2003/Winter 2004): 69–70.

24. Meriwether Lewis personal account book, April 4, 1807, to September 27, 1809, box 1, folder 8, MLC-MHS.

25. JW to TJ, September 15, 1807, document 30145, roll 39, TJ-LOC.

26. *Annals of Congress*, Senate, 10th Cong., 1st sess., pp. 599–621.

27. ML to Mahlon Dickerson, November 3, 1807, Jackson, *LLC* 2: 719.

28. Jackson, *LLC* 2: 697.

29. See full version of "Observations and Reflections" in the appendix.

ELEVEN

Taking Over as Governor

Wide as this wilderness is spread[1]

W inter 1806 was already closing in on Albemarle County when
Meriwether Lewis and his younger brother, Reuben, rode away
from Locust Hill. Over the past three and a half months he had spent some
time with his mother, arranged a promising future as a doctor for his half
brother, John Marks, and set the operation of the plantation in as good
shape as an absentee landowner could expect. For neighboring planters that
would have been enough; they were ready to settle back and enjoy a comfortable winter among congenial and like-minded friends. But a national
hero was driven by more-demanding responsibilities.

What were his feelings? Over the last months he had addressed some
problems of Louisiana territorial government from long distance while
trying to formulate a policy by setting out major objectives and how to
approach them. In doing that he had relied on his own observations, the
recent interview with his predecessor, and access to the information that
the president had been receiving. After two imperfect administrations, no
policy for the transition of authority had been formulated. He seems to have
been a naturally reticent man, but if he was to be governor, then he would
be governor.

It is not unreasonable to suppose that the Lewis brothers started out on the same road that Meriwether used years before to retrieve his widowed mother from Georgia. Likely they turned west through the famous Cumberland Gap, once the pioneer gateway to the wilderness, now a well-worn wagon road far behind a frontier that had already, like the mythic Daniel Boone, crossed the Mississippi. Kentucky was no longer that "dark and bloody ground" where hunters contested with the Shawnee for deer hides—and their lives.

The governor's entourage included his brother, Reuben, and John Pernier, the free mulatto valet whom Thomas Jefferson sent along to look after him.[2] There were wagoners and horse handlers to deal with hauling the governor's papers, the wardrobes of the two young gentlemen, and household furnishings necessary to make life bearable in St. Louis.[3] Lewis carried with him the documents of the exploration of western America that still had to be converted into a narrative of adventure and natural history. But doing that would require stealing time from governing the most challenging territory of the United States.

The slow-moving wagon gave the brothers time to range afield and to look over the seemingly secure lands that belonged to their mother and their half brother, John Marks. But Lewis's holding on Brush Creek in the Ohio Military Reserve, descended from his father's service, was in doubt, and the inheritor was resigned to losing the greater part of it. Science was still on the naturalist's mind on December 20 when they visited and measured a natural bridge near Mr. Paine's land on Stock Creek.

When they reached Lexington on January 14, 1808, the citizens gave Lewis a huge party "in testimony of their regard and respect for him."[4] By mid-February they arrived at Louisville to find that William Clark had been there as late as the third of the month. He was traveling east for his wedding and they had failed to intercept him on the road. When Lewis found an opportunity to write their mother, Reuben had already set out in a flat-bottomed boat with the baggage and carriage. He was accompanied by Major Hughes, Mr. Cox, and the increasingly trail-wise butler, Pernier. After descending the Ohio for 320 miles they would go ashore on the west side of the Mississippi to cover the next 165 miles by land. Lewis expected to start the next day, traveling overland by way of Vincennes and Cahokia.[5]

William Clark was in St. Louis from early May to late July 1807 before Lewis began writing the "Observations" and should have kept his friend updated about developments on the Indian frontier.[6] Now, his friend's brother, Jonathan Clark, gave Lewis a forecast of what to expect in Louisiana. Surely Clark let Lewis know that last May he had assembled and addressed a Yankton and Teton Sioux delegation that seemed amendable to a more friendly relationship.[7] By May St. Louis was aware that Captain McClallen had been deflected from his Santa Fe adventure and after wintering with the Yankton, he had proceeded up the Missouri in the spring. It was supposed that he was headed to the Yellowstone. Another small party led by a Frenchman named Charles Courtin trailed McClallen, but he was going to the Great Falls.

In early May a third combination trading/trapping party had been assembled by the entrepreneurial Manuel Lisa. A good part of the capitalization was provided by the Kaskaskia merchants William Morrison and Pierre Menard, who had designated George Drouillard, the former hunter for the Lewis and Clark expedition, to look after their interests.

Three privately funded trading efforts were already on the river when Clark, in accordance with his instructions from Secretary of War Dearborn, started the recently commissioned Ensign Pryor and a military party to escort the Mandan chief Sheheke-shote to his people. They were accompanied by a private outfit financed by the Chouteau family. Some in St. Louis might have charged that Clark was blending public and private interests as Governor Wilkinson previously tried with Dr. Steele and Captain McClallen. But Clark's orders, to combine a private enterprise with the government party, came directly from the secretary of war.[8]

There had been trouble with western Indians. The Arikara of the upper Missouri, who had been amiable when the Corps of Discovery passed twice, became upset when the news of the death of their chief finally reached them last June. The chief's interpreter, Joseph Gravelines, brought condolence presents from the great father in Washington, but the gift failed to prevent the outraged Arikara from abusing Gravelines and his traveling companion, the trader/trapper Charles Courtin. Incensed by his treatment, Courtin wrote two letters of complaint dated June 22. One of those was sent back to St. Louis with Joseph Dickson, one of the two trappers who induced John Colter to leave the Corps of Discovery and return to the Yellowstone to hunt. The other copy was left with a trustworthy Arikara chief.[9]

Making good time going down the river, Dickson must have met the combination military escort and private trading party that Clark started up the river in May. Following orders from the War Department, William Clark sent Lt. Joseph Kimball and six soldiers to escort the Sioux delegation that came to St. Louis in May to council with the new Indian agent. As those eighteen men, eight women, and six children were only going as far as the Yankton country (in present-day South Dakota), Kimball and his detachment returned from there. The Kimball party was accompanied by a boat and ten men bringing an outfit of trade goods to the eager Yankton.[10]

Nathaniel Pryor, the former sergeant of the Corps of Discovery and now a newly minted ensign, commanded an unnamed sergeant, a corporal, and fourteen privates escorting the Mandan chief Sheheke-shote to his home. René Jusseaume and Pierre Dorion Jr. went along as interpreters. The military escort was accompanied by another trading adventure consisting of thirty-two men, a boat, and a pirogue. Young Pierre Auguste Chouteau Jr. was one of the local lads whom Lewis had recommended in 1804 for an officer's education at the West Point military academy. After graduating he resigned his commission to enter business with his father. Clark had left St. Louis confident that the experienced Pryor and fifty men should be able to handle anything that came up.[11] Around the first of September he was digging up fossils for Jefferson from the Big Bone Lick south of Cincinnati.[12]

If Dickson met the government expedition, he should have tipped them off about the Arikara attitude. By August 2 Dickson had reached St. Louis and given Courtin's letter to Territorial Secretary Bates, who had it translated for forwarding to Secretary of War Dearborn.[13] But the warning came too late. Lieutenant Kimball returned to Cantonment Belle Fontaine on September 27, reporting that everything went well as far as the Yankton were concerned.[14] When he parted company with Chouteau and Pryor at the Sioux village on the twenty-third of August, Kimball believed that "their prospects were flattering for a prosperous and successful voyage."[15]

Seven weeks later a distraught Ensign Pryor straggled in with a boatload of wounded men and the grim news that four of Chouteau's party had been killed in a sharp fight with the Arikara. He reported on October 16 that when the expedition came to the Arikara towns, a chief immediately handed him the other copy of Courtin's complaints. But, as the boats moved to the upper of the three riverside towns, a sharp fight erupted. Trapped in a narrow side channel the boats had been lucky to fall back downstream without all aboard being massacred.[16]

Indian agent Clark received the bad news at his brother Jonathan's home in Louisville and forwarded it to Secretary of War Dearborn in Washington on the thirtieth. Despite what Territorial Secretary Frederick Bates reported as a complete disaster for United States authority, Clark remained calm and was still in Louisville on December 3 when he sent Lt. Joseph Kimball on to Washington with additional information.[17]

Clark told Dearborn to address his letters to Fincastle during the winter. As it turned out, he would not return to St. Louis with his new bride for another six months. Therefore, on assuming his work as governor, Lewis would face the burden of dealing with an increasingly tense situation without his friend. Any other public officer might have questioned why Indian agent Clark failed to return to St. Louis to immediately deal with the Arikara problem, but Lewis and Clark knew from experience that nothing could be done until river navigation opened the following spring.

While he was at the falls of the Ohio, Lewis conferred with John Campbell, who had recently been appointed Indian agent on the upper Mississippi and was now on his way to his post at Prairie du Chien.[18] Campbell was a tough Scotch-Irish Indian trader reputed to have previously beaten a misbehaving Indian to death. Later, when he was justice of the peace for St. Clair County, Indiana Territory, he accidentally shot another, an incident that had not stopped the secretary of war from approving his appointment as the Prairie du Chien agent. Lewis was encouraged to have a good man at that hot spot on the upper Mississippi. Campbell would inhibit any British traders who were still trying to enter and exploit United States territory. If war developed, he might be able to prevent the tribes from joining the British.

Lewis rode on toward Vincennes, towing a pack horse loaded with a case of wine that he bought from Jonathan Clark.[19] No documentary evidence survives showing that Lewis conferred in Vincennes with his Indiana Territory parallel, Gov. William Henry Harrison. But both governors were facing the potential of a British invasion from the headwaters of the Mississippi River, a threat that certainly suggested they should coordinate their efforts.

Nor is there an indication that the incoming governor intercepted the barrage of letters being written by the territorial secretary. In January Bates wrote that "no one feels the want of your superintending presence so much as I." By February 23 he was "every day expected" and on the twenty-sixth, after Reuben and the furniture arrived, the expectation became every hour, every minute.[20]

A British threat from the north was very real for Lewis, who had not forgotten how the trade at the Mandan/Hidatsa villages was being diverted by British intruders. He shared the president's determination to discourage the illicit extraction of United States resources and had outlined a way of doing that in the first letter he wrote after returning from the expedition. Then foreign affairs turned hot the previous summer when a British warship attacked the *Chesapeake*. Even after that national insult, the unapologetic British continued to impress seamen and meddle with Indians.

The nation needed time to prepare for war. President Jefferson and Secretary of State Madison devised a plan to coerce England and France by denying those nations the American resources they needed to continue their continental wars. American ships were prohibited from carrying goods to hostile nations, but the embargo strategy was becoming an economic disaster for the United States as exports dropped from $108 million to $22 million.[21] The policy was crippling the American economy.

It was one thing to control activities in the seaports but quite something else to inhibit returns from the Indian trade that were slipping through the Great Lakes in canoes to Montreal. British traders were still guaranteed access to the tribes in the "Old Northwest" and most frontiersmen were convinced that they were propagandizing disaffected natives. A presidential order to tighten down on British traders still operating under the provisions of Jay's old treaty failed to ease that situation.

Part of the ominous Indian unrest was attributable to Indiana Territory Governor Harrison. In extracting a series of land cession treaties from the tribes still hanging on east of the upper Mississippi, Harrison's techniques ranged from opportunism to outright fraud. Widely resented by the tribes, those methods gave two Shawnee brothers the incentive to circulate among the dissatisfied villages. Tecumseh and his one-eyed brother, known to whites as the Shawnee Prophet, were urging a new tribal confederation strong enough to resist further dispossession.

The prophet's call to reject the new order and return to old ways had taken on religious fervor. There were rumors that adherents were burning those who disagreed with them as witches. Stoking the fires, the unrepentant loyalist and Shawnee squaw man Matthew Elliot hovered at Amherstburg just across the river from Detroit, encouraging the discontented tribesmen to resist the Americans. In 1804, before the expedition had left Wood Creek, Clark encountered Elliot's henchman, Simon Girty, traveling with Indians.

Harrison used his treaty-making talents when he operated as temporary governor of Upper Louisiana. Not long after the Corps of Discovery left, a group of Sac and Fox came down to Portage des Sioux to discuss a totally different matter. Harrison induced them to cede all their lands between the Illinois River and the Mississippi to the United States. Having lost their homes, those tribes moved west of the river and spread as far south as the Des Moines Rapids, which made them the problem of Louisiana Territory. The potential for disorder increased as the Sac raided south across the lower Missouri, striking Osage or any whites who got in their way.

On March 8, 1808, Gov. Meriwether Lewis finally arrived in St. Louis and addressed the problem of finding a place to live. Lewis's presumption that the Gratiot family would give up their home may have been disappointing when he learned that it had been let to a relative and was not available for less than an annual rent of five hundred dollars. The governor settled on a house at the corner of South Main and Spruce, which only cost half that amount. It had a good cellar, four rooms on the first floor, quarters for slaves and servants upstairs, and porches on the east and south sides.[22] Reuben and Pernier set to work putting the place in order while Meriwether assumed the administration of Louisiana Territory, a duty he had evaded, some said neglected, for a year.

Governor Lewis was appalled to find that Secretary Bates had gotten himself in a dither over the legality of Governor Wilkinson's ban on foreign traders. Bates had decided that prohibiting British trade left the tribes of the Des Moines River drainage insufficiently supplied. The previous winter he became concerned that those tribes might not receive supplies to see them through the winter. Bates initially tried to ease tribal concerns by promising them places to trade near the mouth of the Des Moines River and at Prairie du Chien. But Col. Thomas Hunt, the commandant at Cantonment Belle Fontaine, lacked the troops to protect those distant stores or their supply lines.

That gave Bates an excuse to license the British trader Robert Dickson to continue supplying the tribes of that drainage. During the last winter Dickson's traders were *en derouine* (drumming up trade) and continued to propagandize tribes as far west as the middle Missouri. Bates had issued that wrongheaded license in November when Governor Lewis was on the road and unavailable to countermand it. On his arrival Governor Lewis immediately divested Bates of the authority for granting trade licenses.

Lewis recognized that the return of the Corps of Discovery had generated an entrepreneurial surge. Former members of the expedition told large tales about beaver beyond counting on the upper reaches of the Missouri. The demand for fiber for the hat industry was drawing beaver trappers ever deeper into the Indian country. But how would that opportunity of private initiative be received by the self-sufficient and fiercely independent tribes of the northern plains?

After a long experience of trading with British buyers, even distant tribes understood the value of furs as exchange for highly desirable items. They were likely to resent the exploitation of valuable natural resources. During the winter at Fort Mandan, Lewis and Clark had promised that the United States would supplant traders from the north in providing trade goods. But until government trading factories were built, the United States had no facilities in place to counter British inroads. Pryor's unfortunate encounter with the Arikara meant that it would be a long time before any Indians traded at a Mandan government factory. Worse, the Arikara incident was almost four months old and there were ominous possibilities that three trading and trapping expeditions that had gone up the Missouri, ahead of the military party, could very well be marooned above the hostile blockade with no safe way of returning.[23]

Despite Lewis's Anglophobic bias, one of the first licenses he issued went to a young Scot named Ramsay Crooks. Admittedly, Crooks had prior association with Dickson and his wily wintering trader James Aird. But the young man had declared US citizenship and thrown in with the bona fide American trader Robert McClellan. The previous spring when three other parties set out for the upper river, McClellan and Crooks also considered going up the Missouri toward the Great Falls. That plan was put on hold when they were discouraged by disaster to the Pryor party and the depressed price for furs.[24]

The Chouteau family of St. Louis was also inconvenienced. After losing four boatmen in the Arikara fiasco, young Pierre August Chouteau Jr. headed downstream to the overworked Yankton business. What trade he made was mostly mooted because the spring fur market was glutted by unsalable furs. Deerskins had been as good as legal tender, but the only way Auguste Chouteau could realize their value was by resorting to nefarious use of the old Montreal connection. He sent them across the Chicago portage to Michilimackinac and then on to Montreal.[25]

No one doubted that the Chouteau brothers were a force in the Osage trade. When Lewis interviewed General Wilkinson at Richmond, the former governor cautioned against putting to much confidence in them because the family had meddled with Pike's expedition. Pierre Chouteau was protective of the Osage sinecure and maintained that the tribe had given him a large tract of land for trading with them.[26]

The uncertainty of the mails meant that the new governor was on his own. Moses Austin and others had already complained to the postmaster general about the laxity of the mails. Although their complaint reached Washington in less than a month, some winter mail took as long as forty-two days in transit. At the end of March Lewis suspected that his letters had been held up at Cahokia for several days. He had written to Clark's brother-in-law Denis Fitzhugh and to the Louisville publisher Joseph Charless to arrange for a printing press. A press was needed immediately as the Territorial Legislature would meet the second Monday of June to revise the laws of the territory and, no doubt, add others.[27] Citizens needed to be properly informed.

On April 29, Lewis wrote to Fitzhugh at Louisville enclosing funds to enable the newspaper editor Charless to move his press to St. Louis. The governor had solicited $95 in banknotes from other citizens and added a bill of exchange for $100 drawn upon the War Department. He authorized Fitzhugh to add an additional $30 of his funds, making a total of $225 to get the paper started. Perhaps Clark or Fitzhugh would kick in another $30 each.

No matter what the postmaster general promised, post riders could not overcome the difficulties of traveling during a horrendous winter. When the rider drowned trying to cross the swollen Little Wabash River, the funds were lost.[28] Learning of this disaster the governor hoped to intercept Clark at Louisville. Lewis added an addendum that should Clark have left the falls, Fitzhugh was requested to see to the arrangements to get Charless started. This letter was dated May 29 but was still waiting on June 1 when Lewis added the addendum.[29]

Charless performed a small miracle in moving a press, type cases, and other paraphernalia from Louisville to St. Louis in time to publish the first edition of the *Missouri Gazette* on July 12. On July 22 Lewis wrote a government bill of exchange for five hundred dollars and endorsed it in favor of Charless through the facility of Fitzhugh & Rose.[30] On August 18 Fitzhugh advised Secretary of State Madison that he had forwarded that check to the firm of Henry Schroeder & Company of Baltimore.[31] It had taken more than four and a half months to get one important order of territorial business completed. As far as immediate decisions were concerned, Lewis had to make them first and clear the approval of a distant administration later.

Meantime, the governor was obliged to make a private investment. In accordance with the requirements of the Northwest Ordinance that territorial governors own land in their jurisdiction, Lewis purchased, for an unspecified down payment, about 7,100 acres of land in the St. Louis neighborhood for $5,530.[32] When Lewis encouraged their mutual friend Maj. William Preston to take a plunge in real estate, Clark was trying to get a nephew to join him in a mercantile adventure.[33]

Lewis had sent Ensign Pryor, a patroon, and crew of engaged boatmen with a boat to meet the Clark family.[34] William Clark, his bride, and their entourage finally arrived in St. Louis on the first of July. As Lewis had arranged, they initially lived together in what he considered the commodious house at the corner of South Main and Spruce Street.[35] It was a happy time for him in the company of the charming Julia and her husband's niece, Miss Ann Anderson. Merriment may have ended with the emptying of Jonathan Clark's case of wine on the twenty-fifth when Meriwether wrote a chatty letter to Major Preston, who was married to Julia's sister.[36] But Meriwether was still without a wife and the bachelor's presence in those snug quarters became increasingly uncomfortable to the new bride.[37] The close relationship that Lewis initially enjoyed soon had to give way to the pregnant Julia's need for some privacy.

The dedicated researcher Grace Lewis Miller suggested that Meriwether Lewis moved into an office on Main Street but still took his meals with the Clark family.[38] After Clark returned from Fort Osage in October he moved his family into a larger house. But Lewis remained close to the family.

Both men began working together to resolve demanding public problems. For generations the tribes on the lower river and the French population of Louisiana had lived in relative harmony. Now both were being swamped by immigration. As greedy American newcomers overran the land, the old French habitants found their Spanish land titles being challenged. Most of their proofs of prior occupancy were thin or nonexistent, and the governor was not optimistic that the land law and appointed board would resolve those problems.

Delaware and Shawnee fugitives from tribal dispossession had crossed the Mississippi River and resettled to the south, on the fringes of Osage tribal territory. Lewis later admitted that Indians were "exceedingly troublesome during the last winter and spring" but by mid-July he felt that he had "succeeded in managing those on the Mississippi . . . [although] the Osage and others on the Missouri are yet in a threatening position."[39] The Osage and their northern rivals, the Sac, Fox, and Iowa, continued to raid and counterraid. That might have been passed off as the usual war gamesmanship, except that expanding settlement was creeping between them. Incidents between whites and Indians were inevitable.

In 1805 from Fort Mandan, Clark had recommended a string of military posts to pacify the tribes and discourage intrusive British traders. Now was the time to begin. Belle Fontaine was no longer a viable location for the Indian trade factory and needed to be moved to a location more accessible to the tribes. That required a military guard but the federal forces stationed at the cantonment were inadequate. On the excuse that he required definite instructions from the War Department, the veteran officer and old minuteman Col. Thomas Hunt had balked at having to protect the trade factories that Frederick Bates tried to establish on the Mississippi in 1807, or a new place up the Missouri.

On May 17 Secretary of War Dearborn wrote that the decision had been made to build a military post and trading establishment at the Osage River and required the colonel to support it. The military post was meant to interdict vicious exchanges between the tribes.[40] As soon as he had a reliable friend to command that operation, Governor Lewis began planning a post that would plant a barrier across the intertribal war trail.[41] The plans were decided by July 21 when Clark wrote his brother that he would start in mid-August with a reinforced military expedition to build a fort and trade factory up the Missouri River at Fire Prairie.[42]

After encouraging and helping privately finance the establishment of the first printing press in St. Louis, the governor used it to disclose his plans for the territory. On August 2, in the second issue of the *Missouri Gazette*, editor Charless published the first half of Lewis's "Observations and Reflections" on the future of Louisiana. This was prefaced by the statement:

> We shall find this subject of primary importance, whether we consider it as connected with the defence of our much extended and defenceless frontier, the benefits which ought of right to accrue to the United States from the possession of Louisiana, or the future expenditure of blood and treasure, which may be involved in the defence of this country.[43]

Using the blatantly obvious nom de plume "Clatsop," the editor published a long article that amounted to a homily to the practitioners of the old fur trade on the history of their business, its future, and the measures necessary to correct abuses. The reasoned, forward-looking outline was an attempt to inform the public how the government of the territory intended to proceed.[44]

Three days later, the St. Louis entrepreneur Manuel Lisa and the former expedition hunter George Drouillard returned to St. Louis on August 5, 1808. They had built a trading post on the Yellowstone River at the mouth of the Big Horn and generally got on well with the resident Crows. Uninterested in packs of musty beaver, the Arikara had allowed them to pass without incident. When Lisa confirmed that those river towns wanted munitions to resist their enemies and manufactured articles to make their lives easier, he likely didn't emphasize that two other trading parties and his outfit had bypassed those eager customers last year. The Omaha, Yankton, Teton, Arikara, Mandan, and Hidatsa who once controlled river traffic were being neglected in favor of tribes that had beaver to trade. That was what had turned the Arikara sour when the Chouteau party arrived with the intention of going to the Mandans.

George Drouillard, the former hunter for the Corps of Discovery, provided the first description of the expansive Big Horn Country, which Clark transcribed into a rough sketch map. Lewis later made an ink copy that included some notations about the distance to Santa Fe.[45]

The interest in Santa Fe did not depend entirely upon what Lisa and Drouillard told him. There may have been another astonishing report when a former corpsman, John B. Thompson, came to collect his land warrant and immediately sell it for ready cash.[46] Thompson had traveled west of the mountains with the Santa Fe–bound trader that the expedition encountered as they returned in September 1806. After his adventure to New Mexico was diverted, former captain John McClallen went up the Yellowstone in spring 1807 and crossed the Rocky Mountains that fall. That made him the first American officer in the West after the return of Lewis and Clark. Because Thompson traveled with him, the former soldier knew a good deal about British activities west of the mountains.[47]

Meanwhile, on August 20 the two former explorers considered that it might be necessary for Lewis to return east. What he needed to do was to go to Philadelphia and try to get the expedition book back on track. The experts he left working on the natural history and scientific components needed to be consulted and encouraged. More important, Lewis needed some quiet place to write the first two parts that he had described in the prospectus. And a lot of other matters had come up that Lewis would like to discuss with headquarters.

In his role as brigadier general of militia, Clark would take a mounted force of eighty militiamen overland while a company of regulars moved the necessary building supplies by boat. Despite the untimely death of Colonel Hunt, the expedition to Fire Prairie started west on August 24.[48] Although he was seriously ill during the building of the new fort at a place known as Fire Prairie, William Clark exceeded expectations.[49] In addition to bringing the troublesome Kansa to heel, the Brigadier Clark also convinced the Little and Great Osage to accept a treaty ceding their lands between the Missouri and the Arkansas "for three hundred miles back." They agreed to move close to the factory where they were under the protection of the fort.[50]

When William Clark returned to St. Louis in October, difficulties about the treaty immediately developed. Three days after Clark returned, Pierre Chouteau, the authorized Osage Indian agent told Lewis that the Osage were already complaining that they had been deceived. Governor Lewis rewrote Clark's treaty to answer Chouteau's concerns and sent the Osage agent back to have it signed again.[51] In accordance with long-standing federal regulations prohibiting private citizens from dealing directly with tribes, Lewis did not include Chouteau's claim that the Osage had previously ceded him a huge tract of their lands. Clark had created a rift between Chouteau and himself that would have serious future implications.

Preventing intertribal warfare was about all that Lewis could expect to immediately accomplish toward his stated purpose of bringing the western tribes into a harmonious relationship with the United States. But Clark's unilateral treaty was the first taking of tribal territory west of the Mississippi. The fort he built also drove a wedge between the Osage and Spanish meddling with the tribes of the southwestern plains.

Personal initiative was necessary because of the slow communications with Washington. Governor Lewis endured a glacially slow mail service that sometimes delayed or lost his letters. Adding to the confusion of official intentions, messages often passed each other on the trail. In the present time of instantaneous e-mails, faxes, and telephones, it is almost inconceivable that an officer had to wait two or three months for an important exchange with headquarters. Foreseeing a communication problem may have influenced Jefferson's reason for sending Lewis to the distant territory. His protégé had already proved that he was capable of operating beyond supervision.

It was somewhat of a shock in late August 1808 when Lewis received a stern letter from President Jefferson admonishing him for not writing since September 1807. Meriwether was puzzled by that criticism because he sent a long report to the secretary of war on the first of July with the expectation that it would be forwarded to the president. His letter described in detail the initial accomplishments of the first four months. But Dearborn left Washington for the summer and the governor's letter had been held at the War Department instead of being forwarded to Monticello.[52]

Jefferson's apparent loss of patience with the governor became a comedy of misinterpretation when later historians fixed upon this letter to Lewis as proof of a declining relationship between the two friends. Few have studied Lewis's impressive report or bothered to consult the letter that Jefferson wrote on August 21 recognizing the oversight. In that, Jefferson expressed his embarrassment that the reprimand was on its way when he finally received Lewis's report.[53]

In the July report Lewis mentioned difficulties between citizens and wandering Indians. Three apparent murderers of whites had been apprehended and scheduled for trial in St. Louis. Concerned about a harsh reaction, Jefferson the humanist recommended giving the Indians more time "to know our dispositions . . . but if we use forbearance and open commerce with them, they will come to and give us time to attach them to us."[54] Lewis was no more in favor of harsh dealing with Indians than Jefferson, but he felt that firm action was necessary and was prepared to let a court decide.

After speaking with a cousin of Lewis who had been with the governor in July, the president still tried to micromanage Indian affairs from long distance. Jefferson suggested that if only one white man had been killed, only one of the Indian prisoners should be executed, which would demonstrate "that all our dispositions toward them are fatherly."[55]

Jefferson also wrote that he had instructed Secretary of War Dearborn to break up British factories (trading posts) "without our limits on this side of the Mississippi and let them trade in the future only at fixed points, and to suppress their itinerant traders as well as our own."[56] The federal trade factory system had been set up to ensure equitable treatment of Indians with furs to trade, but petty traders off on their own were capable of excesses. Ominously, Jefferson added that if foreign affairs did not clear up "it may be a question for the legislature whether war will not be preferable to a longer continuance of the embargo."[57] Louisiana was very much part of the national strategy and Lewis might be commanding a second front if the British in Upper Canada incited the Indians.[58]

President Jefferson also mentioned that a powerful company was forming to take up the Indian commerce on a grand scale. Conceived by a "most excellent man, a Mr. Astor," the new concern would begin with an initial capitalization of three hundred thousand dollars to be raised to a million as the organization required. The visionary was expected to visit St. Louis and Governor Lewis should pay attention to him, as "Nothing but the exclusive possession of the Indian commerce can secure us their peace."[59]

Astor & Company planned to make a commanding competitive establishment on the upper Mississippi. To protect the American enterprise Lewis suggested posts at the mouth of the Wisconsin and at Dog Meadow (Prairie du Chien). Lewis must have received the president's letter by mid-August when General Clark was preparing to leave to construct Fort Osage at Fire Prairie.

Then Lewis learned of the death of the Prairie du Chien agent John Campbell. In early June, to block any further adventures by Dickson (whom Bates had favored), Lewis had assured Campbell that he would not issue any trading licenses in that part of the country without consulting him. That inspired Campbell to go to the summer rendezvous of Indian traders

at Mackinac Island, where he expressed some strong feelings about the special license from Bates that kept Robert Dickson & Company afloat during
the previous winter. Words were exchanged, and as a consequence, one of
Dickson's friends challenged Campbell to a duel and killed him.[60] Lewis
could not escape wondering what bearing his actions had on the tragedy.

That left Nicholas Boilvin as the governor's man on the upper Mississippi. Boilvin had been around the St. Louis area before the American
Revolution and declared his citizenship after the Louisiana Purchase. At
present he was the agent for the Sac and Fox but would have to inherit the
slain (or maybe assassinated) Campbell's post at Prairie du Chien.[61] In
August an old friend of Bates advised Secretary Dearborn that Dickson
intended to go to Washington and seek the Prairie du Chien agency for
himself. There is no indication that Bates communicated that information
to the governor.[62]

When Clark returned from the newly established Fort Osage, the two
former explorers discussed what had been learned about the upper Missouri
from the return of Lisa and Drouillard. The Indian trade and beaver hunt
was an opportunity for the Louisiana Territory to start paying its way, but
that promise could not be allowed to slip into the hands of British competitors or East Coast financiers like Mr. Astor. Gaining control over the
tribes through commerce required restricting the activities of traders to
places where they could be properly supervised. At the new Osage factory
petty traders and trappers had been left under the supervision of the newly
appointed factor, John Sibley, or his assistant Reuben Lewis.

In May Governor Lewis had authorized the Maha trader Robert
McClellan and his partner Ramsay Crooks to ascend the Missouri with pro-
visions for his trading establishment. The new license restricted "Robert
McClellan & Company; to trade at the Fire Prairie, with authority to the
Agent or Sub Agent of that place, to extend the license, as to embrace such
portion of the upper country as he (said Agent) may judge proper."[63] But
François Robidoux, an established trader at the Blacksnake Hills, and
McClellan and Crooks found it increasingly difficult to contest with an
entrenched competitor.[64] Instead of encouraging the Indian trade, new reg-
ulations were dragging it down.

Trading regulations also applied as far south as the Arkansas River. To
enforce the law, Lewis was lucky that Clark was not the only friend he could
rely on. Not long after he took over as governor, an old association had
reawakened. The name McFarlane seems to bracket Lewis's western career.
The relationship had begun when Lewis was in the Pittsburgh area helping

put down the Whiskey Rebellion. In an earlier riot Capt. James McFarlane, a leader of the rebels, had been shot and killed. As a lesson to trouble-makers, the occupation force went into winter quarters on the farm of the dead captain's brother, Andrew McFarlane. During the winter Lewis became acquainted with the family. In 1803, while waiting for his boats to be completed, Lewis visited the McFarlanes. As he passed down the Ohio the explorer wrote an affidavit recommending that Andrew McFarlane should be reimbursed for losses he suffered during the Whiskey Rebellion.[65]

At some time before 1807 at least three sons of the McFarlane family, James, Lewis, and Andrew, had drifted into the Louisiana Territory. After Governor Lewis arrived, their fortunes improved considerably. On April 14 in response to the War Department authorization to hire someone to examine a reported saltpeter mine on the Osage River, Lewis made out a government draft for $126 to James McFarlane. He also asked the Belle Fontaine blacksmith to shoe the horse of Lewis McFarlane and another man only identified as Mr. Shannon.[66]

The examination of the saltpeter mine was promising and Lewis wrote another draft for McFarlane on July 1. Eleven days later McFarlane was still around the office when he witnessed a small loan that Lewis made to his cousin Isham Lewis.[67]

Before the treaty locking the troublesome Osage to the new fort and factory came into force, the Big Osage band moved to the Arkansas River where they received goods from unlicensed traders. On August 20 Lewis instructed Secretary Bates to warn the temporary Indian agent at the mouth of the Arkansas to deny trade to those dissidents and enforce his order against violators. Much as the whiskey rebels had objected years before, the Arkansas liquor-trading opportunists resented meddling in their business. The governor turned to McFarlane, whom Clark described as "a porticuler friend of his."[68] On September 16 McFarlane was described as a special agent who was being sent to examine disturbing developments on the Arkansas River.

Governor Lewis had set off the district of the Arkansas from the overextended district of New Madrid. That required several new appoint-ments including John Honey, who became clerk of the Courts of Common Pleas and Quarter Sessions, treasurer, and judge of probate for the new dis-trict.[69] Traveling from St. Louis to the Arkansas with secret agent McFar-lane, Honey professed to be relieved when McFarlane broke off to go up the St. Francis River. He found him a boastful, ill-educated companion, too much taken with his new authority.[70]

To the barely concealed indignation of Artillery Capt. George Armistead, Mr. McFarlane arrived on the Arkansas at the end of November. On the way the special agent made a side trip up the St. Francis River to put the fear of the government into some Cherokees and their illicit trader. McFarlane then stalled until the Osage returned from their fall hunt on the plains. After talking to them, he meant to assemble a gang of militia and Indians and sweep the river clear of unlicensed traders. The lack of supplies would force the Big Osage to return to the Missouri and accept the supervision of the new agency. Despite the negative reactions of Honey and Captain Armistead, James McFarlane does not appear to have been a bad choice for an enforcer.[71]

The Osage problems were not part of a larger matter as were the tribes being assembled up the Mississippi and toward the Great Lakes. As Clark saw it, "This Warlike Spirit or Indian Prophet who has his deputies in different parts of this Country destroying the quiet and tranquility of the different Bands and tribes and inducing them to War; is said to be under British influence which extends from the Mississippi quite to Lake Erie."[72]

The administration in Washington was also concerned because of the possibility of war with Britain. President Jefferson wrote from Monticello to Secretary of War Dearborn mentioning a report he had received from Lake Champlain in upper New York. The US customs collector there had occasion to make a visit to Montreal and, as he returned, counted the British garrisons of Chambly, St. Jean's, Oldetown, and Isle aux Noix. There were a total of only 594 soldiers in those decayed old forts and ten thousand men could take the whole country to within a league of Quebec. That must have caused Dearborn, a Maine man, to think that memory was short. In the first year of the Revolution rebels had tried to invade Canada. That near conquest expired, like the enlistments of the militia in the New Year's Eve blizzard under the walls of Quebec.

What that exchange showed was that the Jefferson administration was thinking ahead in case the embargo failed to convince Great Britain. When Dearborn received Jefferson's letter of the twentieth, the old soldier was visiting and checking arsenals and armories in support of the call for the hundred-thousand-man army.[73] But the nation was in no way prepared to conduct an offensive war.

Although neglected in an earlier list, in November, the Louisiana Territory was called upon to furnish its quota of militia for the hundred-thousand-man army. Governor Lewis was required to provide 377 militiamen to serve for twelve months. In his general order of November 28 the former recruiter ended the long specifics with a rousing message.

We are called upon fellow citizens to be a part, when the effort shall be necessary, in defending our liberties and ours from the unhallowed grasp of the modern barbarians of Europe, who insatiate with the horrid butcheries of the eastern world, are now bending their course towards our peaceful and happy shore; we must be prepared to meet them; the cup of accommodation has been drained. . . . National degradation and oppression await a state of inactivity and want of zeal to defend our country and our liberties . . . shrink not therefore, fellow citizens from the task; shielded with the justice of our cause we are doubly armed.[74]

Two weeks after the revised Osage treaty was dated on November 10, Clark wrote a long letter to his brother. "Governor Lewis is here and talks of going to philadelphia to finish our books this winter, he has put if off So long that I fear they will [not] bring us much."[75] The trip was still on Lewis's mind in mid-December when he mentioned in a letter to President Jefferson that Bates claimed to be unqualified for Indian affairs and did not want to assume those duties if the governor went east.[76] Secretary Bates thought that Clark should have the responsibility. By then plans had developed to the point where Clark had agreed to provide Lewis with two of his horses that were in Louisville. The traveler could ride the animals east and sell them there. Jonathan Clark was warned that his brother "wants the horses fatuned" for the long ride ahead.[77]

In a mid-December letter to the president, Governor Lewis explained that the "want of cordiality and confidence" between General Clark and Osage Agent Chouteau had grown as a consequence of the Osage treaty. Because their appointments were distinct, neither had power to control the other. That could be a problem as "I shall be obliged to leave the territory shortly for Washington and Philadelphia" and Secretary Bates refused to accept the duties of the Indian department during his absence. Siding with his friend, Lewis recommended that Clark be invested with some general power of control over the agents and subagents, although Chouteau was still useful and should be retained.[78] By then the lack of cordiality was healing as Chouteau and Clark began working together to organize a new trading company.

As his eventful first year as governor wound down, Lewis looked back on a productive nine months and generally satisfying accomplishments. He had taken action on the Indian problems that faced him when he arrived last March, moving firmly to address the Osage problem and seeing it resolved with a treaty. A strong fort and convenient trade factory should keep them in line. He intended to send his special agent McFarlane back to the Arkansas River to bring the dissidents into the fold. Legal proceedings were under way against scofflaws who failed to get trade licenses. The Sac delivered the murderers to be tried in the court of the territory. After a false start at Bellevue, another new fort and factory was guarding the mouth of the Des Moines River to prevent troublemaking British traders from intruding. He had done what he could from long distance to inhibit the tribal confederation that was gathering on Tippecanoe Creek. Discussions about organizing a large trading expedition for the Yellowstone were under way and, if properly organized and supported, should be strong enough to brush aside the Arikara and return the Mandan chief to his people. In advising Mr. Jefferson that "I shall be obliged to leave the territory shortly for Washington and Philadelphia," Lewis confirmed that he intended to keep the expedition book moving forward.[79]

During this busy time, Lewis also had the satisfaction of helping establish the Masonic Lodge, Saint Louis No. 111. Wearing the symbolic apron of a builder, Lewis was pleased to think that he had done something to foster a benevolent institution and gratified to have been elected its first Worshipful Master. That role involved him in preparations for the Christmas observances and a public display of the brotherhood of man.[80]

On two past Christmases he and Clark had raised a tin cup of whatever they had, whiskey or water, in some god-forsaken place. But William was married now, and his bride heavy with child. Their friend didn't want to intrude in family affairs, so Meriwether Lewis and the valet Pernier may have had a quiet Christmas. Not far away, Frederick Bates spent a pathetic Christmas Day penning a long letter to the Secretary of the Treasury Gallatin.[81]

The town was lively because holidays brought out the French and their quaint customs. After Christmas they would be out on New Year's Eve, dancing their shuffling step as they took La Guignolee—the songs of carolers—from house to house. Pernier had prepared a rum punch to welcome those who called and Meriwether was already a bit heady in his expectations for 1809.

NOTES

1. Alexander Wilson, "Particulars of the Death of Capt. Lewis," Port Folio 7 (January 1812): 39.

2. John Pernier, a mulatto freeman, had worked for Jefferson since the beginning of October 1804. Massachusetts Historical Society, Thomas Jefferson's account book, March 24–May 1805, p. 18: "Servants Wages $14 to John Pernier,"

bottom left corner of page. Photocopies found in GLM, box 34, folder 20, JNEM. He began working for Lewis on July 1, 1807.

3. It appears that other household furniture may have been shipped by boat.

4. *National Intelligencer and Washington Advertiser*, February 22, 1808, p. 3.

5. ML to LM, February 15, 1808, MLC-MHS.

6. Bates had letters from Clark dated July 23 and 24 to which he responded on July 25 with the promise to write Clark in Louisville. On August 2 Bates indicates that Pierre Chouteau is acting as Indian agent in the absence of General Clark. Marshall, *FB* 1: 168–69.

7. WC to WD, May 9, 1807, RG107, M222, roll 2, frame 0772, NARA. For a critical study of William Clark as Indian agent for the Louisiana Territory, see Jay H. Buckley, *William Clark: Indian Diplomat* (Norman: University of Oklahoma Press, 2008).

8. Carter, *TP* 14: 108–109.

9. Dickson and his partner Hancock met the corps as it returned and induced John Colter to return to the Yellowstone with them to trap beaver during the winter 1806–1807.

10. Thomas Hunt to HD, May 23, 1807, RG107, H242, M221, roll 8, frame 2462, NARA.

11. WC to SW, June 1, 1807, Carter, *TP* 14: 126–27.

12. James Holmberg, *Dear Brother* (New Haven, CT: Yale University Press, 2002), p. 126 and notes.

13. FB to HD, August 2, 1807, Marshall, *FB* 1: 168–70.

14. Thomas Hunt to HD, September 27, 1807, RG107, H301, M221, roll 8, frame 2569, NARA.

15. WC to HD, December 3, 1807, RG107, C378, "Kimball's Report," M221, roll 5, frame 1563, NARA.

16. Nathaniel Pryor to WC, October 16, 1807, Jackson, *LLC* 2: 432–38; WC to SW, June 1, 1807, Carter, *TP* 14: 126–27.

17. Nathaniel Pryor to WC, October 16, 1807, Jackson, *LLC* 2: 432–38.

18. John Campbell to HD, April 7, 1808, RG107, H161, M221, roll 23, NARA. William Clark, a longtime friend of Campbell, had sent a letter in April 1804 from River Dubois asking him to be on the lookout for any unusual activity that could interfere with the expedition. Campbell to WC, C350, M221, roll 5, frame 1489, NARA.

19. Personal account book, February 1808, MLC-MHS.

20. FB to these persons: January 16 to ML; February 23 to James Abbott, and February 26, 1808, to Richard Bates, Marshall, *FB* 1: 265, 300, 304. Reuben Lewis and the furniture arrived on February 25. Richard Dillon, *Meriwether Lewis: A Biography* (Santa Cruz, CA: Western Tanager Press, 1965), p. 298.

21. Alexander Balinky, *Albert Gallatin, Fiscal Theories and Policies* (New Brunswick: Rutgers University Press, 1958), pp. 136–37.

22. ML to WC, May 29, 1808, CFC-MHS. This was the Fine-Noise-Campbell

& Matlack house on Block 37B, Map Extension 3 of the St. Louis by the River 1804 map on the National Park Service Web site "The Lewis & Clark Journey of Discovery; St. Louis: The Town as Seen by Lewis and Clark," http://nps.gov/archive Jeff/LewisClark2/Circa1804/Circa1804Main.htm (accessed April 5, 2008). In 1807 Campbell and Matlack had built a stable and an eighteen-by-sixty-foot warehouse. The location is also discussed in detail in Grace Lewis, "The First Home of Governor Lewis in Louisiana Territory," *Missouri Historical Society Bulletin* 14 (July 1958): 360–68.

23. The three were the McClallen party initially headed for Santa Fe but diverted, the small Courtin trapping party, and the larger adventure to the Yellowstone by Manuel Lisa and George Drouillard.

24. David Lavender, *The Fist in the Wilderness* (Garden City, NY: Doubleday, 1964), pp. 88–90, 95–96, 98–99.

25. William E. Foley and David C. Rice, *The First Chouteaus: River Barons of Early St. Louis* (Urbana: University of Illinois Press, 1983), pp. 168–70, 172.

26. Carter, *TP* 14: 243.

27. In his list of bills Lewis drew no. 9 on April 24, 1808, against his second-quarter salary that was not due until the first of July. No. 10 against the second quarter was to Joseph Charless for $100 with an additional $95 in bank bills and an order on General Clark to Fitzhugh. This was a loan to help Charless establish a printing press in St. Louis.

28. ML to SW, August 20, 1808, Carter, *TP* 14: 212.

29. ML to WC, May 29, 1808, CFC-MHS. At the bottom of the letter, Lewis had written an addendum dated June 1, 1808.

30. Denis Fitzhugh to JMA, August 18, 1808, RG59, M179, roll 22, p. 88, NARA.

31. Lewis believed bills for printing the laws were attributable to the State Department and kept a separate list of those numbers. No. 1 to Pierre Provenchere, $71.50 for translating laws of the territory into French. No. 2 on 22 July 22, 1808, to Charless, $500 for paper and printing laws of the territory, $250 in English, and $100 in French. As will be shown later these became the basis of unfounded hype concerning the governor's refused bills.

32. James R. Bentley, "Two Letters of Meriwether Lewis to Major William Preston," *Filson Club History Quarterly* 44 (April 1970): 173.

33. Holmberg, *Dear Brother*, p. 167.

34. ML to WC, May 29, 1808, CFC-MHS.

35. Landon Jones states that Lewis rented a house from John Campbell, the Prairie du Chien agent, but Campbell had been a resident of that place for eighteen years. Landon Y. Jones, *William Clark the Shaping of the West* (New York: Hill and Wang, 2004), p. 172; John Campbell to WC, August 16, 1807, RG107, M221, roll 5, frame 1489, NARA.

36. Jones, *William Clark and the Shaping of the West*, p. 161. Preston had paid Clark's marriage bond.

37. Holmberg, *Dear Brother*, p. 139n3.

38. Stephen Ambrose, *Undaunted Courage* (New York: Simon & Schuster, 1996), p. 438, drawing upon the GLM collection. But it appears that the house Clark rented was later used as Eagle Tavern.

39. Bentley, "Two Letters of Meriwether Lewis to Major William Preston," pp. 173–74.

40. FB to HD, October 22, 1807, Marshall, *FB* 1: 221–24; SW to Thomas Hunt, May 17, 1808, Carter, *TP* 14: 184.

41. John Mason to Rudolph Tillier, May 27; WC to SW, June 25; ML to SW, July 1; and WC to SW, August 18, 1808. Carter, *TP* 14: 188, 194, 200, 209–10.

42. Holmberg, *Dear Brother*, p. 143.

43. Jackson's editorial introduction to "Observations," *LLC* 2: 697.

44. *Missouri Gazette*, August 2, 1808, pp. 2–3.

45. Sketches of the country of the Big Horn obtained from George Drewyer (Drouillard), September 6, 1808, CFC-MHS.

46. This is based on the coincidence that John B. Thompson assigned his land warrant to George Gibson, August 12, 1808, deed book B, p. 152, City of St. Louis.

47. Thompson's attachment to the McClallen party is speculative but based on a growing body of evidence concerning the enigmatic officer's astonishing career.

48. Kate L. Gregg, ed., *Westward with Dragoons: The Journal of William Clark on His Expedition to Establish Fort Osage, August 25 to September 22, 1807* (Fulton, MO: Ovid Bell Press, 1937); Zebulon Pike to Thomas Cushing, August 18, 1808, RG94, M566, roll 1, frame 0197; James House to HD, August 19, 1808, RG107, H171, M221, roll 23, NARA.

49. Gregg, *Westward with Dragoons*, pp. 25–39, 45; Holmberg, *Dear Brother*, pp. 151, 154.

50. Holmberg, *Dear Brother*, p. 154.

51. Jones, *William Clark and the Shaping of the West*, pp. 168–69; ASP, *Indian Affairs*, 1: 766–67.

52. TJ to ML, August 21, 1808, Carter, *TP* 14: 219.

53. ML to SW, July 1 and August 20, 1808, Carter, *TP* 14: 196–203, 212–22.

54. Carter, *TP* 14: 220.

55. TJ to ML, August 24, 1808, Carter, *TP* 14: 221.

56. Carter, *TP* 14: 220.

57. Ibid.

58. HD to TJ, September 4, 1808, document 32017-18, roll 42, TJ-LOC.

59. TJ to ML, July 17, 1808, Jackson, *LLC* 2: 444–45.

60. George Hoffman to HD, August 15, 1808, RG107, H158, M221, roll 23, frame 7358; Stanley Griswold to Thomas Cushing, August 27, 1808, RG94, M566, roll 3, frame 0898, NARA.

61. Nicholas Boilvin to Thomas Cushing, October 8, 1808, RG94, M566, roll 2, frame 0589, p. 173, NARA; Lavender, *The Fist in the Wilderness*, p. 180.

62. After Campbell's death, Robert Dickson left for Washington to seek the job

of Indian agent (Frederick Bates Papers, box 4, letterbook 1795–1809, BFP-MHS). On September 15 seven gentlemen of Michilimackinac warned the secretary of war that Dickson meant to gain a position where he could favor his associates and influence the Indians against the states.

63. Marshall, *FB* 2: 33.

64. See Lavender, *The Fist in the Wilderness*, pp. 106–108, for another perspective on this development. By February 17, 1809, they admitted their breakup although the news was not published in the *Missouri Gazette* until April 12.

65. Moulton, *JLCE* 1: 138.

66. Holmberg, *Dear Brother*, p. 151. This is also discussed in Larry E. Morris, *The Fate of the Corps: What Became of the Lewis and Clark Explorers after the Expedition* (New Haven, CT: Yale University Press, 2004). Could this have been the youngest member of the Corps of Discovery, George Shannon? A native of Washington County, Pennsylvania, Shannon had been one of the first men whom Captain Lewis recruited at Pittsburgh, where the five Shannon brothers were not that distant of neighbors of the McFarlanes. It is possible that one of Shannon's brothers came west to look after George, who lost his leg as a consequence of the Arikara fiasco. William Clark continued George's employment with the War Department until October 1808 when he left for Lexington, Kentucky, to pursue legal studies.

67. In descending from Louisville with the boatload of furniture and household property, Reuben Lewis may have stopped to visit Col. Charles Lewis and his wife, Jefferson's sister Lucy, who had moved from Albemarle County to western Kentucky earlier that year. Sons Randolph and Lilburn purchased considerable tracts of largely undeveloped land along the Ohio in Livingston County. Another of the colonel's sons, Isham, may have joined Reuben or followed later. A second cousin of Meriwether and Reuben Lewis, Isham was also a nephew of Jefferson. On August 24, 1808, Jefferson writes that Isham Lewis had "arrived last night and tells me he was with you at St. Louis" (Carter, *TP* 14: 221). Lilburn and Isham later became notorious for the murder of a slave in 1811, on the day before the famous New Madrid earthquake.

68. Holmberg, *Dear Brother*, p. 218.

69. John Honey appears to have been a former army officer whose resignation opened a slot for Ens. Nathaniel Pryor's promotion to second lieutenant: Nathaniel Pryor to AG, May 3, 1808, RG94, M1094, roll 1, NARA. Honey also appears to have been a half brother of the land board clerk Thomas F. Riddick (Marshall, *FB* 2: 92).

70. John Honey to FB, January 12, 1809, Marshall, *FB* 2: 54–60.

71. George Armistead to FB, November 30, 1808, Marshall, *FB* 2: 44.

72. WC to SW, April 29, 1809, Carter, *TP* 14: 264–70.

73. HD to the governors, October 28, 1808, RG107, M370, roll 3, NARA.

74. Militia Orders, November 28, 1808, Carter, *TP* 14: 236–41; *Missouri Gazette*, February 1, 1809, p. 1.

75. Holmberg, *Dear Brother*, p. 172.

76. Lewis also had sent a letter to his mother informing her that he planned to go east. ML to LM, December 1, 1808, MLC-MHS.

77. Holmberg, *Dear Brother*, p. 187.

78. *ASP, Indian Affairs* 1: 766–67.

79. Ibid.

80. Ray V. Denslow, *Territorial Masonry, the Story of Freemasonry and the Louisiana Purchase, 1804–1821* (Washington, DC: Masonic Service Association of the United States, 1925), p. 19. Saint Louis Lodge No. 111 commenced on November 9, 1808, while December 27 celebrates St. John the Evangelist, which marks the end of the Apostolic age (C. C. Hunt, *The Holy Saints John* [Cedar Rapids: Iowa Masonic Library, 1923], p. 20).

81. FB to AG, December 25, 1808, Marshall, *FB* 2: 47–54.

TWELVE

Reflections in a Cesspool

The anguish that his soul assail[1]

W hat Governor Lewis accomplished during the first ten months of his administration was done under a darkening cloud of his relationship with Territorial Secretary Frederick Bates. Lewis's impressions of St. Louis were like images caught by a dance hall strobe. He had known the place for several months over the winter 1803–1804 while the expedition was being organized, and after a two-and-a-half-year hiatus, he returned in the fall 1806 to quickly catch up on what had transpired. Those were the not entirely heartening observations that he carried to the January 1807 meeting at the president's mansion.

Concern with the future government of Louisiana included Mr. Jefferson, Mr. Madison, Lewis, Clark, and a recently arrived public officer from Detroit, Frederick Bates. Although Secretary of the Treasury Albert Gallatin wasn't present at the gathering, he must have recommended Bates as an experienced official who could be expected to pay close attention to detail.[2]

As the recently returned explorers related their impressions of the political situation in Louisiana, it was apparent that Territorial Secretary Joseph Browne was too closely associated to Aaron Burr and would have to be replaced. That was the immediate order of business but there was a problem. Captain Lewis would be the governor but he needed time to com-

213

plete details relating to the expedition and attend to matters concerning the publication of its results. Until the governor arrived, the new territorial secretary would have to assume the interim control of the territory. Frederick Bates later professed that he really didn't want the assignment, but agreed to go because it was the new hot spot of national interest.[3] When he accepted the appointment he was not entirely innocent of the situation he would face.

Bates was already on the trail west in late February when a former member of the Corps of Discovery, Pvt. Robert Frazer, arrived in Washington with a disturbing report of Burrite activities in St. Louis.[4] Earlier, in October 1806 Aaron Burr's coconspirator and chief of staff, Col. Julien de Pestre, arrived in St. Louis bringing a sheaf of proclamations and commissions to potential filibusters that he presented to David Delaunay, Pierre Provenchere, and Auguste Chouteau. Chouteau made the dramatic gesture of throwing his commission into the fire. When Provenchere traveled east with Pierre Chouteau and the Indian delegation, he carried a letter warning the president that a revolution would occur in the western states by November 15.[5]

De Pestre rode back to Lexington, Kentucky, in mid-October accompanied by militia Maj. Robert Wescott, acting governor Browne's son-in-law. As Wescott set out to return to St. Louis, he carried a letter from Burr to Governor Harrison at Vincennes. The conspiracy came to light on January 19, 1807, when Wescott and General Wilkinson's loyal supporter, Dr. Andrew Steele, rode south toward Ste. Genevieve intending to meet with militia colonel John Smith T. and district sheriff Henry Dodge. The plan was to ship a cargo of lead needed for munitions south to the mouth of the Ohio River to supply the army that Burr was bringing from the east.[6] When President Jefferson read the evidence that Frazer delivered to him in person, he realized that he had sent an unknown quantity to handle disloyalty in the Louisiana Territory.

Frederick Bates was a merchant's son from Virginia, where planters had always been the social elite. He seems to have gone through life with an undefined chip on his shoulder. After the United States finally took over the Great Lakes posts from the British in 1796, Bates's mercantile background led to his appointment in the quartermasters department at Detroit. Riding north from Pittsburgh on trails two feet deep in winter mud convinced Bates that supplying the troops by land was going to be difficult.

Those were the same difficult trails that Meriwether Lewis also traveled as a military courier and later as paymaster of the First Infantry Regiment. As military travelers, their duties took them to some of the same distant posts, but there is no direct proof that their paths crossed. What they shared were similar formative experiences that required attention to "punctuality & fidelity."

Over the next three years Bates's duties took him to the old fur trade depot of Michilimackinac. Although Britain had lost military control of the tribes, the provisions of Jay's Treaty continued to allow British traders access to the Indian trade of the Old Northwest and upper Mississippi River. Americans had to compete within the acknowledged boundaries of their own country. After visiting Fort Wayne in 1800, Bates decided to enter business for himself and obtained credit from a Schenectady, New York, mercantile house. His decision was timely, as within two years the quartermaster's office was superseded by a military agent for the middle department.

In addition to his Detroit business interests, Bates also began climbing the bureaucratic ladder, rising from deputy postmaster to receiver of public monies, land commissioner, and in 1805 associate judge. Those duties required careful accounting and full reports to the Treasury Department.[7] That was how Secretary of the Treasury Gallatin came to appreciate Bates's attention to duty and fiscal responsibility. In November 1806, when Bates left Detroit to deal with the tragic death of his brother Tarleton earlier that year, he also carried land board reports to Washington. Bates arrived about the time that Captain Lewis returned from his heroic exploration.[8] That was why he was available when the Jefferson administration needed someone to send to Louisiana.

Departing Washington almost unnoticed, Frederick Bates must have envied the public attention that Lewis was getting. He had a long winter ride in the cold month of March through endless frigid forests of naked branches with frozen mast from fallen leaves and dead fall crunching under hoof. The inns he found along the way were miserable, vermin-infested holes, and the alternative of approaching a lonely cabin unannounced risked insult, even danger, to get a meal and a decent bed.

Although he had an intellectual bent, Frederick Bates was not the kind of man to see the irony of arriving in St. Louis on April Fool's Day. Five days later he wrote the governor designate that the community already anticipated Lewis's appointment and that "it will be in your power to reunite the contending parties. Even the friends of Wilkinson, will be *satisfied* and perhaps *pleased* with your government." Bates believed that the differences between public officers who discredited the former administration gave Lewis "a fair opportunity of establishing a lasting reputation in Louisiana by composing the unhappy divisions of her Inhabitants."[9] Two days later the unreliable post was still waiting and Bates added that "Many of the Partizans of Gen. Wilkinson calculate on your treading in his footsteps . . . it would be *expedient* to *contradict* expectations . . . allay the fervors of party and take the fiery edge from animosities which have heretofore existed to the disgrace of the Government."[10] Already forming strong opinions, Bates did not suspect that for the next eleven months it would be up to him to resolve those questions.

The first instructions from Governor Lewis arrived with the returning Robert Frazer in early May.[11] Bates was told to leave Indian affairs to William Clark or to the designated Osage agent Pierre Chouteau, who returned to St. Louis on the fifteenth.[12] His first order of business was to politically emasculate Burrites.

Former territorial secretary Joseph Browne had downplayed any emergency but his son-in-law Robert Wescott was the only conspirator to be indicted and Frazer was a witness against him.[13] Bates wasted no time in disposing of "those unprincipled men who have been associated for subversion" and even less to inform the president.[14] But it was a week before he got around to filling in Governor Lewis after making a ten-day tour to acquaint himself with the region.

The lead mines in Ste. Genevieve district were the source of much turbulence and one of the conspirators, the notorious duelist John Smith T., had refused arrest.[15] By spending two days at the home of the most prominent mining entrepreneur, Moses Austin, Bates appeared to have allied himself with another faction. Through a prior Spanish land grant Austin had possession of nine square miles, the largest mine in the district. A progressive man, Austin had built a gristmill, a sawmill, and the area's first reverberatory furnace.[16] Convenient access to an efficient smelter allowed Austin to dominate the adjoining lead claims. It certainly helped their budding relationship that the secretary, through his dual role as a member of the land board, was in a position to dispose of Austin's competitors for lead holdings.

Austin convinced Bates that the former territorial secretary Joseph Browne and his associate John Smith T. were scheming to force miners off lead lands and appropriate those claims. Browne was the legal wizard and Smith T. the strong-arm. After returning to St. Louis, on May 1 Bates stripped Smith T. of his public offices and a week later made James Austin, a cousin of Moses Austin, Justice of the Peace and Justice of the Court of the Common Pleas.[17]

Although Bates warned Lewis that the former partisans of General Wilkinson "calculate your treading in his footsteps," he had immediately initiated what amounted to a new factional relationship. He came away from his conversations with Austin so impressed with the possibilities that he was already considering the purchase of a combination farm and lead lot nearby.[18]

But Bates misread the Jefferson administration's attitude toward former governor Wilkinson, who had been called to Richmond as the main witness in the trial of Aaron Burr. In reconsidering an important action by the Wilkinson administration, Bates questioned the legal basis for denying trading rights that had been given to British interests under Jay's Treaty. Governor Wilkinson had declared that a new purchase like Louisiana was outside that agreement and prohibited foreign access to the Missouri River. Bates wrote:

> I find myself totally in the dark on subjects of very material consequence. — For instance, with respect to the Indian trade on the Missouri: Shall Licenses be granted to trade among those nations with whom the U. States have heretofore had no intercourse: And shall the right to deny to foreigners, a participation in the trade west of the Mississippi be enforced?[19]

That could have been a careful man's review of a legal point. Or was it a holdover from the time he spent in Detroit or at Michilimackinac, where he had been acquainted with the British "southwest traders?" What the previous administration had done was cut off a large part of their business. Bates may have been sympathetic to their predicament but questioning Wilkinson's move to deny outside access to Louisiana was unlikely to be well received by President Jefferson.

By the end of summer, Governor Lewis was in Richmond comparing notes on the territory with General Wilkinson.[20] Having recently assessed the situation in St. Louis for himself, Lewis was not impressed by Bates's consideration of British intruders. His instructions to Bates were in a letter that the territorial secretary uncharacteristically failed to keep.[21]

Despite a poor understanding of the complexities of the Missouri River Indian trade, just eighteen days after he arrived and before he could have received an answer to his question, Bates authorized the St. Louis entrepreneur Manuel Lisa to trade and trap on the upper Missouri. Lisa intended to go as far as the Yellowstone River, among Indians yet unknown to the United States. By authorizing direct trapping of resources that the tribes considered their own, Bates unintentionally set up a disaster for a government party that followed.[22]

Six weeks after Bates took over, the first boats began arriving with the returns of last winter's Missouri River Indian trade. May was the first time that St. Louis became aware that Spanish meddling with the Pawnee had closed the way to New Mexico.[23] Bates should have been sensitive to the arrival of a boat from the Yankton trade where the deflected Santa Fe entrepreneur Capt. John McClallen had wintered. McClallen sent the peltry he had traded in care of former territorial secretary Browne with the explanation that he now intended to proceed up the Missouri River.[24] It is unlikely that the disaffected Browne would have shared that information with Bates, but rumors from returning boatmen certainly circulated around St. Louis.

On May 15 Indian agent William Clark arrived in St. Louis to deal with the western tribes and see to the safe return of the Mandan chief Shehekeshote to his people. Bates sat in when Clark met a Sioux delegation and heard Clark stumble through an officious statement that the interpreter Pierre Dorion translated. What Clark asked Dorion to repeat was probably misunderstood by the audience. Bates wanted no part of Indian affairs but inherited the obligation when, after launching a small military expedition to return a Mandan chief to his people, Clark went off to dig bones and find a wife.[25] As Governor Lewis had not appeared, Bates must have thought that national heroes took a light view of their responsibilities.[26]

The departed Clark was also brigadier general of the militia. Although the militia had been organized by previous administrations, Bates was soon considering a total repeal of the militia law and the vacation of the commissions of worthless men. In the same bundle of letters that he informed Governor Lewis of these adjustments, Bates wrote the secretary of war about problems with the Osage and of rumored Spanish intimidation of the plains tribes.[27] That information came from a letter that Lieutenant Pike wrote to a friend the previous October, but which only reached St. Louis when the upriver trade returns arrived in May.

Secretary Bates had another set of duties. When he left Washington he had been designated as the third member of the board of three commissioners passing on the legitimacy of land claims. The other members were Judge John B. Lucas and Clement Penrose. They were a tribunal with considerable power over the expectations of old French landholders and new arriving American settlers. Bates was also the recorder of the land titles that he helped approve. When his three salaries were combined, he was being paid more than Governor Lewis.[28] And that was nothing compared to the insider information he got as a by-product of his jobs.

The former receiver of public monies at Detroit was trailed west by a letter that Secretary of the Treasury Gallatin dated April 2, 1807.[29] Because the discretion previously allowed to the land board had supported abuse, countenanced fraud, and rapacious speculation, the rules for approving titles were tightened. In March Congress had passed a revised act "respecting claims to Land in the Territory of Orleans & Louisiana."[30] Laxity would be corrected by "a most rigid construction of the law" but the new regulations required proofs that those who settled under the previous Spanish administration found almost impossible to confirm. After proofs to preexisting claims were cleared away, the United States could sell a properly certified title for the price of two dollars an acre. That money would help pay off the large debt from the purchase of Louisiana. As the reform appointee, Bates realized that he was in a position of considerable power.

After receiving Gallatin's letter on May 28, Bates wasted no time in sharing his thoughts with the former governor's enemy William C. Carr. Through a connection to Attorney General Breckenridge, the twenty-two-year-old lawyer had been appointed special agent to investigate abuses in land claims.[31] Since 1805 he had been in a position to pass on the legitimacy of claims being presented to the land board. A vocal opponent of the previous Wilkinson administration, Carr fitted in nicely with what Bates intended to do.[32] After speaking with Bates, Carr immediately wrote to his brother in Lexington that those "who were opposed to the Wilkinson administration were daily receiving instances and marks of approbation from the government . . . and that they [we] are now completely triumphant."[33]

At the end of May Bates also wrote to his brother Richard that "the onward course of Justice must be pursued, uninfluenced by the persuasions or the intimations of those who very foolishly imagined that *I should be compelled to leave the country in six weeks.*" To another correspondent Bates claimed to have disappointed the expectations of both existing cabals by refusing all executive patronage. But in mid-July Bates appointed Carr's close friend Thomas Oliver to receive claims in Ste. Genevieve. Despite his pious pronouncements, the territorial secretary had immediately taken sides and was constructing a cabal of his own.[34]

As a power broker and the highest-paid public officer in the Louisiana Territory, Bates developed a circle of "friends" that reproduced the factionalism he warned Governor Lewis to avoid. After proclaiming the land claims act and requiring those intruding upon government land to be removed, Bates insinuated to Gallatin that the president's forbearance in the execution of previous acts "will in a great degree prevent for the present" the removal of intruders who made their establishments before the March act.[35] Blaming that laxity on former secretary Browne, Bates went so far as to question if "the Executive is the guardian of the Public interests."[36]

Although the land board was slow in addressing other land titles,

Bates's most immediate concern had to do with the Ste. Genevieve leads. That relatively easy-to-produce commodity represented the government's best chance of making this expensive new territory help pay for itself. It also represented attractive opportunities for speculation. After his first visit with Moses Austin, Secretary Bates's immediate interest in purchasing a farm near Austin's smelting operation was held off because the titles were not properly adjusted. In August when Austin tried to encourage the prosecution of his main rival, John Smith T., Bates had to refuse for the lack of anything beyond surmise as evidence.

Devious in their public images, Frederick Bates and William C. Carr were damningly open in the letters they wrote to their brothers. For them, ethics somehow stopped at a family threshold. Carr's letters reveal the depth of collusion infecting the administration of Louisiana. As a special agent of the Treasury Department he was in a position of considerable public power, and private opportunity, too. Carr soon recognized that he could turn insider information to advantage.

Land claimants actually made small down payments in cash and floated the rest on government credit. But the certification process lagged for years and those who became strapped for cash were forced to sell their interest in as-yet-unproven claims for half the value. From the inside information available to him, Carr could identify the most desirable properties, buy at a discount, see to the proof of the title, and then sell the most desirable, certified holdings at a higher price. Of course a good part of that potentially lucrative opportunity depended on the approval of the land board and the registering of the deed, both functions of Frederick Bates.

A loyal man who had delivered evidence against Burr to the president, in an undated private memorial addressed to "Captain" Lewis, Pierre Provenchere pointed out "the injustice to the old inhabitants by the act of the land law which requires proofs of possession they are unable to provide, those were not generated by the Spanish administration, they cannot produce complete titles for the land board."[37] Significantly, the plea was addressed to Governor Lewis rather than to the land board or to the administration.

The plight of the old inhabitants weren't that interesting to a progressive man like Bates. After personal observations in St. Louis, St. Charles, and Ste. Genevieve, he dismissed them as erratic hunters and degraded villagers with no grasp of the meaning of real government. Accustomed as they had been to the dictation of Spanish administrators, "the very name of *liberty* deranges their intellects."[38] What he admired was the superior genius of the Americans.[39]

In letters to his brother Richard, Secretary Bates revealed the character behind the public mask. There is the suggestion that he no longer considered himself a mere proxy and regarded the government of Louisiana as his accomplishment.

On October 16, 1807, when Ensign Pryor returned from the hostile encounter with the previously friendly Arikara, Bates helped him write the report. Pryor was convinced that the upper Missouri River was blockaded and that British traders were still meddling with the tribes along the upper Mississippi.[40] Nor was the relationship with the Osage south of the river all that certain because the Spanish were trying to influence them. Those were potentially serious developments and in his correspondence with members of President Jefferson's cabinet, Bates never missed an opportunity to point out that the designated governor had yet to assume his duties.

In November, after the secretary of war told him to stop pestering that office with his "causeless perplexities," Bates switched to Governor Lewis.[41] After reciting all the problems that he faced, the territorial secretary divulged that he had issued a license to the British trader Robert Dickson to continue supplying the tribes west of the upper Mississippi. His excuse was that the government had failed to build the trade factory promised to the tribes and they were in danger of suffering for the lack of essential supplies. By the time Meriwether received that letter, Dickson had installed his traders for the winter who were likely propagandizing Indians against the United States.

Nevertheless, Bates continued to encourage Lewis to come and relieve him of onerous responsibilities. In January 1808 Bates wrote, "Amidst the disappointments which your absence occasions, no one feels the want of your superintending presence so much as I do." On the twenty-sixth he wrote again that tranquility prevailed despite the bad effect of potential war upon the trade. As a progressive man Bates saw that "as long as we are *Indian Traders* and *Hunters* our settlements can never flourish, and for my own part I care not how soon the savage is left to traverse in solitude his own Desarts."[42]

That was not quite what the president or the governor had in mind. Lewis read into it the insulting implication that the vast territory he had explored was of little consequence. Bates added that several members of the Corps of Discovery had already turned over their land warrants to his friends Thomas Riddick and Alexander McNair and that he had purchased the latter's moiety.[43]

After the turn of the year Bates had another opportunity to make himself useful to Moses Austin by claiming the authority to lease lead lands to individuals. As most of the leases he made were for lands adjoining those of Austin, that made Austin's smelter the most convenient place to take unrefined ore. The price of a lease was one-tenth of the mineral raised, to be paid quarterly to the government. As the government preferred to be paid in best-quality lead, that amounted to a virtual monopoly for Austin. On January 6, 1808, Bates contracted to lease fifty acres of lead land to John Hawkins and Jacob Reed. Lest the treasury see through this cozy arrangement, Bates suggested building an expensive government smelter knowing it was unlikely to be built with the tight-fisted Gallatin.

Given the level of violence concentrated in the lead district of Ste. Genevieve, Bates discouraged his brother from coming to look over prospects for investment until he had it in his power to offer more-advantageous inducements. Near the end of January William Mathers and Michael Hart, who were prior tenants of the United States at *Mine a Renault*, complained to Bates that "we are utterly unable to distinguish public from private claims." An associate of Smith T., appropriately named Cheetham, was surveying five hundred acres that engrossed their claim.[44]

Special agent Carr, who had lived near Austin before his appointment in St. Louis, revisited him about that time. Early the next month Carr came to St. Louis with a letter from Austin complaining about the direction that Breton Township Justice of the Peace John Perry was following. He was making decisions unfavorable to Austin. No surprise that the secretary wasted no time in admonishing Perry against deciding cases in which he or his relations had an interest.[45]

Austin later revealed his interest. "I trust I shall be excused from expressing my solicitude on this occasion as Messrs. Mathews and Hart leased land of the U States by my advice, and in consequence I consider myself in some measure instrumental in placing them in the situation in which they now stand." After the arrival of Governor Lewis, Austin was becoming concerned that matters of his influence were getting out of hand. He wrote that he had always been confident "in the justice of the General Government . . . nor can I yet believe I shall find myself disappointed in my expectations of the just intentions of the Executive of this Territory."[46]

After a delay of eleven months, Governor Lewis was making a winter horseback ride from Louisville by way of Vincennes to take up his post at St. Louis. Solitary days in the saddle gave him time to go over what he had learned in his talks with Indian agent John Campbell.[47] At Prairie du Chien, Campbell would try to counter the activities of British traders.

Although Bates downplayed the growing influence of the Shawnee Prophet and his brother Tecumseh, the Sac and Fox agent Nicholas Boilvin was very apprehensive. In the face of those growing tensions, Bates allowed the British trader Robert Dickson to continue his operations among the tribes of the Des Moines drainage. That was patently wrongheaded.[48]

After Lewis crossed the Mississippi from Cahokia on March 8, 1808, it does not appear that his first meeting with the secretary was entirely pleasant. When Bates turned over his revised version of the laws of the territory, he put it in writing.[49]

That meeting also included a bundle of unresolved complaints about lead claims in the Ste. Genevieve district. Some were about former Burrites, others from opponents of the Wilkinson administration. Their main opponent at the mines was Moses Austin, who Lewis suspected was no better.

When he was organizing the expedition in 1804, Lewis suggested that Capt. Amos Stoddard forward Austin's description of the lead mines to Washington. Six columns of data had appeared in the *National Intelligencer*, along with an editorial note that it had been submitted at the request of Captain Lewis.[50] Now the governor was beginning to regret that endorsement.

On top of those unpleasantries, Bates produced a copy of Private Frazer's prospectus for the publication of his expedition journal, which he had obtained from Maj. Eli B. Clemson. There is no explanation why that document came up at the beginning of their relationship, but it sparked a serious misunderstanding between Lewis and Bates. The secretary immediately wrote to Joseph Charless, the editor and publisher of the *Louisville Gazette*: ". . . procure for me, one, two or three of those western Papers, from different Presses, which contain the Prospectus of Frazier's Journal." Bates would also appreciate something on Lewis's letter condemning the publication of the Gass journal because of "The interest which I take in the compromise of those misunderstandings which have arisen from that Prospectus."[51]

The frustrated author of a potential exploratory masterpiece had spent too much time fending off competitors like Gass or Frazer. Bates left Washington before Lewis published the letter condemning the projected Gass publication and disparaging what Frazer hoped to do.[52] Frazer could only have picked up on that animosity after he returned to St. Louis in April, not long after Bates had arrived.[53] Something in those contentious developments struck a nerve and caused the first unpleasant clash between Lewis and Bates.

By March 24, 1808, Bates complained to his brother Richard that "Affairs look somewhat squally since the arrival of Gov. Lewis. Mighty and extraordinary efforts are making to restore to office some of those worthless men, whom I thought it my duty to remove . . . greatly fear that the Demon of Discord will *again* mount the whirlwind and direct the storm."[54]

The office of the secretary of state was responsible for the administration of the territories. At the end of March Bates sent Madison a half-yearly report, copies of the acts passed up to March 31, 1808, listing appointments in the civil department "together with a list of the civil officers now in commission," and a list of the Indian trade licenses he had issued. Governor Lewis's tardy appearance had given Bates eleven months to entrench himself and he wanted to get everything he had done into the record. Although Bates was covering his behind, many of those names represented individuals beholden to him, an already established faction that the governor would either have to placate or offend.

Buried deeper was the collusion between Bates, Carr, and Austin and their use of insider information for speculative purposes. Real estate was a major concern for old inhabitants, new immigrants, and speculators. The influence that Bates had developed on the land board and as recorder of land titles was more important than his performance as territorial secretary. But whatever the ethical implications of those under-the-table matters, the arrival of a governor with a broader perspective and concern for the security of the territory threatened their narrow interests.

On April 20, 1808, the governor issued a proclamation restricting any further settlements on lands in the Louisiana Territory belonging to the United States. He carefully described those limits using recognized landmarks. To explain this momentous restriction, Lewis reasoned that in evading the existing laws a scattered population was also putting itself beyond the protection of the government. Illegal squatters were ordered to vacate by June 15 or be subject to a fine of a thousand dollars. The restriction would be in effect until the tribes legally ceded their territory.[55]

The proclamation began to pinch when it also inhibited the exploitation of unleased mining claims. That alienated the special interest holders who meant to profit from a situation that had been developing over the past few years. By enforcing the law the governor was sure to generate the same animosity that had spoiled the previous Wilkinson administration.

Military preparedness was a major concern. In the absence of Clark, Governor Lewis made militia appointments. In the appointment of a captain of the St. Charles troop of cavalry, Lewis did not consult Col. Timothy Kibby, who had tried to discredit General Wilkinson during the Burr trial. On the other hand, despite Bates's fears, Smith T. did not regain command of the Ste. Genevieve company. Other civil appointments were also completed by the end of September.[56]

Although the data on licenses issued by his predecessor were missing, Bates produced the list of the Indian trade licenses that he had issued. Most of those were generally concerned with trapping and trading on the lower river, but despite his early reservations, Bates had allowed Manuel Lisa and George Drouillard to take a large party of trappers to the Yellowstone River.[57] In the letter that Bates wrote for him, Ensign Pryor blamed the trouble his expedition ran into with the Arikara on what Lisa might have told them to gain a passage past their villages.

As matters between the governor and the secretary were off to a bad start, Bates soon found an excuse to leave St. Louis by unilaterally deciding to take the business of the land board out of town. Bates, who did not speak French or Spanish, took the St. Louis notary Marie Phillipe Leduc along as his translator. They left on May 24, 1808, to visit Cape Girardeau and New Madrid and continued down the Mississippi as far as the Chickasaw Bluffs.[58]

During the first half of July Bates dealt with irregular claims around the lower Arkansas, discounting many for having missed a filing deadline. Back in St. Louis at the end of August, Bates wrote to Secretary Gallatin proving that he was on the job but admitting that the land problems could not be cleared up in nine months. He also reported that "Since the arrival of Gov Lewis, I have had no interference in the business of the lead Mines—he has however, with great propriety, I think and hope with your approbation, assumed the whole management."[59]

Without the cooperation of the territorial secretary, the administration of Louisiana was a one-man bureaucracy. For Lewis, even meeting with Bates was an emotional trial, more upsetting than constructive. When Lewis sat down to his travel-battered desk, he was already buried under inhabitants' petitions that Bates dumped on him. Those bothersome land matters put him in a bind just when he had more than enough to do dealing with an ominous situation developing on the Indian frontiers.

It had not taken long for the governor and the territorial secretary to become estranged. In a later letter Bates gave his opinion of why antipathy developed:

> At the *first* in *Washington* he made to me so many friendly assurances that I then imagined our mutual friendship would plant itself on rocky [solid] foundations. But a very short acquaintance with the man was sufficient to undeceive me. He had been spoiled by the elegant praises of Mitchell & Barlow, and overwhelmed by so many flattering caresses of the *high &*

mighty, that, like an overgrown baby, he began to think that everybody about the House must regulate their conduct to his caprices.[60]

In implying that their differences were personal, the secretary was not forthcoming about the difficulties that the governor's proclamation and enforcement of the law made to the cozy understanding he had going with special investigator Carr.

In many ways Lewis was out of his depth in political infighting. Although the years he spent as the president's secretary had exposed him to the seamy side of Washington politics, it had always been Jefferson who absorbed the brunt with his calculated aplomb. In St. Louis Lewis realized what it was to be a leader surrounded by conniving enemies.

Perhaps there was a way to restore harmony in the disputatious town of St. Louis. The idealized, shared brotherhood of Freemasonry was a network of trustworthy friends. A St. Louis lodge could become a place to reconcile differences. During the summer Brother Lewis of the Masonic order and others petitioned the Grand Lodge of Pennsylvania for a charter that promised to draw a scrim of fellowship over a contentious community.

The petitioners were an unlikely collection of individuals who already seemed to prove the logic. Territorial justice Rufus Easton had been a founding member of the Kaskaskia lodge. Land board clerk Thomas Riddick helped start the Ste. Genevieve lodge. Other members were editor Joseph Charless, Dr. Farrar, the lawyer Carr, and some of the army officers stationed at Cantonment Belle Fontaine. They represented most of the elite of the St. Louis business community.

The purpose of Masonry was to "spread the doctrine of the Brotherhood of Man, irrespective of race or religious creed." In St. Louis that was not going to be easy. Frederick Bates became a Mason at Detroit in 1802 but his expectation of taking the leadership was topped by the seniority of Meriwether Lewis, who had entered the Door of Virtue Lodge in Virginia in 1797. The members of St. Louis Lodge No. 111 were soon split between those who supported the Worshipful Master Lewis and the aspirations of Brother Bates to that honor. If lodge night was meant to be a moment of moral distraction from the dubious ethics most members practiced during the workday, the ideal was disappointed by apparently inescapable habits of factionalism.

A somewhat bemused William Clark noticed that "the Govr was Installed as master last night." Clark lost most of Saturday, November 9, 1808, observing the procession of the Freemasons and enduring the florid oration of Mr. Bates.[61] Although he and Lewis had named the western tributaries of the Missouri for Masonic virtues—Philanthropy, Philosophy, and Wisdom—it would be another year before the pragmatic Clark would join the lodge.

NOTES

1. Alexander Wilson, "Particulars of the Death of Capt. Lewis," *Port Folio* 7 (January 1812): 39.

2. The correspondence between FB and AG is extensive and begins in 1804 and continues until 1815. Holding appointments governed by the Treasury Department, Bates and Gallatin held a special relationship when overseeing the administration of the Louisiana Territory land claims.

3. Edward Bates, "Letter Giving Sketch of Frederick Bates, February 10, 1859," *Michigan Pioneer Collections* 8 (1907): 563.

4. Robert Frazer to TJ, April 16, 1807, Jackson, *LLC* 2: 409–10. Frazer was bound to give evidence in the trial of Wescott on February 1, 1807, so he made a very fast trip to Washington and spoke directly with the president. Frazer left Washington after March 15 carrying various letters, wrote the president en route on April 16, and was back in St. Louis in time for the trial on the first Tuesday in May, having covered a considerable distance in three months. Whose authorization Frazer traveled under and his reimbursement remain intriguing but unanswered questions.

5. When Madame Provenchere was later called on to provide this evidence for the case against Wescott, she replied that her husband had already taken letters to the president. FB to TJ, May 6, 1807, Carter, *TP* 14: 120–21.

6. Rufus Easton to the SW, July 14, 1807, Carter, *TP* 14: 133–36; Aaron Burr to WHH, October 24, 1806, in Mary-Jo Kline, ed., *Political Correspondence and Public Papers of Aaron Burr*, 2 vols. (Princeton, NJ: Princeton University Press, 1983), 2: 996n1.

7. Marshall, *FB* 1: 8–10, 14.

8. FB to Augustus Woodward, December 3, 1806, Marshall, *FB* 1: 86–87; *ASP, Public Lands* 1: 283–91.

9. FB to ML, April 5, 1807, Marshall, *FB* 1: 99.

10. April 7, 1807, Marshall, *FB* 1: 101.

11. ML to WC, March 15, 1807, Jackson, *LLC* 2: 387.

12. FB to ML, May 15, 1807, Marshall, *FB* 1: 114–15.

13. Frazer's activities can be traced in *United States v. Robert Wescott*, Territorial Supreme Court Records, box 16, folder 10, Missouri State Archives, Jefferson City, MO.

14. FB to TJ, May 6, 1807, Carter, *TP* 14: 120–21.

15. Smith attached the initial T. to indicate he was from Tennessee.

16. ASP, *Public Lands* 2: 554.

17. List of Appointments and Removals, April 1, 1807–March 31, 1808, Marshall, *FB* 1: 320. Smith T. had been lieutenant colonel of militia, justice of the Quarter Sessions and Common Pleas, and commissioner of rates and levies for the district of Ste. Genevieve.

18. FB to Frederick Woodson, May 1, 1807, Marshall, *FB* 1: 112.

19. FB to ML, April 28, 1807, Marshall, *FB* 1: 104–105.

20. JW to TJ, September 15, 1807, document 30145, roll 39, TJ-LOC.

21. FB to HD, May 30, 1807, Marshall, *FB* 1: 132–33.

22. Walter B. Douglas, "Manuel Lisa," *Missouri Historical Society Collections* 3 (1911): 247–49; PC to WHH, May 22, 1805, Jackson, *LLC* 2: 242–43.

23. Speculation hinges on the suggestion that it was May 1807 before a military acquaintance of Lt. Zebulon Pike received a letter reporting the Spanish visit and containing Pike's bills for expenses incurred on the expedition as far as the Pawnee villages. St. Louis was also in the dark and Bates did not inform Secretary of War Dearborn until May 15.

24. Marshall, *FB* 1: 14–41. Uncooperative as late as June 3, Browne impeded Bates's efforts to recover the bonds of persons engaged in the fur trade.

25. WC to SW, June 1, 1807, Carter, *TP* 14: 126–27.

26. WC to SW, May 18, 1807, Carter, *TP* 14: 122–25.

27. FB to HD, May 15, 1807, Marshall, *FB* 1: 119–23.

28. Invoices 21407, 21409, 21410, RG217, M235, roll 65, frames 1191, 1195, 1201, NARA. Bates's annual salary amounted to $2,700! (Secretary of the territory, $1,000; recorder of land titles, $500; land commissioner, $1,200.) Lewis was paid $2,000 annually.

29. AG to FB, April 2, 1807, Marshall, *FB* 1: 93–97.

30. A copy of the act was also forwarded to Carr who received it on June 23 and immediately asked if he should accompany the land board when they held meetings in distant districts. AG to William Carr, August 18, 1807, Carter, *TP* 14: 141.

31. Carter, *TP* 13: 162, 17n.

32. William C. Carr to AG, August 17, 1805, Carter, *TP* 13: 186–87.

33. William C. Carr to Charles Carr, May 28, 1807, Marshall, *FB* 1: 126.

34. FB to Richard Bates, May 31, June 17, 1807; William Hull to AG, July 14, 1807, Marshall, *FB* 1: 136, 146, 160.

35. FB to AG, September 8, 1807, Marshall, *FB* 1: 181.

36. FB to ML, May 15, 1807, Marshall, *FB* 1: 117.

37. This was followed by a petition to Congress signed by Provenchere and others including Auguste Chouteau. Carter, editor of the *Territorial Papers*, guessed that the private memorial was dated in 1807 (14: 156–61). On May 28, 1808, Lewis relied on Provenchere to translate certain laws into French so the inhabitants could understand them (14: 188–89).

38. FB to Richard Bates, December 17, 1807, Marshall, *FB* 1: 242.

39. Marshall, *FB* 1: 239.

40. Nathaniel Pryor to WC, October 16, 1807, Jackson, *LLC* 2: 432–38.

41. FB to ML, November 7, 1807, Marshall, *FB* 1: 228.

42. FB to ML, January 26, 1808, Marshall, *FB* 1: 267.

43. Marshall, *FB* 1: 268.

44. William Mathers to FB, January 29, 1808, Marshall, *FB* 1: 270–72.

45. FB to John Perry, February 8, 1808, Marshall, *FB* 1: 278–79.

46. Moses Austin to FB, March 27, 1808, Marshall, *FB* 1: 318; Eugene Barker, *Austin Papers*, 2 vols. (Washington: Annual Report of the American Historical Association, 1919), 1: 151–52.

47. Bates mentioned on February 23 that Campbell had been appointed Indian agent at Prairie du Chien and was on his way to St. Louis with Governor Lewis (Marshall, *FB* 1: 298).

48. FB to WC, July 25, 1807, Marshall, *FB* 1: 166–67, 307.

49. FB to ML, March 9, 1808, Marshall, *FB* 1: 309.

50. *ASP, Public Lands* 1: 188; Donald Jackson, *Thomas Jefferson and the Rocky Mountains: Exploring the West from Monticello* (Norman: University of Oklahoma Press, 2002), p. 222n22.

51. Marshall, *FB* 1: 309n5.

52. As he raced east to report Burrite activities in St. Louis, Frazer appears to have laid a trail of his prospectus with newspapers in the Philadelphia *Aurora* on December 13, 1806, and January 6, 1807. Lewis dated his critical letter on March 14 but Frazer apparently left Washington the next day without being aware of it and the disclaimer was not published in the *National Intelligencer* until the March 25. Bates's involvement is unclear and it has never been explained how Frazer found backing for his project, which included a large map that was probably drawn for him by the St. Louis cartographer Antoine Soulard. (Jackson, *LLC* 1: 346n; 2: 385–86.)

53. The returning Frazer carried a letter from Lewis to Bates concerning the disloyalty of certain Burrites.

54. FB to Richard Bates, March 24, 1808, Marshall, *FB* 1: 315.

55. Proclamation, April 20, 1808, Marshall, *FB* 1: 337–43.

56. Appointments to Militia Offices by Governor Lewis, Appointments to Civil Offices by Governor Lewis, September 30, 1808, Marshall, *FB* 2: 25–31.

57. Licenses to Trade and to Hunt among the Indians Granted by Governor Lewis, Marshall, *FB* 2: 31–33.

58. Leduc became so sick with intermittent fever that he had to leave his post and Bates later complained of being unwell when he was on the Arkansas. FB to AG, July 22, 1808, Marshall, *FB* 2: 8.

59. FB to AG, August 28, 1808, Marshall, *FB* 2: 22.

60. FB to Richard Bates, November 9, 1809, Marshall, *FB* 2: 108–109.

61. Frederick Bates, "Oration Delivered before Saint Louis Lodge No. 111," *Early American Imprints*, Second series, no. 16954; James Holmberg, ed., *Dear Brother* (New Haven, CT: Yale University Press, 2002), p. 161.

THIRTEEN

Nails in a Coffin

And Desperation triumphed here[1]

Snow bound, ice bound, St. Louis sobered after the excesses of the French traditional celebration *La Guignolee*. William Clark must have been still feeling the effects when he wrote to his brother Jonathan on the second day of January 1809 and came close to breaking his record for misspelling. "A happy new yer [crossed out] year! . . . Every person in this village appear at this time to be gay and barley amuseing themselves visiting Slaying [sleighing] and the like. . . . Slays waggons & horses are driving across the Ice in every Direction—Some horses Slip in but, none have been lost as yet." In addition to the English language, Clark was preparing to butcher nineteen fat hogs and two beefs for his next year's provisions when he wrote that "The weather is exessively Cold, the river Closed and hav been So for a long time we have not recved the mail but once for a long time Seven weeks—every Sunday we anxiously wait for the arrival of the mail to hear of our freinds."[2] He still had not received letters by the twenty-first of January.

Although Clark purchased a large lot and house near the center of town, his family was still living in a rented house where Lewis took meals with them. There on January 10, the mutually cherished Julia Clark gave birth to a baby boy. But the mother and the father didn't get around to christening the "stout portly fellow" for eleven days. When Julia felt strong enough, they went to the St. Louis Catholic church to have Father Flaget bestow the name Meriwether Lewis Clark. The beaming godfather took that as an expression of regard, dare we say love.[3]

The boy had "Strong longues," so neither the mother nor the father were getting much sleep. An outdoor man like Clark didn't hang around to help change diapers. On the twenty-fifth he took a break at the card party Meriwether held in his quarters. The host had to borrow a dollar from his friend to cover his losses.[4]

Sporadic at best, the mail from Washington might take a month, six weeks, or even longer.[5] Until it got through, St. Louisans were uncertain what was happening in distant Washington. Charless wrote an editorial in the *Missouri Gazette* explaining that he had no news to reprint because others along the postal route pillaged the eastern newspapers he intended to copy. Locked away from the world by winter and international politics somehow gone awry, Lewis and Clark had only each other to rely upon.

Before winter closed the trails, Lewis and Clark learned that James Madison had been elected president. Until he took office in March 1809, it was still the familiar Jefferson administration. That indulgent authority was all that Meriwether Lewis had known during the eight years of his political career.

Frederick Bates began the new year alone and feeling sorry for himself. The letter he wrote to his brother James reads like one of Shakespeare's soliloquies: "Most persons in public life have to sustain a load of calumny. I have my full share—and when suspicion once attaches, and the many headed monster in his window, chooses to credit the accusation assure rations of innocence and honor would be of no avail."[6]

In moving positively to discourage unauthorized appropriation of government property, particularly the lead mines, Governor Lewis upset the plans of Bates and Special Agent William C. Carr. Before the winter closed communications they wrote to Washington, attempting to discredit that inconvenient policy. Now they were waiting for an answer from Treasury Secretary Albert Gallatin; they wouldn't have liked what took place in Washington.

On January 6, 1809, Gallatin forwarded the letter from Bates to President Jefferson. The territorial secretary wanted to know if Governor Lewis had received any instructions respecting settlers on the lead mines. If Lewis had no instructions from the treasury and was acting unilaterally, what should be done? Within three days of receiving this message Jefferson replied that he did not recall specific instructions respecting squatters, but there had been discussions and the policy would have been to prohibit them vigorously. The president added, "Carr's story about this has the air of idle rumor, willingly listened to, and shows some germ of discontent existing."[7] Jefferson smelled a rat.

John Mason, the superintendent of the Indian trade, was also locked away from contact with Louisiana. As the head of the factory system Mason was concerned that the embargo was ruining business. The peltry and deerskins stored in his warehouses were in a deplorable state and wasting away.[8] On December 31, 1808, Mason wrote William Clark asking him to take on the additional duty of agent for the office of the Indian trade in St. Louis. Those duties would include accepting and forwarding goods to the two western factories at Fort Osage on the Missouri and Fort Madison on the Mississippi. Clark would receive, store, forward, and sometimes sell the furs coming to St. Louis for a salary of $250 per annum.[9] Mason had picked the best man to resolve those difficulties, but the appointment that he approved in Washington at the end of December did not reach Clark until the first of March 1809. Although the trade factory had been moved from Belle Fontaine to Fort Osage, the former factor, Rodolphe Tillier, continued to create problems.[10]

Three days later, on March 4 in distant Washington, James Madison took the oath of office. As the change of administration proceeded, the transition of similar republican administrations should have gone smoothly. There was a small problem in the War Department because Secretary of War Dearborn resigned early, after recommending that the department rid itself of the presumptuous accountant William Simmons.[11] The damn fellow created more problems than he solved. Given Gallatin's emphasis on economy, that wasn't likely to happen. The former Treasury Department accountant now implanted in the War Department was ready to adhere to what amounted to ill-conceived and impractical regulations. His congressionally approved weapon was the requirement for quarterly estimates of anticipated expenditures. Simmons's use of it would soon demoralize officers in distant posts.

The new secretary of war, William Eustis, was a veteran of the Revolution, a former congressman, and a hospital administrator.[12] But Eustis was unacquainted with present military procedures, practices, or broader policy and was not that inclined to learn. The orders that started going out over his signature were at best ill-informed.

When the mails began getting through to St. Louis, Governor Lewis, Indian agent General Clark, and Belle Fontaine commandant Daniel Bissell found they were dealing with an unexpected problem: how to educate a new secretary of war about operations in Louisiana. And they knew no more about William Eustis than he knew about them.[13]

A year ago, in warning Lewis of Astor's formation of a powerful new trading company, President Jefferson had advised Governor Lewis that "Nothing but the exclusive possession of the Indian commerce can secure us their peace."[14] Lewis could not have received the letter much before the beginning of October 1808 when General Clark was away from St. Louis supervising the construction of a fort and trade factory at Fire Prairie to anchor what amounted to a new Indian territory strung along the Louisiana frontier. Before Clark left on that mission, Manuel Lisa and George Drouillard returned to St. Louis bringing a favorable report of the huge potential of beaver trapping and a question: who was going to exploit it?[15] It was very possible that that trade might be taken over by the New York financier, leaving cash-strapped St. Louis entrepreneurs in his well-capitalized dust.

Not long after meeting the two traders Clark mentioned the fur trade as a business opportunity that might interest his brother Edmund. Clark already had more than enough to attend to. As soon as he had arrived in St. Louis, Clark tried to interest his nephew John Hite Clark in "a propesition from me to join in trade at this place & Camp &c."[16] That didn't work out as he hoped but Clark enlarged upon the opportunities again on November 24.

> The S[t]tores at this place is only Supplied once a year, and great part of the year they have Scercely any goods calculated for the Consumption of the Country. Some money circulates here, The Indian department pays out a large Sum, the offices of government, and the Troops cause much Caish to Circulate, & we may as well as others Ceatch a little.[17]

Meanwhile Manuel Lisa went on to Louisville to improve his connection with Clark's brother-in-law Denis Fitzhugh. At the end of November a now familiar "Manuel" returned after meeting Fitzhugh and Edmund Clark, convinced that what he lightly referred to as "the financial congress held there nightly" only needed a treasurer.[18] Both Lisa and Clark had a long-standing relationship with Drouillard's capitalist, William Morrison of Kaskaskia, who still had an interest in the outfit left on the Yellowstone.[19]

When citing the rates for commodities in St. Louis, Clark thought that the prices paid for previous staples of deerskins and small furs were low and not much in demand. But two dollars a pound for beaver from the upper Missouri was a high price. The plan Clark matured by December was a virtual description of how the western trade was conducted.

my mode of carrying on this trade was, fer John Should lay in the goods in
Baltimore or Philadelphia on the best terms possible, waggon them to the
Ohio, purchase Kentucky Boats and take them down to the falls, take out
all but Such as were necessary for this place, Send them on with Certain
other articles of Kenty. produce to the mouth of the Ohio, write to me by
post when the boats would arrive at the mouth. I would Send one or more
barges (two or three of which I Shall have on hand public) with a Sufficient number of hands to bring up the goods &c.[20]

Clark was beginning to mix private and public business. An altruistic
approach to public service had never impeded the founders of the nation.
Many were significantly involved in the speculative division of the former
Indian lands of the Ohio drainage. Combining public business and private
advantage had crossed the Mississippi, not only with those holding influential offices but also with most of the settlers who claimed more land than
they could possibly farm, with the expectation of eventually selling the surplus for a tidy profit.

Lewis and Clark made investments in land in Louisiana with the confidence that the value of it could only increase. But a significant divergence
of interests was developing as Clark considered attractive opportunities for
business while his partner, in the publication of a book about the exploration, was trying to get back to Philadelphia to write it. The window of
opportunity for a rewarding publication was beginning to close just as they
became aware of recent developments on the upper Missouri, and even
across the Rocky Mountains, that could lessen the impact of their book.

George Drouillard returned with geographical information on the Big
Horn Basin that found its way into Clark's map. Another source of information appears to have been a former member of the Corps of Discovery,
John B. Thompson, who had been in the party that Clark had mentioned
left St. Louis in March 1808. By accident or intent, Thompson had over-
taken former captain John McClallen at the Yankton villages and accompanied him up the Missouri. At the Mandan villages McClallen had taken
on thirty or so Canadian freemen who were hanging around as economic
refugees from the merger of Montreal-based trading companies. Leading a
combined party of about forty-two men, larger than the Corps of Discovery,
McClallen led them up the Yellowstone River and through the mountains
to the lower end of the Bitterroot Valley.[21] Nez Perce returning from the fall
buffalo hunt recognized Thompson and another former corpsman.[22]

When the party broke up in the spring most of the trappers returned to
the upper Yellowstone, where they fell in with and were absorbed into the

trapping force that Lisa and Drouillard left at the mouth of the Big Horn. When the principals left with the first returns in July, Thompson rode in their boat back to St. Louis.

Because he left St. Louis in 1807 before Clark arrived with the expedition land warrants, Thompson claimed his bonus and warrant from Clark on August 12, 1808, and soon sold the warrant to another former corpsman, George Gibson.[23] The transaction meant that Thompson had a face-to-face meeting with the former explorers who could hardly have resisted questioning him about what he had been doing.

Thompson related that he had accompanied McClallen to an intertribal peace council and then they followed the well-traveled Indian road down the Clark Fork as far as what is known today as Lake Pend Oreille, Idaho.[24] The information they extracted from returning buffalo hunters and local fishermen described an easy overland connection to the Fishing Basket Falls on the Columbia River. Having suffered through two tortured trips over the difficult Lolo Trail, Thompson assured his listeners that the Clark Fork was a much better way to the Columbia.

The two former explorers must have been shocked that a private adventurer on his own initiative completed President Jefferson's charge to find a practical connection between the continental rivers. Further, he seemed to have appropriated Indian responsibilities that were their prerogative. Thompson's astonishing revelation was not exactly what Lewis and Clark wanted to hear when they were still trying to publish a narrative of their own accomplishments. As far as can be determined from surviving documents, neither of the two captains ever mentioned what they learned from Thompson.[25]

Like most men of business in St. Louis, William Clark was strapped for cash. Borrowing in anticipation of his quarterly salary he could raise perhaps five hundred to a thousand dollars, and he wished he had some of the money that was tied up in his ownership of slaves. That investment could be better put to trade. As December 1808 ended, Clark was still considering a mercantile combination with John and Edmund Clark. He did not mention a more daring adventure in the fur trade until the first of March 1809, when he told his brother Jonathan that "we have formed a Company to hunt and Trade up the Missouri" and referred him "to my lettr to Bro. E. & John for particulars—"[26]

The idea began in early August when Lisa and Drouillard returned to St. Louis brimming with the potential of beaver trapping on the Yellowstone. St. Louis gossip held that their boat might be carrying as much as ten thousand dollars' worth of furs.[27] By November when Manuel Lisa returned from financial conferences in Louisville, a group of visionaries was already calculating how to enlarge upon that first successful adventure to the Big Horn. A larger outfit would require additional capitalization.

Their enthusiasm was not dampened when the first returns from the Yellowstone trade actually totaled $8,987.50 in beaver that still had to be marketed. After taking $985 off the top for his services as field leader, Lisa divided the rest between the major backers: William Morrison, Pierre Menard, and himself with no retention of capital. Nor was the apparent profit debt free. Some of the returns brought down in August were purchased from trappers at the Big Horn post by giving them notes. And Morrison and Menard still retained an interest in the goods that had been left at Fort Remon at the mouth of the Big Horn River.[28]

According to the Bryan and Morrison Kaskaskia store ledger, the Louisville merchant Denis Fitzhugh (William Clark's brother-in-law) appears to have handled the disposal or forwarding of some of Lisa's returns, an arrangement similar to what the superintendent of the Indian Trade Office assigned to Clark. Superintendent John Mason wanted to divert peltry to New Orleans as the best market for selling or shipping deerskins. He wrote that "The Hatters furs [beaver] I have ordered to Louisville in Kentucky from which point I propose to distribute them in the Country for sale or bring them here by way of Wheelin[g] on the Ohio & Cumberland on the Potomack."[29] To some degree, the extended Clark family was competing with itself.

On a frontier where communications moved at the undependable pace of a post rider, or a favor to an acquaintance, networking was how things got done. Almost as tribal as Indians, the Clarks were functioning quite well in the linear world of Ohio River business. Although the general enthusiastically promoted opportunities in Louisiana to his brothers and nephews, most of them stayed put in Indiana and Kentucky and those who came west turned out to be a bother. No matter, by December 1808 William Clark had a spoon in several pots.

After years of battling the Chouteau lock on St. Louis, Lisa had penetrated another important family network. He led Clark to participate in the early discussions for another trading and trapping expedition. The "long Story to tell you Shortley in the public way—it is not ripe yot & paper full" that William mentioned to Jonathan on December 10 had to do with the formation of the Missouri Company.[30] By the first of March 1809 Clark confirmed the formation of a partnership of ten shares, one that he had taken for himself and another reserved for his Louisville kinsman Denis Fitzhugh.

[W]e have formed a Company to hunt and Trade up the Missouri to be Called the St. Louis Missour fur Compny. —of 10 Shares, and 140 men with the view to hunt & Trap th Beaver &c. Mr. Wilkinson [written above "Beaver &c" with no indication where it should be placed] on this Subject I must refur you to my letter to Bro. E & John for particulars—[31]

Another prospective partner, Benjamin Wilkinson, carried the letter to Louisville to explain the details in person to Fitzhugh, who might furnish supplies for the outfit.

A week later Clark and Pierre Chouteau were buying goods for the venture that were intended for sale to the men or traded to Indians. Some of those items suggest they were scooping up whatever Bernard Pratte had available in his store. Questionable purchases were forty-four pairs of women's shoes, six of men's, men's silk stockings, spectacle cases, and twenty-five pounds of hair powder. The bill totaled $6,271.14 ¼ , for which they gave four notes of $1,489.52 each and another for $1,300.[32]

Clark's attempt to bring his brothers or brother-in-law into the partnership was unsuccessful, and by May 28, 1809, he had to admit,

I have given up one Shere in the fur Company which I had taken fer Mr. Fitzhugh or John &c. but have been oblige[d] to retain the other which I calculate on makeg. a prophet [profit]. The goods which have been put in to the company was generally as it was purchased by the quantity at this place—[33]

Fortunately that opened a place for the Ste. Genevieve lead miner and natural leader Andrew Henry, who would turn out to be the best man in the organization.

Lewis and Clark were close, and Clark certainly shared his growing interest with his friend the governor. If John B. Thompson had indeed reported accurately on his experiences, they had a good idea of what had developed in the upper country. Men were already trapping beaver on the upper Yellowstone, at the Three Forks of the Missouri, and across the mountains in the Bitterroot Valley. As long as the western tribes tolerated trapping, it was not a matter of exploring but rather of exploiting before others cut into a potential bonanza.

In the winter 1808–1809 St. Louis was a small town. The office of the governor was on South Main Street, and he knew most of those who came there. Although the dignity of his position required a certain amount of decorum, visitors were likely to pop in for a moment, and Pernier didn't always intercept them. Given that casual intimacy, it is not surprising that Lewis was personally acquainted with the prospective partners forming the new company, and well aware of what they were doing.

The unlikely combination ranged from the near-aristocratic Pierre Chouteau and his son Pierre August Chouteau Jr. to that down and dirty, competitive parvenu Manuel Lisa. Between those extremes of social acceptance were such pillars of the establishment as Sylvestre Labbadie, William Morrison, Pierre Menard, Benjamin Wilkinson, and Andrew Henry. William Clark and Lewis's brother, Reuben, were direct connections to the governor.

William Morrison and Pierre Menard stayed in the new syndicate to protect their remaining interest in the previous Lisa-Drouillard adventure, the untraded goods left at the mouth of the Big Horn. But their former representative George Drouillard was left out.[34] Although he was still at odds with Clark over the Osage Treaty, Pierre Chouteau Sr. came in to keep his old rival Lisa from stealing a march. His son Pierre Chouteau Jr. was eager to go back and repay the Arikara for what they did to him two years before. Sylvestre Labbadie was an experienced St. Louis trader, and Benjamin Wilkinson, the former governor's nephew, would be the intermediary between St. Louis and Louisville.[35]

Those visionaries intended to finance a massive beaver trapping expedition sure to decimate the animal colonies along the rivers. No one seems to have questioned if taking resources from unceded Indian land was legal. It was true that individual trappers or small parties had been infiltrating tribal territory along the lower river for some time, but that impact was gradual. Most Indian hunters, who preferred to trade deerskins or buffalo robes, didn't take beaver in productive quantities. Financing large-scale trapping far from home depended on a high return of the best-fibered beaver pelts to satisfy the felting industry.[36]

The partners were getting in over their heads. Most St. Louis capitalists were inexperienced in operating a trapping expedition. Nor would the number of new recruits have experience in that kind of hunting. Recognizing the organizers as merchants and facilitators, Lewis saw that Manuel Lisa was the exception, a tough, experienced river trader and transporter. Whatever complaints about his leadership in the field, he had taken a party higher on the rivers than any other St. Louis operation. Lisa had established amiable relations with indulgent Crows and Drouillard had scouted expansion possibilities. After Morrison and Menard paid him for looking after their interests, Drouillard had enough money to equip himself and some of his Shawnee kinsmen as trappers.

Governor Lewis recognized the difficulties that the entrepreneurs were undertaking and the larger implications because he was still charged with getting the Mandan chief safely past the belligerent Arikara. The large expedition of the St. Louis MFCo. would test the acceptance of territorial tribes only "supposed" to be at amity with the United States. What recourse would a governor of Louisiana have if they objected?

Indians were not the only concern because information came down the river that British traders had invaded the upper Columbia. Restraining them could not be left to a private individual like past captain McClallen, who was masquerading as an official of the United States. Despite those reservations, Lewis was as high on expectation as Clark. They were helping to launch a new industry.

Five of the partners were old hands in the Indian trade, unlikely to trust each other in a dark room if the lights suddenly went out. Lisa's biographer Richard Oglesby puts it best:

> The most noteworthy feature of the Articles of Agreement was the way in which it concretely delineated the aura of distrust which hung about this heterogeneous collection of merchants banded together to exploit the riches of the Northwest. . . . Although the business mores of that day were no better, or worse, than our own, the lengths to which these men went to insure each other's honesty not only were absurd but were partly the cause of the company's failure to take full advantage of its prospects.[37]

Those precautions led to a contractual obligation to actively participate in field operations and avoid the temptation to trade on their own. The twenty articles of Association and Co-partnership of the St. Louis Missouri Fur Company (hereafter MFCo.) reflected the legal brilliance of Attorney General Edward Hempstead that Clark dutifully copied at the beginning of the ledger in which, as downstream agent, he would record transactions.[38]

The expedition would be more than a fur trade venture because Lewis and Clark also saw it as a way of getting the Mandan chief Sheheke-shote back to his people. As early as August 20, 1808, General Clark had written to the secretary of war

> . . . if the Government does not intend to send a military command with the Mandan Chief next spring, and you think it necessary that arrangements should be made in this country for to send him up his nation (Govr. Lewis will be absent about that time,) if I am to make the arrangements for to get him to his Country I must request the favour of you to inform

me. That timely preparations may be made by some party so as to let out early in the spring—My former plan has been defeated for the want of a few more regular troops, or a sufficient time for a large company to equip themselves. I think a Company can be formed of Hunters & Traders attached to a few troops who will take up the Indian (Mandan chief), if Government should not send a large command into that country.[39]

What concerned Lewis and Clark was Ensign Pryor's previous hostile encounter with the Arikara. But did that disaster justify gambling US funds on what was essentially a private enterprise? Even an expedition as large as the MFCo. could run into another hostile reception. Governor Lewis did not like the idea of sending men in harm's way. Neither could he allow one tribe to deny access to others that he hoped to reconcile to a new government. The private expedition had to be strong enough to uphold the dignity of the nation.

If the party was to get up the river to its destination before winter set in, it had to start early. There was no time to clear what Governor Lewis intended to do, or the amount he was willing to pay, with Washington. The government contract for the return of the Mandan chief was dated February 24, 1809, and the price of doing it set at seven thousand dollars.

Although the figure of seven thousand dollars would surely shock Washington accountants, it was not unreasonable. Ensign Pryor returned from his bad experience with the Arikara claiming that it might take four hundred men to force a passage through to the upper Missouri.[40] Pierre Chouteau, who had a personal interest in how things developed, stated that the strength of a party to open a passage with the sword might require five hundred men, even ten thousand could be found insufficient.[41] Experienced traders might have thought that sum extreme, as they could pretty well calculate to the last pound of powder or twist of tobacco what had always been necessary to buy passage past the river tribes. But twice embarrassed by the failures to get tribal leaders back to their people, the Jefferson administration was willing to assume the cost. The secretary of war had already authorized another attempt without setting a cap on expenditures.[42]

Governor Lewis steered clear of a compromising position by limiting funding to a military response to the Arikara. He carefully laid out in a lengthy contract what the government expected to get for the investment. He contracted for 125 men, a force acting as a body of properly armed militia, "of Whom Forty shall be Americans and expert Riflemen." Fifty-six dollars a man was not unreasonable pay for two or three months' service and subsistence, perhaps at risk to their lives if the Arikara turned bel-

A newly discovered letter that Meriwether Lewis wrote to Henry Dearborn, secretary of war, in June 1807, making various "observations and remarks" regarding letters from William Clark and trading practices. The letter is several pages in length. (Public domain)

President Thomas Jefferson's handwritten document to the Senate of the United States on February 28, 1807, nominating Meriwether Lewis of Virginia to governor of the Louisiana Territory and William Clark to the rank of lieutenant colonel. Clark's appointment was upgraded to brigadier general. (Public domain)

A sample of Jeremiah Connor's handwriting showing that the "L" in Louis and the flamboyant style of the "r" in Sir prove the handwriting. Sheriff Connor of St. Louis was a close friend of Meriwether Lewis and wrote the August 18, 1809, letter for him. This newly discovered letter suggests that either Lewis was so enraged over the July 15 letter that he couldn't write legibly, or that he was ill and couldn't hold a pen. (Public domain)

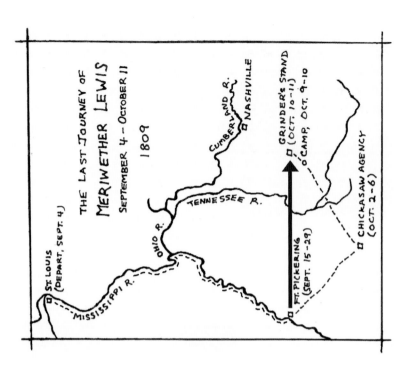

Map of Meriwether Lewis's last journey from St. Louis to Fort Pickering and then to Grinder's Stand. The authors believe that Lewis went directly from Fort Pickering to Grinder's Stand and bypassed the Chickasaw Agency. (Courtesy of Jim I. Merritt)

One of the most important letters of Meriwether Lewis's career. Dated August 18, 1809, Lewis is replying to a letter that presumably William Eustis, secretary of war, wrote to him on July 15 refusing to pay certain bills. New evidence shows that William Simmons, the accountant for the War Department, not William Eustis, wrote the letter. (Public domain)

The type of cabin in which Meriwether Lewis stayed on the Natchez Trace on his last night. (Courtesy of Thomas Danisi)

Meriwether Lewis Site and Memorial Monument commemorating the explorer and governor of the Louisiana Territory. The monument is located near Hohenwald, Tennessee, in a pioneer cemetery on the grounds of the National Park Service along the route of the Natchez Trace Parkway. (Courtesy of Thomas Danisi)

Meriwether Lewis Monument with inscriptions. Erected in 1848 by the state of Tennessee, two sides of the monument bear words: a short statement in Latin and on this side, "An officer of the Regular Army / Private Secretary to President Jefferson / Commander of the Expedition to the Oregon in 1803–1806 / Governor of the Territory of Louisiana / His melancholy death occurred where this monument now stands and 'under' which rest his mortal remains." (Courtesy of Thomas Danisi)

ligerent. The legal input from Attorney General Edward Hempstead was made clear: the MFCo. had to accomplish the mission if it expected to be paid. Specific deadlines of April 20 and May 10 were set as demonstrations of progress.[43]

Making the trip upriver, an official project infused badly needed capital by helping to meet the cost of getting potential trappers to the harvest. That could be seen as a contrived subsidy to a private enterprise. Lewis could justify it, not as most have concluded, just to return the Mandan chief—but more important, to get a large force of Americans in the upper country to discourage British inroads.[44]

At the risk of his reputation, Governor Lewis was devising a continental strategy, a daring move to deny British traders the privileges they had previously taken around the Mandan/Hidatsa villages and were now trying to extend to the Great Falls or Pacific slope. There are few clues to that vision, because the discussions between Lewis and Clark and the other principals were face to face. The existing documents do not contain records of those conversations.

Only after Lewis made that risky commitment to return Sheheke-shote were the Articles of Association and Co-partnership of the MFCo. signed on March 3.[45] Four days later Governor Lewis made an initial down payment of $1,500.[46] That was the first of four drawn-in amounts that were small enough to be negotiated in the largely cashless frontier economy. The first bill of exchange was in favor of Benjamin Wilkinson, the agent for the company, who immediately left for Louisville to make arrangements with Clark's brother-in-law Denis Fitzhugh.

To avoid any misunderstanding the interpreters included subagent Pierre Dorion and his son Baptiste Dorion, both fluent in the Sioux language, and Chouteau's speaker, Noel Mongrain. The Arikara interpreter was Joseph Gravelines, and the Mandan interpreter René Jusseaume, whose family was returning home. On May 13 Jusseaume and Governor Lewis made an indenture for the education of thirteen-year-old Toussaint Jusseaume, who would remain in St. Louis as Meriwether's ward.[47]

The men who left St. Louis in thirteen barges in April and May believed the operation had a $10,000 capitalization. From personal experience Lewis knew that recruiting often involved enlargement of the truth. Specific examples of recruiting men include Richard Ward, who was engaged for three years in Louisville in early April by Benjamin Wilkinson. For $150 a year Ward was to help move a company boat to the headwaters of the Missouri, trap there, and help bring the returns back to St. Louis. At St. Louis on the nineteenth Auguste Pierre Chouteau agreed to pay Henly Donnalson $500 for work and labor. Thomas James was living in Florissant, fifteen miles northwest of St. Louis, when he signed on to steer the boat of twenty-four "Americans" under the supervision of Reuben Lewis.[48] None of the above appear to have been the experienced riflemen that the contract specified, but they would have to do in order to meet the governor's deadline.

The partnership held back until a codicil was written into the contract that Governor Lewis signed on February 24, 1809.

> Second. The said Lewis shall not before the last day fixed herein for the departure of said expedition, License or <permit> authorize any other person or persons to ascend the Missouri any higher or farther up said River, than the Mouth of the River La Platte, for the purpose of Trading with the Indians. Nor permit any party accompanying the said detachment or any other party, to ascend the river, go before or in advance of the said detachment commanded by said Choteau from the mouth of the said River La Platte, to the Mandan village.[49]

In guaranteeing that the MFCo. would enjoy the exclusive business of the upper river, Lewis provided the new operation with a monopoly that escaped the ambitions of many previous St. Louis traders. In creating a sinecure for his associates Governor Lewis made sure that the potential returns would be far more valuable than the seven-thousand-dollar direct government subsidy to get it started.

In a town of many merchants, news of a major new endeavor was not kept secret. On March 1 the *Missouri Gazette* announced the company.

> The Missouri Fur Company, lately formed here, has every prospect of becoming a source of incalculable advantage, not only to the individual's engaged in the enterprise, but the community at large. Their extensive preparations, and the respectable force they intend to ascend the Missouri with, may bid defiance to any hostile band they may meet with: — the streams which descend from the Rocky Mountains afford the finest hunting, and here we learn they intend to build their fort. They have engaged to convey Shehekah, the Mandan chief, to his nation.[50]

Critical townsmen also read between the printed lines. The investment was protected by a sweet deal with the governor, and those seven thousand federal dollars would go a long way toward covering the costs of moving a large outfit to the hunting grounds. No one complained because most St. Louis outfitters had some stake in the new adventure. Supplying the large number of hunters and boatmen being signed up was profitable to the merchants. Before the fleet of the MFCo. straggled away, St. Louis enjoyed a miniboom and those who gained saw no reason to question the financing. Exploiting public funds for private ambitions was on the way to becoming a western tradition.

The first concern was getting past the Arikara. Lewis gave Pierre Chouteau a temporary militia command. If he thought that the combined military and private parties were not strong enough to force a passage of the Arikara, Chouteau was authorized to engage three hundred of "the most friendly and confidential Indian nations . . . to cooperate with the detachment against the Aricares."[51] In actuality that meant the Yankton or Teton, who were not known as Sioux ("enemies" in Algonkian) for nothing. Clark felt that he had finally overcome the mistrust of the Tetons, and a combined army of 550 scheduled to assemble for battle at the mouth of the Cheyenne River should be sufficient to deal with the same number of poorly armed Arikara.

The governor's approach to uncooperative tribes was hardening. In his July 1808 report to the secretary of war he had been ready to sanction war using the Shawnees, Delawares, Kickapoos, Iowas, and Sioux as an extreme force to march against the uncooperative Little Osages.[52] If the Arikara put up a fight, they were to be cut off and the prisoners (if any) given to the Mandan and Hidatsa to be incorporated into those tribes. Only three years after preaching peace all across the continent, Lewis was ready to use a heavy hand on a people he had previously trusted. As historian and editor Donald Jackson pointed out, Lewis's call for their extirpation went further than Jefferson's recommendation of August 1808 that they be severely punished.[53] During the first months of his administration, Governor Lewis addressed several troublesome Indian problems and dealt with them firmly. Just before the MFCo. left, the governor added $500 in tobacco and munitions for Indian allies, and next day $440 worth of what was called Indian presents, which actually meant powder and lead, with the addition of tobacco and vermillion.[54]

The long list of military instructions that Meriwether wrote out in detail for the commander did not allow Pierre Chouteau much wiggle room. Governor Lewis was careful to ensure that the private enterprise would not deviate from the primary mission.

As a former army officer Lewis thought to provide a medical kit and supplies worth $220 in case there was action. Dr. William Thomas was going along as field surgeon for the militia and planned to return from the Mandan villages. After that the fur traders and trappers were on their own.[55]

By the end of May the first contingents of the MFCo. were under way with an impressive fleet of thirteen keelboats and barges. The actual number of men is difficult to determine because there were stragglers and deserters. Lewis dated his final order to Pierre Chouteau as late as June 8.[56] To ensure that the military party was as contracted, it would be inspected by Capt. Eli B. Clemson when passing Fort Osage.[57]

It was some months later that a description of the arrival was published in a Nashville newspaper.

Extract of a letter from Fort Osage, near the Fire Prairie, Missouri, July 11

On the 8th instant. The St. Louis Missouri Fur company arrived at this post, on their passage to the Rocky Montains, and this day their boats to the number of ten, got under way for their destination. This company consists of an incorporated body of Merchants, who have associated together for the purpose of carrying on the Indian trade, trapping and hunting on the head waters of the Missouri, and have organized a body of militia of 140 and upwards in number, under the command of Major Chouteau, for the purpose of conveying the Mandan Chief to his nation, and under the orders of the governor of the territory of Louisiana until this service is performed; after which they proceed on their original destination and pursuits.

This detachment appear to be well armed and equipped, and leave this in perfect good order and high spirits, and have no doubt but they will be quite competent to pass (or chastise should it be found necessary) any tribe of hostile Indians if any such they should meet with, on the Missouri.

P.S — This post is situated on the Missouri river, 350 miles above St. Louis, and is central to the Osages, Kenasas, Ottas, Missouris, Ioways, and Pewanies nation of Indians. Those nations of Indians are quite peaceable and friendly disposed, except the Kenasas, who at times commit depradations on the other tribes. The United States have erected a trading house here for their accommodation.[58]

There were already hints that all was not going well in the upper country. On May 29 after the flotilla was under way Clark wrote that "a man has just Come down the missouri who informs us that one man was killed by the Blackfoot Inds. last fall on the head of the Jefferson River and others robed."[59] He may not have known that the slain trapper was the former corpsman John Potts.

British traders on the upper Saskatchewan River confirmed that by an entry in the *Edmonton House Journal*.

The Falls Indians have likewise plundered a small American settlement on the Missoury & they confess themselves killed two of the men that belonged to it. Amongst other plunder, they have brought us a rifle Gun which on account of its weight they consider of little Value. Traded 70 beaver of inferior quality. The beaver that the Indians are bringing in may have been of a bad quality because they were poorly conditioned by the unlucky Americans.[60]

An earlier entry on October 2, 1808, appears to have resolved the problem of a loose cannon in the mountains.

> Several Blood Indians arrive'd with provisions &c. These People it appears from a variety of Accounts, & from the spoils now in their Possession, discovered in their Summer War excursions, on a southern branch of the Missoury, two small settlements which they plundered of goods to a considerable amount, besides about 300 Beaver Skins. One of the men belonging to these settlements was killed & the rest (ten in number) after being stripped were permitted to escape—From some papers brought in by the Indians, the immediate Traders seem to have been Canadians; but from the situation of the Houses, & from the American Colors, which were taken from them, it is concluded that they must have been Subject to the United States.[61]

Lewis and Clark's loose cannoneer in the mountains, former captain of artillery John McClallen had been killed.

Another North West Company trader on the Saskatchewan below Edmonton also recorded indignities that had fallen upon the party that Charles Courtin took above the Great Falls toward the Three Forks. However, the Canadians mentioned may have been some of the thirty who had thrown in with the McClallen party as it passed the Mandan/Hidatsa towns.

Unaware and certainly not informed of ominous developments, the militia moving up the river began having second thoughts. By July William Clark had six deserters from the expedition in jail and outfitting them was a dead loss to the company.[62] As the summer progressed Clark became increasingly pessimistic and would have given up his three-thousand-dollar commitment to the partnership if he could have found a buyer.[63]

For the past year Meriwether Lewis had been planning to return east. In the fall of 1808 Clark had arranged for his friend to use horses he had at Louisville. But the departure continued to be delayed, and Clark wrote to his brother, "I wish my horses wase here. Govr. Lewis talks of Going on but I think he will not untll July. if you meet with an oppertunity prey Send thum on to me partcularly the publc Horse."[64]

As far as Lewis and Clark were concerned, the travel plan had to do with the completion of the expedition narrative. But that kept being put aside by pressing matters of government. Clark related to his brother:

> we have been thretened by the Indians Some time ago, but every thing is like to turn out well, as Soon as ther plans and intentions was well understood, the Govr. ordered out the militia, and the regulars garresoned at Bellfontain near this place moved, those movements Confused the Stimulators (British) of the Indians flusterated their plans and the most of the bands broak of[f] from the Connection and well [we] Shall have tranquility. 100 Militia is Still up the Mississippi at the fort on that river placeing it in a complete State of Defence. they will be down in a fiew Days.[65]

It had been three years since St. Louis was sensitized to the melding of public and private interests. The secretary of war had condoned former governor Wilkinson's use of a military expedition to escort a private adventurer toward Santa Fe, but the troublesome commandant of the Ste. Genevieve district, Maj. Seth Hunt, found that an excuse to discredit Wilkinson.[66] Hunt was now an agent for Moses Austin and his activities would not bear close scrutiny.

That left it to the former factor of the Belle Fontaine Indian store to find fault with the arrangement. Rodolphe Tillier's quarrels with his assistant George Sibley had discredited him with Superintendent John Mason. When the new factory was built at Fort Osage, Mason pulled the rug from under Tillier by appointing Sibley factor, seconded by the governor's brother, Reuben Lewis. When William Clark assumed the administration of activities in St. Louis, it was no surprise that Tillier tried to blow the whistle on the funding of the MFCo. After the formation of the MFCo. became public, on April 27, 1809, Tillier wrote to President Madison, "Is it proper for the public service that the U.S. officers as a Governor or a Super Intendent of Indian Affairs & U.S. Factor at St. Louis should take any share in Mercantile and private concerns."[67]

Because the governor's contribution to the launching of a joint military/private enterprise had been authorized by the previous secretary of war, the new administration had to honor the seven-thousand-dollar commitment. But no matter what the president was led to think, the governor was doing his duty.

Outfitting the MFCo. expedition sucked up the stock of the mercantile community. Manuel Lisa spent or made promises to recruits but not many of them ever trusted him completely. The company purchasing agent Benjamin Wilkinson traveled as far as Louisville to complete the outfit. A good part of that economic boost was based on the expectation of the seven thousand dollars that Governor Lewis had authorized. But when the mail blocked by winter began getting through, it brought rejections of other previously submitted, legitimate government bills. If some War Department accountant refused to pay Pierre Provenchere $18.75 for translating the laws of the territory, what would that office do when it received four drafts to finance the return of an Indian chief?[68]

During the first seven months of 1809 the St. Louis business community simmered in an increasing stew of uncertainty. It didn't take much cracker barrel calculation to see that it was highly unlikely that the governor would be able to meet that debt from his own resources. Over the spring and summer those burdened businessmen began losing their nerve. A "run" began on "the bank of Meriwether Lewis."

Through the connection with his best friend Clark, the St. Louis entrepreneurs led Lewis into a compromising position. The governor provided a cash infusion that the MFCo. needed to get started. It is hard to conceive in modern times of instant plastic credit, but in 1809 St. Louis business ran on scraps of paper either carefully penned by a cautious merchant or hastily scribbled on a makeshift desk. This was instant currency but it was only as good as the man who signed the paper. Such arrangements were not limited to an exchange between two individuals, because markers passed from hand to hand were bartered or negotiated in payment for things far from the original obligation. Merchants essentially operated on faith, and a weak link in those long chains of promises put everyone in jeopardy in a society that did not ordinarily rely on specie as a source of funds.

Not until August 18, 1809, after enduring months of uncertainty, was Lewis relieved to receive confirmation that the MFCo. bill would be paid. But the government refused the bill that he wrote on May 13 for $500 worth of "Tobacco, Powder, &c. intended as Presents for the Indians, through which this expedition was to pass."[69] Lewis knew that two other bills were buried somewhere; one he had written on the first of May for medical supplies for Dr. Thomas, and another written on May 15 for $440 that was also described as additional Indian presents.[70] They would surely be refused.

The outraged governor responded immediately.

Those protested Bills from the Departments of War and treasury have effectively sunk my Credit: brought in all my private debts, amounting to about $4000, which has compelled me, in order to do justice to my Creditors, to deposit with them, the landed property which I had purchased in this Country as Security.[71]

Lewis was also enraged about a complex chain of bureaucratic buckpassing that had been going on since 1808 over the costs of printing the laws of the territory.[72] That was a temporary setback that he would resolve when he went to Washington. But he could not help feeling insulted by unjustified insinuations that emanated from the office of the former secretary of state, James Madison, who was now the president.

NOTES

1. Alexander Wilson, "Particulars of the Death of Capt. Lewis," *Port Folio* 7 (January 1812): 39.

2. WC to Jonathan Clark, January 2, 1809, in James Holmberg, ed., *Dear Brother* (New Haven, CT: Yale University Press, 2002), pp. 189–90.

3. An appreciative tip of our hat to Landon Jones for his description of that time in his fine book *William Clark and the Shaping of the West* (New York: Hill and Wang, 2004), p. 171.

4. Ever a defender, Grace Lewis Miller pointed out that Clark owed Lewis something for his half of the rent on the first house.

5. Lewis's letter to Dearborn on October 3, 1808, was received on March 20, 1809; Clark's letter to Dearborn on December 2, 1808, was received on January 19, 1809; Bates's letter of February 7, 1809, left with the mail on the eleventh and was received on March 30. RG107, M22, roll 4, and Carter, *TP* 14: 242–43, 257.

6. FB to James Bates, January 1, 1809, letterbook 1801–1809, BFP-MHS.

7. TJ to the secretary of the treasury, January 9, 1809, Carter, *TP* 14: 248–49.

8. John Mason to Thomas Newton, January 16, 1809, RG75, M16, roll 1, pp. 310–13; John Mason to SW, RG107, M342, M221, roll 33, frame 1246, NARA.

9. John Mason to WC, December 31, 1808, Carter, *TP* 14: 247.

10. Dispute between Tillier and the Office of Indian Affairs: John Mason to Rodolphe Tillier, June 21, 1809, RG75, M16, roll 2, pp. 13–17, NARA.

11. HD to TJ, February 16, 1809, document 33040, reel 42, TJ-LOC; HD to TJ, February 16, 1809, reel 10, document 5985 1/4, JMA-LOC.

12. Orchard Cook to TJ, December 24, 1807, RG59, M418, roll 4, frame 0157, NARA.

13. The president's secretary regularly delivered messages to the House and Lewis may have known Eustis when he was a representative from 1801 to 1804.

14. TJ to ML, July 17, 1808, Jackson, *LLC* 2: 444–45. As it turned out Astor went to Montreal instead of St. Louis.

15. Lisa and Drouillard returned by August 5. On that day, Drouillard bought

a hat, shoes, and suspenders from Philipson's store. Joseph Philipson's account book, August 5, 1808.

16. Holmberg, *Dear Brother*, pp. 141, 142nn4, 6.

17. Ibid., p. 168.

18. Ibid., pp. 170–71.

19. William Morrison was a nephew of the Philadelphia Quaker merchant Guy Bryan who sent Morrison west in 1790. See Daybooks 1805–1808, Bryan and Morrison Business Records, University of Illinois.

20. Holmberg, *Dear Brother*, p. 182. See p. 185n3 for author's interpretation of mixing private and public business.

21. John C. Jackson, "Captain John McClallen," in *The Louisiana Purchase: A Historical and Geographical Encyclopedia* (Santa Barbara, CA: ABC-Clio, 2002).

22. Joseph B. Tyrrell, "Letter of Roseman and Perch, July 10th, 1807," *Oregon Historical Quarterly* 38 (December 1937): 394–95.

23. John B. Thompson to George Gibson, August 12, 1808, deed book B, 152, recorder of deeds, City of St. Louis, St. Louis, MO.

24. "Journal of the Rocky Mountain House Occurrences, October 11, 1806, to July 26, 1807, by David Thompson," Archives of Ontario MS, DT book 18, microreel 2, np. Lt. Jeremy Pinch to the British Mercht., Poltito Palton Lake, September 19, 1807; T. C. Elliott, "The Strange Case of David Thompson and Jeremy Pinch," *Oregon Historical Quarterly* 40 (June 1939): 190–91.

25. Admittedly, this speculation hangs on the thinnest threads of deduction but is explained in John Jackson's reconstruction of McClallen's activities in a book-length manuscript.

26. Holmberg, *Dear Brother*, p. 197.

27. Actually $8,987.50 before they were divided.

28. Richard Edward Oglesby, *Manuel Lisa and the Opening of the Missouri Fur Trade* (Norman: University of Oklahoma Press, 1963), pp. 65–67.

29. John Mason to Governor Lewis, May 17, 1809, Carter, *TP* 14: 275. Mason expected that the embargo would soon be lifted.

30. Holmberg, *Dear Brother*, p. 184.

31. Ibid., p. 197.

32. St. Louis MFCo. record book 1809–1812, Chouteau Family Collection, MHS.

33. Holmberg, *Dear Brother*, p. 201.

34. Drouillard's previous duty watching Lisa may not have been entirely voluntary as there is a record that Morrison took him to court for unspecified damages on March 9, 1807. Drouillard may have been working off that debt. See GLM, box 47, folder 23, JNEM.

35. Oglesby, *Manuel Lisa*, pp. 66–70.

36. See Murray G. Lawson, "The Beaver Hat and the North American Fur Trade," and John C. Ewers, "The Influence of the Fur Trade Upon the Indians of the Northern Plains," 27–37, in *People and Pelts: Selected Papers. Second North American Fur Trade Conference* (Winnipeg: Peguis Publishers, 1972).

37. Oglesby, *Manuel Lisa*, p. 70.

38. Ibid., p. 68n6.

39. WC to HD, August 20, 1808, RG107, C197, M221, roll 19, frame 5842, NARA. Note the timing of Clark's letter after Lisa and Drouillard returned on the fifth and Thompson reported before August 12.

40. Nathaniel Pryor to WC, October 16, 1807, Jackson, *LLC* 2: 437.

41. *Frankfort (KY) Palladium*, December 30, 1809, p. 2.

42. SW to WC, March 9, 1807, Carter, *TP* 14: 108–109.

43. Agreement for Return of the Mandan Chief, February 24, 1809, Jackson, *LLC* 2: 447.

44. WC to HD, August 20, 1808, RG107, C197, M221, roll 19, frame 5842, NARA.

45. Oglesby, *Manuel Lisa*, p. 68n6. Author cites three copies of this agreement, the last in French for the Chouteaus.

46. ML to SW, March 7, 1809, RG107, L299, M221, roll 25, frame 8477, NARA.

47. René Jusseaume to ML, May 13, 1809, French and Spanish Archives, roll F523, item 2982, State Historical Society of Missouri, Columbia, MO.

48. Thomas James, *Three Years among the Indians and Mexicans* (repr., Lincoln: University of Nebraska Press, 1984), p. 4.

49. Agreement for Return of the Mandan Chief, February 24, 1809, Jackson, *LLC* 2: 449.

50. *Missouri Gazette*, March 1, 1809, p. 3.

51. ML to PC, June 8, 1809, Jackson, *LLC* 2: 452.

52. ML to SW, July 1, 1808, Carter, *TP* 14: 197–98.

53. TJ to ML, July 17, 1808, Jackson, *LLC* 2: 445n1.

54. ML to WD, May 15, 1809, RG107, L1809, M22, roll 4, frame 1535, NARA.

55. RG107, L340, NARA. The bill upon the government for medicines was dated May 1.

56. ML to PC, June 8, 1809, Jackson, *LLC* 2: 451–56.

57. Eli Clemson to William Linnard, November 18, 1809, RG107, L366, M221, roll 25, frame 8526, NARA.

58. *Democratic Clarion (TN)*, December 8, 1809, col. 4.

59. Holmberg, *Dear Brother*, p. 201.

60. Entry for October 31, 1808, *Edmonton House Journal*, July 30, 1808, to August 2, 1809, HBCA B.60/a/8, fo.4, Manitoba Provincial Archives. The Indians were mistaken; John Colter had escaped. The heavy rifle was his, the same he had carried during the expedition.

61. October 2, 1808, HBCA B60/a/8, fo.4, Manitoba Provincial Archives.

62. The deserters Charles Bourguion, François LeMichel, Nicholas Brazeau, and Joseph Richard were taken to court in November. L. Ruth Frick, *Courageous Colter and Companions* (Washington, MO: Colter-Frick, 1997), p. 248.

63. Holmberg, *Dear Brother*, p. 210.

64. Ibid., p. 201.

65. Ibid., pp. 201–202.

66. Dr. Andrew Steele accompanied Lieutenant Wilkinson's expedition to the mouth of the Platte. How McClallen's plan to go to Santa Fe related to Lieutenant Pike's 1806 expedition was another unanswered question.

67. Rodolphe Tillier to John Mason (forwarded to President Madison), April 27, 1809, RG107, T1809, M222, roll 4, frame 1628, NARA. For an abridged version of this letter, see Robert Rutland et al., *The Papers of James Madison: Presidential Series*, 5 vols. (Charlottesville: University of Virginia Press, 1984), 1: 141–42.

68. ML to secretary of state, May 28, 1808, Carter, *TP* 14: 188–89.

69. SW to ML, July 15, 1809, Carter, *TP* 14: 285.

70. Two bills written on May 1 and 15, 1809, were received by the War Department on the same date of October 7. But the bill for $500 dated May 26 was received June 20 (RG107, M22, roll 4).

71. ML to WE, August 18, 1809, Jackson, *LLC* 2: 459–61.

72. That ultimately hurt Pierre Provenchere, who was not being paid. Pierre Provenchere to his father, July 29, 1809, Provenchere Collection, MHS.

Fourteen

Beginning a Fatal Slide

None but unfeeling strangers knew[1]

F or two months winter-bound St. Louis received no mail at all.[2]
Relying on local news to fill his four small pages, the editor of the *Missouri Gazette* was forced to declare that "the *Gazette* is under certain control" and was not the mouthpiece for the administration.[3]

But Joseph Charless owed a lot to Governor Lewis for helping him set up the press and for feeding him public business to be printed. The price for printing the laws of the territory came to five hundred dollars, a figure that eventually rose threefold. Unfortunately, the jobs that set Charless's press on solid footing created difficulties for Lewis with the man who was now president elect.

As fellow Virginians, James Madison and Meriwether Lewis should have been friends. Eight years before, when President Jefferson's new secretary had been getting his feet under himself, Mr. and Mrs. Madison had lived in the president's house through May. Over the next two years they shared stimulating dinners with the president. Mrs. Madison sometimes acted as hostess for more formal functions. Lewis looked to her health when fever struck.

During the intervening years, in some ways Captain Lewis knew more about what President Jefferson was thinking than did his secretary of state.

As the purchase of Louisiana moved forward Madison dismissed the new territory as a place to shuffle off increasingly inconvenient Indians. After questioning the legality of an exploring expedition, Secretary Madison suggested the benefit to commerce should be stressed to Congress as a justification for the expenditure. When asked to provide Captain Lewis with a question to add to his list, Madison only inquired if it would be convenient to occasionally measure the heads of the Indians.[4] Not a particularly enthusiastic endorsement of the plan.

More direct evidence of Madison's stand regarding Louisiana as room for displaced Indians (not for new states) was defined in a twenty-seven-page pseudonymous pamphlet, signed and dated Sylvestris (aka St. George Tucker, aka James Madison), August 10, 1803.[5] That pamphlet appeared when the expedition was already being organized. But in a year-end letter to Mr. Jefferson from St. Louis, Lewis gave three definite reasons why it was impracticable to relocate settlers and tribesmen. It may have been a mistake to enclose a transcript for Mr. Madison.[6]

Because the territorial governor reported to the secretary of state, Madison was not entirely pleased when the popular hero dawdled away a year in Washington, Philadelphia, and Virginia instead of rushing to take hold in St. Louis. When Meriwether put in for the first quarterly payment of his salary, the secretary of state's office deducted $5.55 for an overcharge.[7]

A more telling fiscal friction with the State Department began after Lewis took over as governor and engaged Pierre Provenchere to translate certain sections of the laws of the territory into French for the modest sum of $18.75. It was only fair that all the laws should be available to the French-speaking citizens. Uncertain what to charge, Provenchere queried his father in Philadelphia who estimated that the translation of the 370 pages ought to be worth $560.[8] When Lewis learned that the Department of State refused to pay that first modest charge, he immediately stopped Provenchere, who was halfway through the full translation. That meant there was a debt for perhaps $280 for the work already performed. On February 6, 1809, Lewis resubmitted the Provenchere bill to the State Department without realizing that the piddling amount was the tip of a larger problem.[9]

Although the administration of the territory was a State Department obligation, Secretary Madison further embarrassed the governor by rejecting a five-hundred-dollar bill of exchange for providing an advance to buy paper and ink to print the laws of the territory. On Madison's recommendation to hold Lewis accountable, the treasurer of the United States returned that perfectly legitimate bill. In all there would be six bills of exchange relating to the publication of 250 copies in English and 100 in French. The total cost for the printing and publishing totaled $1518.95, all of which was refused.[10]

The November 1809 election of James Madison seemed to promise a continuation of the Jefferson administration's policies. Unfortunately the former government went out under the cloud of the ill-conceived Embargo Act and the expense of calling up a hundred-thousand-man army. The embargo blocked the income derived from foreign commerce at the same time that Congress increased defense spending dramatically. In a report dated December 10, 1808, Secretary of the Treasury Gallatin relayed the bad news that government revenue had fallen by six million from the previous year and was "daily decreasing."[11]

Mr. Jefferson's parting gift to Madison was the repeal of the embargo three days before Madison took office. The restriction was replaced with the Non-intercourse Acts, which reopened trade with all nations except England and France. The country was in business again.

Another carry-over expense inherited by the new administration was the cost of calling for a huge army when war with Great Britain seemed imminent.[12] It didn't matter that it had really been a political gesture and that most of the militiamen were paper soldiers; the call-up was expensive and the cost had to be met. The last contribution of the outgoing Jefferson administration was the submission of a budget for the next year, a work of creative imagination apparently designed by the Treasury Department.

The last budget from the Jefferson administration limited the government of Louisiana to an appropriation of $6,600 for salaries of the governor, judges, and territorial secretary, with a munificent sum of $350 for office expenses.[13] The salary of the governor was $2,000 and that of the territorial secretary, $1,500. Salaries for the judges and other public officers soaked up the rest of the fund, leaving nothing appropriated to run the government. Governor Lewis had already committed more than $7,000 to send Sheheke-shote home.

Politics entered into the creation of the Madison cabinet because Sen. William B. Giles and his followers were determined to prevent a foreigner from holding the important office of Secretary of State. Opposed to the appointment of Albert Gallatin, as a compromise Giles was willing to have Gallatin to continue as secretary of the treasury.[14]

Madison's political advisors also rejected the appointment of Michigan Territorial Gov. William Hull as secretary of war.[15] Instead, a former Massachusetts congressman and lately Boston hospital administrator William

Eustis was suggested. Three days after his inauguration on March 4, 1809, President Madison named Eustis to that important responsibility. Henry Dearborn had already departed on February 17 and the new secretary of war did not appear until the fifth of April. There seems to have been no plan for a transition program and for six weeks, day-to-day operations were left to Chief Clerk John Smith and accounting to William Simmons.

National security seemed assured when the British minister David Erskine told the president that his government had rescinded the orders in council that had created past abuses, and a special envoy would be sent to adjust differences. Greatly encouraged, on April 19 Madison proclaimed an end to the ban on trade with England. The extensive and expensive troop buildup in anticipation of war with Great Britain would end in July. But it turned out that Mr. Erskine had exceeded his authority and there would be no agreement with England.[16]

Retained at Treasury, Albert Gallatin continued working with his former associates on the Committee on Ways and Means to streamline the War and Navy departments. Promptness and real accountability was intended to check abuses by officers of the government. Seeking the means to impose economy Gallatin devised a system to bring free-wheeling disbursing officers to heel. Henceforth, they would be required to make estimates and have expenditures approved before writing any checks.[17] Although it was international relations that had disrupted the national economy, he looked to the War and Navy departments as a way of decreasing the bourgeoning debt. Gallatin wrote:

> It is believed that the present system of accountability of the military and naval establishments may be rendered more prompt and direct, and is susceptible of improvements which, without embarrassing the public service, will have a tendency more effectually to check any abuses of subordinate agents. Provisions to that effect are rendered more necessary by the probable increase in those departments.[18]

A concerned Congress cooperated by approving a measure that seemed reasonable on the surface but failed to consider important actualities. The flaw in the effort to control expenditures was the distance to frontier establishments. At best it took a month or more for letters to travel between the capital and the western posts—in winter, two or even three months while correspondence moldered in some snow-blocked riders' dispatch case. Consideration and a response doubled the time lag.

Had Governor Lewis known that he was supposed to wait for the approval of Indian gifts necessary to draw tribal allies into the Arikara campaign, that response would have been delayed for another year. Another drawback was the implication that officers serving at distant posts with heavy responsibilities could not be trusted to act decisively when the situation required an immediate response. Waiting two or three months for the approval of some closeted accountant eroded initiative.

Then on May 18, 1809, Secretary Gallatin divulged to President Madison that "government expenses will not be able to be paid this year. The suspension of commerce and the consequent decrease of importation during the last twelve months will necessarily cause a great diminution in the receipts."[19] Lacking the funds to pay its bills, the Madison administration had to impose economies.

However, Secretary Gallatin rationalized that land board expenditures in Louisiana were justified because the sale of public lands, authorized and recorded by three commissioners, was supposed to generate income. In addition to his $1,500 salary as territorial secretary, Frederick Bates was paid $500 as recorder of land titles and $1,200 for his role as land board commissioner from a separate treasury office account.[20] Thomas Riddick, the favored clerk of the land board, received $1,500.[21]

As the mails between Washington and St. Louis began moving again, Governor Lewis realized the earthquake shift in the comfortable relationship that he previously enjoyed with the Jefferson administration. He was already having problems with the State Department and now trouble with the War Department loomed. Eustis came to the War Department from previous service as a hospital administrator, with little understanding of what was required to deal with a widely scattered, poorly supported military stationed on distant frontiers.

Military historian Theodore Crackel, author of *Mr. Jefferson's Army*, wrote that "the new administration was both indifferent and inadequate" to the maintenance of the army. "Eustis—with the apparent support of Madison—undid much of what Jefferson and Dearborn had created."[22]

That extended beyond stopping recruiting or making appointments to the military academy because the government of Louisiana still reported to the secretary of war in matters dealing with the Indian tribes. In November 1808 Secretary of War Dearborn wrote a letter to William Clark that the western Indian agent did not receive until after the winter broke. When Clark answered on April 29, 1809, he may not have known he was addressing a new secretary. A month later, Eustis read a recapitulation of the developments of the past year and an overview of the present situation with the tribes. Filling in details that might have been lost in the transition of the office, Clark showed that those actions were perfectly consistent with what Governor Lewis was doing.[23]

When Clark's letter reached Washington on May 11, Secretary Eustis responded that estimates of expenses would have to be submitted and approved before action could be undertaken. Eustis pointed out that expenditures for the past year had totaled an outrageous twenty thousand dollars.[24] Presumably Governor Lewis was also informed of this new regulation. If not, Clark made him aware.

With his letter Clark forwarded an analysis of the situation along the lower Arkansas River, where settlers and opportunists were illegally dealing with the dissident Osage who refused to accept the Fort Osage Treaty. Governor Lewis appointed his friend James McFarlane to go to the Arkansas River and corral them. In December 1808 McFarlane reported "that the civil and Military cannot understand each other as well as they aught to do for the safety of the country and our frontiers."[25]

Capt. George Armistead refused to recognize the authority of the governor to control immigrant Indians or intrusive whites, and the militia could not be depended upon because they were often the same men who were involved in illicit trading.[26] However, when impoverished Osage came to the temporary Indian agent at Fort Madison on the Arkansas, John Breck Treat refused to deal with them in order to force them to look to Fort Osage for their supplies.[27]

At the Arkansas River in mid-February 1809, McFarlane assembled a delegation of Osage to take to St. Louis. It was not a pleasant trip as tribal cultures were fragmenting. When the party arrived on the White River, McFarlane learned that Maj. Seth Hunt told the displaced Cherokee living there that they were at liberty to kill the Osage in his party. Passing from the Cherokee village to a refugee Delaware town, "I found them burning their friends and relations, which they said were bad persons, such horrid seens I never heard of before this."[28] The dark influence of the Shawnee Prophet had invaded Louisiana.

On March 31, 1809, on the oath of James McFarlane, Governor Lewis issued a warrant for the arrest of whiskey traders supposed to be agents of an unlicensed trader. Attorney General Edward Hempstead warned Secretary Bates not to interfere with the trial of some of the miscreants that was due to be held on the fourth Monday of the next month at New Madrid.[29]

A week later Lewis noted that intruders were settling near the Shawnee villages on the Merrimac River and near the Delaware towns on the St. Francis

River above New Madrid, and he required Bates to prepare a proclamation ordering those squatters to remove and the sheriff to enforce it. Through his special agent and enforcer, Lewis was dealing firmly with scofflaws.

The governor had acted decisively to solve the Osage problem. But when McFarlane was among the Cherokee and Delaware he observed the growing influence of the Shawnee Prophet, whose adherents were burning unbelievers.[30] Soon there were ominous rumors from the north that a band of Winnebago had descended the Illinois River with the intention of attacking the outpost near the mouth of the Des Moines. When the trustworthy Lt. Nathaniel Pryor reported that place was in a bad state of defense, Governor Lewis called for volunteers to protect the frontier.

At that time the country was still under the general order of November 1808 calling on Louisiana for its quota of 377 men as part of the hundred-thousand-man national army.[31] On April 3, in keeping with discussions with the previous administration, Lewis asked for two companies from St. Louis and St. Charles, which would be designated the "Louisiana Spies." But volunteers for those scouts were reluctant to engage, and after a week the disappointed governor was obliged to order out the existing militia companies of St. Louis and St. Charles.[32]

On April 21 Indian agent Nicholas Boilvin reported from Prairie du Chien that "I am at present, in the fire, receiving Indian news every day that a Puant (Winnebago) chief was employed by the British to get all nations to go to Detroit to see their British father."[33] Two days later Capt. James House of the United States Army arrived at the Des Moines outpost and found that Alpha Kingsley had abandoned that installation and moved into a new Fort Madison. But Kingsley was a poor military engineer, and that place was still indefensible because it lay under high ground.[34]

Tension had eased somewhat by May 16 when Indiana Territorial Gov. W. H. Harrison wrote Eustis from Vincennes that the threat of trouble from the Prophet's town seemed to be receding. He couldn't quite put his finger on the reason and had planted a confidential Frenchman in the Indian town as a spy. It would have been about a month before Eustis received this and he may have been led to doubt if what Governor Lewis was doing in Louisiana was really justified. But there was still the possibility of a major Indian outbreak in the Northwest.[35]

In his first full year as governor, Meriwether Lewis brought a number of Indian problems under control, moved to stop random crimes by tribesmen or whites, resolved the old Osage problem, confronted illicit activities on the Arkansas River, and did what he could to answer the growing threat of a major tribal insurrection in the Northeast. And he finally had the return of the Mandan chief Sheheke-shote under way, guarded by a temporary militia force under the command of the experienced Indian agent Pierre Chouteau. The chief's return had been ordered by the previous administration but what would the new, budget-minded secretary of war think about the seven-thousand-dollar cost? Or of the supplemental bills of four or five hundred dollars for Indian presents to be distributed by Chouteau as needed?[36]

In the spring of 1809 land speculators seemed curiously disinterested in the security of the territory. At a time when Governor Lewis was dealing with frontier defense, Secretary Bates was receiving, and not discouraging, letters meant to discredit those efforts.

During the previous summer Lewis appointed John M. Heath to several civil offices in the St. Charles District. Heath appeared to be a forward-thinking man who in association with William Christy established a salt works in what would be later known as Blackwater Township, Cooper County. On February 7, 1809, Heath wrote Bates a fawning letter trying to excuse himself from what might have been an attempt to defraud private individuals "and if possible Saddle the odium and responsibility upon the Executive." He confessed that he disclosed the key of the plan to Bates and was now trying to retract statements that might have involved the secretary. Three days after Bates "parried the unwarrantable aims" Heath asked him "if the child had not better be smothered in its infancy!"[37]

Bates kept letters critical of the governor's firm action in dealing with the Osage on the Arkansas. When special agent McFarlane demanded troops to help him clean up illicit activities, the commandant at Fort Pickering complained that he "has excited much allarm among the inhabitants from his threats and bosting authority."[38] After the turn of the year another Lewis appointee, John Honey, went farther in accusing McFarlane of outrageous dealings among the Cherokee. His appearance on the Arkansas had inspired "universal terror."[39] But Honey and Captain Armistead did not take their complaints to the governor. Instead they went to Secretary Bates, giving that jealous subordinate an excuse to claim Lewis was losing the confidence of the citizens.

In mid-April Bates spilled his bile to his brother Richard:

I have spoken my wrongs with extreme freedom to the Governor—It *was* my intention to have appealed to *his* superiors and *mine*; but the altercation was brought about by a circumstance which aroused my indignation and the overflowings of a heated resentment, burst the barriers which Prudence and Principle had prescribed. We now understand each other much better. We differ in every thing; but we will be honest and frank in our intercourse. . . . I lament the unpopularity of the Governor; but he had brought it on himself by harsh and mistaken measures. He is inflexible in error, and the irresistable Fiat of the People, has, I am fearful, already sealed his condemnation. Burn this, and do not speak of it.[40]

But another denunciation of the governor soon went east to Bates's brother:

I never saw, after his arrival in this country, anything in his conduct towards me, but alienation and unmerited distrust. I had acquired and shall retain a good portion of the public confidence, and he had not generosity of soul to forgive me for it. . . . I bore in silence the supercilious air of the Governor for a long time; until last summer [1809] he took it into his head to disavow certain statements which I had made, *by his order* from the Secretary's Office. This was too much—I waited on him,—told him my wrongs—that I could not bear to be treated in such a manner—that he *had* given me the orders & as truth is always eloquent, the Public *would believe* it on my assurances. He told me to take my own course—I shall, Sir, said I, and I shall come, in future to the Executive Office when I have *business* at it.[41]

The quarrel between the governor and the territorial secretary came to a head in late June during the Masonic celebration of the Festival of St. John the Baptist.[42] Brother Charless saw that the *Gazette* published an invitation to those who were not brethren to attend. The procession would form at the lodge room at noon and march to the church, where a brother (presumably Bates) would deliver the oration. Dinner was scheduled for three o'clock, followed by a ball.[43]

The description of what happened at the festival depends entirely upon the unforgiving bias of Brother Bates.

. . . there was a ball in St. Louis. I attended early, and was seated in conversation with some Gentlemen when the Governor entered. He drew his chair close to mine—There was a pause in the conversation—I availed myself of it—arose and walked to the opposite side of the room. The dances were now commencing—*He* also rose—evidently in passion, retired into an adjoining room and sent a servant for General Clark, who refused to ask me out as he foresaw that a Battle must have been the consequence of our meeting. He complained to the general that I had treated him with contempt & insult in the Ball-Room and that he could not suffer it to pass. He knew my resolutions not to speak to him except in business and he ought not to have thrust himself in my way. The thing *did pass* nevertheless for some weeks when General Clark waited on me for the purpose of introducing me to make some advances. I replied to him "*NO*, the Governor has told me to take my own course and I shall step a *high* and a *proud* Path. He has *injured* me and he must *undo* that injury or I shall succeed in fixing the stigma where it *ought* to *rest*."[44]

These were serious matters. Clark managed to steer his friend away from something rash and potentially fatal. Not long after the ballroom incident, he went further in trying to effect a reconciliation, which the supercilious Bates rejected in an insulting way that Clark chose to overlook. Lewis also made an attempt to reconstruct the relationship. According to Bates, when he went to the executive office on business, the governor made another placative gesture. Considering himself the injured party, Bates refused to accept the overture unless his confederate Carr and some other gentlemen were called in as witnesses. He wrote later, "*this* particular misunderstanding [was] adjusted to the entire satisfaction of Carr and myself."[45] If the word of a declared enemy is true, then Meriwether Lewis had made a humiliating effort to keep his administration functioning.

When the terms of the government had been decided in the president's mansion, Lewis had expected something better from Frederick Bates who would be a useful addition to his government. For a year while Lewis attended to more pressing matters, Territorial Secretary Bates was the only authority in Louisiana. But those distractions had dragged on too long, and the subordinate developed a proprietary interest in his temporary authority. It was unfortunate that they had gotten off on a sour note causing Bates to turn sulky, then belligerent, and finally insulting. Now they were traveling hopelessly divergent paths.

The lawyer and special agent of the Treasury Department William C. Carr was less concerned about ethical considerations when he wrote to his brother Charles:

> I think the day is now close at hand when a fortune may be made by the purchase of lands in Louisiana. It is true that they have risen a little already. But the circumstance will be no disadvantage to a purchaser.— On the contrary, it will serve as a direction to those quarters of the territory, where the greatest current of immigration has heretofore been and where monied men or those able to purchase the best farms would first settle themselves provided the lands were for sale—
>
> An effect has now taken place, which without my vanity, I think I may say was foreseen by several years past—The introduction of the

American government here (as is the case) perhaps on a greater or less degree upon all material revolutions in a country brought into circulation a considerable quantity of cash; which was a medium, until then not very common in Upper Louisiana. This in a measure intoxicated many persons & plunged them directly into excesses, which their fortunes & a greater scarcity of cash would not support—This added to the natural & obvious effects of the American government on the Commerce of the Country, by discountenancing monopolies & granting no exclusive privileges, produced a brisk exchange of property, whilst it has exposed many individuals to law suits & a total sacrifice of their property. In consequence of this there is a great quantity of land for sale in this territory, both cultivated and uncultivated. The most common price for that sold at private sale is $2.00 an acre . . .

Good lands must greatly increase in value here in the course of a few years—I shall certainly purchase if I can do so without involving myself—They are offered to me every day on a long credit, by paying a little cash in hand. I expect Mr. Bates our Secretary will join me in some purchases we contemplate making in a short time—If therefore you think proper to vest any of your money in property of that kind & can trust it with me I flatter myself I could employ it to a great advantage for you.

I have made more important contracts in six months past than I ever made in all of my life before—I have bought two negro fellows, one last spring—another a few weeks since for $333.33 part on a credit of 12 months—This last I sold again directly for one of those land warrants issued by the late Secy of War to the followers of Lewis and Clark for 320 acres each—payable at the land office at $2 an acre.[46]

Through a tumultuous time Meriwether Lewis was as reticent to reveal his feelings on paper as he had been to make regular entries in the expedition journals. He wrote, when it was necessary, with precision and even brilliance but was usually conservative of unnecessary words or personal expression. Does that make him a lazy penman? Or was he a self-contained leader who preserved the dignity of his office in contrast to the blustering of lesser men? It is an irony of that expressive restraint that his biographers have been obliged to depend on the biased words of others to reconstruct a private man.

At the beginning of July, War Department accountant William Simmons informed Clark that Indian department expenditures in the Louisiana Territory had exceeded expectations. The Indian agent was directed to send specific quarterly estimates "in sufficient season" to enable the department to advise Clark before any bills are drawn on the department. When Clark received this directive, he responded that he had been instructed by the Secretary of War to pay the accounts authorized by himself as necessary. "I do not recolect to have exceeded what appeared to be necessary."[47] In August Clark was reprimanded for hiring subagents without authority. But an internal 1809 memo from the secretary of war to the superintendent of Indian trade shows that Eustis agreed that the local supervisor should appoint the agents "to whom they ought to be well known . . . and accountable."[48] That memo apparently never reached Simmons's desk, because he told Clark that several agents and interpreters had not been authorized or approved by the department and he would not pay their salaries, thereby crippling the Louisiana Indian agency.

On July 26, 1809, Governor Lewis announced that the militia Washington had called for in the hundred-thousand-man army could stand down. Filling the territorial quota of 377 men had been disappointing, as there were only 50 heroes to release. In making that call on the order from the president and secretary of war, Lewis had put his heart into a patriotic appeal. If there was a lesson to draw from the disappointing response, it had to be that citizens of Louisiana were more interested in themselves than in the nation.

NOTES

1. Alexander Wilson, "Particulars of the Death of Capt. Lewis," *Port Folio* 7 (January 1812): 39.

2. *Missouri Gazette*, January 25, 1809, p. 3.

3. *Missouri Gazette*, January 4, 1809, pp. 2–3.

4. James Madison's Notes, April 14, 1803, Jackson, *LLC* 1: 34.

5. Sylvestris, *Reflections on the Cession of Louisiana to the United States* (Washington City: printed by Samuel Harrison Smith, 1803).

6. ML to TJ, December 28, 1803, Jackson, *LLC* 1: 148–55.

7. Governor Lewis to the secretary of state, June 28, 1807, Carter, *TP* 14: 131–32.

8. Peter Provenchere to his father, July 29, 1809, Provenchere Papers, MHS. Provenchere became aware that the State Department was refusing the governor's bills and expressed doubts whether he would be paid.

9. ML to JMA, February 6, 1809, MSS 9041, 9041-a, papers of the Lewis, Anderson, and Marks families.

10. Expenses for printing the laws were detailed through Lewis's six bills of exchange. No. 1 to Pierre Provenchere, $71.50 for translating the laws of the territory into French; No. 2 to Joseph Charless, $500 on July 22, 1808, for paper and printing

the laws of the territory; No. 3 to Francois V. Bouis, $18 on December 28, 1808, for translating additional laws into French; No. 4 to Charless, $88.75 for printing certain laws necessary for immediate distribution; No. 5 to Provenchere, $18.70 on February 6, 1809, for additional translation; No. 6 to Charless, $822 on May 5, 1809, for printing laws, territorial general orders, and blanks for militia returns.

11. AG to the Committee of Ways and Means, December 10, 1808, RG233, M1268, roll 7, frame 0084, p.180, NARA.

12. US Statutes at Large 2 (1964): 478, http://memory.loc.gov/ammem/amlaw/lwsl.html (accessed April 8, 2008).

13. Ibid., p. 523.

14. Dice Robins Anderson, *William Branch Giles* (Gloucester, UK: Peter Smith, 1965), pp. 148–49.

15. William B. Giles to JMA, January 10, 1809, document 965 and February 1809, document 988 and February 27, 1809, document 1011-1014, series 2, reel 25, JMA-LOC.

16. James Morton Smith, *The Republic of Letters: The Correspondence between Thomas Jefferson and James Madison, 1776–1836*, 3 vols. (New York: Norton, 1995), 3: 1569–71, 1597.

17. *ASP, Finance* 2: 335–36.

18. AG to the Committee of Ways and Means, December 10, 1808, RG233, M1268, roll 7, NARA. In this time of austerity, Gallatin gave a bonus, "an additional allowance" of $550 to the clerks in the treasurer's, accountant's, and comptroller's office in August 1809, RG217, M235, roll 67, documents 22277-78, frames 0850-53, NARA.

19. AG to JMA, May 18, 1809, RG217, M235, roll 19, frame 0363. Halting exports affected the Office of Indian Trade, which needed an immediate infusion of fifteen thousand dollars and asked for an additional twenty-five thousand dollars two months later. John Mason to SW, July 19, 1809, RG75, M16, roll 2. It also promised to be a difficult year for army personnel, who would not be fully paid until 1810. Maj. William McRae at New Orleans wrote that from June 1809 to March 1810, the troops did not receive compensation even though the law required payment every two months: RG107, M1810, M222, roll 4, frame 1728.

20. Frederick Bates, recorder of land titles, RG217, invoice 21409, M235, roll 65, frame 1195 and commissioner of land titles, Invoice 21410, frame 1201.

21. Thomas F. Riddick, clerk to the land commissioners, Invoice 21403, frame 1175.

22. Theodore J. Crackel, *Mr. Jefferson's Army: Political and Social Reform of the Military Establishment, 1801–1809* (New York: New York University Press, 1987), p. 182.

23. WC to SW, April 29, 1809, Carter, *TP* 14: 264–67.

24. WC to WE, May 11, 1809, RG75, M15, roll 2, frame 0190, p. 436.

25. Carter, *TP* 14: 266.

26. George Armistead to FB, November 30, 1808, Marshall, *FB* 2: 44–45.

27. John Breck Treat to HD, September 25, 1808, RG107, T134, M221, roll 32. Starving, a term used in Indian relations, ranges from actual lack of food to the way tribesmen expressed a need for munitions for hunting, or goods in general. Treat's middle name is Breck, not Burke. Territorial Supreme Court Records, box 29, folder 8, Missouri State Archives.

28. James McFarlane to Governor Lewis, December 11, 1808, Carter, *TP* 14: 266–69. McFarlane was back in St. Louis by March 15. He was an intelligent, educated man and the atrocities McFarlane reported were also being observed at the White River, Indiana, or at Sandusky Indian settlements. See Helen Hornbeck Tanner, ed., *Atlas of Great Lakes Indian History* (Norman and London: University of Oklahoma Press for the Newberry Library, 1987), pp. 103–104.

29. FB to WHH, November 9, 1809, Marshall, *FB* 2: 107–108.

30. The term refers to the practice of torturing a prisoner to death by burning at the stake. The practice that once might have held some religious significance had by now degenerated into political sadism.

31. Militia Orders, November 28, 1808, Carter, *TP* 14: 236–41.

32. April 3, 10, 1809, Carter, *TP* 14: 258, 262.

33. Nicholas Boilvin's Report, April 21, 1809, RG107, C523, M221, roll 20. The letter is enclosed with William Clark's correspondence to SW.

34. James House to WE, April 10, 1809, RG107, H392, M221, roll 23; Alpha Kingsley to WE, April 19, 1809, K89, roll 25, frame 8176, NARA.

35. The military commander at Cahokia warned SW of threatening dangers from hostile Indians in St. Clair County (Whitesides to SW, April 19, 1809, RG107, W531, M221, roll 33). It is also interesting to note that on September 18, 1811, Secretary Bates issued James McFarlane a license to trade on the waters of the Mississippi above the mouth of the Missouri on the security of Sam Solomon. On November 11 William Henry Harrison attacked the Prophet's town on the Tippecanoe Creek branch of the Wabash, defeating the Indian coalition although not decisively.

36. PC to SW, May 15, 1809, RG107, C1809, M222, roll 4, frame 1535; ML to SW, May 13, 1809, L1809, M222, roll 4, frame 1565; ML to SW, May 15, 1809, L341, M22, roll 4, NARA.

37. John Heath to FB, February 7, 1809, letterbook 1801–1809, BFP-MHS. In August 1810 Heath tried to get a license from Bates to hunt beaver in the Osage country. John Heath to FB, August 23, 1810, Marshall, *FB* 2: 159.

38. George Armistead to FB, November 30, 1808, Marshall, *FB* 2: 45.

39. John Honey to FB, January 12, 1809, Marshall, *FB* 2: 54–60. Discovering a white man trying to defraud the Cherokee, McFarlane summarily whipped and drove him away.

40. Extract from a Letter to Richard Bates, April 15, 1809, Marshall, *FB* 2: 64.

41. FB to Richard Bates, November 9, 1809, Marshall, *FB* 2: 108–12.

42. Freemason Lodge Account with Hunt & Hankinson dated June 12, 1809, for $42.72 and authorized by Meriwether Lewis, BFP-MHS.

43. *Missouri Gazette*, June 21, 1809, p. 3. Festival of St. John the Baptist, June 24, St. Louis Lodge No. 111 celebrating the "Baptist," preparing the way for the light, the arrival of Christ.

44. FB to Richard Bates, November 9, 1809, Marshall, *FB* 2: 109–10.

45. Marshall, *FB* 2: 110.

46. William Carr to Charles Carr, August 25, 1809, William Carr Papers, MHS.

47. WC to SW, July 1, 1809, RG107, C581, M221, roll 20, frame 6275, NARA. However, the department valued Clark's opinion on the cost of several buildings for the Indian department and asked Lewis for an estimate of the reasonable compensation for the rations of the troops being sent up the Mississippi. SW to ML, April 28, 1809, Carter, *TP* 14: 263.

48. WE to John Mason, April 25, 1809, RG75, M15, roll 2, p. 434, NARA.

FIFTEEN

Documents of a Decline

... this high destiny so dear[1]

O n the expedition William Clark was usually the practical partner who attended to the day-to-day operations while Lewis ranged afield, dazzled by what he was finding. They made a perfect team for the challenges of discovery. But Captain Lewis also had the ultimate responsibility of answering to the nation for the realization of President Jefferson's great continental dream. And the kindly, almost fatherly, mantle that Jefferson used to shelter his protégé from the harder realities of fiscal responsibility did not shield the young governor from the insidious persistence of enemies.

Exchanges between Louisiana and Washington crawled at a pace that could be six weeks to as long as two or more months during a difficult winter. Even a prompt reply doubled the time lag. The winter of 1808–1809 was no exception, when drafts and bills of exchange written by Lewis and sent to Washington averaged three months.[2] What that meant was that there wasn't time between the inauguration of the president and the arrival of bills for one complete exchange.

It was April when the first mail got through to St. Louis, and in mid-May Governor Lewis and Gen. William Clark were still unaware of the new Madison administration policy requiring quarterly estimates before expenditures could be made.[3] By then they had submitted a number of bills of exchange for payment and confidently proceeded with expenses necessary for the operation of the territory.

The scarcity of money in St. Louis was another problem. During the first fateful eight months of 1809, Governor Lewis and General Clark were constantly inconvenienced by the lack of cash. As there was no real budget for the operation of the Louisiana Territory, Lewis had to risk his personal credit to keep the government afloat. As refused bills returned for further explanation, Lewis and Clark realized that until someone in Washington could be brought to understand the real situation, they were backing government bills with their own purses.

When he was secretary of state, James Madison had refused several bills from Governor Lewis concerning the printing of the laws of the territory and their translation into French.[4] On February 6 Lewis resubmitted a small bill that Madison had refused. Consistent with the policy of his predecessor, on May 5 the new secretary of state Robert Smith also refused to pay it. That minor exasperation returned to St. Louis at the end of the first week of July. Lewis could not make sense of the rejected draft. The laws were printed for a murder case that Judge Lucas said he would not try unless he had a copy. Clearly that was a necessary expenditure. Lewis could also see that if this measly draft was rejected, what others would not be honored?

> [T]his occurrence has given me infinite concern as the fate of other bills drawn for similar purposes to a considerable amount cannot be mistaken; this rejection cannot fail to impress the public mind unfavourably with rispect to me, nor is this consideration more painfull than the censure which must arise in the mind of the executive from my having drawn for public monies without authority, a third and not less imbarassing circumstance attending the transaction is that my private funds are entirely incompetent to meet those bills if protested.[5]

On March 7, 1809, Lewis had forwarded to the War Department the cost of returning the Mandan chief Sheheke-shote to his people. That added up to a total of six drafts broken in increments of a thousand to fifteen hundred dollars, to a total of seven thousand because a single order on the government for that large amount would have been impossible to negotiate in cash-short St. Louis. Those drafts began arriving in Washington: two on May 1, three on May 4, and one on July 1. It must have seemed like a creeping barrage of fiscal bombshells.[6]

Although new regulations requiring quarterly estimates had been invoked earlier, the seven thousand dollars went toward the quarter ending on March 30 and had to be paid. Later expenses would be posted to the second quarter, which opened the cost of "Indian presents" and medical supplies to challenge by the new administration. It was no concern of great minds or small that the several months needed to submit a proposal and receive approval would have postponed the expedition up the Missouri River for another year.

On May 13, 1809, Governor Lewis sent in another bill for five hundred dollars.[7]

> My bill of exchange No. 26 of this date in favor of Peter Chouteau or order, is on account of, and in past for, certain ammunition Tobacco and Paint, which has been furnished by the Said Chouteau, and which under my orders has been appropriated in the following manner.——— It is deposited with Major Chouteau who has been appointed to the command of a detachment of the Militia of this Territory, who are directed to convey the Mandan Chief to his Village, to be transported at the expense of the Missouri St. Louis fur Company who constitute that body of Militia, and under the direction of the Major, is to be expended if necessary by being distributed among such friendly Indians as he may think proper to take with him as auxiliaries to Insure the safe conveyance of the Mandan chief in passing the Aricara Villages, if the ammunition &c, is not thus expended it is to be returned to this place for the use of the United States or to be paid for by said Chouteau out of his annual compensation as Indian agent. Note after this there was another bill No. 27, 15th May for 440 dollars for the balance of this account amounting to 940 dollars.[8]

While the administration shuddered at what it perceived as the cost of just returning an Indian to his home, on May 18 Secretary of the Treasury Gallatin told President Madison that the nation was out of money.[9]

The expenditure of government funds was not unnoticed by enemies of the territorial government. When General Clark accepted additional responsibilities in the government factory system, he took over the job previously performed by the Belle Fontaine factor Rodolphe Tillier. Tillier retaliated by writing to President Madison and claiming that the governor was awarding special favors to the MFCo.[10] Tillier prefaced his letter by piously claiming that "To represent the present situation of these remote parts of the United States Territory may be of public service, to the wise administration of your Excellency; and can give no offence if founded on Fact & real Truth."[11]

Tillier claimed that the plan of the Pryor party failed "on account of being coupled with a private expedition" and condemned Clark for not making inquiries into the cause of the failure. He accused Lewis of waging war on the Osage "to destroy them without ever manifesting any plausible ground or reason." Tillier protested that Lewis and Clark had established a factory at the Osage nation and convinced the Osage "to resign to the U.S. on the bare demand of an Indian Agent the greatest part of their land & Inheritance."[12]

Tillier charged that enormous sums of money from the US Treasury had been needlessly consumed when the governor forced the militia to enlist under the auspices of the MFCo. After the Mandan chief was safely returned, the real design of the fur company would let out "about 200 men to hunt Beaver in the upper part of the Missouri." Tillier wrote that Lewis put the expedition on public account, "man'd & officered and paid as U.S. militia &c," and then asked, "Is it proper for the public service that the U.S. officers as a Governor or a Super Intendant of Indian Affairs & U.S. Factor at St. Louis should take any share in Mercantile and Private concerns."[13] Two weeks later Tillier followed up with another letter stating that the expedition was about to depart but "afeared not a creditable one."[14] Taken at face value by an administration already facing a fiscal crunch, what Tillier sent to Washington was a powerful indictment.

Another weak link in St. Louis also enjoyed a connection to Washington. Although Pierre Chouteau's family was involved in the new company, his brother-in-law Charles Gratiot was angling for a job with John Jacob Astor. As early as December 9 Gratiot wrote to Astor revealing plans for the new MFCo.[15]

As an avowed enemy of the Indian trade factory system, Astor wrote Gallatin in May 1809 complaining of the MFCo.'s competitive edge:

> Another circumstance I wish'd to have mention'd to you, of which however you are no doubt long since inform'd, that a Brother of Gov. Lewis's with some traders, Mr. Chouteaux & others have form'd a company to push up the Missouri. It is of some interest for me to know whether this Company has form'd itself under the auspices of Government whether they are to have any particular patronage to expect more than the American Fur Company—Mr. Chouteaux being as I am told the agent of Indian Affairs for the Osage Nations & Mr. Lewis one of the concerns being Brother of the Govr & Superintendant of that Territory it is presum'd that they will at least receive all the friendly aid which can be afforded them from that quarter & indeed I should rather regret to go in opposition to an American concern.[16]

After telling Gallatin about the size and routes of the two parties he intended to send west, one by sea and the other overland up the Missouri and down the Columbia, Astor inquired if the MFCo. enjoyed special favor from the government and asked for that standing for his enterprise. On May 16 he forwarded Gratiot's early warning letter to Gallatin, who made a note at the bottom of the page urging that the president read it, and sent the letter on to Secretary of War Eustis. Mail delivery between New York and Washington was a lot faster than the time it took Governor Lewis to communicate from St. Louis.

Tillier's letter reached Washington on June 8, probably in the same post rider's pouch as Lewis's two bills. It was forwarded to President Madison, and others in the War Department were also appraised of the contents. Although it came from a disenfranchised public officer with some dark secrets about his own performance, Tillier directed the administration's attention on an expensive project. Taken at face value, those were powerful charges meant to destroy the president's confidence in Governor Lewis.

The War Department waited over a month before responding. Time was taken up with discussions between the secretary of war and the president on how to deal with the Louisiana money drain. Madison had already experienced that problem when he was secretary of state. He saw the support given Charless for the publication of the laws of the territory as a conflict of interest for a press that Lewis helped establish. Now there were warnings of another suspicious combination of public and private interests in the return of the Mandan chief. Facing a monetary crisis, Madison was in no mood to continue authorizing expenditures from Mr. Jefferson's protégé.

There was a bureaucratic hit man. In previous efforts to deal with a massive million-dollar annual debt from the frontier Indian wars, Rep. Albert Gallatin of the House Ways and Means Committee had convinced the House to create a separate office within the Treasury, accountant of the War Department.[17] Making the secretary of the treasury responsible for the expenses of the War Department effectively "tied the hands of the Secretary of War."[18] With a staff of eight clerks, the duties of the accountant's office were so wide-ranging that only one financial task remained for the secretary of war—setting the department's annual budget.

William Simmons had been the accountant of the War Department since the administration of President George Washington.[19] In settling the public accounts of the department, he was required by law to refer all disputes to the comptroller of the treasury for decision. But over the years William Simmons saw that as an impediment to the efficient operation of his office and often judged and settled them himself.[20]

In the late 1790s, Meriwether Lewis was a young recruiting officer in the field when he first came into contact with Simmons.[21] Settling the accounts of the Corps of Discovery in 1807 had been difficult. The daily accounts were often scribbled notes meant to be copied later. The proofs that Captain Lewis retained to back up his claims against the government were a mess of unbound material, some barely credible as evidence to justify a payment voucher. But Lewis came from the academy of a military paymaster, a duty that required perfect accounting, and no omissions or failures marred his service record.

The organization and accountability of the Corps of Discovery had been a field of the unforeseen. How should an officer account for a buffalo skin bag of Mandan corn purchased from an Indian who knew neither written word nor signature? What is the procedure for dealing with the value of a branded horse that wandered off in the night, or was eaten out of desperation? The consequences of difficult situations were inexplicable to a man like William Simmons, who had never seen the sun set west of the Appalachians or the heights of the Rocky Mountains.

Had there been overspending? Although an old term not in much use in the first decade of the nineteenth century, President Jefferson seems to have given Captain Lewis *carte blanche*. In some expenses, Meriwether probably overspent, not irresponsibly but to buy necessities for a one-of-a-kind expedition. Most of the notes and payment orders that he wrote were for legitimate expenses, but there were others that a Washington accountant might find objectionable.

Growing impatient, on June 17, 1807, Simmons suspended action on the expedition account until Lewis returned from Philadelphia to prove it to him personally.[22] By late July Lewis was back in the Capitol clearing up the final accounts with Simmons.

In documenting the intricate expenses of the expedition, the historian Donald Jackson assumed that Simmons found little to object to when reviewing Lewis's own accounting. But if Simmons decided that a voucher was not properly supported, he could charge that sum against Lewis personally! In his July 31 letter, Simmons affirmed that "you should say in writing . . . whether you consider yourself or Capt. Clarke chargeable with any part of the provisions supplied . . . & . . . to what amount."[23] Lewis was given a schedule of items purchased on the expedition and told to note which had been used for the expedition, which he still possessed, and for which he should be held accountable.[24] On August 5 Simmons submitted the voluminous schedule to Dearborn and, according to Donald Jackson, approved the account.[25] When Lewis departed the Capitol he was aware that he still had to justify a zero balance to Simmons but he needed time to work out the numbers. In the meantime, Simmons had tabulated that Lewis owed the US government $9,685.77.[26]

The War Department accountant was required to provide a quarterly statement of unsettled accounts in arrears, to the Treasury Department. Every three years a new schedule exhibited the outstanding expenditures. At the end of that period, the US government could then institute lawsuits against those individuals with interest accruing daily.

Unconvinced by Lewis's accounting, Simmons reported that Lewis was in arrears for thousands of dollars. On September 30, 1807, a long month after appearing to have approved the list, Simmons reported that a balance was due to the government for $8,749.36 and an additional $571.50 from Lewis's contingent account.[27]

Simmons was not conducting a vendetta against Lewis; he showed the same amount of fanaticism toward anyone who could not produce exacting records. Other military officers at distant posts felt Simmons's power to block legitimate expenses.[28] Even the commanding general of the army who described him as "a despotic vindictive executive & a military panderer" was subjected to Simmons, who ignored direct commands from Secretary of War Dearborn and from President Jefferson about compensating General Wilkinson and then, self-righteously, went public by providing the entire account to a Washington newspaper.[29] Later, when soldiers were dying in fever-ridden New Orleans and General Wilkinson doing his best to care for them, Simmons blocked the funds necessary to construct a hospital.[30]

Because Simmons had complete autonomy, his practices escaped scrutiny for a long time.[31] Moving at his own measured pace, he exasperated a preferred clerk in his office until the man complained that Simmons exhibited a "perplexing incapacity in the settlement of public accounts."[32] On his last day as secretary of war, Dearborn urged President Jefferson to fire Simmons.

> It was early perceived that the passions, prejudice, general disposition and character of the Accountant of this Department, rendered him very unsuitable for the office he holds; and I should have applied for his removal several years ago . . . of late the conduct of Mr. Simmons has been such . . . as to compel me in justice to that Department and to the office I have had the honor of holding, as well as to my successor, to request that he be removed; and I am fully persuaded that the opinion of the public officers generally, who have been acquainted with his character and conduct accords with mine,—that he ought not to be continued in office.[33]

All that Jefferson could do was forward Dearborn's letter to the succeeding administration. James Madison filed it and allowed Simmons's practices to continue, now backed by the new requirement for estimates before expenditures. How fully the new regulation requiring quarterly estimates was initially circulated is a question. Nor did the schedule for compliance make an allowance for officers operating at a distance. Unaware of the tightening of the purse strings, honest officers had already made expenditures before they were informed of the rules and many, including the commanding general of the army, found their legitimate bills protested. The strict reporting and accounting that slowed the drain on a depleted treasury would embarrass and in some cases essentially destroy the careers of loyal army officers.

It has been assumed that the secretary of war refused to pay what he saw as an extravagance. Closer examination shows that the devastating refusal was not written by William Eustis. On July 15, 1809, when the rejection was dated, the secretary was preparing to leave on summer vacation and the accountant William Simmons was left to compose that poison arrow.[34] He wrote:

> After the sum of seven thousand dollars had been advanced on the Bills drawn by your Excellency on account of your Contract with the St. Louis Missouri Fur Company for conveying the Mandan Chief to his Village . . . Your Excellency will not be surprized that your Bill of the 13th of May . . . has not been honored. In the instance of accepting the volunteer services of 140 men for a military expedition to a point and purpose not designated, which expedition is stated to combine commercial as well as military objects, and when an Agent of the Government appointed for other purposes is selected for the command, it is thought the Government might, without injury to the public interests, have been consulted. As the object & destination of this Force is unknown, and more especially as it combines Commercial purposes, so it cannot be considered as having the sanction of the Government of the United States, or that they are responsible for the consequences. The President has been consulted and the observations herein contained have his approval.[35]

It would have been sufficient to just refuse the bill. But Simmons had imbibed larger implications that verged on policy.[36] On August 18 Meriwether passed his thirty-fifth birthday. As a present he received a letter purporting to be from the secretary of war but smelling strongly of the insufferable William Simmons. The expensive Mandan expedition was approved for payment but the War Department wasn't going to spend a penny more for Indian presents. The refusal was written in terms that could only be taken as insulting. So Meriwether spent his natal day in exasperation that must have come close to a red rage, feeling that his character as much as his actions had been challenged. Lewis's response was unreserved:

> Yours of the 15th July is now before me, the feelings it excites are truly painful. With respect to every public expenditure, I have always accompanied my Draft by letters of advice, stating explicitly, the object of the expenditure: if the object be not a proper one, of course I am responsible; but if on investigation, it does appear to have been necessary for the promotion of the public Interests, I shall hope for relief.
>
> I have never received a penny of public Money, but have merely given the Draft to the person who had rendered the public service, or furnished articles for public use, which have been invariably applied to the purposes expressed in my Letters of advice.
>
> I have made advances for the Public from time to time in small sums for recovering of public horses which have been lost, for forage for them, expenses attending Sales &c. and have retained from the sales of those horses the sum of eighty five Dollars, for which I have ample vouchers. In these transactions I have drawn no draft, calculating on going forward long since and settling my Accounts with the Public. The balance of Sales in Money and Bonds have been lodged with General Clark by the Vendue-Master; —to the correctness of this statement, I call my God to witness.
>
> I have been informed Representations have been made against me, — all I wish is a full and fair Investigation. I anxiously wish that this may reach you in time to pr[e]vent any decision relative to me.
>
> I shall leave the Territory in the most perfect state of Tranquility which I believe, it has ever experienced. I find it impossible at this moment, to explain by letter, and to do away by written explanation the impressions which I fear, from the tenor of your letter, the Government entertain with respect to me, and shall therefore go on by the way of New Orleans to the City of Washington with all dispatch.[37]

Written immediately upon receiving the refused bill, the letter was not in Meriwether's hand; it appears to have been written from dictation or was a scrawled draft by a close friend.[38] Perhaps Meriwether did not trust himself to make a fair copy. Nor could he rely on Territorial Secretary Frederick Bates, who was now a confirmed enemy. Lewis saw an insinuation in the rejection that the MFCo. was something beyond a trapping adventure. Perhaps he felt that he was being accused of plotting another filibuster. Unwilling to trust his own handwriting, he paced in frustration and vowed,

"Be assured Sir, that my Country can never make a Burr of me—She may reduce me to Poverty; but she can never sever my Attachment from her."[39]

The source of that insinuation was close to home. Before the Missouri expedition departed Bates informed the War Department about the contract being transmitted by the governor. In giving the principles of the arrangement, Bates could not resist adding, "You will have observed that it is as well *mercantile* as *military*."[40] Bates mentioned that in taking command of the expedition, Pierre Chouteau would not be performing his duties as Osage agent. That prompted Simmons to assume in the July 15 letter that Chouteau's agency had become vacant and the governor needed "to appoint a suitable character to supply his place."[41] In his response Lewis repeated the terms of Chouteau's orders and his hope that the Osage agent would not be removed.[42]

The refusal of the Indian presents was a breaking point for the governor and although it was about additional expenses, that wasn't the real issue. Lewis was confident that he could resolve the question of denied drafts, but what could he do about the blank indifference of a president and a secretary of war who were unwilling to step up to the problems of managing Indian affairs. Benign neglect was not the answer.

Whatever came over Meriwether Lewis in mid-year 1809 was not a precipitous decision to go to Washington about his debts. For almost a year he and Clark had been discussing a trip east to complete the publication of their joint expedition book. As far as Clark knew, Lewis had a plan to accomplish that and had already arranged for respected experts to provide scientific supplements. Some of those contributors had already been paid, and others needed additional supervision.[43]

Over the eighteen months since he had actively taken over the government of the Louisiana Territory, Lewis had generated many pages of intelligent, well-thought-out, and clearly expressed writing. But that creative energy had been devoted to official correspondence, reports, or chatty exchanges with distant relatives and friends. He wrote through the distractions of the day or by candlelight far into the humid nights. Most public men would have been satisfied to generate a record of the performance of their duty and accomplishments. But a creative author with a masterpiece in his mind must have thought that much official correspondence was mostly a wasteful expenditure of ink and paper. Lewis needed to go to some quiet place where he could draw the mass of uncataloged, sometimes nearly incomprehensible, data in the raw journals and notebooks into an intelligently comprehensive and readable whole.

Time. Time was all he needed.

In his August 18 letter, Lewis wrote that the protested bills "from the Departments of War and Treasury have effectively sunk my Credit: brought in all my private debts amounting to about $4000, which has compelled me, in order to do justice to my Creditor, to deposit with them, the landed property which I had purchased in this Country, as Security." Lewis and his loyal friend Clark began methodically preparing for his absence by setting up guarantees for those creditors whose expectation of prompt payment had stalled.[44]

Always behind the gap in communications, both Lewis and Clark were finding it increasingly difficult to continue floating expenditures with paper promises for which they were personally responsible. Lewis had been using his governor's salary as a temporary expedient with the expectation of being properly reimbursed. Only one five-hundred-dollar bill had been refused, but he realized that two others sent later would also be protested. Lewis considered the situation as a short-term inconvenience until he cleared up the matters in Washington.[45] Although exasperated by the difficulties that the accounting process was creating, he was not hysterical.

Until the fiscal matters were resolved, Lewis put up his real estate in St. Louis as a guarantee to those who were holding unpaid debts. That was not an irrational act of a desperate man; it was just what an honorable man would do to reassure debtors against the vagaries of federal accounting.

In William Clark's memorandum book describing his journey to Washington, there are entries from others like Edward Hempstead as reminders of services Clark might do for them on the journey. One entry is in Lewis's hand.

> M. Lewis will thank Genl. Clark to obtain from Judges Lucas and Coburn their opinions and impressions relative to the publication of the laws of the territory of Louisiana. whether they did receive that at the time they were enacted that the general government would pay the same and [in . . . crossed out] then [want of the . . . crossed out] genl. government has not paid or in the event of their not paying the amount of the expenses attending the same, that they would consent that the legislature of the territory should make provisions for the payment of the expenses incurred on that subject.
>
> The General will be pleased to forward whatever he may obtain from the judges on this subject to me at Washington, All letters [and papers . . . crossed out] to be returned to the city of Washington which may arrive addressed to me at this place.[46]

The measures that Governor Lewis and General Clark took after the decision was made for Lewis to go east were sensible and appropriate. Of course Lewis was exasperated to have another problem inserted, unnecessarily, between him and getting away to complete the narrative, which he had been trying to arrange for the past year.

Both Lewis and Clark had plunged into land acquisition. Under the Northwest Ordinance of 1787, the governor of a territory was required to own a thousand acres.[47] Lewis had gone well beyond that in providing what may have been a nest egg for his mother or place for her if she wanted to relocate. There were other parcels too. As he prepared to leave for the capital, Lewis set up those investments as a guarantee to his debt holders. That surety was not liquid, but it also wasn't going to walk away. There is no certain evidence that he actually intended for any land to be sold.[48]

Because his investments included business enterprises, William Clark was actually balancing a more complex debt load. In a pressing situation his investments could demand cash, as was the case with the MFCo. But Clark was accustomed to operating that way and most of his deals involved members of his extended family who were unlikely to become unreasonable when government bills were temporarily refused. For Clark, as for Lewis, the unaccountable reluctance of the government to answer its just obligation was a momentary inconvenience.[49]

The two men made what appears to have been a mutual decision to send their 1,600-acre land warrants down to New Orleans to be sold in a better speculative market. That was not so much an admission of debt as an attempt to get some cash actually in hand. Title still depended on waiting until surveys were made and property could be located in the Louisiana Territory. At the pace the land board was moving, that was still far in the future. As it turned out no buyers in New Orleans could be found for such large blocks of land, even at a discount, and neither Lewis nor Clark's warrants were sold.[50]

The collusion between members of the land board resurfaced in a letter that Bates sent to John R. Cabanné of New Orleans. On August 10 he wrote:

> It is possible that I may have been uninformed as to the high prices of land warrants in New Orleans. They are intrinsically worth no more than $2.00 per acre—and if you find that they are not valued in market above that sum, I am desirous that you should accept it. Nothing less than two dollars ought to be taken, for they can be sold or located here without a sacrifice. Mr. Carr does not join with me in this reduction of price, he still hopes that speculation [speculators'] objects detached from the nominal value of the warrants will enable you to sell them for three dollars.[51]

Those must have been the warrants sold by three members of the Corps of Discovery in which Bates had developed a speculative interest.

Two weeks later Carr wrote:

> Our Governor left us a few days since with his private affairs altogether deranged. He is a good man, but a very imprudent one—I apprehend he will not return—He has drawn on the general government for various & considerable sums of money which have not been paid: of course his bills have been protested—He has vested Judge Stuart of Kaskaskia, General Clark and myself with full powers to adjust and liquidate all demands against him & left in my hands all his land titles, to be sold for that purpose. . . . Some of these lands situated about 10 miles from this place near a little village called St. Ferdinand will be sold.[52] The title is complete and the quality of the land excellent. It is also situated on the bank of the Missouri—If I had the money I would give it for the land instantly.[53]

Moses Austin penned a letter from the mines on August 27 that must have given Bates a chill when he received it. Austin pretended to be concerned that those who were preparing a memorial petition to Congress had access to the books of the land board. From a member of the board he extracted enough clues to fear that a false impression could be detrimental to the reputation of Judge Lucas. Austin feared that there might be a "mole" or informer connected with the board. That did little to encourage peace of mind in Bates, particularly when the governor was leaving to go to Washington. Who knew what he would tell the Madison administration?[54]

Bates usually rewrote letters translated from French into English, including several letters for Pierre Chouteau.[55] Before leaving as the commander of the militia, Chouteau had given power of attorney to his son Pierre Chouteau Jr. to continue drawing his compensation as Indian agent. As the order to appoint a new agent was a direct challenge to the Chouteau family's control of the Osage business, on the first of September young Chouteau wrote to the War Department to protect his father's position:

> By the last communication made me by his Excely Govr Lewis, I have reason to believe that you were not pleased that my Father was employed to reconduct the Mandane Chief, and that you consider this mission as being inconsistent with his place of Agent in the Indian department for the Osage Nation. Perhaps, also, you do not approve the manner in which the affairs of that Department have been managed for some time past. . . . During a long time past my father has been only *nominally* Indian Agent,

and that the direction of the Osage Nation has been entirely with the Governor & his two Agents.[56]

In his effort to cast his father in a good light, Chouteau threw doubt on the governor's role in launching the expedition. Bates must have been delighted to recopy it in English. The letter would be traveling east at the same time Lewis was headed for Washington.

NOTES

1. Alexander Wilson, "Particulars of the Death of Capt. Lewis," *Port Folio* 7 (January 1812): 39.

2. WC to SW, April 29, 1809, Carter, *TP* 14: 264. "I had the honor of receiving your letter of the 17th of November which is the last I have received from you." ML to WE, RG107, L264, 299, 340, 341, 339, M22, roll 4. The lesson for a historian trying to reconstruct a sequence of events is that documents arranged by the date of the writing can be misleading. A letter does not become effective until it is received.

3. WC to WE, May 19, 1809, RG107, C541, M221, roll 20, frame 6231.

4. *Early American Imprints*, Second series, no. 15451.

5. ML to unknown addressee, July 8, 1809, MSS 9041, 9041-a, papers of the Lewis, Anderson, and Marks families.

6. RG107, M22, roll 4.

7. ML to WD, May 13, 1809, RG107, L1809, M222, roll 4, frame 1565 for $500 and May 15, 1809, for $440. The breakdown of the amount paid to Chouteau: 400 lbs. gunpowder $600, 100 guns $100, 1,250 lbs. lead $100, 20 lbs. vermillion $50, 600 lbs. tobacco $90; RG107, C1809, frame 1535. Lewis suggested that the $940 could be considered as a loan to bridge an unfortunate omission.

8. ML to WE, May 13, 1809, Jackson, *LLC* 2: 451; ML to WD, May 13, 1809, RG107, L295, and May 15, 1809, L341, M222, roll 4, frame 1566. There was an additional bill of $250 for medicines for the expedition surgeon.

9. AG to JMA, May 18, 1809, RG217, M235, roll 19, frame 0363.

10. The factory at Cantonment Belle Fontaine was closed in the winter of 1809. As factor from 1805 to 1809, Tillier believed that the closure occurred because of his altercation with George Sibley, the assistant factor whom he fired in November 1807. (George Sibley to SW, November 6, 1807, RG107, S442, M221, roll 2 and FB to SW, November 7, 1807, B314, roll 4; John Mason to Rodolphe Tillier, April 12, 1808, RG75, M16, roll 2, p. 153.) Governor Wilkinson had recommended that the factory at Belle Fontaine be closed and a new one opened nearer the location of the Indian villages (Carter, *TP* 13: 239).

11. In 1811 it was discovered that Tillier had been cooking the books at Belle

Fontaine. He had fired Sibley for accusing him of using the factory to his advantage but his daybook revealed that Sibley had been correct. (Sundry charges in Tillier's daybook, which appeared to be unauthorized as sundries furnished Indians as presents, 1807–1809, RG75, T58, roll 1, frame 0083.)

12. Robert J. Brugger et al., eds., *Papers of James Madison*, Secretary of State series, 8 vols. (Charlottesville: University Press of Virginia, 1986), 1: 141–42.

13. Rodolphe Tillier to John Mason, April 27, 1809, RG107, T1809, M222, roll 4, frames 1582 and 1628. This letter is in two large fragments on the microfilm and the one printed by University of Virginia, cited above, has been edited and does not contain the second fragment.

14. Rodolphe Tillier to SW, May 12, 1809, RG107, T273, M221, roll 32, letter received June 10, 1809.

15. Charles Gratiot to John Jacob Astor, December 9, 1808, Charles Gratiot Papers, box 1, MHS.

16. John Jacob Astor to AG, May 16, 1809, Albert Gallatin Papers, reel 19, New York University Archives.

17. Raymond Walters Jr., *Albert Gallatin, Jeffersonian Financier & Diplomat* (New York: Macmillan, 1957), pp. 43, 90.

18. Harry M. Ward, *The Department of War, 1781–1795* (Pittsburgh: University of Pittsburgh Press, 1962), p. 144.

19. George Washington to the Senate, June 12, 1795, Nominations, series 2 letterbooks, letterbook 27, LOC. Simmons would hold the position until 1814.

20. *Early American Imprints*, Second series, no. 7471, pp. 1–2, and no. 32773, p. 11; *ASP, Finance* 2: 339.

21. Lewis had his first exchanges with Simmons on December 19, 1797. Other communications are dated March 10, 1798, March 22, 1798, and June 19, 1799.

22. WS to ML, June 17, 1807, Jackson, *LLC* 2: 417. Simmons ordered the national hero to bring any papers related to expedition expenditures "to explain such of the charges as may require it."

23. July 31, 1807, Jackson, *LLC* 2: 419.

24. Ibid.

25. Financial Records of the Expedition, August 5, 1807, Jackson, *LLC* 2: 419–30.

26. *Early American Imprints*, Second series, no. 21675, pp. 4, 14, and no. 24153, p. 6.

27. Simmons allowed Lewis's unresolved accounting of the debts of the expedition to remain on the official record until 1810, including accrued interest in the amount of $364.91.

28. Simmons, well known to War Department personnel, objected to the accounts of numerous officers in the field. For examples: RG107, M221, rolls 21 (Dinsmoor), 29 (Abrahams), 32 (Van Dyke), 33 (Wilkinson), and 36 (Gratiot, Gravelines, Neelly). The War Department accountant brought suit for $16,919.64 against Moses Hooke, who had been the military agent at Pittsburgh trusted by no

less than the commanding general of the army (*Early American Imprints*, Second series, no. 21675, p. 6). In 1809 Simmons rejected several bills that Capt. Gilbert Russell submitted as legitimate expenses for moving his company to a new post: GR to SW, RG107, R209, 219, 235, 244, M221, roll 29.

29. JW to AG, September 5, 1807, Gallatin Papers, 1807, # 77, NYHS; ASP, *Finance* 2: 337–52; *Early American Imprints*, Second series, no. 18893; An American Time Capsule: Three Centuries of Broadsides and Other Printed Ephemera, LOC, "Public Plunder."

30. RG107, M6, roll 4, pp. 170, 180, 182, 196.

31. The accountant's office was housed in a separate building from the War and Treasury departments. (RG217, M235, roll 67, frame 1202).

32. *Early American Imprints*, Second series, no. 11805, p. 2. Simmons submitted protested accounts to the comptroller of the treasury in an untimely manner and, ironically, there was no provision in the law to enforce it.

33. HD to TJ, February 16, 1809, reel 10, document 5985 1/4, JMA-LOC.

34. James Morton Smith, ed., *The Republic of Letters*, 3 vols. (New York: Norton, 1995), 3: 1595. War Department letterbooks do not contain Eustis's signature after July 9 (RG75, M15, roll 3, frame 0019-20) and after July 13 (RG107, M6, roll 4, pp. 170–89). Eustis also writes on July 12 that he is preparing to leave Washington shortly; arrives in New York on July 26. Rutland et al., *Papers of James Madison*, 1: 308.

35. WE to ML, July 15, 1809, Jackson, *LLC* 2: 456–57; original letter, see WS to ML, July 15, 1809, RG107, M6, roll 4, p. 177, frame 0104.

36. Simmons had also been sparring with WC over Indian expenses since May. On August 7 Simmons responded to Clark's letter of 1 July advising of expenses ". . . it does not appear to be necessary that the expense attending our Relations with the Indians in the Territory of Louisiana, should be four times as much as the whole expense of supporting its civil government . . ." His solution effectively gutted the Indian agency of its most useful people. Carter, *TP* 14: 289–90. For the full exchange: WC to WD, 1 July 1809, RG107, C581, M221, roll 20, frame 6275.

37. ML to WE, August 18, 1809, Jackson, *LLC* 2: 459.

38. ML to WD, August 18, 1809, RG107, L328, M221, roll 23, frame 8501. Comparison with other letters show that this letter was not in Lewis's hand but written by Jeremiah Connor, sheriff of St. Louis, RG233, M1708, roll 6, frames 497–99.

39. ML to WE, August 18, 1809, Jackson, *LLC* 2: 460.

40. Even though PC was the addressee, Bates penned this letter. PC to WD, June 14, 1809, RG107, C562, M221, roll 20, frame 6255.

41. WE to ML, July 15, 1809, Jackson, *LLC* 2: 457.

42. Ibid., p. 461.

43. Bernard McMahon to TJ, January 17, 1809, Jackson, *LLC* 2: 446; Bernard McMahon to TJ, December 24, 1809, pp. 484–86; WC to BSB, May 22, 1810, pp. 548–49; James Holmberg, *Dear Brother* (New Haven, CT: Yale University Press, 2002), pp. 201, 210.

44. ML to WE, August 18, 1809, Jackson, *LLC* 2: 460. The Missouri State Archives has a number of lawsuits filed against Meriwether Lewis in the Territorial Supreme Court Records spanning from 1809 to 1812. Some of these cases can be found in the following boxes and folders: 29-7; 30-22; 31-15; 34-23, 32, 34; 35-17; 48-2, 3. The MFCo. is also represented: 45-44.

45. Beyond the $940 for Indian presents, the list of bills was for small amounts: $18 for printing the laws; $81 for an assaying furnace; $1 for incidental expenses.

46. Clark's memorandum book, p. 31, Lewis and Clark Collections, C-1075, microfilm 1, Western Manuscript Collection, Columbia, MO.

47. Ordinance of 1787, July 13, 1787, Carter, *TP* 2: 41.

48. Lewis bought many tracts of land in St. Louis city and county. These sales span the dates from May 3, 1808, to April 1, 1809. For more information on those transactions see, Collet's index, MHS.

49. Clark's memorandum book, Lewis and Clark Collections, C-1075, microfilm 1, Western Manuscript Collections. Clark's close relationship's with his family is presented convincingly in Holmberg, *Dear Brother*.

50. Richard Gearey to George Graham, Commissioner of the General Land Office, December 31, 1826, GLM, box 8, folder 14, JNEM. It took an act of Congress, twenty-one years after Meriwether Lewis received his original land warrant, to authorize "the right of entering any of the public lands of the United States, subject to entry at private sale, to the amount of the residue of the warrant of 1600 acres." Prior to that year, the General Land Office had never seen a warrant of that size. A *Bill for the Relief of the Legal Representatives of Meriwether Lewis*, 20th Cong., 1st sess., HR 282, April 28, 1828.

51. FB to John Cabanné, August 10, 1809, letterbook 1801–1809, BFP-MHS.

52. This was the tract that Meriwether Lewis bought for his mother. ML to LM, December 1, 1808, MLC-MHS.

53. William Carr to Charles Carr, August 25, 1809, William Carr Papers, MHS.

54. Moses Austin to FB, August 27, 1809, Marshall, *FB* 2: 77–79.

55. PC to WD, June 14 and August 12, 1809, RG107, C562 and C612, M221, roll 20, frames 6255, 6310.

56. Pierre Chouteau Jr. (Auguste Pierre) to SW, September 1, 1809, Carter, *TP* 14: 315–19. Chouteau Jr. was referring to Indian agents William Clark and James McFarlane.

SIXTEEN

Appointment with Destiny

Fell, friendless and unhonored here[1]

Meriwether Lewis had been considering a return east for the past
year. Almost as soon as the newly wed Clarks arrived in St. Louis,
Lewis spoke about returning to Philadelphia to finish the expedition book.
Thomas Jefferson had written, "Your friends are all well, & have been long
in expectation of seeing you. I shall hope in that case to possess a due portion of you at Monticello . . . be assured yourself of my constant & unalter-
able affections."[2]

When Governor Lewis and General Clark began receiving disturbing
letters from the War Department stopping the payment of certain disputed
bills, the decision to leave for Washington could no longer be postponed.[3]
A sympathetic Clark wrote to his brother that "Several of his Bills have
been protested and his Crediters all flocking in near the time of his Setting
out distressed him much, which he expressed to me in Such terms as to
Cause a Cempothy [sympathy] which is not yet off."[4]

The first step in the arrangements to leave for Washington was recon-
ciling matters between two friends. Lewis and Clark sat down together and
listed the accumulated debts and credits, right down to the dollar that
Lewis borrowed playing cards last January. This friendly accounting concluded with Clark's observation, "Settled this 21st of August agreeably to

the above settlement, $554.43."[5] Next day in his personal account book
Lewis drew up the bills.

> A list of private debts due . . . To John G. Commegys—$331.45 ½. To
> Benjamin Wilkinson—$151.60. To Col. August Chouteau—$10. To
> James McFarlane—$657.95 To same by Dubill [Due bill?] $60.50, [subto-
> taled $728.45 (minus $10), totaled $718.45, and then all crossed out]. To
> Issac Miller of which a note is left with General Clark, $202.87 ½. Lud-
> well Bacon payable on demand given for disappointment on a sum of
> money paid 7th June 1808, to be first paid. [Apparently that was what
> happened as the entry is crossed out.] I owe John Colter this sum having
> recieved the same for him at the War office as the gratuity allowed by the
> government of the Ustates for his services on a tour to the Pacific ocean—
> $320. To [paid overwritten] your order in favor of Charles Sanganet—
> $125. I have agreed to pay Mr. J. Baban the sum of one hundred dollars
> next spring or to his order in full for the inconvenience sustained by him
> in not receiving the amount of a note given him for $450 agreeable to
> contract.[6]

It appears that the total of the debts was $2,310.37. Lewis also put his
landed property into the hands of William Clark and two attorneys whom
he believed he could trust. The arrangement meant that Judge Alexander
Stuart and William C. Carr were authorized to hold the property as security
for the debtors until he settled the problem in Washington. The arrangement with Judge Stuart was complex and suggests that Lewis did not expect
to sell any land: "Gave Judge Stewart a deed for 708 Acres of land at
portage DeSous—conditional that if I return him $750 with interest
thereon before the 1st of October 1810, then the deed will be voyd."[7]

On the nineteenth Carr was deeded "a parcel of land situated on the
hill, back of the town of St. Louis."[8] As he scrambled to finish letters that
the governor would carry to Washington, Carr had unusual insight into
Lewis's money problems.[9] An intimate of the vindictive Secretary Bates, it
is possible that Carr was the source of embarrassing leaks about the governor's financial situation.

Lewis solved a $4,355 debt to Pierre Chouteau with young Pierre
Chouteau on the twenty-third. Written in French, the document was witnessed by Bates and the notary Marie Phillipe Leduc.[10] In his memorandum
book Lewis noted that this was accomplished by returning the land with the
note and paying the money by the following May. In Clark's mind that
meant after matters in the east were resolved, his friend intended to return

to St. Louis. "I think all will be right and he will return with flying Colours to this Country."[11]

Both Lewis and Clark needed some immediate cash. That was why Lewis gave a receipt for Clark's land warrant number 2, which he promised to sell in New Orleans, or that failing, turn it over to Daniel Clark to be sold.[12] Lewis planned to take his own land warrant for sixteen hundred acres to Bomby Robertson to be disposed of for two dollars an acre or more, if it could be obtained.[13]

After those arrangements were completed Clark wrote his brother, "I have not spent Such a Day as yesterday fer maney years, busily employed untill Dinner writing my Dispatches, and then took my leave of Govr. Lewis who Set out to Philadelphia to write our Book."[14]

Clark paused to consider his own financial situation, which also included a number of debts. He was uncertain how his bills from the Indian agency would be received in Washington. "I have sent on my accounts to the 1st of July with vouchers for all to about $1800 which is not yet expended in totl. I am under no apprehention, they Settled my Acts. To the 30t. Decr. laist and a ballance was in my faver of $17.68." But with a number of business deals up in the air Clark would gladly have sold his share of the MFCo. for the three thousand dollars it had cost him.[15]

Through those last days in St. Louis Lewis kept a to-do list in his memo book, which he stressed by drawing a little hand with a pointing finger: "Enquire of Brown at Orleans for the bones of the mamoth sent him by Genl. Clark for the president of the Ustates." "Directed my letters to be returned to the City of Washington." "Deliver a receipt from Mr. McFarlane to Capt russell at Chickaway Bluffs."

Lewis may have had a premonition or was already feeling a malarial attack coming on because he sent Pernier to Dr. Saugrain with a thirty-dollar note for medicine.[16] It was curious that a close friend like Clark, or an interested observer like Carr, believed that Lewis left St. Louis on August 25. But two days later Lewis was still attending to some unfinished business.[17]

The packet that Meriwether Lewis put together on the twenty-seventh was one of the most important in his career because those letters gathered together matters that he wanted to discuss with his old friend Thomas Jefferson. Showing that his relationship with his mentor was still active and mutual, they disprove endlessly repeated assumptions that Jefferson had given up on him.[18]

Lewis meant to answer Jefferson's apprehensions about his Indian policy. The first part of the packet appears to have been something Lewis had worked up previously and had Bates recopy. Lewis now addressed it to the president, dating the page at the top and signing his name at the bottom. But it was not meant for the present executive. It was for an old friend who was now a private citizen and concerned the discussion between them that had been moving in slow motion since last summer. They debated how to deal with Indians who committed hostile acts against US citizens. After two Iowas and a Sac were apprehended and tried before Judge Lucas for killing a white man, the former president suggested that showing mercy might make a more lasting impression on a tribe.[19]

Lewis wanted Jefferson to see how the trial had gone and the steps of the defense that postponed a verdict. Convinced of judicial error or mistaken principles, Lewis raised larger questions about the government's ability to deal with violations and what constituted boundaries between the territory and the tribes. This carefully reasoned and well-expressed letter was accompanied by a complete transcript of the trial and legal proceedings, made by the clerk of the court.

Lewis also bundled up accounts of two councils that had been held with Osage Indians who were brought to St. Louis by special operative McFarlane: "the undersigned chiefs of the Osage residing on the Arkansas River having had the treaty read to them and explained by M. Lewis acknowledge, consent to and confirm all stipulations to the treaty of November 10, 1808, done at St. Louis August 31, 1809."[20] That was rightfully War Department Indian business but Lewis included it in the packet he meant to take with him to Monticello.

The last page and a half written in Meriwether's hand was about observations on how to deal with the problem of setting a boundary between the Indians and the government. He had been thinking about that problem and decided to include his views with the other related materials.

Taking the time to tidy up a difference of opinion with his former mentor showed that Meriwether was in complete command of his faculties. The packet was not the work of a man driven to the edge, but carrying those documents to his mentor implied that the governor of Louisiana had lost confidence in the present administration. The plan to go east and forward the publication of a narrative of the expedition now included a confrontation with the secretaries of War and State and even President Madison if necessary.

Lewis had to convince those chair-bound bureaucrats that a frontier government required immediate decisions. Louisiana could not be directed at long distance over an imperfect system of communication. He had to have sufficient funds in order to deal with the specific problems of the territory. Lewis enclosed the packet with other papers in a trunk, including the journals of the expedition needed to complete the narrative that he would take with him as soon as a suitable boat became available.

Governor Lewis was still in St. Louis on September 2 when he sent Pernier with a note to Pierre Chouteau Jr. "I will thank you to furnish me with the following articles by two o'clock this evening." From the Chouteau storehouse he requested chief's coats, pants and hats, calico and scarlet cloth, blue strouding, blankets, ornaments, weapons, and ammunition. These were presents to repay the reticent Osage for signing the treaty. "The Indians will be dispatched to their respective villages the day after tomorrow with some trusty interpreter to conduct them beyond the settlements with provisions until they pass the inhabitants."[21]

On the same day he ordered Bates to advise Indian agent John Breck Treat that the accustomed trade with the Indians of the Arkansas River and its waters could be reopened.[22] Then he gave James McFarlane a bond for $800.08 to cover the $718.45 expenses of the two missions to the Arkansas and St. François rivers. Governor Lewis's actions in those last days were not those of a man whose world seemed to be crumbling around him.[23]

On the humid morning of September 4, Governor Lewis boarded a boat going to New Orleans. The first part of the voyage from St. Louis to the mouth of the Ohio was the reverse of that which Lewis and Clark traveled five years before, and at about the same time of the year. They had been on their way to organize the expedition and the future had been all before them, an unknown world waiting to be discovered. Now that adventure was beginning to dim. To revitalize it Lewis had to write a masterpiece.

New Madrid was about 250 miles downstream. As the boat floated down the river they drifted slowly past a dull panorama of brushy riverbanks and fetid backwaters. In early September the crew nodded off in the warm sun, leaving the helmsman to watch well ahead for changes in the current or dangerous obstacles. If he called, they had to up and row furiously to avoid getting set in a dangerous bend or under tall trees leaning over the water. It was a slow drift on those olive waters.

Drifting logs, sinkers, and sawyers everywhere made it inadvisable to risk traveling in the dark. At nightfall, they tied up to willows or a heavy log near a bit of a beach where they could start a fire. They were not alone on the river. Other fires winked in the distance. The Mississippi was the channel of commerce that four nations had lusted after and traitors had tried to monopolize.

Keelboats built on the distant Monogahela drifted downstream to New Orleans where they might be fitted out as sailing ships to carry the commodities of the Ohio drainage to a waiting world. Some of those were like the keelboat Lewis contracted for the expedition but most of the watercrafts that they passed, or that overtook them, were clumsy barges, broadhorns, or rafts carrying the produce from farms that were growing into real homes and fields tilled by the yeoman farmers who Mr. Jefferson dreamed would inherit this earth. Crude boats would be broken up and sold for lumber at New Orleans. Many of the voyagers were sacrifices to the notorious fevers of the lower Mississippi. Those that survived would hike home along the Natchez Trace. Boats working up the river were rowed by sun-blasted river men who found relief only when there was wind enough to sail. Headwinds could force a boat to tie up until they blew out.

Along the way Lewis saw small groups of Indians traveling in canoes or camping along the riverbank or on islands. Even from a distance he could see that they were a sullen, degraded people whose faded trade clothing and cheaply made ornaments were a poor reward for having lost everything. Meriwether could not avoid drawing a comparison between those dazed refugees and the proud horsemen he and Clark had known in the West. Was this what the Osage and the Sac had been reduced to?

For Meriwether Lewis a lazy drift nodding in the warm sun should have been a welcome rest. Actually the torturous pace prolonged his tension. In a fog of daily boredom and increasing pain Lewis tried to contain his growing sense of urgency, but the slow trip gave him too much time to churn matters over and over. Dark thoughts came on him from every direction, neglected responsibilities and failures heaping up. The demon ague was closing in on him again.

After seven days they slipped past Bayou St. Jean and saw a two-mile-square plain dotted with cattle. New Madrid amounted to about two hundred houses scattered along the ever-encroaching river. Because of the civil appointments he made, Governor Lewis knew that the jobs of French Creoles had been given away to American and German immigrants. As the wagon-road distance of 240 miles to St. Louis overreached the arm of the law, the United States had given them a court of common pleas and quarter sessions, but at the cost of their old ways.[24]

Lewis sent Pernier ashore to locate someone to help with a legal matter and to collect something for their supper. The valet found the prices rather high: milk a half dollar a gallon, butter or a dozen eggs cost a quarter, and a nice chicken might command as much as three-quarters of a dollar.

But Pernier had gone ashore with more to do than collecting a few groceries. He returned with a man named François Trenchard to witness the will that Meriwether had composed. It was not more than a line or two and not unusual for a traveler in those times of uncertainty to make. He bequeathed his estate, real and personal, after his private debts had been paid, to his mother, Lucy Marks. That included his expedition land warrant, which, along with Clark's, he had intended to take to New Orleans for sale. The precaution was necessary because Lewis had decided to leave the slow boat and risk the sometimes dangerous Natchez Trace.

Before they reached New Madrid they met boats coming up the river. From shouts as the boats passed, there were dire warnings that fever was raging below.[25] That was enough to cause Lewis to reconsider going to New Orleans and returning to the East Coast by sea. Other writers like Stephen Ambrose and Dawson A. Phelps have speculated that the reason given for this change of plan was that he feared for the safety of his journals.[26] Fearing interception by British ships wasn't a matter of paranoia in those trying times as the overbearing British continued to drive the nation closer to the brink of war. But his trunk also contained a number of documents attesting to the correct governance of Louisiana and the resolution of the refused warrants of exchange. He still needed to resolve Simmons's lingering questions about the expenses of the expedition, a matter of honor as much as fiscal accountability. Proofs of his integrity were in those dispatch boxes and he meant to keep them safe.

Lewis also needed to warn Clark about the change of plan to go overland from Fort Pickering. Very likely he did that in hope that they might reconnect along the trail to Washington and be prepared to present a united front to detractors. At New Madrid, Lewis was thinking clearly because he wrote a letter to Clark and had made a will, and those facts refute later newspaper accounts that he was in any way deranged.

But his companion the valet Pernier could see another ague episode coming on. He had been trained since 1804 in the courtly school of Monticello, and sent by Jefferson to look after his friend and protégé. As Lewis's valet and confidente, Pernier felt closer to a kindly employer than the few dollars of the salary he was paid could buy. Those duties had included carrying sometimes bitter exchanges to those who tried to drag the governor down. If the free mulatto man risked looking slyly into the faces of the likes of Mr. Bates, he kept his feelings to himself. When the severe chill came on, Pernier wrapped Lewis in blankets to warm him. When that turned into a fever, he wiped his brow and applied cooling cloths. In this small way he did what Mr. Jefferson or a mother would have done.

But Pernier was no doctor and Meriwether was showing the effect of a malarial attack of the most virulent kind. Both of them knew how an episode of the ague would ravage him. If he had been dosing himself with Dr. Rush's calomel-laced pills, as was his usual practice, those mercury-laden little bombs had no actual effect on the condition. What they did was contribute to an accumulating case of mercury poisoning. In this episode the pills had failed to cut the symptoms and Lewis was driven to drinking a decoction of Peruvian bark so bitter it had to be disguised with wine. Lacking wine, Pernier may have tried cutting it with whiskey. Weakened and desperate, the chronic sufferer was close to exhausting his tolerance of the monster. Unable to bear it any longer, in a complex state of inescapable pain and intoxication, stepping over the side into the enveloping waters may have seemed the only way to end the torture.[27] Pernier and the boatmen twice had to restrain him.[28]

After four days of that torture, the boat reached the first of the four Chickasaw Bluffs. The third bluff was the highest, the fourth two miles long and sixty perpendicular feet high. Pernier helped the ailing Lewis struggle up the 120 squared log steps to Fort Pickering. The tottering governor saw a pleasant green fronting the stockade where a sentinel paced back and forth between the small cannon and piled shot bracketing the gate.

Commanding officer Capt. Gilbert Russell was appalled to see a man who was obviously so sick. The boat crew told him that Lewis had made two attempts to kill himself.[29] Captain Russell was no doctor but he had seen many men, himself included, suffer from the ague. Incapable of imagining mercury poisoning or grasping evidence of depression, as the commander of his company, Russell knew a drunk from a sick soldier. He put Lewis under the care of surgeon's mate W. C. Smith. The ailing Lewis was set up in the captain's own quarters which were presumably better than the earth-floor huts of the soldiers.

On the next day, September 16, Lewis summoned the strength to write a short note to President Madison informing him that he had changed his plans and would travel overland to Washington. The shaky penmanship and structure of that letter has been used to demonstrate the author's condition. However, it has been overlooked that Lewis wrote that as a cover letter for the printed laws of the Territory of Louisiana that he enclosed.[30] That was Lewis's answer, sent ahead, to those State Department bills that Madison continued to refuse, a matter of honor and withheld respect as much as accounting.

Historical speculation, based on the shaky handwriting of the short

cover note, has tried to show that Lewis was either emotionally disinte-
grating or a hopeless drunk. Russell in later descriptions of that trying time
tried to explain his failure in caring for the sick man and intimated that he
had denied liquor to Lewis, except for a small amount of wine.[31] But he was
dealing with a sick man, not an alcoholic, and the wine may have been used
to cut the bitter taste of Peruvian bark. After five days of battling a malarial
episode, the most distressing symptoms disappeared and for the next ten or
twelve days Lewis's health improved. Because Lewis was lodged in Russell's
room, the two officers had opportunities to talk.

Captain Russell certainly wasn't looking for another invalid to heal.
When he took over the post on June 10 it was in a deplorable condition,
the palisades rotten, the huts of the soldiers without floors, no serviceable
chimneys. Efforts to repair the defenses and provide decent living conditions for his men were frustrated when the garrison was laid low with fever.
At one point out of forty-eight men and officers, only eight or nine were fit
for duty. Four men drowned when they were sent across the Mississippi on
an errand and six others deserted. Lacking money, Russell paid some men
with his own funds.[32] Then, near the end of August, he had been informed
that the War Department accountant had refused his bills of $1,798 for
moving his company to the new post.[33]

Russell was particularly sensitive to that refusal. In the past it had taken
an act of Congress to relieve him of a similar debt that the War Office
accountant refused.[34] Like many other field officers, the captain was aware
that problems covering legitimate debts incurred in the line of duty
emanated from William Simmons. Russell's reaction was not as restrained as
the indignant letter Governor Lewis had written on August 18. Reading the
refusal in his quarters, Russell exploded. His "unguarded expressions of the
moment" were overheard by a civilian who immediately peddled what he
heard to the factor of the nearby Indian trade house, David Hogg. The army
officer had previously fallen out with civilian Hogg over a demand to arrest
a man accused of illicit trading. Refusing to act on insufficient evidence, Russell didn't have to look far to find his enemy. It would be November before
Russell learned that Hogg wasted no time in reporting that reaction to
Superintendent Mason and to Russell's superior, Col. Thomas Cushing.[35]

There must have been moments in a candlelit evening when the two
soldiers compared the abuses of the accounting department and damned
William Simmons to a bean counter's hell. The fellow had been causing
trouble for too long to attribute the latest refusals to the faltering economy.[36]
After his exasperated outburst, Russell sent an application downstream to

regimental headquarters asking permission to go to Washington and clear up his bills. If orders arrived in time, they could travel together.

When his patient was feeling better, Russell mentioned that Maj. Amos Stoddard was posted at Fort Adams below on the river. Meriwether wrote to his old associate on the twenty-second to arrange payment of an old debt of two hundred dollars. That letter was clear and well phrased. As an after-thought he added that Stoddard should address him in the city of Wash-ington until the last of December, "after which I shall be on my return to St. Louis."[37]

Ironies were beginning to compound. On the day that Lewis prepared to leave Fort Pickering, Stoddard was already in Nashville. Coming up the Natchez Trace from Fort Adams, Major Stoddard intercepted an unnamed traveler just from the Chickasaw Bluffs with a description of Governor Lewis's condition. In Nashville Stoddard shared this ominous rumor with a man named James Howe, who wasted no time informing Frederick Bates.

> Governor Lewis had arrived there (some time previous to his leaving it) in a state of mental derangement, that he had made several attempts to put an end to his own existence, which this person had prevented, and that Capt. Russell, the commanding officer was obliged to keep a strict watch over him to prevent his committing violence on himself and had caused his boat to be unloaded and the key to be secured in his stores.[38]

Sadly, the two men who helped found a US presence in Upper Louisiana, and who had endured the trials that went along with that duty, just missed reconnecting with each other by a few days. But Lewis had no way of knowing that a sympathetic friend was just ahead.[39] He was hoping to reconnect with Clark.

Eighteen days after Lewis left town, as receiving agent for the Indian factories, William Clark started the last of the public peltry downstream to New Orleans. That cargo was traveling under the supervision of several people, including the ever-handy James McFarlane, who planned to accom-pany the cargo of furs to the East Coast by sea.[40] Clark also planned to go to Washington and had promised to take Julia and the baby to see her father. When the Clarks started out from St. Louis on September 21, they were escorted across the river and as far as Cahokia by A. P. Chouteau, Clement Penrose, Sheriff Jeremiah Connor, David Delaunay, and several others who were also loyal supporters of the governor.[41] Those friends had no way of knowing that a very sick Governor Lewis "was much indisposed at New Madrid" and had recovered sufficiently to have set-off in good health for New Orleans but by the time he had reached Fort Pickering, he was forced to stop to recover his strength yet again.[42]

On October 12 the Clark entourage reached his brother Jonathan's home above the falls of the Ohio where they stayed for two weeks. They were there when the letter that Lewis wrote on September 11 caught up with Clark. Lewis announced that he had given up the plan to go down the river to New Orleans and instead would take a faster overland route to the Natchez Trace. Clark was puzzled by his friend's comment that he had made his will and had it witnessed.[43]

If the governor was worried about the valuable papers he was carrying, Clark guessed that McFarlane, who was also on his way east but by boat, might overtake his friend Lewis somewhere between New Madrid and the fourth Chickasaw Bluff. As McFarlane was "a pertcular friend of his," Clark imagined that Lewis might consign the documents to him and ride light to Nashville.[44]

Clark folded that letter into a bundle of other documents, including his copy of the MFCo. agreement, but when he went on with his family, he forgot to take them. Hearing disturbing reports about Lewis, Clark feared what he had failed to read between the lines.

NOTES

1. Alexander Wilson, "Particulars of the Death of Capt. Lewis," *Port Folio* 7 (January 1812): 39.

2. TJ to ML, August 16, 1809, Jackson, *LLC* 2: 458. Lewis never received this letter.

3. Ibid., pp. 459–61. Previous writers had framed these exchanges to create the impression that Lewis's response was desperate, but careful examination of all the circumstances seems to disprove it.

4. James Holmberg, ed., *Dear Brother* (New Haven, CT: Yale University Press, 2002), p. 210.

5. Lewis and Clark: Settlement of Account, August 21, 1809, Jackson, *LLC* 2: 462.

6. Personal account book, April 1807–1809, box 1, folder 8, MLC-MHS. Lewis paid off his debts to shopkeeper Joseph Philipson on August 22, Joseph Philipson's account book.

7. Ibid. Following a date of August 22, Judge Alexander Stuart spelled his name "Stuart." Historians have taken Lewis's lead of spelling it Stewart but that is incorrect. See his signature in RG217, M235, roll 66, frame 0524.

8. ML to William Carr, August 19, 1809, box 1, folder 11, MLC-MHS. Witnessed by Jeremiah Connor and Sam Solomon.

9. Carr still reported to Treasury Secretary Albert Gallatin.

10. Following a date of August 22. Personal account book, MLC-MHS.

11. Holmberg, *Dear Brother*, p. 210.

12. The receipt is reproduced in Lillian R. Frick, *Courageous Colter and Companions* (Washington, MO: Colter-Frick, 1997), pp. 339–40.

13. Thomas Bolling Robertson of New Orleans.

14. Holmberg, *Dear Brother*, p. 210. Like Carr, WC believed that Lewis left St. Louis about the twenty-fifth, but that was incorrect.

15. Ibid.

16. Lewis bought a medicine chest from Dr. Saugrain, August 24, 1809, for $30.75. June–September 1809, CFC-MHS.

17. Lewis to the President, August 27, 1809, Carter, *TP* 14: 293–312. Carter did not publish the entire document in *TP*. The remaining twelve pages cover two Indian councils and notes by Meriwether Lewis, RG107, L101, M221, roll 38, frames 4907–31.

18. TJ to ML, August 16, 1809, Jackson, *LLC* 2: 458.

19. TJ to ML, August 24, 1808, Carter, *TP* 14: 221.

20. RG107, L101, M221, roll 38, frames 4907–31; *ASP, Indian Affairs* 1: 764.

21. ML to A. P. Chouteau, September 2, 1809, deed book B, 378, Recorder of Deeds.

22. FB to John Breck Treat, September 2, 1809, Marshall *FB*, 2: 79.

23. His personal account book reflects the long chain of expenses, another proof of Lewis's methodical actions as he prepared to leave St. Louis. Meriwether Lewis, personal account book, 1807–1809, MLC-MHS.

24. The description of the river is drawn from Reuben Gold Thwaites, ed., *Early Western Travels*, vol. 4, *Cumings, Sketches of a Tour of the Western Country 1807–1809* (Cleveland: Arthur H. Clark, 1904).

25. Testaments of a serious and lethal malarial outbreak from St. Louis to New Orleans in the summer of 1809 killed hundreds of people: RG94, M1136, roll 1, frames 0837–40, pp. 45–49.

26. Stephen Ambrose, *Undaunted Courage* (New York: Simon & Schuster, 1996), p. 463; Dawson A. Phelps, "The Tragic Death of Meriwether Lewis," *William and Mary Quarterly* 13, no. 3 (July 1956): 314.

27. A malarial outbreak in New Orleans that same summer caused many soldiers to wander off and die in the swamps: JW to SW, August 19, 1809, RG107, W658, M221, roll 33, frame 1564; RG94, M1136, roll 1, frame 0832, p. 39.

28. Authors' interpretation of Russell's account when Lewis arrived at Fort Pickering.

29. Lewis was not traveling with McFarlane, who would have discussed a friend's condition with the captain. McFarlane had commanded a boat to New Orleans, a week after Lewis departed St. Louis.

30. ML to JMA, September 16, 1809, box 1, folder 11, MLC-MHS.

31. GR to TJ, January 31, 1810, document 33657, roll 45, TJ-LOC. An abridged and paraphrased version in Jackson, *LLC* 2: 748.

32. RG107, M221, R235 and 244, roll 29.

33. RG107, R244. Passing through Nashville last May on his way to take over the command of Fort Pickering from Captain Swan, Russell sent in his accounts and vouchers for the expenses of recruiting and moving the troops. RG217, M235, roll 67, document 22209, frame 0636.

34. US Congress, *House Journal*, 9th Cong., 1st sess., p. 3; GR to SW, March 15, 1808, RG107, R133, M221, roll 12, frame 3623. As a captain of Tennessee militia in 1803 Russell had been ordered to proceed with his company to Natchez, then had to sue the government to recover the expenses. March 1808 he wrote to Dearborn charging that the accountant Simmons was defrauding the government. He was a captain in the regulars when he moved his company to Fort Pickering only to run into the same problem again. RG94, M566, roll 2, frame 0322.

35. GR to SW, January 2, 1810, RG107, R14, M221, roll 39, frame 6095. It may go to Russell's state of mind that in early September an altercation with David Hogg of the nearby Indian factory was protested to Superintendent Mason. His drafts had still not been paid when he explained his difficulties with Hogg to the SW.

36. RG107, R219, 235, 240, 244, roll 29. Two days later he wrote the first of the two letters to TJ.

37. The note is reproduced in Frick, *Courageous Colter*, p. 340.

38. James Howe to FB, September 28, 1809, BFP-MHS. Letter printed in *Missouri Historical Society Collections* 4 (1912–1923): 472.

39. The facility with which the informant traveled across country from the bluffs or Stoddard's trip up the trace disproves claims of the danger of those passages.

40. Near New Orleans the trade factory boat ran into a storm that led McFarlane to file a protest on November 3 against claims for damages suffered by his passengers or freight. From there he continued to the East Coast. French and Spanish Archives, C-2965, roll F523, no. 2990, Western Manuscripts Collection.

41. French and Spanish Archives, Clark's memorandum book, Lewis and Clark Collections, C-1075, microfilm 1, Western Manuscripts Collection.

42. *Missouri Gazette*, October 4, 1809, p. 3.

43. Excerpts from Clark's 1809 Journal, October 12, 1809, Jackson, *LLC* 2: 724. Holmberg, *Dear Brother*, pp. 218, 224, 228.

44. Holmberg, *Dear Brother*, p. 218.

SEVENTEEN

Last Journey

This lonely grave—this bed of clay[1]

A day or so after the arrival of the seriously indisposed Governor Lewis, Maj. James Neelly, the new Indian agent, came to Fort Pickering.[2] As the representative of the federal government he had recently taken under his protection four thousand Chickasaw Indians. About a quarter of them were mixed-bloods who had an advantage as middlemen in running tribal affairs. Few were more influential or as wealthy as the Colbert brothers. Last February, after the previous agent succumbed to malaria, they recommended "an old gentleman of our acquaintance that is not so fond of speculation as our former agents have been."[3] But the appointment was far from a sinecure.

Major Neelly had the job since early July and was still settling into his new responsibilities when he left the Chickasaw agency and came to the government factory near Fort Pickering on September 18. One of the other applicants whom Neelly had beaten out for the appointment was the spiteful factor David Hogg. It was unlikely that Neelly found much hospitality at the government house.[4] He had been appointed to that post about the same time that Captain Russell assumed command of Fort Pickering. Together they were facing the difficult task of ejecting as many as four or five thousand illegal squatters from the Chickasaw lands. Some coordination was certainly justified.

Neelly may not have seen Meriwether during the worse time of this episode but over the next ten days he picked up the gossip circulating the garrison. The hero of western exploration was a very sick man. Captain Russell was waiting for permission to travel east concerning his refused bills, and Neelly may have stalled in hope that they could travel together. During that time Lewis recovered, and in their conversations Neelly got a sense of his intentions. The agent was planning to go to Nashville on agency business and if Meriwether appeared to be well enough, they could travel together. There was nothing sinister in a courtesy to a fellow federal officer.

Disappointed in his own expectations, the best Captain Russell could do was provide two government horses and riding gear for the governor and his servant Pernier. Neelly furnished a "horse to pack his [Lewis's] trunks, &c, and a man to attend to them." There may have been another horse for Neelly's gear. But before Lewis could undertake a pack trip, he had to reduce his baggage. Two trunks, an empty liquor case, a bundle of sheets, blankets, and coverlet were left at Fort Pickering, all of which Captain Russell would send back to William C. Carr in St. Louis.[5] Lewis had been taking a trunk to New Orleans as a favor to the Belle Fontaine officer Captain House, and Russell also agreed to forward it downstream.[6]

On September 27, Lewis executed a promissory note to Captain Russell as security for the two government horses. The amount of $379.58 was to be repaid on the first of next January. At the bottom of the small page Russell added a reminder to Lewis that the saddle was to be left at Talbot's in Nashville. The governor carried with him two trunks containing all his papers relative to the expedition to the Pacific, General Clark's land warrant, a portfolio, memo, and notebook, and many papers of a public and private nature. A rifle, two pistols, pipe tomahawk, and a dirk should be weapons enough to defend the $220 cash that Lewis was carrying, and $99 of that was a treasurer's check on the United States bank at New Orleans endorsed by Russell.[7]

The party left Fort Pickering on September 29 taking a direct overland route toward Nashville. On the first leg of the journey the party may have been accompanied by several Chickasaw returning to their homes. Riding a hundred miles in three days at a steady pace brought them to some Indian cabins strung along the upper reaches of Beech Creek.[8] The hard ride and a malarial relapse exhausted Lewis and they stopped to rest for several days.

Their accommodation must have been similar to what the traveling ornithologist Alexander Wilson described a year and a half later. The Chickasaw camp he visited was two or three solitary huts with a few acres of open land where the "wretchedly cultivated" corn nodded in the Indian summer awaiting a hardening frost. Wilson's hosts spread a deerskin on the floor for a bed and he used his portmanteau for pillow.[9] Neelly had a working command of the Chickasaw language but whether he could have arranged much better accommodations for the exhausted Lewis is unlikely.

The rapidly deteriorating Lewis was aided by sympathetic strangers unable to interrupt the tragic slide. If Neelly realized how bad the situation was as the governor sagged in his saddle, there wasn't much that he could do to head it off. He was not a Mason but in that final passage he was as good a brother to Meriwether Lewis as most, but not all of the lodge members back in St. Louis. Captain Russell had been horrified when Meriwether staggered to the head of the long stairway, supported by his body servant. A sufferer of the ague himself, and responsible for a command laid low by fever, Russell did what he could to get the poor devil into shape to ride.

Now Meriwether relied on Pernier. Trailing behind on the other government horse, Pernier must have had a growing sense of hopeless apprehension. A free mulatto, he owed his training as a butler, body servant, and all-around personal assistant to the careful household of Thomas Jefferson.[10] Pernier tried to make their rude accommodations in St. Louis as comfortable as possible, sometimes fulfilling duties that might have been required of an aide. Although he spoke French better than most of the French habitants, he was still a free black man in a slave society. It was a point of feeling for Pernier that the man he served could not accept the harsh discipline that William Clark inflicted upon his household slaves.[11] In his reconstruction of the fate of John Pernier, Donald Jackson suggested that the servant had a sensitive soul and was loyal to the man he had lived with intimately for the previous two years.

After resting in "the Chickasaw Nation" for two days, they continued on to find a crossing at the Tennessee River. Unless Neelly knew of a boat along the shore, they had to swim the river. Alexander Wilson described his crossing of the Buffalo River in 1811. He had no alternative but to plunge in on his horse and try to keep its head upstream so they wouldn't drift down too far. Boatmen returning on foot on the trace searched for a driftwood log that they could paddle across. If not, they swam.

Crossing the Tennessee was a challenge and even in drowsy late summer weather, getting immersed must have been a shock to a malaria-weakened traveler like Lewis. His wet underclothing had to dry on him. They traveled for another day before making camp.[12]

On the morning of October 10 two of the horses had wandered off after being turned out to graze. The governor wanted to press on but one of the missing animals was government property and Neelly had to stay to search for them. Lewis agreed that he would wait for the agent at the first habitation he came across. Having traveled this trail before, Neelly knew that would be Grinder's Stand, an inn on the Natchez Trace where a respectable family would make the ailing man relatively comfortable. Meriwether rode on, trailed by Pernier and the packer riding double and leading the pack horse with Lewis's trunks.[13] Although it has been generally understood that Lewis traveled on the Natchez Trace, we think he actually came to it overland very near Grinder's Stand.

There was only one direct witness to the worn traveler's arrival at a two-cabin and connected-roof dogtrot and barn just off the trail. Mr. Grinder was away, but his wife was a frontier woman living along a well-traveled route and accustomed to accommodating travelers. Although it is possible she didn't recognize the significance of her guest, Mrs. Grinder soon rustled up some supper while her guest sat in a chair by the door in the sunset making comments on the beauty of the evening. He also rose and paced restlessly while talking to himself. Mrs. Grinder became so uncomfortable with the situation that she gave up her house to the guest who preferred his own buffalo robe and bearskin to a bed. She slept across the dogtrot in the other cabin, and Pernier and the packer bedded down in the barn loft above the horses.

This is how Priscilla Grinder remembered the events of that evening and sleepless night that she related to Alexander Wilson sixteen months later.

> Governor Lewis, she said, came there about sun-set, alone, and inquired if he could stay for the night; and, alighting, brought his saddle into the house. He was dressed in a loose gown, white, striped with blue. On being asked if he came alone, he replied that there were two servants behind, who would soon be up. He called for some spirits, and drank very little. When the servants arrived, one of whom was a negro, he inquired for his powder, saying he was sure he had some powder in a canister. The servant gave no distinct reply, and Lewis, in the mean while walked backwards and forwards before the door, talking to himself. Sometimes, she said, he would seem as if he were walking up to her; and would suddenly wheel round, and walk back as fast as he could. Supper being ready he sat down, but had not eat but a few mouthfuls when he started up speaking to himself in a violent manner. At these times, she says, she observed his face to flush as if it had come on him in a fit. He lighted his pipe, and drawing a chair to the door sat down, saying to Mrs. Grinder in a kind tone of voice,

"Madam this is a very pleasant evening." He smoked for some time, but quitted his seat and traversed the yard as before. He again sat down to his pipe, seemed again composed and casting his eyes wishfully towards the west, observed what a sweet evening it was. Mrs. Grinder was preparing a bed for him; but he said he would sleep on the floor, and desired the servant to bring the bear skins and buffaloe robe, which were immediately spread out for him; and it being now dusk the woman went off to the kitchen, and the two men to the barn, which stands about two hundred yards off. The kitchen is only a few paces from the room where Lewis was, and the woman being considerably alarmed by the behaviour of her guest could not sleep but listened to him walking backwards and forwards, she thinks for several hours, and talking aloud, as she said, "like a lawyer." She then heard the report of a pistol, and something fall heavily on the floor, and the words "O Lord." Immediately afterwards she heard another pistol, and in a few minutes she hear him at her door calling out "O madam! Give me some water, and heal my wounds." The logs being open, and unplastered, she saw him stagger back and fall against a stump that stands between the kitchen and room. He crawled for some distance, raised himself by the side of a tree, where he sat about a minute. He once more got to the room; afterwards he came to the kitchen door, but did not speak; she then heard him scraping the bucket with a gourd for water, but it appears that this cooling element was denied the dying man! As soon as day broke and not before, the terror of the woman having permitted him to remain for two hours in this most deplorable situation, she sent two of her children to the barn, her husband not being at home, to bring the servants; and on going in they found him lying on the bed; he uncovered his side and shewed them where the bullet had entered; a piece of the forehead was blown off, and had exposed the brains, without having bled much. He begged they would take his rifle and blowout his brains, and he would give them all the money he had in his trunk. He often said, "I am no coward, but I am so strong, so hard to die." He begg' d the servant [John Pernier] not to be afraid of him, for that he would not hurt him. He expired in about two hours, or just as the sun rose above the trees.[14]

The scene that morning was ghastly and the despairing Pernier close to shock. Somehow he steeled himself to make the packer help him move the body of Governor Lewis and get it arranged in a more respectable manner. Then they waited until Major Neelly arrived, leading the one horse he had recovered. He had to leave the government horse lost in the woods.[15]

Most accounts discreetly overlook what those secondary victims of the tragedy had to do. There was a grim search for enough boards to cobble together a crude box. The shredded, blood-crusted clothing had to be removed, the wounded body washed, and the corpse redressed in something suitable for a tolerable burial. That was just what frontier countrymen of the period would have done for a deceased relative or neighbor.

Mrs. Grinder was a decent woman who went on to bear several children and raise a respectable family. She knew what was necessary, although it was more decent for Pernier to handle the intimate details. Cleansing the bloody corpse was an experience that marked him in a way he never escaped. By the time Priscilla Grinder was interviewed by Lewis's friend Alexander Wilson, Pernier had died in Washington.[16] He had a lot of bad memories from the death of Lewis to forget.

After taking several days to deal with the tragedy, Neelly and Pernier, trailing with the baggage, rode on to Nashville.[17] The seventy-two-mile ride took two or three days. In Nashville Neelly quickly consigned the two trunks to the care of William C. Anderson, a distant relative of the Clark family. Anderson called upon Thomas Freeman, the same man who had participated in the government exploration of the Red River in 1808. Because he had connections in Washington, Freeman agreed to see the property safely conveyed to President Madison. But before he would proceed they made an inventory of Lewis's personal effects.[18]

The trunks were opened and the contents carefully noted by Anderson, Freeman, and two officers stationed at Nashville, Captain Boote of the First Infantry Regiment and Capt. John Brahan, an officer of the Fifth. A Virginian, Captain Brahan wrote letters to the secretary of war and President Madison while Neelly composed an almost identical statement to send to former President Jefferson. All were dated October 18, seven days after the tragedy.[19]

After years of publishing stale material copied from other newspapers, the editor of the Nashville *Democratic Clarion* finally had a scoop. The October 20 edition appeared with columns edged in mourning black, describing in lurid detail "the untimely end of a brave and prudent officer." That became the source of the ghastly details about Lewis's last agony, particularly the details about cutting himself.[20] The knife wounds story appeared in the *Democratic Clarion* two days after Neelly and Brahan wrote their reports and was soon reprinted in Frankfort. Eventually it was published in the *National Intelligencer* and many other eastern newspapers, each version profiting from editorial embellishment.[21]

The circle was complete when William Clark and his party arrived at Shelbyville, Kentucky, and read a copy of the Frankfort *Argus* newspaper.

Nashville, October 20—It is with extreme regret we have to record the melancholy death of his excellency Meriwether Lewis, Governor of Upper Louisiana, on his way to the City of Washington. The following particulars, are given us by a gentleman who travelled with him from the Chicasaw Bluffs.

The governor had been in a bad state of health, but having recovered in some degree, set out from the Chicasaw Bluffs and in travelling from that to the Chicasaw nation, our informant says, he discovered that the governor appeared at times deranged, and on their arrival in that nation, having lost two horses, the governor proceeded on, and the gentleman detained with a view of hunting the horses. The governor went on to a Mr. Grinder's on the road, found no person at home but a woman: she observed something wild in his appearance, become frightened and left the house to sleep in another near it, and the two servants that was with him went to sleep in the stable. About three o'clock the woman says she heard the report of two pistols in the room where he lay, and immediately awakened the servants, who rushed into the house, but too late! He had shot himself in the head and just below the breast, and was in the act of cutting himself with a razor. The only words he uttered, was "It is done, my good servant give me some water," and expired in a few moments after. He was as decently intered as the place would admit.[22]

Clark rode on another eight miles trying to wrap his mind around the shocking possibility that his friend might be dead, then stopped at Shannon's tavern an hour after dusk where he wrote to his brother Jonathan:

[W]hen at Shelbyville to day I Saw in a Frankfort paper called the Arguss a report published which givs me much Concern, it Says that Govr. Lewis killed himself by Cutting his Throat with a Knife on his way between the Chickaw Saw Bluffs and nashville, I fear this report has too much truth, tho' hope it may have no foundation—my reasons for thinking it possible is founded on the letter which I recved from him at your house.[23]

President Madison had the shocking news by October 30, then he passed it on to Jefferson:

We just learn the melancholy fate of Governor Lewis which possibly may not have travelled so quickly into your neighborhood. He had, it seems, betrayed latterly symptoms of a disordered mind: and had set out under the care of a friend on a visit to Washington. His first intentions was, to make the trip by water; but changing it, at the Chickasaw Bluffs, he struck across towards Nashville. As soon as they had passed the Tennessee, he took advantage of the neglect of his companion, who had not secured his arms, to put an end to himself. He first fired a pistol, at his head, the ball of which glancing, was ineffectual. With the 2d. he passed a Ball thro' his body, wch. being also without immediate effect, he had recourse to his Dirk with wch he mangled himself considerably. After all he lived till the next morning, with the utmost impatience for death.[24]

On October 19 the *Missouri Gazette* was still catching up on the ominous symptoms about the governor that had appeared at Fort Pickering. It quoted information that Colonel Bissell had received from Major Stoddard, dated September 28 at Nashville. As the report was serious, editor Charless added, "we sincerely hope that the next communication may bring the agreeable news of Gov. Lewis's health being perfectly restored."[25] Given the coincidence, the letter that James Howe wrote to Bates on September 28 must have arrived at the same time but was not mentioned. It was November 2 when the *Gazette* published the sad news in St. Louis.[26]

Ever the careful bureaucrat, Frederick Bates kept the documents that damned him. By the end of October 1809 St. Louis had learned the fate of Governor Lewis. But there was no sympathy in the secretary. In a few days, on November 2, he coldly informed the Prairie du Chien subagent Nicholas Boilvin that "Gov Lewis is no more. He died in Tennessee about 20 days ago."[27] In observing that Boilvin had lost a friend, Bates implied that he had better step carefully in the future. But in the letters that followed, Bates quickly shored up his connections with those who could influence his future.[28]

A week later the full gush of Bates's bile was regurgitated to his brother Richard in the condemnation of someone no longer around to defend himself.

> You have heard no doubt of the premature and tragical death of Gov. Lewis. Indeed I had no personal regard for him and a great deal of political contempt. Yet I cannot but lament that after all his toils and dangers he should die in *such a manner.* . . . I never saw after his arrival in this country, anything in his conduct towards me, but alienation and unmerited distrust. I had acquired and shall retain a good portion of the public confidence, and he had not generosity of soul to forgive me for it. . . . Oh Lewis, how from my Love, I pity thee! "Those who stand high, have many winds to shake them. And if they fall, they dash themselves to pieces."[29]

NOTES

1. Alexander Wilson, "Particulars of the Death of Capt. Lewis," *Port Folio* 7 (January 1812): 38.

2. August 27, 1809, RG107, N94, M221, roll 27.

3. Malcolm McGee to SW, September 27, 1808, RG107, M221, roll 26, frame 8765, and George Colbert to SW, February 18, 1809, C469, roll 20, frame 6146.

4. James Robertson to SW, January 22, 1809, RG107, R198, M221, roll 29, frame 9719.

5. James Neelly to TJ, October 18, 1809. Memorandum of Lewis's personal effects, November 23, 1809, Jackson, *LLC* 2: 467, 470–74.

6. GR to TJ, January 4, 1810, document 33616-7, roll 45, TJ-LOC.

7. Ibid.

8. The party took a direct route to the Natchez Trace. Taking the Chickasaw Nation statement at face value meant an unnecessary detour that would have required a fifty-mile-a-day pace to reconcile with the known timeline.

9. Wilson, "Particulars of the Death of Capt. Lewis," p. 40.

10. Donald Jackson, "On the Death of Meriwether Lewis's Servant," *William and Mary Quarterly* 21 (July 1964): 445.

11. William E. Foley, *Wilderness Journey: The Life of William Clark* (Columbia: University of Missouri Press, 2004), pp. 166, 168.

12. For background on Lewis's trip to Grinder's Stand (inn), letters from Neelly, Russell, and Brahan provide insightful information.

13. James Neelly to TJ, October 18, 1809, Jackson, *LLC* 2: 467–68.

14. Wilson, "Particulars of the Death of Capt. Lewis," pp. 36–38. Claims have been made that Mrs. Grinder could not have seen what she reported on such a dark night but at that time people were accustomed to getting about without light. That was a lesson learned during the Korean War when enemy soldiers moved under cover of darkness and US soldiers had to be trained how to do that by protecting their night vision.

15. John Brahan to JMA, October 18, 1809, document 33520-1, roll 44, TJ-LOC. Mrs. Grinder reported that two men slept in the stable. That means Pernier was with the packer.

16. Jackson, "On the Death of Meriwether Lewis's Servant," pp. 445–48.

17. If Neelly had already made his agency at Duck River, he may have stopped to share his experience with his wife.

18. Edward Coles, who had stayed on as President Madison's secretary, had them in Washington by the first week in January. Isaac A. Coles to TJ, January 5, 1810, Jackson, *LLC* 2: 486–87.

19. John Brahan to SW, October 18, 1809, RG107, B589, M221, roll 18, frame 5632; James Neelly to TJ, October 18, 1809, Jackson, *TP* 2: 467–68.

20. Richard Dillon, *Meriwether Lewis: A Biography* (Santa Cruz, CA: Western Tanager Press, 1965), p. 338. See also comments by Jackson, *LLC* 2: 746–47.

21. *National Intelligencer (Washington, DC)*, November 13, 1809, p. 3.

22. *Argus of Western America (KY)*, November 4, 1809, p. 2. The *Argus* was published in Frankfort, Kentucky, and was known also as the *Frankfort Argus*. This was the second printing of the *Argus* article and probably the same that was printed

on October 28; however, it is not a direct copy of the original *Nashville Clarion* newspaper report. Editorial embellishments were added to the *Argus* article and this elaboration continued as other newspapers reprinted the story.

23. WC to Jonathan Clark, October 28, 1809, in James Holmberg, ed., *Dear Brother* (New Haven, CT: Yale University Press, 2002), pp. 216–23.

24. Robert A. Rutland et al., *The Papers of James Madison*, 5 vols. (Charlottesville: University of Virginia Press, 1984), 2: 48–49.

25. *Missouri Gazette*, October 19, 1809, p. 3. In the way papers were made up in times of limited amounts of type, front and back pages would be made up ahead of time and the latest news printed inside.

26. James Howe to FB, September 28, 1809, BFP-MHS.

27. FB to Nicholas Boilvin, November 2, 1809, Marshall, *FB* 2: 104.

28. FB to John Coburn, November 2, 1809, Marshall, *FB* 2: 104; November 10, 1809, to William O. Allen; December 14, 1809, to Alexander McNair, 2: 114, 120.

29. FB to Richard Bates, November 9, 1809, Marshall, *FB* 2: 108–10. Portions of this damning letter have been cited previously in order to establish the sequence of events.

EIGHTEEN

Devils in the Blood

Poor Reason perish'd in the storm[1]

The details of the death of Meriwether Lewis have been of considerable, sometimes insensitive interest to historians and often repeated
in sanguinary detail. But his bones deserve to rest in peace. A fuller examination of the causes may be a last respect. What happened to Meriwether
Lewis to tip him from a productive year and a half into what appears to be
the depths of depression? There had been more trying times. A winter in
the rainforest on the Pacific Coast should have been enough to depress
anyone, but there are no indications that Lewis suffered from what is now
known as a mood disorder.[2] William Clark did not hold back from mentioning his own health problems, but during their time together he never
noted more detail about his friend except that he was feeling unwell or had
recovered.

In trying to rationalize the tragic death of his friend, Thomas Jefferson
used a term that has since been widely misunderstood. He wrote, "Governor Lewis had from early life been subject to hypocondriac affections. It
was a constitutional disposition in all the nearer branches of the family of
his name & was more immediately inherited by him from his father."
Reflecting on Lewis's death, Jefferson repeated, "We have all to lament that
a fame so dearly earned was clouded finally by such an act of desperation.
He was much afflicted & habitually so with hypocondria."[3]

307

But hypochondria, in the usage of the time, described a set of physical symptoms. Medical understanding of that day made no attempt to identify an emotional condition as the term is used today.

The term *hypochondrium* referred to the anatomical region seated in the abdominal area and *hypochondria* included the cartilage, viscera, muscles, and organs located there.[4] *Hypocondriac affections* actually referred to the disease known as *hypochondriasis*, a complex, physical sickness.[5] Ailments ascribed to the *hypochondrium* meant a cluster of chronic illnesses manifested by a fever stemming from an unknown cause.

American medicine was in its infancy and no authority of Jefferson's time could accurately describe Lewis's illness or state, whether it was mental, physical, or a combination of both. In 1809 American doctors held that *melancholia* was a mental illness while *hypochondriasis* was a physical condition with unknown causes. However, better-qualified European doctors recognized hypochondriasis as real and physical, sometimes occurring in tandem with melancholia. The distinction between melancholia as a mental disease and hypochondriasis as a physical disease would take centuries to unravel and comprehend.[6]

Melancholia had been a term for one of the principal forms of madness for centuries. It referred to a severe mental disorder entailing a significant degree of dejection, sadness, a gloomy cast of mind, and also a pattern of complaining about an array of physical symptoms.[7]

Jefferson recalled that when Lewis served as his secretary, the president had at times observed his "depressions of mind." But Jefferson was iron-willed about his own afflictions and regularly bathed his feet in cold water for purposes of health. Beyond being incapacitated with a periodical headache that may have been migraine but could also represent a reaction to his own malarial episodes, Jefferson was reluctant to admit physical weakness in himself, or in others.[8] So the former president guessed that Lewis "was in a paroxysm" of one of those afflictions at the time of his death.[9] The term *paroxysm* may seem to describe a mental condition, but in the usage of the seventeenth and eighteenth centuries it denoted a fit or rigor (tremors induced by chills).[10] That was understood to be a stage, an outward affection (symptom) of a more serious but unidentified malady generally called "the ague."[11] The Greeks knew intermittent fever, which the physician Galen called *signa febrium intermittentium*, the ancient name for malaria.[12] Over the centuries other names were periodic fever, bilious fever, or the ague.[13]

The ague that disordered those internal organs was later understood to be malaria but no one could have guessed that a person suffering with untreated malaria could unintentionally kill himself. It was not until 1828 that a British doctor treating uncured ague patients found that a "disorder of the mind" is an effect of intermittent fever.[14] Additionally, hypochondriasis sufferers also had dark urine, which dovetailed with the symptoms of malaria.[15] When Lewis was in a malarial paroxysm, this meant the length of a certain type of fever that displayed three stages: cold, hot, and sweating or fits. Six years before Lewis died, an American medical student said that patients could experience great anxiety "at the height of the fit, as to feel like an intolerance of life itself."[16]

Far from being the melancholic disposition that gave rise to imaginary illnesses, as American doctors had latterly considered it, the hypochondriasis that afflicted Meriwether was a debilitating complication of chronic untreated malaria. In malaria, mature parasites residing in the gut of mosquitoes are discharged during the insect's blood meal, invade the liver, hatch in the blood, and over a short lifetime cause the enlargement of the spleen and the liver. The disease then progresses through severe anemia, delusions, high fever, and delirium to death. There was no cure.

Similar in appearance, the parasites belong to the genus *Plasmodium* and are known by their specie names, *falicparum*, *vivax*, *malariae*, and *ovale*. The main reason why malaria went unidentified for centuries was that "the fevers caused by those four organisms vary enough in their clinical presentations that different labels evolved for their symptom complexes."[17] The nature of the disease establishes "long-term chronic infections, in which the host stays infectious to ensure that sufficient transmission . . . can occur to guarantee survival."[18]

Malaria is a disease fitted with a hydra-head of painful secondary complications that mimic other conditions like anemia, jaundice, migraine-type headaches, and enlarged liver and spleen.[19] Yet for all of its mimicry, those tiny monsters in the blood had been the scourge of Upper Louisiana years before the arrival of Lewis and Clark. The inhabitants may not have known its formal name but they must have recognized the pattern of the fever without being able to do much about it. It is appalling to realize how prevalent malaria was in the population, and how debilitating.

In September 1794 the Spanish lieutenant governor residing in St. Louis wrote about an epidemic "where the fevers have gotten everyone down." Surveyor General Antoine Soulard had succumbed several times and in mid-October fell ill again, "more seriously than ever . . . it is his 6th bout of most violent fever."[20] Four years later, a French engineer visiting St. Louis attributed the sickly summer conditions to recurring fevers that "lower your resistance, leaving you for some time during convalescence in a sort of melancholy stupor."[21] In November 1803, Capt. Amos Stoddard reported that the Upper Louisiana population suffered from intermittent fever.[22] Four years later a captain reported on an army officer who, after suffering horribly and begging not to be deserted by his doctor, died at Cantonment Belle Fontaine.[23]

Nor was the fever localized. Capt. Daniel Bissell in 1805 was ready to resign his commission "because of his determination not to Serve in a Southern clime."[24] In August 1808 the Chickasaw Indian agent had an attack of "ague and fever" that lingered on for six weeks until "the ague quit him but the fever turned more severe and [he] died."[25] A year later, on August 26, 1809, Capt. Gilbert Russell told the secretary of war "such has been the unhealthiness of the season that with the troops I have as yet have been unable to make no improvement [to the deplorable condition of Fort Pickering]—Out of forty eight officers & men I have sometimes had but eight or nine fit for duty."[26]

Meriwether was one of many sufferers. The commonness of the disease in the population is appalling by today's standards. Most malarial Americans were silent victims, barely admitting to an episode beyond measuring how long it took for someone to recover. Personal accounts don't describe the sequence of symptoms beyond some vague reference to the ague or the fever. It isn't clear if they linked one bout to another, much as we don't track recurring colds. Given the likelihood of worms, ticks, fleas, and other parasites they couldn't effectively combat, demons in one's liver was just another burden of lives often cut short.

Malaria was the most common disease during the early colonial and frontier periods: "So inescapable that many refused to regard it as a disease, but like hard work, a concomitant [accompaniment] of the frontier."[27] That history carries pertinent information from an early period before a cure was found for the disease. Modern-day scientists tend to doubt the accuracy of diagnosis in earlier times because the surviving information, written by uncured sufferers, was based on inference.[28] It is claimed by some that in the past, malaria was a collection of symptoms that went by a myriad of archaic names like autumnal fever, bilious fever, remittent fever, intermittent fever, bilious remittent fever, the chills and fever, or, simply, the ague. Those names were used in different parts of the country because malaria is not a single disease but "a family of four different diseases caused by four different parasites."[29] Sufferers of that terrible time, and their doctors, may not have known exactly what they were trying to treat.

Ague was an imprecise diagnosis. Modern physicians who have not wit-nessed a full-blown attack of untreated malaria have rejected the eighteenth-century sufferer's descriptions as imprecise language for genuine verification of the disease. That misses important clues from those close to the suffering, like Meriwether Lewis, who regularly witnessed the course of the disease in others and still could not scientifically name it in himself.[30]

Malariologist Margaret Humphreys makes a distinction between sick-nesses that look like malaria and malaria itself: "How a particular writer ap-plied the phrase needs to be determined from other evidence, such as the asso-ciation with swampy ground, the appearance of the disease in summer months, and the display of the 'tawny tone' or skin color that suggests jaundice."[31]

Although most sufferers could not accurately name what they had or how to treat it, Jesuit missionaries in South America had stumbled upon something. Most commonly used as a treatment, Peruvian bark or *cinchona*, brewed as a tea, had an ingredient that was a dozen years later isolated as qui-nine.[32] The brewing could take as long as forty-five minutes and soon lost its strength. The decoction was so bitter that it had to be mixed in a quart of claret, port wine, or brandy that the sufferer drank at regular intervals for a number of days.[33] By the time this treatment began to have some effect, the episode had probably run its course. Over time, large doses could produce serious side effects, including tinnitus (ringing in the ears) and deafness.

Sometimes taken as a fault, Meriwether's journalistic lapses on the expedition may have reflected times when malaria immobilized him. That he or Clark for that matter didn't make much of it was not particularly heroic in a time when many of the others in the party also suffered. Recon-structing Meriwether's activities during the last months he spent in St. Louis provides reliable clues to his health.

At the beginning of 1809 there was a ten-day lapse when Clark per-formed some duties for him. That could have been the consequence of a massive *La Guignolee* hangover or a malarial episode. Some of his last let-ters appear to be in another hand, which suggests that the governor needed additional help completing his work, didn't trust Bates, or couldn't hold a pen. At some point the valet Pernier was sick and had to be attended by Dr. Farrar, who charged Lewis an exorbitant fee "but which my situation com-pells me to pay."[34]

From midsummer 1809 on a momentum began building in the body of Meriwether Lewis. In addition to other physical and emotional stresses, he had to endure the punishing torment of recurring malaria. To resist it, Meri-wether Lewis listed a potential medicine chest in the small account book that he carried in the last two years of his life. Although he may not have understood it, those recipes did more harm than good because some included calomel, a mercury derivative. If Lewis had stuck to the Peruvian bark, he may not have suffered as intensely.[35]

Receipt for the best Stomachic

¼ oz. of Cloves/ ½ oz. of Columbo/ 1 oz Peruvian bark/ 1 quart of Port Wine.

These ingredients to be well pounded and shook when taken—a wine glass twice or thrice a day may be taken with good effect, it is an excellent restorative.

Receipt for making wine from Mr. King of Washington. Cask of 30 gallons filled with grapes common, Brandy one or two gallons, fill with cider after formented and clear or in the state for bottling.

Method of treating billious fever when unattended by Typhus or nervous symptoms—

Get the patient [to] taken as strong puke of tarter Ametic, the second day after a purge of Calomel and Jallop which should be repeated after two days more, to be taken in the morning, and no cold water to be used that day a pill of opium and tartar to be taken every night and after the purgatives ten grains of Rheubarb and 20 grs of Barks should be repeated every morning & at 12 o'ck.

Emetic: 4 grs Tartar to be desolved in 3 table spoonfulls of water warm one spoonfull to be taken every five minutes to procure at least five pucks or a motion.

Pill of Opium and tartar: Nine grains of Tartoar Emetic and 12 grs of Opium made into 18 pills—one every night at bedtime.

Dose of Calomel and Jallap: 6 grs of Calomel & 15 of Jallap

Antibillious pills: 20 grs of Vitrolated Tartar & 40 of Jallap made into 12 pills—3 to be taken at night to which if they do not operate by morning two more are to be taken to facilitate their operaton.

Alloe pill: The size of an english pea made up with molasses and flour to be given at night then at bedtime.[36]

There is a curious discrepancy between the day that his close friend Clark and the less intimate Carr thought the governor left St. Louis, August 25, and the actual departure on September 4.[37] Perhaps for those ten days he was secluding himself from clamoring creditors, waiting for a boat, or suffering from another bout of malaria. At the height of the summer infection season, the likelihood is strong in favor of malaria.

Although ague and pneumonia both exhibit chills and fever, Lewis could tell the difference. The ague was periodic, presented itself with violent paroxysms, and usually ended within a day or two. On November 13, 1803, Meriwether Lewis described what appears to be a malarial relapse:

> left (Fort) Massac about five oclock—descended about three miles and encamped on the S.E. shore raind very hard in the eving and I was siezed with a violent ague which continued for about four hours and as is usual was succeeded by a feever which however fortunately abated in some measure by sunrise the next morning.[38]

The entry is telling because his phrase "as is usual" indicates both frequency and familiarity with the illness. Lewis stated that he took a dose of Dr. Rush's pills "which operated extremely well," and he was "entirely clear of fever" by that evening. However, it was days later before Lewis was well enough to write about the incident in his journal.

One of the most complete descriptions of a malarial outbreak occurred at the presidential mansion during most of March 1807. Several persons staying with President Jefferson experienced a synchronous attack. Beyond demonstrating that malaria can strike in the middle of winter as easily as in the summer months, the malarial parasite synchronizes with the host's circadian rhythm.[39] Infected persons are subject to the maturation cycle of the parasite, which can happen at any time although the summer months were usually the most dangerous period because the presence of mosquitoes is greatest then and "coincides with the usual time of biting by the mosquito vector."[40]

On March 2, 1807, President Jefferson reported that his son-in-law, Thomas Mann Randolph, had succumbed to a "chill and fever" that lasted a day and then returned the following evening. Four days later Meriwether Lewis was attending to Randolph along with Dr. Jones and the president's secretary, Isaac Coles.[41] Jefferson remarked that he caught "a very bad cold, which laid me up with a fever one day" and prompted historians to conclude that everyone at the president's house had caught his cold.[42]

In reality Jefferson had been infected with malaria since at least 1792 and was suffering from a malarial relapse.[43] In March Jefferson wrote that "The remains of a bad cold hang on me, and for a day or two past some symptoms of periodical headache. Mr. Coles and Capt. Lewis are also indisposed, so that we are but a collection of invalids."[44]

The illness that affected several persons at the same time was a classic presentation of the ague. It appears that Meriwether relied on Dr. Rush's pills instead of the Peruvian bark. On March 11, Lewis wrote to Clark that he had been indisposed and "took some pills last evening after your departure from which I found considerable relief, and have no doubt of recovering my health perfectly in the course of a few days."[45] Neither Jefferson, his son-in-law, nor Lewis recovered in a few days. It was weeks before Lewis departed Washington and, after resting a few days in Baltimore, finally arrived in Philadelphia in the second week of April.

On March 20, Jefferson, the iron-willed man, complained that he was in the seventh day of a periodical headache. That was his way of explaining away the "intermittent headaches or agues in the head" that are also described as a retro-orbital headache.[46]

> I write this in the morning before the fit has come on. The fits are by no means so severe as I have felt in former times, but they hold me very long, from 9 or 10 in the morning till dark. Neither Calomel nor [Peruvian] bark have as yet made the least impression on them. Indeed we have quite a hospital, one half below and above stairs being sick.[47]

The next day Jefferson again complained about his ailment. "I am writing under a severe indisposition of periodical headache, with scarcely command enough of my mind to know what I write."[48] Malaria hung onto Jefferson longer than he expected and finally the sufferer had to leave Washington for Monticello to recuperate.

It was the third week of May before Jefferson felt well enough to return to the capitol.[49] He had actually been sick with malaria for almost three months and was suffering from the same malady that he later ascribed to Lewis: hypocondria as well as sensible depressions of mind. The man who fought illness square in the face could not admit that he had been stricken with the ague because he too was unaware of malaria's myriad symptoms.

In June 1813, President James Madison also succumbed to malaria's remittent fever and was laid up for nearly thirteen weeks. Every day for three weeks, Dolley believed he would die. The *Federalist Republican* reported that when leaving Madison's chamber, witnesses were "under a full conviction of the derangement of his mind." Yet Madison would not admit that the illness was a recurrent form of the ague, the same that tortured Jefferson, Lewis, and even Secretary of War Dearborn for many years.[50]

By the time Captain Lewis became Jefferson's secretary and then governor in St. Louis, he had traveled great distances for a man of his time. Military and private life had taken him from Georgia to Michigan, from the Atlantic Ocean to the Pacific Coast. Those wide travels meant that Lewis was probably exposed to several mosquito genotypes and was a likely candidate for mixed infections, the type of malaria when more than one *Plasmodium* parasite invades its host.[51] The episodes he must have suffered during those years have escaped the record.

How violent were Lewis's reactions to ague? Humphreys says that the two dominant malarial organisms in North American history were *falciparum* and *vivax*, while a third, *malariae*, showed up less than 1 percent of the time. *Falciparum* ws the most dangerous: "the victim suffers from intermittent high fevers, with a severe retro-orbital headache, parched throat, and diffuse body aches. The body can be wracked with abdominal cramping, diarrhea, and vomiting." *Vivax* caused a high fever, "skull-splitting headache and icy pains throughout the skeleton." The body's own thermostat sensed, falsely, that it needed to increase temperature, and the ensuing fight led to paroxysms of shivering and rising fever. Once that plateau was reached, the "patient feels terribly hot, and then as the temperature falls, profuse sweating follows, leaving the sufferer washed out and exhausted."[52]

As familiar as Lewis was with the illness, in his confusion, he could not accurately convey the sequence of chills and fever because of impaired memory, another feature of the disease.[53] Because he failed to grasp that the natural course of an attack would lessen with time, Lewis attributed his recovery to the effect of the remedy.[54] Even though Lewis believed that Dr. Rush's pills were "sovereign" in curing him, his reliance on them was sheer folly.[55] He was slowly poisoning himself. Rush's pills were composed of calomel, the crystalline form of mercury, and jalap, a herbal purgative from Mexico. Rush believed that his "prescription of 10 grains of calomel and 15 of jalap thrice a day" would rid the body of bilious fever.[56] By 1809 Lewis had modified Rush's formula to six grains of calomel, as often as needed. Regardless of that reduction, Lewis was not only a victim of chronic malaria but probably also of mercurial toxicity that had been building up over the previous six years. Twentieth-century medical books discouraged the use of calomel and only in obstinate cases recommended one to four grains, on an infrequent basis.[57]

During the year 1808 Lewis did not record any hint of illness, just the usual perfunctory remarks to his mother that he enjoyed generally good health.[58] But for William Clark it was a different story. On his way up the Missouri by boat at the end of August he was stricken with a severe illness. On September 13 he recorded "a Dysentary, which I have had for Some time," had "now become very serios." Five days later he remarked that the illness caused him to land frequently. Although he was seriously ill, probably with chronic malaria, Clark continued keeping a journal. But for part of that journey upriver he could not recall the correct month or day.[59]

Stress began to impact Lewis in mid-1809, particularly after the Masonic celebration on June 21 when Bates accused Lewis of provoking a fight.[60] Right after that bitter encounter, things began moving obliquely for Lewis. Soon, the governor began receiving correspondence from Washington admonishing him for overspending.[61] Then Lewis received a refusal from the War Department accountant Simmons who would not pay two considerable bills. When he indignantly replied on August 18, it was his friend, Sheriff Jeremiah Connor, who penned the letter.[62]

Besides Lewis being sick in August and September, many of his friends had come down with the ague too: Alexander Stuart and his wife, Benjamin Wilkinson, William and Julia Clark, Joseph Charless, and even the untrustworthy William C. Carr.[63]

A clue to how Meriwether tried to deal with the onset of what he must have realized was another torture of ague is lost with the list of the medicines that he obtained from Dr. Antoine Saugrain. The doctor also acted as post-surgeon's mate at the Cantonment Belle Fontaine, where medical supplies were in short supply.[64] As the fever season peaked, the governor was not the only sufferer. Saugrain had filed a medical report in June that the military stores were depleted and that the barracks were in deplorable condition.[65] As Saugrain's supply to treat his civilian patients was low, the doctor may have been unable to provide much Peruvian bark or calomel.

Whatever his physical condition, on the twenty-ninth and thirtieth of August, Lewis attended an Indian conference with the Osage. In the first two days of September, he approved reopening the trade with them and delegated Bates to do the paperwork. In the meantime, Lewis prepared for his departure, took a day to sign agreements, make hasty goodbyes, and then floated off downriver.

During the ten-day boat ride from St. Louis to New Madrid, Lewis may have felt another attack coming on. A later report in the *Missouri Gazette* was that "he was much indisposed."[66] But what does indisposed really mean? Witnesses to the suffering of several military officers described a fearsome but invisible opponent.

There was the example of Capt. Russell Bissell, who performed his duties on the frontier during the same years as Lewis. In 1805 his brother Officer Daniel Bissell had threatened to resign his commission rather than serve in the fever death trap on the lower Mississippi.[67] After assuming command of Cantonment Belle Fontaine, Capt. Russell Bissell experienced a bilious colic on the night of December 11, 1807. Other officers saw him suffer excruciating pain from which medicines gave no relief. After three days the pain eased somewhat. As his doctor prepared to return to St. Louis, the sick man begged that he not be left in that condition. On the evening of the seventeenth Bissell "relaps'd with such violence as baffled the powers of medicine." He died the next morning.[68]

Several years later, in the summer of 1811, another officer, Capt. Joseph Cross, became debilitated at Belle Fontaine. Cross was afflicted with a delirium that was mentally serious, abstract, and he was "averse to company or conversation which was no doubt mistaken for continuance of mental disease by my military brethren." In the fall of that year, he became indisposed again but in a short time reported himself well. His commanding officer had him arrested because he was mentally deranged. Dr. Antoine Saugrain verified that he was incapable of performing any duty and remanded him to quarters for more than six months.[69]

If Lewis was suffering and weakened by recurring attacks of malaria, why did he give up a slow but relatively comfortable boat ride down the Mississippi for a physically challenging overland journey? In the last letters he wrote, Meriwether explained that he did not want his papers and the expedition journals falling into the hands of the British whose ships were still stopping United States vessels. But that was a remote possibility; a more immediate fear was the malarial epidemic raging in Lower Louisiana.[70]

Already a victim, Lewis realized that striking overland might avoid potentially fatal complications lower on the Mississippi. The letter he wrote to Clark informing him of the change of plans did not alarm his friend. Making that brief will was a reasonable precaution—or was it a premonition of something worse yet to come?

The traveler departed St. Louis with thirty dollars' worth of ineffectual medicines unlikely to relieve the return "recrudescence" of those interior monsters.[71] During the trip to New Madrid he suffered from a malarial episode, which convinced him to abandon the river and ride overland. When a recrudescence of malaria struck him again, the impact was so overwhelming that, mad with pain and panicked with anticipation of a continued attack, because he was on a boat he probably tried to throw himself overboard twice.

Pity Pernier who had been with Lewis for the past two years and had learned to recognize the symptoms. But he and the boat crew were unprepared to handle a deranged, delirious, and strong passenger demonstrating unpredictable, wild, and erratic behavior. The valet may have been set to brew a dose of Peruvian bark, a cocktail that had to be drunk quickly before the brew lost its effectiveness.[72] But it had to be mixed with wine or whiskey to cut the extremely bitter taste. The sick man could have been imbibing enough alcohol to make him drunk.

On the other hand, Lewis may have restricted himself to Rush's "sovereign" remedy. The pills he took were mercurial and opiate—a bad combination because the opiate allows deep absorption of mercury.[73] By the time the boat pulled under the last Chickasaw bluff, Meriwether Lewis was a wreck.

But inebriation does not explain the reported suicidal attempts. When the familiar signs of the onset of an episode appeared, anticipating the attack was terrifying. The English military physician John Pringle described soldiers who succumbed to the first stage of the ague:

> There were some instances of the head being so suddenly and violently affected, that without any previous complaint the men ran about in a wild manner, and were believed to be mad, till the solution of the fit by a sweat, and its periodic returns, discovered the true nature of their *delirium*. That a few returns of the paroxysms reduced their strongest men to so low a condition as to disable them from standing. That some became at once delirious . . . and would have thrown themselves out the window, or into the water, if not prevented.[74]

Other victims suffered excruciating pain above the eye, one "so dreadfully tormented with a pain of this kind, as to be rendered almost insane."[75] The prolonged cold and sweating stages were accompanied by an agonizing pain in the *epigastrium*, another term for the *hypochondrium*.[76] After repeated attacks the spleen, typically the size of a fist and weighing five ounces, enlarges to fill the abdominal cavity and weighs in excess of seven pounds![77]

Another physician, John Macculloch, caring for chronic malarial patients, stated that remittent fevers produced a disorder of mind that is "mistaken for hypochondriasm." Macculloch was the first to connect symptoms of the ague to the hypochondrium, wherein both the liver and the spleen become enlarged due to the constant strain of malarial parasites upon those organs. In serious cases of chronic episodes, he reported that it stimulates the patient "to think of suicide. This insane desire is a very common complaint of patients labouring under intermittent, and a very frequent source of great alarm and horror." Macculloch reasoned that delirium played a pivotal role especially when coupled with solitude, that the desire of suicide is strongest "should night chance to be the period in which this fit occurs."[78]

Macculloch wrote his observations from the descriptions of what his malarial patients told him when they suffered from an attack. The worst part for them included the anticipation because they knew what would happen. Macculloch described the reasoning experienced by chronic malarial sufferers:

> As relates to the desire, the simple fact is, that the patient feels a species of antipathy against some peculiar part of his body . . . or he longs to commit the act by wounding that particular point . . . whether his aberration amounts to the desire of suicide or not, this very point or place is the one eternally forcing itself on his imagination as an object of hatred and revenge. And so perfectly insane is this feeling, that I have been informed by more than one patient . . . that there is no conviction . . . that death would follow; or rather that the impression is as if the offending part could be exterminated or cured by the injury, and that the patient would then be well.[79]

This remarkable statement shows that reason can be overwhelmed by morbid suffering. Macculloch concluded that his patients were not committing suicide because of depression or mania. But Macculloch goes much further in his observations as if he were writing about Lewis and others who had experienced such unspeakable misery and who were clearly unable to help themselves.

A sufferer of the ague himself, Capt. Gilbert Russell of Fort Pickering should have recognized the symptoms. Most of his garrison had been down with the ague just before the governor arrived. But documentary clues to malaria often show a lack of sympathy from those presently well for those afflicted. Each sufferer of the common demon had to bear it alone.

Russell recognized that Lewis was seriously sick and assigned him to the care of surgeon's mate W. C. Smith. From dealing with the previous epidemic Smith should have recognized the symptoms of malaria but he lacked any effective medicine. Brewing Peruvian bark, if he had any, into a decoction that was so bitter that the sufferer could not retain it, required diluting it in wine or whiskey. Sick soldiers took it for the alcohol, and maybe the doctor as well.[80]

Relieving pain depended on laudanum. If there was a drinking component complicating the condition, chasing alcohol with an opiate was not much of a treatment.

Captain Russell was stern in his later appraisal of Lewis.

The fact is . . . that his untimely death may be attributed solely to the free use he made of liquor which he acknowledged very candidly to me after his recovery & expressed a firm determination never to drink any more spirits or use snuff again both of which I deprived him of for several days & confined him to claret & a little white wine. But after leaving this place by some means or other his resolution left him.[81]

After almost two hundred years, it is the description of the experienced Dr. John Macculloch that restores the honor of a sufferer whose reputation has been recast by too much guesswork:

[W]hile the irritable, or jointly despairing and raging or angry state of this chronic fever is present, there is also a particular part of the body affected by an uneasy but undefinable sensation, such that the mind constantly reverts to it as a source of suffering. And if this local affection is not a Neuralgia, or a condition of absolute pain, yet it is a local and nervous one of an analogous nature, always returning to that one point under the same stage of the fever or delirium. When, as is not unusual, it is seated in the head, it is even distinguishable by a dull pain, or a confusion, or a sense of "buzzing" (for it is described by patients) in one fixed place. . . . I have the assurance of such patients, that the suicidal desire is exclusively directed to that spot, and that while a pistol would be the only acceptable mode, there would also be no satisfaction unless that were directed to this actual and only point.[82]

Reconsidering malaria is not an apology for what followed. That was an accident as unfathomable as a crash on the highway. But there is that bothersome matter of a man's honor being tarnished by uninformed, irresponsible speculation.

NOTES

1. Alexander Wilson, "Particulars of the Death of Capt. Lewis," *Port Folio* 7 (January 1812): 39.

2. David L. Nicandri, "The Columbia Country and the Dissolution of Meriwether Lewis: Speculation and Interpretation," *Oregon Historical Quarterly* 106 (Spring 2005): 7.

3. TJ to Paul Allen, August 18, 1813, and John H. Marks on Lewis's debts, 1811, Jackson, *LLC* 2: 591–92, 728.

4. Stanley W. Jackson, *Melancholia and Depression* (New Haven, CT: Yale University Press, 1986), p. 274.

5. Robert Hooper, *Medical Dictionary* (New York: Harper & Bros., 1841), pp. 442–43; William Cullen, *First Line of the Practice of Physic*, 4th ed., 4 vols. (Edinburgh: C. Elliot, 1784), 4: 178; George Motherby, *Medical Dictionary*, 3rd ed. (London: George Wallis, 1791), p. 429.

6. Esther Fischer-Homberger, "Hypochondriasis of the Eighteenth Century— Neurosis of the Present Century," *Bulletin of the History of Medicine* 46 (July-August 1972): 394–97.

7. Stanley W. Jackson, "Melancholia and Mechanical Explanation in Eighteenth-Century Medicine," *Journal of the History of Medicine and Allied Sciences* 38 (July 1983): 298; Stanley W. Jackson, "Melancholia and the Waning of the Humoral Theory," *Journal of the History of Medicine and Allied Sciences* 33 (July 1978): 369.

8. For discussion of Jefferson's headaches (but no mention of malaria) see Brodie, *Thomas Jefferson: An Intimate History*, pp. 43, 115, and index "Health Problems," p. 581.

9. TJ to Paul Allen, August 18, 1813, Jackson, LLC 2: 591–92. In her insightful analysis of this statement Grace Lewis Miller points out that Jefferson based his conclusion on the two periods when he was intimately connected with Lewis, the years as his secretary and after the return from the expedition. GLM, box 39, folder 13, JNEM.

10. Kurt J. Isselbacher et al., *Harrison's Principles of Internal Medicine*, 13th ed., 2 vols. (New York: McGraw-Hill, 1992), 1: 889.

11. William Cullen, *First Line of the Practice of Physic*, 4th ed. 4 vols. (Edinburgh: C. Elliot, 1784), 1: 10, 13; William Cullen Brown, *The Institutions of the Practice of Medicine*, 5 vols. (Edinburgh: 1801), 3: 354; Daniel Drake, *The Principal Diseases of the Interior Valley of North America*, 2nd ed. (repr., Philadelphia: Lippincott, Grambo & Co., 1854), pp. 49–73; Bruce Chwatt, "Ague as Malaria," *Journal of Tropical Medicine and Hygiene* 79 (August 1976): 174.

12. Leennius Andreas Galen, ed., *Claudii Galeni . . . Opera, nunc demum a clarissimus iuxt a & eruditis viris latinate donata, iam vero ordine iusto, & studio exquis-itore in lucem recens edita. Basileae, per Andream Cratandrum, mense martio* (Basileae, per Andream Cratandrum, mense martio, 1529), pp. 455–56.

13. Bruce Chwatt, "Ague as Malaria," p. 168.

14. John Macculloch, *An Essay on the Remittent and Intermittent Diseases*, 2 vols. (London: Longman, Rees, Orme, Brown, and Green, 1828), 1: 247. Prevalence of the disease extended through the nineteenth century.

15. Pigmentation of the blood became known as melanemia. Charles Poser and G. W. Bruyn, *An Illustrated History of Malaria* (New York: Parthenon Publishing Group, 1999), p. 23.

16. William Cullen, *First Line of the Practice of Physic*, 4th ed., 4 vols. (Edinburgh: C. Elliot, 1784), 1: 13; Henry Ashton, *An Inaugural Essay on the Remitting and Intermitting Bilious Fever* (Philadelphia: Eacum & Mecum, 1803), p. 39 (*Early American Imprints*, Second series, no. 3692).

17. Margaret Humphreys, *Malaria, Poverty, Race, and Public Health in the United States* (Baltimore: John Hopkins University Press, 2001), p. 8.

18. Allan Saul, "The Role of Variant Surface Antigens on Malaria-Infected Red Blood Cells," *Parasitology Today* 15 (November 1999): 455.

19. The condition of an enlarged liver and spleen is known today as hepatosplenomegaly.

20. Zenon Trudeau to Francisco Louis Hector Carondelet, September 8, 1794, AGI PC 208a-446; Pierre Deluzieres to Zenon Trudeau, September 28, 1794, AGI PC 208a-453; Pierre Deluzieres to Francisco Louis Hector Carondelet, October 17, 1794, AGI PC 209-666, Papeles de Cuba Collection, MHS. Soulard was appointed surveyor general in February 1795.

21. William E. Foley and Carl J. Ekberg, ed., *An Account of Upper Louisiana by Nicolas de Finiels* (Columbia: University of Missouri Press, 1989), p. 130.

22. *New-England Palladium (MA)*, December 30, 1803, p. 1.

23. Capt. Eli Clemson to SW, December 11, 1807, RG107, C1808, M222, roll 3, frames 1145–47.

24. JW to SW, July 27, 1805, Carter, *TP* 13: 167.

25. George Colbert to WD, February 18, 1809, RG107, C469, M221, roll 20, frame 6146.

26. GR to SW, August 26, 1809, RG107, R244, roll 29, frame 9756.

27. R. Carlyle Buley, "Pioneer Health and Medical Practices in the Old Northwest prior to 1840," *Mississippi Valley Historical Review* 20 (March 1934): 502; Edward F. Maguire, "Frequent Diseases and Intended Remedies on the Frontier, 1780–1850," (master's thesis, St. Louis University, 1953), p. 6.

28. Darrett B. Rutman and Anita H. Rutman, "Of Agues and Fevers: Malaria in the Early Chesapeake," *William and Mary Quarterly* 33 (January 1976): 33.

29. Humphreys, *Malaria*, p. 8.

30. Eldon Chuinard, *Only One Man Died* (Glendale, CA: A. H. Clark, 1980), p. 27.

31. Humphreys, *Malaria*, p. 26. Dr. Humphreys was not the first medical doctor to associate swamps and marshes with malaria. See A. W. Ratcliffe, "The Historical Background of Malaria—A Reconsideration," *Journal of the Indiana State Medical Association* 39 (July 1946): 339.

32. William J. Fitzgerald, "Evolution of Use of Quinine in Treatment of Malaria," *New York State Journal of Medicine* 68 (March 1968): 800–802.

33. John Redman Coxe, "Cinchona-Peruvian Bark," in *The American Dispensatory*, 5th ed. (Philadelphia: Thomas Dobson and Son, 1822), pp. 195–96; A. P. Philip, *A Treatise on Febrile Diseases*, 1st ed., 2 vols. (Hartford, CT: Cooke & Hale, 1809), 1: 130.

34. Personal account book, November 8, 1808, MLC-MHS.

35. Rush should have reminded Lewis of Benjamin Franklin's proverb: "An ounce of prevention is worth a pound of cure." Franklin was referring to Peruvian bark, "a little of which will do more in preventing the Fits than a great deal in

removing them." Leonard Woods Labaree and Whitfield Bell Jr., *The Papers of Benjamin Franklin*, 37 vols. (New Haven, CT: Yale University Press, 1959–2006), 4: 63.

36. Personal account book, MLC-MHS.

37. WC to Jonathan Clark, August 26, 1809, in James Holmberg, ed., *Dear Brother* (New Haven, CT: Yale University Press), p. 210 and n6.

38. ML, November 13, 1803, Moulton, *JLCE* 2: 86. Daniel Goldberg, a malariologist on the faculty at Washington University School of Medicine in St. Louis, notes that the fever precedes the chills (personal interview on December 3, 1998).

39. Frank Hawking, Michael J. Worms, and Kenneth Gammage, "Host Temperature and Control of 24-Hour and 48-Hour Cycles in Malaria Parasites," *Lancet* 7541 (March 1968): 506.

40. Ibid. "24- and 48-Hour Cycles of Malarial Parasites in the Blood; Their Purpose, Production, and Control," *Transactions of the Royal Society of Tropical Medicine and Hygiene* 62 (June 1968): 747.

41. TJ to MJR, March 6, 1807, in Betts and Bear, *FL*, pp. 298–99.

42. Ibid.

43. Jefferson believed he suffered from migraines but the periodical headache that he described in various occasions was always accompanied with fits or paroxysms. Notes on headache remedy called the sun-pain, April 10, 1792, document 41873, roll 16, TJ-LOC.

44. TJ to MJR, March 16, 1807, Betts and Bear, *FL*, p. 302.

45. ML to WC, March 11, 1807, Jackson, *LLC* 2: 385.

46. Abraham Rees, "Hemicrania," in *The Cyclopaedia; or, Universal Dictionary of Arts, Sciences, and Literature*, 45 vols. (London: Longman, Rees, Orme & Browne, 1819), 19: n.p. Humphreys, *Malaria*, p. 9.

47. TJ to MJR, March 20, 1807, Betts and Bear, *FL*, p. 304.

48. TJ to JMO, March 21, 1807, document 29195-6, roll 38. If Jefferson would have read his own letters, this was a recurring illness. On March 12, 1806, document 27547, roll 35, he complained that he was "incapable of business." Jefferson had another attack of periodical headache about a year later that "disabled me from business" for seven weeks. TJ to JMO, February 18, 1808, document 30989, roll 40, TJ-LOC. April 11, 1808, letter 169, Thomas Jefferson and James Monroe Correspondence, transcribed and edited by Gerard W. Gawalt, Manuscript Division, LOC.

49. TJ to MJR, April 2, 1807, Betts and Bear, *FL*, p. 306. Daniel Drake, the preeminent physician, reported on ague cases in spring 1828. "The symptoms which they exhibited were various. In some cases they assumed the character of periodical headache or sun-pain." Daniel Drake, "Report on the Diseases of Cincinnati in the spring of 1828 . . . for Ague and Fever," *Western Journal of the Medical and Physical Sciences* 2 (1828–1829): 217.

50. Gary Wills, *James Madison* (New York: Henry Holt, 2002), p. 124; Robert Allen Rutland, *The Presidency of James Madison* (Lawrence: University Press of Kansas, 1990), p. 130; JMA to HD, August 8, 1813, document 737, series 1, roll 15, JMA-LOC; Elswyth Thane, *Dolley Madison* (New York: Crowell-Collier, 1970), p. 99.

51. Marian C. Bruce and Karen P. Day, "Cross-Species Regulation of Malaria Parasitaemia in the Human Host," *Current Opinion in Microbiology* 5 (August 2002): 431–37.

52. Humphreys, *Malaria*, p. 9.

53. Refer to the event of November 13 in Moulton, *JLCE* 2: 86.

54. Thomas C. Danisi, "The 'Ague' Made Him Do It," *We Proceeded On* 28 (February 2002): 10–15.

55. Moulton, *JLCE* 4: 436.

56. Ibid., 2: 86n1; Benjamin Rush, *An Account of the Bilious Remitting Yellow Fever* (Philadelphia: Thomas Dobson, 1794), pp. 200–201; Drake W. Will, "The Medical and Surgical Practice of the Lewis and Clark Expedition," *Journal of the History of Medicine and Allied Sciences* 14 (July 1959): 282.

57. A. S. Blumgarten, *Textbook of Materia Medica, Pharmacology and Therapeutics* (New York: Macmillan, 1939), p. 221; Oliver T. Osborne, *The Principles of Therapeutics* (Philadelphia: W. B. Saunders Company, 1922), p. 339.

58. ML to LM, December 1, 1808, MLC-MHS.

59. Kate L. Gregg, *Westward with Dragoons* (Fulton, MO: Ovid Bell Press, 1937), pp. 7, 10, 16, 39, 45.

60. FB to Richard Bates, November 9, 1809, Marshall, *FB* 2: 109.

61. During that same time frame, Gallatin approved a bill from Bates for $134 to remove desks and benches for the purpose of hearing land grant testimony: RG217, M235, roll 63, document 20476, frame 1062.

62. ML to SW, August 18, 1809, RG107, L328, M221, roll 23, frame 8501.

63. William Clark's memorandum book, 1809, microfilm C-1074, p. 3, Western Historical Manuscripts; Holmberg, *Dear Brother*, p. 210; Benjamin Wilkinson to ML, September 1, 1809, MLC-MHS; William Carr to Charles Carr, August 25, 1809, William Carr Papers, MHS.

64. Antoine Saugrain to DB, June 16, 1809, Carter, *TP* 14: 278–89.

65. Ibid.

66. *Missouri Gazette*, October 4, 1809, p. 3.

67. JW to SW, July 27, 1805, Carter, *TP* 13: 167.

68. Capt. James House, Capt. E. B. Clemson, and Lt. Alpha Kingsley to SW, January 12, 1808, RG107, C1808, M222, roll 3, frames 1145–47.

69. Capt. Joseph Cross to SW, January 9, 1812, RG107, C192, M221; February 22, 1812, C219; and June 7, 1812, C366, roll 43. It was reported by Dr. J. S. Cool in the summer of 1811 that he found "the remitting and intermitting fevers prevailing among the troops" at Fort Osage. He was informed by the officers at the fort that the fevers were the worst since the fort opened. Cool to SW, September 18, 1811, RG107, C5.

70. Before the end of October, General Wilkinson would lose more than one thousand troops to malaria in New Orleans and Wilkinson was sick for the entire month of September. JW to WE, August 19, 1809, RG107, W658, M221, roll 33, frame 1564–65; James Ripley Jacobs, *The Beginning of the US Army, 1783–1812*

(Princeton, NJ: Princeton University Press, 1947), p. 352; RG233, M1268, roll 12, frame 0399; RG94, M1136, roll 1, frames 0837–40, pp. 45–49.

71. Recrudescence is defined as a return of fever within six weeks of a malarial attack while a relapse is characterized as returning to a morbid condition from which there had been a partial or complete recovery. George Sibley, the factor at Fort Osage, described a recrudescence. "I am perpetually annoyed with feebleness, want of appetite, nausea, indigestion etc. I am getting weaker and worse every day. Sometimes I have an ague and am seldom if ever without some fever more or less— I am still about however, but am not able to do anything." George Sibley to Rufus Easton, 1815, Lindenwood College Collection, MHS.

72. In the summer months, "infusions of bark undergo . . . putrefactive fermentation . . . in so short a time . . . that the first infusion only can be used." Clark Sanford, "Observations on the Peruvian Bark," *Medical Repository* 3 (1812): 244.

73. J. G. O'Shea, "Two Minutes with Venus, Two Years with Mercury— Mercury as an Antisyphilitic Chemotherapeutic Agent," *Journal of the Royal Society of Medicine* 83 (June 1990): 393.

74. John Pringle, *Observations on the Disease of the Army* (Philadelphia: Fry and Kammerer, 1810), p. 157. Early American Imprints, 21145.

75. Jean Senac, *A Treatise on the Hidden Nature and the Treatment of Intermitting and Remitting Fevers* (Philadelphia: Conrad & Co., 1805), p. 82.

76. Andrew Davidson, ed., *Hygiene & Diseases of Warm Climates* (Edinburgh: Young J. Pentland, 1893), p. 171. Because of the pooling of blood, "pain may be in the splenic region alone, across the upper abdomen, or in lower abdominal quadrants." Barry S. Zingman and Brant L. Viner, "Splenic Complications in Malaria: Case Report and Review," *Clinical Infectious Diseases* 16 (February 1993): 227.

77. William Osler, *The Principles and Practice of Medicine*, 2nd ed. (New York: D. Appleton and Company, 1895), p. 162; U. V. Gopala Rao and Henry N. Wagner, "Normal Weights of Human Organs," *Radiology* 102 (February 1972): 337.

78. John Macculloch, *Essay on the Remittent and Intermittent Diseases*, 2 vols. (London: Longman, Rees, Orme, Brown, and Green, 1828), 1: 247, 249.

79. Ibid., 1: 249–50.

80. Before the year was over Captain Russell would write a court-martial charge against the doctor accusing him of neglect of duty, failure to issue medicines, and keeping a mistress in quarters: GR to SW, November 29, 1809, RG107, R14, M221, roll 39, frame 6025.

81. GR to TJ, January 31, 1810, document 33657, roll 44, TJ-LOC. An abridged letter is in Jackson, *LLC* 2: 748.

82. Macculloch, *Essay on the Remittent and Intermittent Diseases*, 1: 252–53.

Nineteen

Echoes of a Tragedy

No eye, save that of Heaven, beheld[1]

O n October 30, 1809, a ten-day-old copy of the Nashville *Democratic Clarion* reached Washington. This described in lurid detail "the untimely end of a brave and prudent officer."[2] What President Madison might have thought is unknown but it appears that he had received the note Lewis wrote from Fort Pickering. After reading the newspaper account, or the letter from Captain Brahan, he sent a rather coldhearted account on to Monticello.

The impact of Madison's letter may have been lessened by a comment editor Thomas G. Bradford added in the *Clarion* report. "In the death of Governor Lewis the public beheld the wreck of one of the noblest of men—he was a pupil of the immortal Jefferson—by him he was reared—by him he was instructed in the tour of the sciences—by him he was introduced to public life."[3]

Jefferson was in Richmond on October 20 when he received an invitation to join the Council of State at the Eagle Tavern the next day. There he received a laudatory address by the citizens of Richmond to which he replied on the twenty-second. Three days later he went to his Eppington estate and did not return to Monticello until November 2.[4]

There is the possibility that Jefferson already knew, as a report of the death may have reached Staunton, Virginia, as early as October 27 and was published in the *Republican Farmer* on November 4. On that day Jefferson wrote to Gallatin seeking employment for the son of a mechanic in his neighborhood. Two years before he had heard of a backwoods boy who had gotten a book and was trying to self-educate himself. Jefferson brought him to Monticello, gave him the use of his books, and provided his board, lodging, and some wages while giving him the liberty of dividing his time between reading and working. After two years he had improved himself in mathematics and might find employment as a surveyor. That was touchingly similar to the assistance he had given to another promising neighborhood boy years before, and cruelly coincidental in light of what was developing.[5]

November was a difficult month for Thomas Jefferson. He received Madison's letter reporting the death of Lewis on November 5 and responded the next morning with a note that answered some minor business between them and ended with a short paragraph about the weather and temperature. He did not mention Lewis.[6]

Jefferson wrote that he left Monticello the next day and was away for a "fortnight" (two weeks), returning on November 21. Although he penned a note concerning insurance on November 7, there were no other significant letters from Jefferson during that period.

Riding the governor's horse, the valet Pernier had stopped at Locust Hill to relate the terrible story to the family.[7] After that ordeal he went to Monticello, delivered the letter from Neelly, and recited his own version to Jefferson. The copy of the Neelly letter in the National Archives bears the endorsement "received 21 November." The saddened master of Monticello waited five days before forwarding the letter to Madison.[8] Pernier carried it on to Washington on November 26.[9] Jefferson remained at Monticello awaiting the arrival of William Clark.

On November 12 his former secretary Isaac Coles notified him that a number of items that had been left at the president's house in Washington were being forwarded to Monticello. Included was "a large skin of the grisly bear," a sad reminder of the expedition. Next day in Philadelphia, Conrad & Company, the contracted publishers of the expedition narrative, also wrote Jefferson asking how to proceed since Lewis was dead. Jefferson replied on November 23 that those matters would have to wait until William Clark arrived to deal with whatever was in Lewis's trunks.[10]

Letters must have crossed in the mail, as by then Madison had written Jefferson asking him to feel out James Monroe for the appointment as governor of Louisiana.[11] Monroe had previously refused an appointment as gov-

ernor of the Orleans Territory, but would he consider the vacancy occasioned
by the death of Lewis as it was in the more suitable climate of St. Louis? That
must have tried the grieving Jefferson, who had to put duty to the nation
above his personal feelings. He rode the few miles to Monroe's home on the
thirtieth and had a frank discussion with him for an hour or two.

> The catastrophe of poor Lewis served to lead us to the point intended. . . .
> The sum of his answers was, that to accept that office was incompatible
> with the respect he owed himself, that he would never act in any office
> where he would be subordinate to any body but the President himself.[12]

Until another candidate could be identified, the government of Louisiana
would have to remain in the hands of Territorial Secretary Bates.

By then newspaper accounts copied and recopied from each other had
spread from Virginia to Vermont. Most of the stories concentrated on the
gory details. The mortuary notices in the distant *Connecticut Courant* of
November 29 began with the death of a thirty-year-old hatter, who "in a fit
of insanity" had leaped from a second-story window. That item was followed
by an account of the death of Meriwether Lewis, Esq., of Upper Louisiana.
The proximity of two apparent sufferers of mercury poisoning was particularly curious.[13]

The story edged in black that was published in the *Democratic Press* of
Philadelphia enlarged on details. The editor, John Binns, was a thirty-
seven-year-old Dublin man with an Irish sense of the tragic. The additional
information that he used to enlarge the obituary could only have come from
someone who had been in contact with Lewis. The informant must have
been Mahlon Dickerson, who cut out the item and kept it for the rest of his
life as a lasting memento of the friend who had continued to correspond
with him.

> A gentleman from Nashville informs me that he conversed with a person
> who had seen Governor *Meriwether Lewis* buried on the 12th inst. About
> forty miles beyond Nashville, on the Natchez road.—The accounts are,
> that Governor *Lewis* arrived at a house very weak, from a recent illness at
> Natchez, and shewed marks of mental derangement. After a stay of a few
> hours at the above house, he took his pistols and shot himself twice, and
> then cut his throat.
>
> The above unfortunate intelligence is confirmed by a gentleman at
> present in this place. It is added, that governor Lewis, in addition to
> shooting himself twice in the body, and cutting his throat, shot himself in
> the head, and cut the arteries in his thighs and arms.

We have been unable to procure any satisfactory intelligence of the circumstances which led to this unhappy event—We have only heard it stated, that Governor Lewis drew bills to a considerable amount on the government of the United States, for which there had been no specific appropriations and which came back protested. We can hardly suppose, however, that an incident of this kind, alone, could have produced such deplorable consequences.[14]

The above was followed by a second column edged in black taken in part from the Nashville paper of October 20.

To record the untimely end of a brave and prudent officer, a learned scholar and scientific gentleman this column of the Clarion is ushered to the world in black—On the night of the 10th instant, Meriwether Lewis, Esq. Governor General of Upper Louisiana, on his way to Washington city, came to the house of Mr. Grinder, near the Indian line in this state—called for his supper and some spirits, of which he partook and gave some to his servants, Mr. Grinder not being at home. Mrs. Grinder retired to the kitchen with her children, and the servants (after the governor went to bed, which he did in good order) went to a stable about three hundred yards distant to sleep—no one in the house with the governor—and some time before midnight, Mrs. Grinder was alarmed by the firing of 2 pistols in the house—she called to the servants without effect—and at the appearance of day light the servants came to the house, when the governor said he had now done for himself—they asked what, and he said he had shot himself and would die, and requested them to bring him water, He then laying on the floor where he expired about 7 o'clock in the morning of the 11th—he had shot a ball that grazed the top of his head and another through his intestines, and cut his neck, arm and ham with a razor. When in his best senses he spoke about a trunk of papers that he said would be of great value to our government. He had been under the influence of a deranging malady for about six weeks—the cause of which is unknown, unless it was from a protest to a draft which he drew on the secretary at war, which he considered tantamount to a disgrace by government.

In the death of governor Lewis the public behold the wreck of one of the noblest of men—he was a pupil of the immortal Jefferson—by him he was reared—by him he was instructed in the tour of the sciences—by him he was introduced to public life, when his enterprising soul, great botanical knowledge, acute penetration, and personal courage soon pointed him out as the most proper person to command a projected exploring party to the N.west coast of the American continent, he accepted the

arduous command on condition that he might take Mr. Clarke with him—
they started; the best wishes of the American people attended them. After
an absence of two years, to us of anxious solicitude we were cheered with
the joyful return of our countrymen. A new world had been explored—
additional knowledge in all the sciences obtained, at a trifling expense of
blood and treasure. The voice of fame echoed the glad tidings through the
civilized world—the name of Lewis was the theme of universal praise.—
The national legislature voted a complimentary donation of the brave
little band. Scarcely had the governor time to pay his respects to a widowed mother, before he was again called into public service. The Upper
Louisiana had been torn to pieces by party feuds, no person could be more
proper to calm them—he appeared and all was quiet.

The limits assigned this notice do not admit of a particular detail of
his executive acts—suffice it to say that the parties created by local circumstances and Wilkinson were soon united—the Indians were treated
with and large purchases of valuable land made of them—the laws were
amended, and judicious ones adopted—to the securing the citizens of the
territory from a renewal of the scenes of 1806.

During the few leisure moments he had from his official duties, he
was employed in writing the particulars of his celebrated tour up the
Missouri—to complete which appears to have been the wish nearest his
heart—and it gives us much pleasure, if we can feel pleasure in the present melancholy instance, to state that we have it from a source which can
be depended upon, that he had accomplished the work in three very large
volumes, with an immense number of painting—and all was ready for the
press. We hope these volumes may be the means of transmitting to pos-
terity the worth of a man whose last act cast a gloom over the fair pages
of his early life.[15]

As William Clark continued east, he realized that he had left the last
letter from Lewis at his brother's. Anxious about that oversight, he wrote,
"I wish much to get the letter I receved of Govr. Lewis from N. madrid,
which you Saw it will be of great Service to me. prey Send it to Fincastle as
Soon as possible." He also wrote to William Anderson "to Send the Govrs.
paipers to me if they were yet in his part of the Conntry." By November 8,
as the entourage struggled across the terrible turnpike north of Clinch
Mountain, Clark still had not received more "perticular[s]" on the death of
his friend.[16]

Clark had been at the home of his father-in-law, Colonel Hancock, for
about a week, yet as late as November 26 he was still "expecting to receive
Govr. Lewis papers by Mr. Whitesids, a Seneter from Tennessee, whome I

am in formed by Mr. W. P. Anderson, will take Charge of those papers for me and bring them on. " By then Clark had received a letter from Captain Russell.

> Capt. rusell Sais he made his will at the Bluffs and left Wm. Merrewether & myself Execeters and derected that I Should dispose of his papers &c. as I wished—pore fellow, what a number of Conjecturral reports we hear mostly unfavorable to him. I have to Contredict maney of them.[17]

Despite what Russell wrote to Clark, or what Clark misunderstood, Lewis made his will at New Madrid, not Fort Pickering.

William Anderson passed on to Clark a small comfort he extracted from Pernier: "his Servent reports that on his way to nashvill, he would frequently Conceipt [conceive] that he herd me Comeing on, and Said that he was certain [I would] overtake him, that I had herd of his Situation and would Come to his releaf."[18]

After waiting four days in the vain hope of getting more information, Clark continued on toward Washington. According to his memorandum book, when he visited the Lewis family at Locust Hill Clark must have been relieved that Lucy Marks was not there. "I shewed young Mr. Marks all the letters I had about his Brothers situation and told him my oppinion on that subject. He distressed."[19]

Continuing to Charlottesville on December 7, Clark ran into former president Jefferson. "He invited me to go and stay at his house, &c. I went with him and remained all night, spoke much on the af[fairs] of Gov. Lewis &c. &c. &c."[20] Clark could only hope that Lewis's protested bills would be accepted by the government but feared that the $940 submitted for Indian presents was going to be a stumbling block. Just before leaving St. Louis Clark had received a letter from the War Department, checking him about expenses and dismissing many of the trustworthy interpreters and subagents. The War Department also withheld judgment on James McFarlane's role in resolving the problem of dissident Osage on the Arkansas.[21] Clark knew that Lewis had given McFarlane a bond for eight hundred dollars to assure that he would be paid.

Riding on to Richmond, Clark "met with Mr. Merriwether with whom I had much Conversation about Govr. Lewis—expressed some doubts as to the Legality of Gov. Lewis Will, he agreed that I should take such papers as Concerned me out of the Govr. papers if they were brought to the City &c. and agreed to get Mr. Coal [Cole] to assist on the point to examine them."[22]

The traveler finally arrived on December 18 in Washington, where the boxes that had been inventoried and packed in Nashville had been delivered to the presidential mansion. Edward Coles, who was serving his second president as personal secretary, assisted Clark as they opened each box and sorted the contents. Coles informed Jefferson that "all the public papers were turned over to the War Department," everything related to the expedition was taken by Clark, "& all that remained is contained in five little bundles now directed to you" to remain at Monticello until William Meriwether called for them.[23] On that same day, William Meriwether wrote to John Marks that he had already received a letter from Coles and that they had found a will dated September 11 giving everything to Lewis's mother. Although Clark supposed that might not be his last will, he was obligated to a last service to his friend.[24] In cooperation with William Meriwether, Clark administered the estate and would see to the publication of their book.

Forgotten in the fixation with the recovery of the journals of the expedition are the public papers that were sorted out and sent to the proper departments of government. Coles and Clark noted a bundle of documents relative to the mines, a bundle dealing with McFarlane's equipment to explore the saltpeter mines including his journal, a bundle labeled "Ideas of the Western Expedition," and a bundle of vouchers for expenditures that were sent to the State Department.[25]

Those vouchers were the evidence to answer the rejection of the governor's accounts. Lewis had included them confident that he had sufficient documentation to answer any objections. He departed St. Louis believing that he was in the clear, and as the cogs of bureaucracy slowly turned over the next several years, he was.

The proofs should have singed the conscience of those who had tormented the governor with refused bills and insults. Accountant William Simmons was probably incapable of toting a moral debt but Secretary of War Eustis indirectly revealed some feeling. When Clark appeared to reconcile his own bills, problems were resolved without a hitch.[26]

There was a particular bundle among the papers Clark and Coles sorted from Lewis's baggage that was sent on to Mr. Jefferson. Included was the August 27 packet Lewis put together before leaving St. Louis that was intended for Jefferson. The thirty-nine pages remained at Monticello until Jefferson was satisfied he understood the contents. Eventually he sent them on to the War Department, where a clerk entered the packet in the register of letters received under the date October 6, 1810. After that they dropped through a crack and have been rarely, if ever, consulted.[27] Due to clerical neglect, a good deal of what Lewis had accomplished in St. Louis has been overlooked.

Two other documents had entered the postal system at the beginning of September 1809. One was the letter from Pierre Chouteau Jr. defending his father's role in the return of the Mandan chief, which the War Department found inconsistent with the duty of an Osage agent. Young Chouteau wrote, "Last spring the governor thought to ingratiate himself with the Band of the Osage established on the River Arkansas, but still without communicating his projects to my Father, he sent to them Mr. McFarlane second agent to the Osages." According to Chouteau, McFarlane made immense promises to the Osage and when their delegation arrived in St. Louis, "it was immediately proposed to them to proceed to Washington City with Mr. McFarlane." The Indians refused because the promises to them had not been fulfilled and their confidence was destroyed.[28] That wasn't quite correct but could be excused as a son's loyalty to his father. Bates had been party to it.[29] Young Chouteau's letter made it east to Eustis in a fast twenty-two days.

While William Clark was in Washington settling the matter of his protested bills, his partner in the MFCo., Pierre Chouteau Sr., returned from the Mandan villages. That matters hadn't gone very well with the company would filter through newspapers throughout the West. A Nashville paper published the experience of two of the men in mid-December:

> On Monday last, two men belonging to the party who conducted the Mandan chief to his nation, arrived here in 43 days from the Mandan village. They say they arrived at the village on the 24th of September last, all well, having a passage of 101 days from this place. From the mouth of the Missouri to the village is 1610 miles, and calculating their being obliged to stop for several days on their journey to procure provisions, progressed upwards of twenty miles per day.
>
> The men report that they arrived at the Ricaree village on the 12th of Sept. and experienced a considerable degree of hospitality from these people; the Seaux appeared very hostile and nothing but fear prevented stopping the party. These men left the hunting party about 25 miles of the mandan village on their way to the hunting ground, at the foot of the mountain, they expressed great apprehension from the Blackfoot Indians who swarm in those regions, and who appear entirely in the interest of the British factors, who have trading houses on the Yellow stone river, and other streams which empty into the head waters of the Missouri.
>
> Messrs. Crook's, Miller, and M'Clelland who had permission to ascend the Missouri to its head, were stoped by the Titons and escaped by stratagem otherwise was expected they would have been cut off. These gentlemen are now trading with the Mahas on the river Platte. Messrs. Pierre Chouteau and two sons; Auguste, son of col. Auguste Chouteau,

Mr. Manuel Lisa & doctor Thomas are expected daily; from them we expect a more particular detail of the voyage.[30]

On November 22 the elder Chouteau addressed a short "information" to Eustis and followed that on December 14 with a long, detailed description of the return of the Mandan chief. After five years his relationship with the US government was crumbling, and Pierre wrote to redeem himself.[31]

Informed that his services to the government were no longer required, Chouteau had no way of knowing that Governor Lewis had supported him in the same letter that responded to the protested bills. Chouteau described the return of the Mandan chief in considerable detail to authenticate the relationship with the MFCo. The latter part of that letter was an apology for the problems arising from the Osage Treaty and an appeal to retain his station. Chouteau failed to grasp that the new administration was cutting expenses and, like the Prairie du Chien agent Boilvin, he had to convince the new regime that he was essential to the conduct of Indian affairs.[32]

Truth was, the secretary of war didn't care. His obligation was to reduce expenses. For the West this was disastrous because Eustis didn't understand the Indian trade or Indian relations and, with the government running out of money, he wasn't interested in learning. Clark had a small, sweet revenge when he confronted his detractors in Washington.

> My accounts are all Settled without much dificuelty. I found the president & Secty. of war reather favourably disposed towards me & in place of my haveing lost Confidence, I feel flattered from the attention & refurences that I am reather a faverite. I have hot [not] the good wishes of the anl. [animal] who I treat like a puppy—as he is.[33]

Accountant William Simmons's only admission of an error had to wait until March 4, 1812.

> [T]here is due to the Estate of the late Meriwether Lewis, deceased—the sum of Six hundred & thirty six Dollars 25/100 being the balance of his Account for disbursements made for the conveyance of the Mandan Chief, and his family to his Village on the Missouri River—including the Damages, Interest and Cost of the Protest of three Bills of Exchange drawn by him on this Department, in May 1809, for said purposes, which were protested for non-payment—now admitted in conformity to the decision of the Secy. Of War; which Sum is to be transmitted by the Treasurer of the United States to Edward Hempstead, Administrator of the Estate of the said Lewis, deceased, at St. Louis. W. S.[34]

When the War of 1812 began in July, Secretary of War Eustis soon proved his incompetence and was replaced by John Armstrong, a tough man who wasted little time in also ridding himself of William Simmons. The accountant wrote to President Madison complaining that he had been discharged after twenty years of faithful service and attributing his dismissal to Armstrong's fraudulent and personal motives. Two years later Simmons still considered himself a champion of right, as he alone could see it. He charged a professor at West Point of abusing and degrading cadets for trivial offenses. In May he expected to be called to give his evidence about the accounts of a quartermaster at Fort Niagara.[35] To the very end he was a demon accountant.

Frederick Bates was, judging by his own documents, a jealous and disloyal secretary who encouraged dissension among others and took delight in reporting it. Although he was the governor's main reliance in handling the details of Louisiana government at a time when unity was necessary, Bates had found excuses to set himself apart from Lewis. The criticism of the governor came from a faction that coalesced around the territorial secretary.[36]

Not quite three weeks after Lewis departed for Washington, Frederick Bates occupied the role of Worshipful Master at Saint Louis Masonic Lodge No. 111 and signed William Clark's diploma on September 18, 1809. With the governor out of the way, Bates enjoyed a heavy hand with the land board and the power of an acting governor. He soon turned on Clement Biddle Penrose for sometimes opposing him on the land board.[37] In October Penrose expressed his opinion that Bates's "motives of my misunderstandings with Govr. Lewis, were, the hopes of acquiring the Executive Office on his removal." An indignant Bates called that statement "impudent stupidity" and tendered to Penrose "my most hearty contempt."[38]

By the end of the month Bates found an excuse to insult then discharge another of Lewis's friends. Sheriff Jeremiah Connor was replaced with Bates's adherent Alexander McNair. In January 1810, when Edward Hempstead defended Connor against aspersions, Bates threatened him, then on the twenty-second informed him, "You are no longer Attorney General of the territory of Louisiana."[39]

William Clark was made of sterner stuff. When he returned to St. Louis in July 1810, Bates could not understand why the government hadn't acted on his letter critical of Lewis. Clark had outmaneuvered him in the Capitol.

I find that Mr. Bates has disapproved of the proceeding in the Indian departmt. and in addition to his Complaints against Govr. Lewis he has laid in Complaints against me to the government, the amount of which he has not Shewn me, but Sais he is ready to do it at any time I am at Some loss to determine how to act with this little animale whome I had mistaken as my friend, however I Shall learn a little before I act.[40]

As the Lewis estate administrator, William Clark had taken on the responsibility of dealing with his friend's debts. In conjunction with Carr they sold some land in September 1809 to answer the most demanding creditors. A year later, on November 3, 1810, Clark sold more of the land. The delighted buyer who got sixty-four acres for the bargain price of sixty-four dollars was Frederick Bates.[41]

A rationale for Governor Lewis's death began to emerge in January 1810. At Fort Pickering Capt. Gilbert Russell had read the news of the death in a worn copy of the Nashville paper. He was a soldier, which in the western army meant burying men who died of the fever. The captain knew their terrible sufferings, but he had never seen a man kill himself because of them. Had he somehow failed a brother officer?

After the departure of Lewis and Neelly, Russell was beset by problems with surgeon's mate W. C. Smith, who was accused of neglect of duty, failure to give out medicines, and keeping a mistress in quarters. That must have led to a row, because next day Russell was aware that factor Hogg had tried to discredit him with his superiors by claiming that the captain neglected his duty and spoke disrespectfully of the government. Russell laid those matters out in a thirteen-page letter to the War Department dated January 2, 1810.[42]

Lewis had given Russell a verbal order to hold his expedition land warrant instead of sending it on to New Orleans. The post still hadn't left two days later when Russell saw an opportunity to rid himself of that responsibility. In the cover letter to Thomas Jefferson, Russell volunteered a description of the circumstances while Lewis was at Fort Pickering. He described helping Lewis to prepare for the overland trip and that he had intended to accompany him. Because he had helped the weakened man repack, the captain knew quite a bit about what was taken in the two trunks. Russell was aware that Lewis carried $220 in notes, specie, and a $99.58 treasurer's check that he endorsed in case Lewis needed to convert it to cash.[43]

The captain was discreet about the governor's condition and the steps he had taken to get the man back on his feet. Still expecting permission to return and clear up his refused bills, Russell promised to give Mr. Jefferson a more complete description in person. But by the end of December Russell was still disappointed in his travel plans and was increasingly concerned about rumors that Agent Neelly had taken advantage of the situation at

Grinder's Stand. Neelly was said to be making unjustified claims and had appropriated Lewis's weapons.

Russell wrote Jefferson again. This second explanation may have been fact, partial truth, or an effort to discredit Neelly by making him accessory to what Russell now claimed was Lewis's alcoholism. Pernier and even the unlucky Mrs. Grinder were included in Russell's charge.[44] This letter became the basis for much speculation about Lewis's condition, but it has the tone of a man covering for himself. When Jefferson received those two letters, he responded with his comments on hypocondria.[45]

The *Republican Star or Eastern Shore General Advertiser* took issue with rumors about the death of Lewis in its February 13, 1810, issue.

> We lose no time in doing an act of justice, by contradicting a report which was published as the supposed cause of late Governor Lewis. It appears that from a child, when ever attacked with sickness, that the fever generally affected his brain—and the fatigue and heat of his water passage from St. Louis to the Chickasaw Bluffs threw his symptoms into a very high fever, and it was impossible to procure the necessaries of life, much less medical aid to combat the disorder. These facts we have from several sources.[46]

It was late in 1811 before Captain Russell finally received permission to return east. At army headquarters in Fredericktown on November 26 the captain took the trouble to write a long statement of the whole experience leading up to the death of Governor Lewis. It is not clear why he felt that this was required, but it reiterated his belief that the governor's "state of mental derangement appeared to have been produced by indisposition as other causes." His description of the tragedy at Grinder's Stand repeated the widely circulated accounts, but the previous charges against Neelly and others had disappeared.[47]

As late as 1813 Russell was still trying to get paid for the government horses he had provided to Governor Lewis and for the check he endorsed. Russell neglected to mention that he had canceled the check. With interest the total bill was now $379.58. Three years later that debt against the Lewis estate was settled for $255.61.[48] For Gilbert Russell, who had done his best, Meriwether Lewis was a hard man to forget.

Clark's prolonged stay in the East was the beginning of the drawn-out process of getting the expedition book written and published. *Lewis and Clark's Travels* was advertised to consist of three volumes; narrative, meteorological and astronomical, and scientific. Untrained as a scientist, Clark lacked the ability to write a masterful narrative. All he could do was fall back on what he had—the field journals—and what he understood—the adventure. The creation of the narrative came to depend upon Clark's daily records, as edited by a series of writers with no firsthand experience or sense of it beyond what they deciphered. Historians would follow those sixteen red morocco–bound notebooks and the associated papers to the neglect of the man who was central to their creation.

Clark asked Jefferson to guide him and inquired if Congress would help with the financing. The talents of botanist Benjamin Smith Barton "were exclusively solicited" for that third volume on natural history. American Philosophical Society member Henry Muhlenberg was disheartened when he heard that "Lewis's Travels, will for some secret reason not be published at least not in the proposed manner."[49]

That began a process that reduced the work of Meriwether Lewis to an unfortunate abstraction. As a subject of learned or amateur speculation, Lewis had become a frame on which to hang personal opinions. For two hundred years the journals of the Corps of Discovery have commanded so much attention that few have questioned whether their mission was properly completed.

According to Jefferson, Lewis, Clark, and several APS members, the journals were essentially private notes. Only the map and summary of the tribes made at Fort Mandan rightfully belonged to the US government. Shifting attention to the journals created the prevailing belief that they were the only worthwhile story about the expedition and obscured Lewis's original intention of producing an important scientific publication. This fixation led to unwarranted criticism of Lewis.

It has been charged that Lewis omitted about four hundred entry dates from his journals. The omission of so many dates and the fact that he ordered other expedition members to write journals caused some historians to argue that Lewis was remiss in his duties and they even suggest "a larger pattern of negligence."[50] But Lewis performed other necessary tasks that account for more than 150 dates that are entirely separate from the journal entries.[51] The separate body of codices detailing the performance of those tasks has been overlooked, underestimated, and ultimately consigned as miscellaneous documentation.

Those who feel disappointed that Lewis omitted to write on the remaining 250 days fail to grasp that commanding officers must delegate chores. Lewis had delegated the daily log to Clark. Had Lewis written as much every day with as much enthusiasm as he did on the occasions when he felt compelled to describe a special something, the expedition would have exhausted its paper supply and the resulting pages would have been so voluminous that they would have had to be cut in order to be published. The fault lies not with Lewis, but with ourselves.

However, there was a living legacy. The expedition journals were still being edited in 1812 when Bernard McMahon wrote Jefferson that plants Lewis had collected were fully mature. McMahon praised some of the more elegant specimens. One shrub had a dark purple color with yellow flowers that were "showey and extremely fragrant." He also described a shrub from the Columbia River and a yellow currant from the Jefferson River. Later, Jefferson wrote that Lewis's journey had added a number of new plants to "our former stock. Some of them are curious, some ornamental, some useful, and some may be made acceptable to our tables." Those gifts spread further when McMahon made gifts of the Lewis seeds to European friends. The list and Jefferson's gifts went on from there.[52]

In 1813, Jefferson expressed disappointment that the expedition narrative had still not been published. Finally, in utter exasperation, he pressed Barton: "When shall we have your book on American botany, and when the 1st volume of Lewis & Clark's Travels? Both of these works are of general expectation, and to no one of more than myself."[53] Jefferson already knew the zoological discoveries would "experience greater delay."

Three years later Barton, McMahon, and Muhlenberg had all died and Jefferson found himself complaining to Clark. Although the narrative had been printed, he still hoped to see something on the astronomical observations, the geographical chart, and the Indian vocabularies. But Clark was in St. Louis acting as governor of the territory and the most that he could do was to send "plenty of seeds from those hitherto unknown parts" of the Missouri Territory.[54]

Jefferson donated the botanical work to the APS, where it was lost for many years. In 1898, Thomas Meehan, curator at the Academy of Natural Sciences in Philadelphia, found the dried specimens: "With the freedom of three quarters of a century the museum beetles had made sad work in the bundles. In a few cases the specimens had been wholly reduced to dust, and only fragments were left in other cases. Generally, however, they were in fair condition."[55]

The APS wisely accepted a proposition to deposit them and other collections with the Academy of Natural Sciences in Philadelphia, where they have remained to this day. Meehan, with help from academy botanists, attended to the detailed work of putting the collection in order. His work evolved into a scholarly and scientific collection that allows botanists from all over the world to view plants more than two hundred years old.[56]

Sadly, what was published was not the masterpiece that Lewis had envisioned—as late as 1816, Thomas Jefferson chided William Clark on what was lacking.

> The travelling journal of Govr. Lewis and yourself having been published some time ago, I had hoped to hear that something was doing with the astronomical observations, the Geographical chart, the Indian vocabularies, and other papers not comprehended in the journal published, with a view to have these given to the public according to the original intention. ... I hope the part I have had in this important voyage, will excuse the interest I take in securing to the world all the beneficial results we were entitled to expect from it, and which would so fully justify the expences of the expedition incurred by the United States in that expedition.

In response Governor Clark explained what he had tried to do and added:

> The Missouri River on which there is much emence tracts of fine Country calculated for rich & populous settlements, and watering an emence space in which there is much welth in furs, Peltres, minerals, dies &c. is tolerable well understood but not in sufficient use. The Lands on the lower portion of that river is settling fast, the middle portion (or as high up as the Big Bend or White River) is Crowded with Traders, but the upper and richer portion has had no American citizen since the falue [failure?] of the Missouri Co. in 1811 and I am under great apprehentions that the British will take possession of that rich Tract by way of Assinniboin & Saskassion rivers as they have done at the mouth of the Columbia, and on Lewis & Clarks rivers.[57]

Three editions of the complete set of journals plus countless paraphrases, excerpts, and interpretations have failed to do what Lewis might have done had he lived. Late nineteenth- and twentieth-century historians have been disappointed that the author died without meeting that challenge. As the explanations sometimes took strained flights of imagination, interpreting the Lewis and Clark materials became a minor industry.[58]

Clarification requires following the surviving government documents in a labyrinth of bureaucratic back files. These show that the public career of Meriwether Lewis was bracketed by the commanding presence of Thomas Jefferson. In the lead-up to the continental exploration and in the initial returns Jefferson and Lewis were in agreement. But something happened after the return of the expedition that caused a subtle alteration of their relationship.

In allowing the first reports from Fort Mandan to be printed and widely circulated, Jefferson acted precipitously. That undercut the first part of Lewis's projected three-volume publication but could be remedied by what Lewis intended to do with the rest of the manuscript. Then the president denied that opportunity by appointing Lewis governor of Louisiana, delaying his departure to Philadelphia, and in the next year intercepting Lewis and sending him to observe and report on the increasingly embarrassing Aaron Burr trial. The only writing that Lewis managed to do during the fall of 1807 concerned the present state and future prospects of the Louisiana Territory, which he might have intended to use as an analysis to complete the projected book.

Jefferson, the amateur scientist, was really a tinkerer with household conveniences, natural science, agriculture, native peoples, and educating young men. Unable to admit Lewis took radical measures to alleviate his pain, Jefferson found it necessary to rationalize the act of Lewis's death. The term *hypocondria* that Jefferson emphasized about Lewis put the character of the man in doubt. In the final accounting Thomas Jefferson, the man who molded the boy and launched him on the road to greatness, failed his own creation.

That does not mean his lifelong mentor was directly responsible for Lewis's death, anymore than Madison can be held accountable for the economic measures he was forced to take. They were all good men doing their best as a new continental nation stumbled forward. Lesser public servants like Bates, Carr, or Simmons were just small, jealous men with selfish goals. But each in his unintended way contributed to the tragic loss of one of the most promising men of the period. What they did created stresses, but Lewis left St. Louis confident that he could resolve difficulties by visiting Washington. It was an impartial parasite in his blood that cut him down.

Later in the nineteenth century, theories about Lewis being a victim of foul play were viewed as more acceptable than an accident that looked like suicide. In his 1956 article, "The Tragic Death of Meriwether Lewis," published in the *William and Mary Quarterly*, National Park Service historian Dawson A. Phelps effectively refuted the murder conspiracy stories by pointing out that those did not begin to appear until thirty-five years or so after Lewis's death.[59] But popular writers like Vardis Fisher in 1962 and Richard Dillon in 1965 enlivened their books with the murder theory. Dillon wrote, "Was Meriwether Lewis murdered? Yes. Is there proof of his murder? No." After admitting "No government inquiry, official or otherwise, was made into Lewis's death," seven pages later Dillon alludes to how an 1809 coroner's jury, "whose records have all been lost," felt about unproven murder. Conspiracy theorists continue to deviate from the documented evidence. Lacking actual facts those inventions depend upon attacking the contemporary evidence of what happened or the character of individuals close to the event.

There are several theories that attempt to find why Lewis killed himself. It is impossible to recover what Meriwether Lewis thought in those last tortured moments. Our evidence points to what he did to alleviate his suffering from malaria, like what other victims were sometimes driven to do. He tried to end the suffering and in that last treatment, accidentally, ended his life.

It was the failure of his body, not his mind, nor his dedication, that cut him down. Lewis was simply unable to continue treating a lifelong, incurable illness. His death cannot be attributed, as many have tried to do, to personal weakness or to the failure to rise to a challenge. It was the result of unforgiving nature, the work of an impartial centuries-old protozoa as indifferent and final as a bullet.

But this was not an acceptable end for a national hero. Lewis was many years in his nearly forgotten grave when respectable editors published more complete versions of the great adventure and conquest of the continent, but they still found it difficult to excuse a hero who they believed had killed himself. Strained rationalizations challenged his sanity or his courage in the face of adversity but consistently ignored his health.

Despite the absence of credible evidence, a body of conspiracy theories has contested the plain facts of suicide. Some authors have resorted to the dramatic possibility of murder, which took hold with a public unable to accept the bleak truth that a national hero could meet with such a tragic end. The controversy continues to haunt the memory of a sufferer who had no idea how to treat his own physical torment. Lewis's contemporaries believed that he put an end to himself. What they lacked was the medical understanding to see why.

Oh, there was a murder all right, committed by a colony of *Plasmodia*, microscopic demons that had infiltrated Lewis's liver years before and periodically came out to swim in his bloodstream. Over a lifetime they wore him down. And there was an accessory. Dr. Benjamin Rush dispensed mercury-laced pills that were not just ineffective but actually harmful. Careless authors have been amused to refer to those pills as Thunderbolts.[60]

In the medicine chest of the expedition, which Dr. Rush put together, Lewis included fifty dozen of Rush's pills.[61] Whether or not Rush recommended them for the treatment of malaria, Lewis used them to combat attacks of the ague. The pills had no effect on the infestation but their use coincided with the temporary remission of the disease. Twice a day during one of his malarial episodes, Lewis might throw down as many as a half dozen of Rush's pills, twelve poisonous grains of mercury. That diverted Lewis from ingesting a decoction of boiled Peruvian bark, a remedy that he readily prescribed to others.

What Meriwether Lewis might have been is something to ponder. That he died a victim of an overpowering disease is in the final accounting not that critical. But it matters that the tragedy resulted in ideas that diminish him. For just over two hundred years, enthusiasts have settled for the adventure and failed to lament the missing hand and inspired pen. The death of a suffering man was converted into the loss of what he might have written.

Eighteen months after the news of Lewis's death reached the East, the young ornithologist Alexander Wilson decided to travel down the Ohio River. Wilson was an admirer and friend of the explorer because Lewis had generously allowed him access to the western bird specimens in Charles Willson Peale's museum. Wilson rode alone down the Natchez Trace in search of birds and new experiences. Although well armed, he found no great threat in the bands of boatmen he encountered who were returning home after a long river trip to New Orleans.

> These men were as dirty as Hottentots; their dress a shirt and trowsers of canvass, black, greasy, and sometimes in tatters; the skin burnt wherever exposed to the sun; each with a budget, wrapt up in an old blanket; their beards eighteen days old, added to the singularity of their appearance, which was altogether savage. These people came from the various tributary streams of the Ohio, hired for forty or fifty dollars a trip, to return back on their own expenses. Some had upwards of eight hundred miles to travel.[62]

Stopping at Grinder's Stand Wilson got a firsthand report. His interview with Mrs. Grinder recovered the best first-person account of the fatal night. It seems unlikely that the authenticity of the vivid details that he took down were colored by sympathy or retelling. Mrs. Grinder's husband wasn't all that pleased to cooperate because the gossip mill was circulating stories that embarrassed the family. Wilson arranged and paid for a fence to be built around Lewis's grave to keep wild animals away and then rode on, composing a poem in his mind to a tragic ending.[63]

> *Lone as these solitudes appear*
> *Wide as this wilderness is spread*
> *Affection's steps shall linger here*
> *To breathe her sorrows o'er the dead.*

NOTES

1. Alexander Wilson, "Particulars of the Death of Capt. Lewis," *Port Folio* 7 (January 1812): 39.

2. Robert A. Rutland et al., eds., *The Papers of James Madison*, 5 vols. (Charlottesville: University of Virginia Press, 1984), 2: 48–49.

3. *(Nashville) Democratic Clarion*, October 20, 1809, p. 3.

4. Jackson, *LLC* 2: 746–47. TJ to the following: October 22, 1809, to citizens of Virginia; October 25 to JMA; November 2 to John Porter, roll 44, TJ-LOC.

5. TJ to Gallatin, November 4, 1809, document 33548, roll 44, TJ-LOC. Another wounding reminder was written in Knoxville on November 5. David Campbell wrote that his son, Thomas Jefferson Campbell, was eighteen now and undecided whether to study law or physics. The father asked Jefferson to advise him when he visited Monticello to meet the man he had been named for.

6. TJ to JMA, November 6, 1809, document 39-55, series 1, roll 11, JMA-LOC; for a printed version, see James Morton Smith, *The Republic of Letters*, 3 vols. (New York: Norton, 1995), 3: 1606.

7. James Holmberg, ed., *Dear Brother* (New Haven, CT: Yale University Press, 2002), p. 231n4. Pernier's good intentions went for nought; members of the family later concocted the story that Pernier had stolen Meriwether's watch and was seen wearing it in Mobile. When Neelly wrote Jefferson he spoke of holding the watch but must have reconsidered as it was in the boxes when Coles and Clark opened them in Washington.

8. John Brahan to JMA, October 18, 1809, document 33520-21, and James Neelly to TJ, October 18 1809, document 33522-23, roll 44, TJ-LOC. Neelly's letter in Jackson, *LLC* 2: 467–68.

9. Pernier claimed that Lewis owed him $240 for his services. Jefferson provided him with some cash against that debt and told Pernier to sell the horse and also credit that to the account.

10. TJ to C. and A. Conrad and Co., November 23, 1809, Jackson, *LLC* 2: 474–75.

11. JMA to TJ, November 27, 1809, in Smith, *The Republic of Letters*, 3: 1609; http://memory.loc.gov/ammem/collections/madison_papers/index.html (accessed April 8, 2008).

12. JMA to TJ, November 30, 1809, in Smith, *The Republic of Letters*, 3: 1610.

13. *Connecticut Courant*, November 29, 1809, p. 3. In the nineteenth century, Danbury, Connecticut, had fifty-six hat factories where hatters working in close, poorly ventilated shops inhaled the mercury fumes used in the felting process and were poisoned.

14. *Democratic Press (PA)*, November 13, 1809, column 1, "Lexington (KY)," October 28. Extract of a letter from a gentleman in Russelville, to his friend at present in Lexington, dated "Russelville, 20 October 1809."

15. Ibid., column 2.

16. October 30 and November 8, 1809, Holmberg, *Dear Brother*, pp. 224–26.

17. Ibid., November 26, 1809, p. 228.

18. Ibid.

19. Excerpts from Clark's 1809 journal, Jackson, *LLC* 2: 724.

20. Ibid., 2: 725.

21. SW to WC, August 7, 1809, Carter, *TP* 14: 289–90; Clark's reply to the August 7 letter: WC to SW, September 21, 1809, RG107, C644, M221, roll 20, frame 6357.

22. Excerpts from Clark's 1809 journal, Jackson, *LLC* 2: 725.

23. Isaac A. Coles to TJ, January 5, 1810, Jackson, *LLC* 2: 486–87.

24. William D. Meriwether to John Marks, January 5, 1810, Jackson, *LLC* 2: 487–88.

25. William D. Meriwether to WC, January 22, 1810, and WC to William D. Meriwether, January 26, 1810, Jackson, *LLC* 2: 489–91; Isaac Coles and WC to John Marks, January 10, 1810, MSS 9041, 9041-a, papers of the Lewis, Anderson, and Marks families.

26. WC to Jonathan Clark, January 12, 1810, in Holmberg, *Dear Brother*, p. 234.

27. ML to the president, August 27, 1809, Carter, *TP* 14: 293–312. Carter omitted the last twenty-one pages from the packet. ML to TJ, August 27, 1809, RG107, L101, M221, roll 38, frames 4907–31.

28. A. P. Chouteau to WE, September 1, 1809, postmarked Cahokia September 2, 1809, and received at WD, September 23, 1809, Carter, *TP* 14: 315–19.

29. Bates wrote two letters for Chouteau in 1809. PC to WD, June 14 and August 12, 1809, RG107, C562 and C612, M221, roll 20, frames 6255, 6310.

30. *(TN) Review*, December 15, 1809, p. 2.

31. PC to SW, November 22, 1809, RG107, C671, M221, roll 20, frame 6377; PC to SW, November 22, 1809, letterbook, p. 104, Chouteau Collections, MHS.

32. PC to SW, December 14, 1809, Carter, *TP* 14: 343–52.

33. Holmberg, *Dear Brother*, p. 234.

34. Termination of Lewis's account, March 4, 1812, Jackson, *LLC* 2:576. The difference between the total debt of $1,120 and $636.25 suggests that the two later bills had been quietly adjusted and paid.

35. *Calendar of the Correspondence of James Madison: Bulletin of the Bureau of Rolls and Library of the Department of State* (Washington, DC: Department of State, 1894), pp. 619–20.

36. Many letters from Frederick Bates to his friends show favoritism. See Marshall, *FB*.

37. A nephew of General Wilkinson, Penrose had arrived in St. Louis in 1805 with the general's entourage and, like Judge Lucas, survived the disputes of the land board. Bates took over the third position on the board.

38. FB to Clement Penrose, October 20, 1809, Marshall, *FB* 2: 99.

39. Ibid. Jeremiah Connor, November 29, December 3, 14, 1809; Alexander McNair, December 14, 1809; Edward Hempstead, January 20, 22, 30, 1810; FB 2: 99, 116–18, 120–22, 123, 126–27.

40. Holmberg, *Dear Brother*, p. 248.

41. The sale is recorded in the court of common pleas, GLM-JNEM.

42. GR to SW, January 2, 1810, RG107, R14, M221, roll 39, frame 6095.

43. GR to TJ, January 4, 1810, document 33616-17, reel 45, TJ-LOC.

44. GR to TJ, January 31, 1810, document 33657, TJ-LOC.

45. TJ to GR, April 18, 1810, Jackson, *LLC* 2: 728.

46. *Republican Star or Eastern Shore General Advertiser (MD)*, February 13, 1810, p. 3.

47. Statement of Gilbert Russell, November 26, 1811, Jackson, *LLC* 2: 573–75.

48. GR to William D. Meriwether, April 18, 1813, Jackson, *LLC* 2: 732n.

49. Henry Muhlenberg to Stephen Elliott, June 16 and November 8, 1809, January 11, 1810, November 11, 1812, typescripts in Academy of Natural Sciences.

50. Moulton, *JLCE* 2: 18.

51. Moulton, *JLCE* 3: 450–72; 12:1–14; Paul Russell Cutright, "Meriwether Lewis: Botanist," *Oregon Historical Quarterly* 69 (June 1968): 148–70; Earle E. Spamer and Richard M. McCourt, "The Lewis and Clark Herbarium of the Academy of Natural Sciences," *Notulae Naturae* 475 (December 2002): 2–16.

52. Rodney H. True, "Some Neglected Botanical Results," *Proceedings of the American Philosophical Society* 67 (1928): 14–17.

53. TJ to BSB, April 3, 1813, document 35182, roll 46; TJ to Madame de Tesse, December 8, 1813, document 35557-58, roll 47, TJ-LOC.

54. TJ to Alexander von Humboldt, December 6, 1813, and TJ to WC, September 8, 1816, Jackson, *LLC* 2: 596, 619; Henry Muhlenberg to Stephen Elliott, January 11, 1810, typescripts in Academy of Natural Sciences. Thomas Meehan, "The Plants of the Lewis and Clark's Expedition across the Continent, 1804–1806," *Proceedings of the Academy of Natural Sciences of Philadelphia* 50 (January–March 1898): 12–49.

55. Thomas Meehan, "The Plants of the Lewis and Clark's Expedition across the Continent, 1804–1806," *Proceedings of the Academy of Natural Sciences of Philadelphia* 50 (January–March 1898): 14.

56. Elliott Coues, "Notes on Thomas Meehan's on the Plants of Lewis and Clark's Expedition across the Continent, 1804–1806," *Proceedings of the Academy of Natural Sciences of Philadelphia* 50 (April–September 1898): 291–315.

57. TJ to WC, September 8, 1816, and WC to TJ, October 10, 1816, Jackson, *LLC* 2: 619, 623–26.

58. Nicholas Biddle, *History of the Expedition under the Command of Captains Lewis and Clark, to the Sources of the Missouri River, thence across the Rocky Mountains and down the River Columbia to the Pacific Ocean. Performed during the years 1805-5-6, by Order of the Government of the United States*, 2 vols. (Philadelphia: Paul Allen,

1814); Reuben Gold Thwaites, ed., *Original Journals of the Lewis and Clark Expedition, 1804–1806*, 8 vols. (New York: Dodd, Mead, 1904–1905).

59. Lewis's champion, historian Grace Lewis Miller, responded with a long rebuttal to Phelps that the *William & Mary Quarterly* refused to print. On some points she corrected misconceptions, but other objections of Miller's were too biased to be considered.

60. Stephen Ambrose, *Undaunted Courage* (New York: Simon & Schuster, 1996), p. 89; Paul Russell Cutright, "I gave him barks and saltpeter," *American Heritage: The Magazine of History* 15 (December 1963): 98. Cutright resurrected the term in 1969 and in subsequent book publications. Paul Russell Cutright, *Lewis & Clark: Pioneering Naturalists* (Lincoln: University of Nebraska Press, 1989), p. 175. Rush's thunderbolts or thunderclappers were not terms used during Lewis's time. They were first described in a series of essays on quackery by Dr. Morris Fishbein, editor of the *American Medical Association Journal*, and later in several books that he authored. Morris Fishbein, *Frontiers of Medicine* (Baltimore: Williams & Wilkins Company, 1933), p. 179. None of the authors provided citations.

61. Ambrose, *Undaunted Courage*, p. 90. Supplies from private vendors, Jackson, *LLC* 1: 80.

62. Wilson, "Particulars of the Death of Capt. Lewis," p. 36.

63. Ibid., p. 40.

Appendix

Observations and Reflections on the Subject of Governing and Maintaining a State of Friendly Intercourse with the Indians of the Territory of Louisiana.[1]

MERIWETHER LEWIS

Annotated by Thomas C. Danisi and John C. Jackson

W e shall find this subject of primary importance, whether we consider it as connected with the defence of our much extended and
defenceless frontier, the benefits which ought of right to accrue to the
United States from the possession of Louisiana, or the future expenditure of
blood and treasure, which may be involved in the defence of this country.
In treating this subject, I have deemed it expedient in the commencement
for its more complete development to state the leading measures pursued by
the Spanish provincial government in relation to their intercourse with the
Indians of Louisiana, and point out the evils which flowed from those measures as well to the Indians as the whites, to the end that we may profit by
their errors and be ourselves the better enabled to apply the necessary cor-
rectives to those evils which their practices introduced.[2]

From the commencement of the Spanish provincial government in
Louisiana, whether by the permission of the crown or originating in the
pecuniary rapacity of the governor's general of the province, this officer
reserved to himself exclusively the right of trading with all the Indian
nations in Louisiana, and therefore proceeded to dispose of this privilege to
individuals for certain stipulated sums; his example was generally imitated
by the governor of upper Louisiana, who made a further exaction;[3] these

exclusive permissions to individuals varied as to the extent of country or nations they embraced and the periods for which he granted, but in all cases those exclusive licenses were offered to the highest bidder, and consequently the sums paid by the individuals purchasing, were quite as much as the profits of the trade would bear, and in many instances, from a spirit of opposition between contending applicants, much more was given than the profits of the traffic would justify and the individual of course became bankrupt, this however was among the least of the evils flowing from this system of exclusive trade to the Indians it produced the evils of an extravagant advance on the price of their merchandize, corrupted their morals and subjected them to the rigour of those measures of coertion which have been and still must be practised with a view to reduce them to order. The Indians were compelled to pay such extravagant prices for the articles they purchased, that their greatest exertions would not enable them to purchase as much as they had previously been in the habit of consuming, and which they consequently conceived necessary to their well being, for as this system progressed, the demands of the governor become more exorbitant and the traders to meet their engagements, exacted higher prices from the Indians, altho' the game became more scarce in their country. The morals of the Indians were corrupted by placing before them the articles they viewed as of the first necessity to them, at such prices that they had it not in their power to purchase; they were therefore induced in many instances to take by force that which they had not the means of paying for; consoling themselves with the idea, that the traders were compelled from necessity to possess themselves of their peltries and furs, in order to meet their engagements with those from whom they had purchased their merchandize, as well as those who had assisted him in their transportation, and consequently could not withdraw themselves from their trade without sustaining much injury.[4] The prevalence of this sentiment among the Indians, was very forceably impressed on my mind, by an anecdote related to me by a gentleman of my acquaintance who had for several years enjoyed the exclusive privilege of trading with the Osage Indians;[5] it happened that after he had bartered with them for all the peltries and furs which they had on hand, that they seized forceably on a number of guns, and a parcel of ammunition which he had still remaining; he remonstrated with them against this act of violence, and finally concluded by declaring that he would never return among them again, nor would he suffer for any person to bring them merchandize thereafter. They heard him out very patiently, when one of their leaders pertly asked him if he did not return as usual the next season, to obtain their peltries and furs, how he intended to pay the persons from whom he had purchased the merchandize which they had then taken from him.

The Indians believed implicitly that the traders were the most powerful persons in the country, and that they had the power of withholding merchandize from them, but the great thirst displayed by the traders for the possession of their furs and peltries, added to their belief, that they were compelled to continue their traffic, was considered by the Indians as a sufficient guarantee for the continuance of their intercourse, and therefore felt themselves at liberty to practice aggressions on the traders with impunity, thus governing the traders by what they conceived their necessities to possess their furs and peltries, rather than being themselves governed by their own anxiety to obtain merchandizes, which they may most effectually in my opinion by well regulated system.[6]

The Indians found by a few experiments of aggressions on the trader that as it respected themselves, it had a salutary effect, and altho' they had mistaken the legitimate cause of action on the part of the traders, the result being favourable to themselves, they still continued their practices. The fact is, that these merchants were obliged to continue their trade under every disadvantage, in order to make good their engagements to the governors; whose protection being secured, they were safe both in person and property from their other creditors.[7] The first effect of these depradations of the Indians, was the introduction of a ruinous custom among the traders, of extending to them a credit, which I shall hereafter notice more particularly as it relates to our future view of commerce with those nations. The traders who visited the Indians on the Missouri, usually arrived at their wintering stations from the 1st of September to the 15th of October, here they carried on their traffic until the month of April or beginning of May,[8] in the course of the season they had possessed themselves of every skin the Indians could procure, and of course there was an end of trade: but previous to their return the Indians insist upon a credit being given them, on the faith of payment being made when they returned the next season. The traders on those occasions well understood their situations, and knowing as they did, that this credit was nothing less than the price of their passports, or the privilege of departing in safety to their homes, of course narrowed down the amount of their credits, by concealing so far as they could, to avoid the suspicions of the Indians, the remnant of their merchandize; but the amount offered or given to the Indians, was always such as constituted a considerable proportion of their whole stock in trade, or say the full amount of the summer or redskin hunt.[9] The Indians well knew that the traders were in their power, and the servile motives which induced them to extend their liberality to them, and were thereof no the less solicitous to meet their engagements on the day of payment; to this indifference they were further urged, by the traders distributing among them on those occasions, many articles of the least necessity to them: the consequence was that when the traders returned the ensuing fall if they obtained only half their credits they were well satisfied, as this covered their real expenditure.[10] Again, if it so happened in the course of the winter's traffic, that the losses of the trader, growing out of the indolence of the Indians and their exorbitant exactions, under the appellation of credits should so reduce their stock in trade, that they could not pay the governors the price stipulated for their licences, and procure a further supply of merchandize in order to prosecute their trade, their finances were immediately revoked, and the privilege granted to other individuals, who with ample assortments of goods, visited the rendezvous of their predecessors without the interpolation of a single season; and it did not unfrequently happen that the individuals engaged in this commerce, finding one of their number failing from the rapacity of the Indian nations with whom he had been permitted to trade, were not so anxious to possess themselves of the privilege of trading with that nation; the governors of course rather than loose all advantages, would abate of their demands considerably; the new trader thus relieved from a considerable proportion of the tax borne by his predecessor, and feeling disposed to make a favourable impression on the minds of the Indians, to whom he was about to introduce himself, would for the first season at least, dispose of his goods to those Indians on more moderate terms than his predecessor had done. The Indians consequently found that the aggressions they had practiced on their former trader, so far from proving injurious to them, had procured for them not only their exoneration from the payment of the last credit given them by their former trader, but that the present trader furnished them with goods on better terms than they had been accustomed to receive them. Thus encouraged by the salutary effects of their rapacious policy, it was not to be expected that the Indians would alter their plan of operation as it respected their new trader, or that they should appreciate the character of the whites generally, in any other manner than as is expressed in a prevailing sentiment on this subject now common among several nations on the Missouri, "that the white men are like dogs, the more you beat them and plunder them, the more goods they will bring you, and the cheaper they will sell them." This sentiment constitutes at present the rule of action among the Osage, Kanzas, Soos and others,[11] and if it not be broken down some efficient measures shortly, it needs not the gift of prophesy, to determine the sum of advantages which will result to the American people from the Indian trade of Louisiana.

CLATSOP[12]

These aggressions of the Indians were encouraged by the pusillanimity of the engageés, who declared that they were not engaged to fight.

The evils which flowed from this system of exclusive trade were sensibly felt by the inhabitants of Louisiana. The governor, regardless of the safety of the community, sold to an individual the right of vending among the Indians every species of merchandize; this bartering, in effect, his only efficient check on the Indians. The trader, allured by the hope of gain, neither shackled with discretions nor consulting the public good, proceeded to supply the Indians, on whom he was dependent, with arms, ammunition, and all other articles they might require. The Indian, thus independent, acknowledging no authority but his own, will proceed, without compunction of conscience or fear of punishment, to wage war on the defenceless inhabitants of the frontier, whose lives and property, in many instances, were thus sacrificed at the shrine of an *inordinate thirst for wealth* in their governors, which in reality occasioned all those evils. Although the governors could not have been ignorant that the misfortunes of the people were caused by the independence of the Indians, to which they were accessory, still they were the more unwilling to apply the corrective; because the very system which gave them wealth in the outset, in the course of its progress afforded them many plausible pretexts to put their hands into the treasury of the king their master. For example: the Indians attack the frontier, kill some of the inhabitants, plunder many others, and, agreeably to their custom of warfare, retire instantly to their villages with their booty. The governor, informed of this transaction, promptly calls on the inhabitants to aid and assist in repelling the invasion. Accordingly a party assemble under their officers, some three or four days after the mischief had been done, and they pursue them, as they usually did, at no rapid pace, three or four days, and returned without overtaking the enemy, as they might have well known before they set out. On their return the men were dismissed, but ordered to hold themselves in readiness at a moment's warning. When, at the end of some two or three months, the governor chose to consider the danger blown over, he causes receipts to be made out for the full pay of two or three months' service, to which the signatures of the individuals are affixed; but as those persons were only absent from their homes ten or twelve days, all that was really paid them did not amount to more than one-fourth or one-fifth of what they receipted for, and the balance, of course, was taken by the governor, as the reward for his faithful guardianship of the lives and property of his majesty's subjects.

The Spaniards, holding the entrance of the Missouri, could regulate as they thought proper the intercourse with the Indians through that channel; but from what has been said, it will be readily perceived that their traders, shackled with the pecuniary impositions of their governors, could never become the successful rivals of the British merchants on the west side of the Mississippi, which, from the proximity to the United States, the latter could enter without the necessity of a Spanish passport or the fear of being detected by them. The consequence was that the trade of the rivers Demoin, St. Peter's, and all the country west of the Mississippi nearly to the Missouri, was exclusively enjoyed by the British merchants. The Spanish governors, stimulated by their own sordid views, declared that the honour of his majesty was grossly compromitted[13] by the liberty that those adventurers took in trading with the natives within his territory without their permission, and therefore took the liberty of expending his majesty's money by equipping and manning several galleys to cruise in the channels of the Mississippi in order to intercept those traders of the St. Peter's and Demoin rivers, in their passage to and from the entrance of the Oisconsing river; but after several unsuccessful cruises, and finding the Indians so hostile to them in this quarter that they dare not land nor remain long in the channel without being attacked, they therefore retired and gave over the project.[14] The Indians were friendly to the British merchants, and unfriendly to the Spanish, for the plain reason that the former sold them goods at a lower rate. The Ayaways, Sacks, Foxes, and Yanktons of the river Demoin, who occasionally visited the Missouri, had it in their power to compare the rates at which the Spanish merchant in that quarter and the British merchant on the Mississippi sold their goods; this was always much in favour of the latter; it therefore availed the Spaniards but little when they inculcated the doctrine of their being their only legitimate fathers and friends, and that the British merchants were mere intruders and had no other object in view but their own aggrandizement. The Indians, deaf to this doctrine, estimated the friendship of both by the rates at which they respectively sold their merchandise, and of course remained the firm friends of the British. In this situation it is not difficult for those to conceive who have felt the force of their machinations that the British merchants would, in order to extend their own trade, endeavor to break down that of their neighbours on the Missouri. The attachments of the Indians to them afforded a formidable weapon with which to effect their purposes, nor did they suffer it to remain unemployed.

The merchants of the Dog Prairie, rivers Demoin and Ayaway,[15] stimulated the nations just mentioned to the commission of acts of rapacity on the merchants of the Missouri, nor was Mr. Cameron and others, merchants of the river St. Peter's, less active with respect to the Cissitons, Yanktons of the plains, Tetons, etc., who resort to the Missouri occasionally still higher up. War parties of those nations were consequently found lying in wait on the Missouri to intercept boats of the merchants of that river at the seasons they were expected to pass, and depredations were frequently committed, particularly by the Ayaways, who have been known in several instances to capture boats on the Missouri in their descent to St. Louis, and compelled the crews to load themselves with heavy burdens of their best furs across the country to their towns, where they disposed of them to the British merchants. In those cases they always destroyed the periogues, and such of the peltries and furs as they could not carry off. It may be urged that the British merchants, knowing that the United States, at present, through mere courtesy, permit them to extend their trade to the west side of the Mississippi; or rather they are mere tenants at will, and that the United States possesses the means of ejecting them at pleasure; that they will, under these circumstances, be induced to act differently towards us than they did in relation to the Spanish government. But what assurance have we that this will be the effect of the mere change of governments without change of measures in relation to them. Suffer me to ask what solid grounds there are to hope that their gratitude for our tolerance and liberality on this subject will induce them to hold a different policy towards us.[16] None, in my opinion, unless we stimulate their gratitude by placing before their eyes the instruments of our power in the form of one or two garrisons on the upper part of the Mississippi. Even admit that the people were actuated by the most friendly regard towards the interests of the United States, and at this moment made a common cause with us to induce the Indians to demean themselves in an orderly manner towards our government, and to treat our traders of the Missouri with respect and friendship, yet, without some efficient check on the Indians, I should not think our citizens nor our traders secure; because the Indians, who have for ten years and upwards derived advantages from practice on lessons of rapacity taught them by those traders, cannot at a moment be brought back to a state of primitive innocence by the united persuasions of all the British traders. I hold an axiom, incontrovertible, *that it is more easy to introduce vice into all states of society than it is to eradicate it*; and that this is still more strictly true when applied to man in savage than in his civilized state. If, therefore, we wish, within some short period, to divest ourselves of the evils which flowed from the inculcation of those doctrines of vice, we must employ some more active agent than the influence of the same teachers who first introduced them. Such an agent, in my opinion, is the power of withholding their merchandise from them at pleasure; and to accomplish this, we must first provide the means of controlling the merchants. If we permit the British merchants to supply the Indians in Louisiana as formerly, the influence of our government over those Indians is lost. For the Indian in possession of his merchandise feels himself independent of every govern-ment, and will proceed to commit the same depredations which they did when rendered independent by the Spanish system.[17]

The traders give themselves but little trouble at any time to inculcate among the Indians a respect for governments, but are usually content with proclaiming their own importance. When the British merchants give them-selves trouble to speak of governments, it is but fair to presume that they will teach the natives to respect the power of their own. And at all events, we know from experience that no regard for the blood of our frontier inhab-itants will influence them at any time to withhold arms and ammunition from the Indians, provided they are to profit by furnishing them.[18]

Having now stated, as they have occurred in my mind, the several evils which flowed from that system of intercourse with the Indians pursued by the Spanish government, I shall next endeavor to point out the defects of our own, and show its incompetency to produce the wished-for reform; then, with some remarks on the Indian character, conclude by submitting for the consideration of our government the outlines of a plan which has been dictated as well by a sentiment of philanthropy towards the aborigines of America, as a just regard to the protection of the lives and property of our citizens; and with the further view also of securing to the people of the United States, exclusively, the advantages which ought of right to accrue to them from the possession of Louisiana.[19]

We now permit the British merchants of Canada, indiscriminately with our own, to enter the Missouri and trade with the nations in that quarter. Although the government of the United States has not yielded the point that, as a matter of right, the British merchants have the privilege of trading in this quarter, yet from what has been said to them, they are now acting under the belief that it will be some time before any prohibitory measures will be taken in respect to them; and are therefore making rapid strides to secure themselves in the affection of the Indians, and to break down as soon as possible, the American adventurers by underselling them, and thus monopolize that trade. This they will effect to an absolute certainty in the course of a few years. The old Northwest company of Canada have, within the last two years, formed a union with the Newyork[20] company, who have previously been the only important rivals in the fur trade; this company, with the great accession of capital brought to them by the Newyork company, have, with a view of the particular monopoly of the Missouri, formed a con-nexion with a British house in Newyork, another at New Orleans, and have sent their particular agent, by the name of Jacob Mires, to take his station at St. Louis.[21] It may be readily conceived that the union of the Northwest and Newyork companies, who had previously extended their trade in opposition to each other, and to the exclusion of all unassociated merchants on the upper portion of the Mississippi, the waters of lake Winnipec and the Athe-baskey country, would, after their late union, have a surplus of capital and a surplus of men which they could readily employ in some other quarter: such was the Missouri, which from the lenity of our government, they saw was opened to them; and I do believe, could the fact be ascertained, that the hope of future gain from the fur trade of that river was one of the principal causes of the union between those two great rivals in the fur trade of North America.[22] That this trade will be nurtured and protected by the British gov-ernment I have no doubt, for many reasons which it strikes me could be offered, but which, not falling immediately within the purview of those observations on the fur trade of Louisiana, I shall forebear to mention.[23]

As the Missouri forms only one of four large branches of the commerce of this united, or, as it is still called, the Northwest company, they will have it in their power not only to break down all single adventurers on the Mis-souri, but in the course of a few years to effect the same thing with a com-pany of merchants of the United States, who might enter into a competition with them in this single branch of their trade. Nor is it possible that our mer-chants, knowing this fact, will form a company for the purpose of carrying on this trade, while they see the Northwest company permitted by our gov-ernment to trade on the Missouri, and on the west side of the Mississippi; therefore, the Northwest company, on the present plan, having driven the adventurers of small capitals from those portions of our territory, will most probably, never afterwards have a rival in any company of our own mer-chants. By their continuance they will acquire strength, and having secured the wished-for monopoly, they will then trade with the Indians on their own terms; and being possessed of the trade, both on the Mississippi and the Missouri, they can make the price of their goods in both quarters similar, and though they may be excessively high, yet being the same they will run no risk of disaffecting the Indians by a comparison of the prices at which they receive their goods at those places. If, then, it appears that the longer we extend the privilege to the Northwest company of continuing their trade within our territory the difficulty of excluding them will increase, can we begin the work of exclusion too soon?[24] For my own part I see not the necessity to admit that our own merchants are not at this moment competent to supply the Indians of the Missouri with such quantities of goods as will, at least in the acceptation of the Indians themselves, be deemed satisfactory and sufficient for their necessaries. All their ideas relative to their necessities are only comparative, and may be tested by a scale of the quantities they have been in the habit of receiving. Such a scale I transmitted to the government from fort Mandan. From a regard to the happiness of the Indians, it would give me much pleasure to see this scale liberally increased; yet I am clearly of opinion that this effect should be caused by the regular progression of the trade of our own merchants, under the patronage and protection of our own governments.[25] This will afford additional security to the tranquility of our much extended frontier, while it will give wealth to our merchants. We know that the change of government in Louisiana, from Spain to that of the United States, has withdrawn no part of that capital formerly employed in the trade of the Missouri; the same persons still remain, and continue to prosecute their trade. To these there has been an accession of several enterprising American merchants, and several others since my return have signified their intention to embark in that trade within the present year, and the whole of those merchants are now unembarrassed by the exactions of Spanish governors. Under those circumstances is it fair for us to presume that the Indians are not now supplied by our own merchants with quite as large an amount of merchandize as they had been formerly accustomed to receive? Should the quantity thus supplied not fully meet our wishes on liberal views, towards the Indians, is it not sounder policy to wait the certain progress of our own trade, than, in order to supply this momentary deficiency, to admit the aid of the Northwest company, at the expense of the total loss of that trade; thereby giving them a carte blanch on which to write in future their own terms of traffic with the Indians, and thus throwing them into their hands, permit them to be formed into a rod of iron, which, for Great Britain, to scourge our frontier at pleasure?[26]

If the British merchants were prohibited from trading in Upper Louisiana, the American merchants, with the aid of the profits arising from the trade of the lower portion of the Missouri and the western branches of the Mississippi, would be enabled most probably to become the successful rivals of the Northwest company in the more distant parts of the continent; to which we might look, in such case, with a well-founded hope of enjoying great advantages from the fur trade; but if this prohibition does not shortly take place, I will venture to predict that no such attempts will ever be made, and, consequently, that we shall for several generations be taxed with the defence of a country which to us would be no more than a barren waste.[27]

About the beginning of August last two of the wintering partners of the Northwest company visited the Mandan and Minnetaree villages on the Missouri, and fixed on a site for a fortified establishment. This project once carried into effect, we have no right to hope for the trade of the upper portion of the Missouri until our government shall think proper to dislodge them.[28]

This season there has been sent up the Missouri, for the Indian trade, more than treble the quantity of merchandise that has ever been previously embarked in that trade in any one period. Of this quantity, as far as I can judge from the best information I could collect, two-thirds was the property of British merchants, and directly or indirectly that of the Northwest company. Not any of this merchandise was destined for a higher point on the Missouri than the mouth of the Vermillion river, or the neighborhood of the Yanktons of the river Demoin; of course there will be a greater excess of goods beyond what the Indians can purchase, unless they sell at one-third their customary price, which the American merchant certainly cannot do without sacrificing his capital.

On my return this fall I met on the Missouri an American merchant by the name of Robert M'Clellan, formerly a distinguished partisan in the army under General Wayne. In a conversation with this gentleman, I learned that during the last winter, in his trade with the Mahas, he had a competitor by the name of Joseph La Croix (believed to be employed by the Northwest company, but now is an avowed British merchant); that the prices at which La Croix sold his goods compelled him to reduce the rates of his own goods so much as to cause him to sink upwards of two thousand dollars of his capital in the course of his trade that season; but that as he had embarked in this trade for two years past, and had formed a favourable acquaintance with the Mahas and others, he should still continue in it a few seasons more, even at a loss of his time and capital, in the hope that goverment, seeing the error, would correct it, and that he might then regain his losses from the circumstance of his general acquaintance with the Indians.[29]

I also met, on my way to St. Louis, another merchant, by the same name, a Captain M'Clellan, formerly of the United States corps of artillerists. This gentleman informed me that he was connected with one of the principal houses in Baltimore, which I do not now recollect, but can readily ascertain the name and standing of the firm if it is considered of any importance; he said he had brought with him a small but well assorted adventure, calculated for the Indian trade, by way of experiment; that the majority of his goods were of the fine, high-priced kind, calculated for the trade with the Spanish province of New Mexico, which he intended to carry on within the territory of the United States, near the border of that province; that, connected with this object, the house with which he was concerned was ready to embark largely in the fur trade of the Missouri, provided it should appear to him to offer advantages to them. That since he had arrived in Louisiana, which was last autumn, he had endeavored to inform himself of the state of this trade, and that from his inquires he had been so fully impressed with the disadvantages it laboured under from the free admission of the British merchants, he had written to his house in Baltimore, advising that they should not embark in this trade unless these merchants were prohibited from entering the river."[30]

I have mentioned these two as cases in point, and which have fallen immediately under my own observations: the first shows the disadvantages under which the trade of our own merchants is now actually labouring; and the second, that no other merchants will probably engage in this trade while the British fur traders are permitted by our government to continue their traffic in Upper Louisiana. With this view of the subject, it is submitted to the government, with whom it alone rests, to decide whether the admission or non-admission of those merchants is at this moment most expedient.[31]

The custom of giving credits to Indians, which grew out of the Spanish system, still exists, and agreeably to our present plan of intercourse with these people, is likely to produce more pernicious consequences than it did formerly. The Indians of Missouri, who have been in the habit of considering these credits rather as a present, or the price of their permission for the trader to depart in peace, still continue to view it in the same light, and will therefore give up their expectations on that point with some reluctance; nor can the merchants well refuse to acquiesce, while they are compelled to be absent from the nations with which they trade five or six months in the year. The Indians are yet too vicious to permit them in safety to leave goods at their trading houses, during their absence, in the care of one or two persons; the merchant, therefore, would rather suffer the loss by giving the credit, than incur the expense of a competent guard or doubling the quantity of his engagees, for it requires as many men to take the peltries and furs to market as it does to bring the goods to the trading establishment, and the number usually employed are not found at any time more than sufficient to give a tolerable security against the Indians.

I presume that it will not be denied that it is our best policy, and will be our practice, to admit, under the restrictions of our laws on this subject, a fair competition among all our merchants in the Indian trade. This being the case then, it will happen, as it has already happened, that one merchant having trade with any nations, at the usual season gives them a credit and departs; a second knowing that such advance had been made, hurries his outfit and arrives at the nation perhaps a month earlier in the fall than the merchant who had made this advance to the Indians; he immediately assembles the nation and offers his goods in exchange for their redskin hunt; the good faith of the Indians, with respect to the absent merchant, will not bind them to refuse; an exchange, of course, takes place; and when the merchant to whom they are indebted arrives, they have no peltry, either to barter or to pay him for the goods which they have already received; the consequences are that the merchant who has sustained the loss becomes frantic; he abuses the Indians, bestows on them the epithets of liars and dogs, and says a thousand things only calculated to sour their minds and disaffect them to the whites; the rival trader he accuses of having *robbed* him of his credits (for they never give this species of artifice among themselves a milder term), and call him many opprobrious names; a combat frequently ensues, in which the principals are not the only actors, for their men will, of course, sympathise with their respective employers. The Indians are the spectators of those riotous transactions, which are well calculated to give them a contempt for the character of the whites, and to inspire them with a belief in the importance of their peltries and furs. The British traders have even gone farther in the northwest, and even offered bribes to induce the Indians to destroy each other; nor have I any reason to doubt but what the same thing will happen on the Missouri, unless some disinterested person, armed with authority by government, be placed in such a situation as will enable him to prevent such controversies. I look to this custom of extending credits to the Indians as one of the great causes of all those individual contentions, which will most probably arise in the course of this trade, as well between the Indians and whites, as between the whites themselves; and that our agents and officers will be always harassed with settling these disputes, which they never can do in such a manner as to restore a perfect good understanding between the parties. I think it would be best in the onset for the government to let it be understood by the merchants that if they think proper to extend credits to the Indians, it shall be at their own risk, dependent on the good faith of the Indians for voluntary payment; that the failure of the Indians to comply with their contracts shall not be considered any justification for the maltreatment or holding abusive language to them, and that no assistance shall be given them in any shape by the public functionaries to aid them in collecting their credits. If the government interfere in behalf of the traders by any regulation, then it will be the interest of every trader individually to get the Indians indebted to him, and to keep them so in order to secure their peltries and furs exclusively to himself. Thus the Indians would be compelled to exchange without choice of either goods or their prices, and the government would have pledged itself to make the Indians pay for goods of which they cannot regulate the prices. I presume the government will not undertake to regulate the merchant in this respect to law.[32]

The difficulties which have arise, and which must arise under existing circumstances, may be readily corrected by establishing a few posts, where there shall be a sufficient guard to protect the property of the merchants in their absence, though it may be left with only a single clerk; to those common marts, all traders and Indians should be compelled to resort for the purposes of traffic.[33]

The plan proposed guards against all difficulties, and provides for a fair exchange, without the necessity of credit; when the Indian appears with his peltry and fur, the competition between the merchants will always insure him his goods on the lowest possible terms, and the exchange taking place at once, there can be no cause of controversy between the Indian and the merchant, and no fear of loss on the part of the later, unless he is disposed to make a voluntary sacrifice, through a spirit of competition with others, by selling his goods at an under value.

Some of the stipulations contained in the licenses usually granted our Indian traders are totally incompatible with the local situations and existing customs and habits of almost all the Indian nations in Upper Louisiana.[34] I allude more particularly to that clause in the license which compels them to trade at Indian towns only. It will be seen by reference to my statistical view of the Indian nations of Upper Louisiana, that the great body of those people are roving bands, who have no villages or stationary residence. The next principal division of them, embracing the Panias, Ottoes, Kanzas, etc., have not their villages on the Missouri, and the even pass the greater portion of the year at a distance from their villages, in the same roving manner. The third and only portion of those Indians who can with propriety be considered as possessed of such stationary villages as seems to have been contemplated by this clause of the license is confined to the Ayaways, Sioux, and Foxes of the Mississippi, and the Ricaras, Mandans, Minnetarees and Ahwahaways of the Missouri.[35] The consequence is that until some further provision be made, all the traders who have intercourse with any nations except those of the last class will form their establishments at several points on the Missouri where it will be most convenient to meet the several nations with whom they wish to carry on commerce. This is their practice at the present moment, and their houses are scattered on various parts of the Missouri. In this detached situation, it cannot be expected that they will comply with any of the stipulations of their licenses. The superintendent of St. Louis, distant eight hundred miles or a thousand miles, cannot learn whether they have forfeited the penalty of their licenses or not; they may, therefore, vend ardent spirits, compromit the government or the character of the whites, in the estimation of the Indians, or practice any other crimes in relation to those people, without the fear of detection or punishment. The government cannot with propriety say to those traders that they shall trade at villages, when in reality they do not exist; nor can they for a moment I presume, think of incurring the expense of sending an Indian agent with each trader, to see that he commit no breach of the stipulations of his license. These traders must of course be brought together, at some general points, where it will be convenient for several nations to trade with them, and where they can be placed under the eye of an Indian agent, whose duty it should be to see that they comply with the regulations laid down from their government.[36] There are crimes which may be committed without a breach of our present laws, and which make it necessary that some further restrictions than those contained in the present licenses of our traders should either be added under the penalties in those licenses, or punished by way of a discretionary power, lodged in the superintendent, extending to the exclusion of such individuals from the Indian trade. Of this description I shall here enumerate three:

First, That of holding conversations with the Indians tending to bring our government into disrepute among them, and to alienate their affections from the same.

Second, That of practising any means to induce the Indians to maltreat or plunder other merchants.

Third, That of stimulating or exciting, by bribes or otherwise, any nations or bands of Indians to wage war against other nations or bands, or against the citizens of the United States, or against citizens or subjects of any power at peace with the same.

These appear to me to be crimes fraught with more real evil to the community, and to the Indians themselves, than vending ardent spirits, or visiting their hunting camps for the purpose of trade; yet there are no powers vested in the superintendents, or agents of the United States, to prevent their repeated commission; nor restrictions or fines imposed by our laws to punish such offences.

It is well known to me that we have several persons engaged in the trade of the Missouri who have, within the last three years, been adopted as citizens of the United States, and who are now hostile to our government.[37] It is not reasonable to expect that such persons will act in good faith towards us. Hence, the necessity of assigning metes and bounds to their transactions among the Indians. On my way to St. Louis, last fall, I received satisfactory evidence that a Mr. Robideau, an inhabitant of St. Louis, had, the preceding winter, during his intercourse with the Ottoes and Missouris, been guilty of the most flagrant breaches of the first of those misdemeanors above mentioned. On my arrival at St. Louis I reported the case to Mr. Broom [Browne] the acting superintendent, and recommended his prohibiting that person from the trade of the Missouri unless he would give satisfactory assurances of a disposition to hold a different language to the Indians. Mr. Broom informed me that the laws and regulations of the United States on this subject gave him no such powers—and Mr. Robideau and sons still prosecute their trade.[38]

The uncontrolled liberty which our citizens take of hunting on Indian lands has always been a source of serious difficulty on every part of our frontier, and is evidently destined to become quite as much so as in Upper Louisiana, unless it be restrained and limited within consistent bounds.[39] When the Indians have been taught, by commerce, duly to appreciate the furs and peltries of their country, they feel excessive chagrin at seeing the whites, by their superior skill in hunting, fast diminishing those productions to which they have been accustomed to look as the only means of acquiring merchandise; and nine-tenths of the causes of war are attributable to this practice. The Indians, although well disposed to maintain a peace on any other terms, I am convinced will never yield this point; nor do I consider it as of any importance to us that they should; for with what consistency of precept and practice can we say to the Indians, whom we wish to civilize, that agriculture and the arts are more productive of ease, wealth, and comfort than the occupation of hunting, while they see distributed over their forests a number of white men engaged in the very occupation which our doctrine would teach them to abandon. Under such circumstances it cannot be considered irrational in the Indians to conclude that our recommendations to agriculture are interested, and flow from a wish on our part to derive the whole emolument arising from the peltries and furs of their country, by taking them to ourselves.[40]

These observations, however, are intended to apply only to such Indian nations as have had, and still maintain, a commercial intercourse with the whites; such we may say are those inhabiting the western branches of the Mississippi, the eastern branches of the Missouri, and near the main body of the latter as far up as the Mandans and Minnetarees. Here it is, therefore, that it appears to me expedient we should draw a line, and temporarily change our policy. I presume it is not less the wish of our government that the Indians on the extreme branches of the Missouri to the west, and within the Rocky Mountains, should obtain supplies of merchandise equally with those more immediately in their vicinity. To effect this, the government must either become the merchant themselves, or present no obstacles to their citizens which may prevent their becoming so with those distant nations; but as the former cannot be adopted (though I really think it would be best for a time), then it becomes the more necessary to encourage the latter. Policy further dictates such encouragement being given, in order to contravene the machinations preparing by the Northwest company for practice in that quarter.[41]

If the hunters are not permitted in those distant regions, the merchants will not be at the expense of transporting their merchandise thither, when they know that the natives do not possess the art of taking the furs of their country. The use of the trap, by which those furs are taken, is an art which must be learned before it can be practised to advantage. If the American merchant does not adventure, the field is at once abandoned to the Northwest Company, who will permit the hunter to go, and the merchant will most probably be with him in the outset; the abundance of rich furs in that country hold out sufficient inducement for them to lose no time in pressing forward their adventures. Thus those distant Indians will soon be supplied with merchandise; and while they are taught the art of taking the furs of their country, they will learn the value, and until they have learnt its value, we shall run no risk of displeasing them by taking it.[42] When the period shall arrive that the distant nations should have learned the art of taking their furs, and know how to appreciate its value, then the hunter becomes no longer absolutely necessary to the merchant, and may be withdrawn; but in the outset he seems to form a very necessary link in that chain which is to unite these nations and ourselves in a state of commercial intercourse.

The liberty to our merchants of hunting, for the purpose of procuring food, in ascending and descending the navigable water-courses, as well as while stationary at their commercial posts, is a privilege which should not be denied them; but as the unlimited extent of such a privilege would produce much evil, it should certainly be looked on as a subject of primary importance; it should, therefore, enter into all those compacts which we may think proper to form with the Indians in that country, and be so shaped as to leave them no solid grounds of discontent.

The time to which licenses shall extend.

A view of the Indian character, so far as it necessary it should be known, for the purposes of governing them, or maintaining a friendly commercial intercourse with them, may be comprised within the limits of a few general remarks.

The *love of gain* is the Indians' ruling passion, and the fear of punishment must form the corrective; to this passion we are to ascribe their inordinate thirst for the possession of merchandise, their unwillingness to accede to any terms, or enter into any stipulations, exceptt such as appear to promise them commercial advantages, and the want of good faith, which they always evince by not complying with any regulations which in practice do not produce to them those expected or promised advantages. The native justice of the Indian mind will always give way to his impatience for the possession of the goods of the defenceless merchant, and he will plunder him, unless prevented by the fear of punishment; nor can punishment assume a more terrific shape to them than that of *withholding every description of merchandise from them.* This species of punishment, while it is one of the most efficient in governing the Indians, is certainly the most humane, as it enforces a compliance with our will without the necessity of bloodshed. But in order to compass the exercise of this weapon, our government must first provide the means of controlling their traders. No government will be respected by the Indians until they are made to feel the effects of its power, or see it practiced on others; and the surest guarantee of savage fidelity to any government is a thorough conviction in their minds that they do possess the power of punishing promptly every act of aggression which they may commit on the persons or property of their citizens. If both traders and Indians throughout Upper Louisiana were compelled to resort to regulated commercial posts, then the trader would be less liable to be pillaged, and the Indians deterred from practicing aggression; for when the Indians once become convinced that in consequence of their having practised violence upon the persons or property of the traders, that they have been cut off from all intercourse with those posts, and that they cannot resort to any other places to obtain merchandise, then they will make any sacrifice to regain the privilege they had previously enjoyed; and I am confident that in order to regain our favour in such cases they would sacrifice any individual who may be the object of our displeasure, even should he be their favorite chief, for their thirst for merchandise is paramount to every other consideration; and the leading individuals among them, well knowing this trait in the character of their own people, will not venture to encourage or excite aggressions on the whites when they know they are themselves to become the victims of its consequences.

But if, on the other hand, these commercial establishments are not general, and we suffer detached and insulated merchants, either British or American, to exercise their own discretion in setting down where they may think proper on the western branches of the Mississippi, for the purposes of trading with the Indians; then, although these commercial establishments may be so extended as to embrace the Missouri, quite to the Mandans, still they lose a great part of their effects; because the roving bands of Tetons and the most dissolute of the Siouxs, being denied the permission to trade on the Missouri at any rate, would resort to those establishments on the Mississippi, and thus become independent of the trade of the Missouri, as they have hitherto been. To correct this, we have three alternates: First, to establish two commercial posts in this quarter. Secondly, to prohibit all intercourse with the Sisitons and other bands of Siouxs on the river St. Peter's and the Raven's-wing river, informing those Indians that such prohibition has been the consequence of the malconduct of the Tetons, and thus leave it to them to correct them; or, Thirdly, to make an appeal to arms in order to correct the Tetons ourselves.

Impressed with a belief, unalloyed with doubts, that the ardent wish of our government has ever been to conciliate the esteem and secure the friendship of all the savage nations within their territory by the exercise of every consistent and pacific measure in their power, applying those of coercion only in the last resort, I here proceed with a due deference to their better judgment, to develop a scheme which has suggested itself to my mind as the most expedient that I can devise for the successful consummation of their philanthropic views towards those wretched people of America, as well as to secure to the citizens of the United States all those advantages which ought of right exclusively to accrue to them from the possession of Upper Louisiana.[43]

The situation of the Indian trade on the Missouri and its waters, while under the Spanish government

The exclusive permission to trade with nations.

The giving by those exclusions the right to individuals to furnish supplies, which rendered the Indians independent of the government.

The times of sending goods to the Indians, and of returning to St. Louis—the necessity of giving credits; therefore the disadvantages of:

The evils that grew out of the method pursued by the Spaniards, as well to themselves as to the Indians.

The independence of individuals of their own government.

The dependence of the Indians on those individuals, and their consequent contempt for the government, and for all other citizens, whom they plundered and murdered at pleasure.

The present rapacity of the Indians, owing to this cause, aided also by the system of giving credits to the Indians, which caused contentions among the traders, which terminated by giving the Indians a contempt for the character of the whites.

The permission to persons to hunt on Indian lands, productive of many evils, the most frequent causes of war, hostile to the views of civilizing and of governing the Indians.

The first principle of governing the Indians is to govern the whites—the impossibility of doing this without establishments, and some guards at those posts.

The Sisitons may be made a check on the Tetons by withholding their trade on the Mississippi.

Having stated the several evils which flowed from the Spanish system, I now state the Indian character, the evils which still exist, and what they will probably terminate in if not redressed—the plan recommended to be pursued and the benefits which may be expected to result therefrom, conclude thus, it may be pretty confidently believed that it is not competent to produce the wished-for reform among the Indians.

Hunters permitted in the Indian country pernicious-frequent cause of war between us.

Some of the stipulations of the licenses granted the traders, in application to the state of the Indians on the Missouri, of course not attended to. The incompetency of the Indian agents to see that any of the stipulations are complied with. Whiskey or ardent spirits may, therefore, be introduced, and other corruptions practised without our knowledge. There is not at

present allowed by law to the superintendent of Indian affairs any discretionary powers by which he can prohibit our newly acquired citizens of
Louisiana, who may be disaffected to our government, from trading with
the Indians; the law says that any citizen of the United States who can give
sufficient security for the sum of five hundred dollars for the faithful compliance with the stipulation of his license shall be permitted to trade. An
instance has happened in Mr. Robideau, etc.[44]

NOTES

1. This annotated version begins with the portion of the "Observations" that
was published in the *Missouri Gazette*, August 2, 1808, pp. 3–4. Those first pages
represent Governor Lewis's thinking a short five months after he arrived in St.
Louis. In a curious twist of circumstance, the excerpt was presented to the public
just three days before the arrival of the first returns from a trading and trapping
expedition on the Yellowstone River when Governor Lewis learned that many of
the concerns he foresaw were already occurring.

2. Surviving records are not very clear on how well prior governor Wilkinson
and Territorial Secretary Joseph Browne, or Browne's replacement, Frederick Bates,
were instructed in their duties before being sent to administer Louisiana. In the
matter of issuing Indian trade licenses, there were technicalities of law that needed
to be observed and forms to be followed. Previous histories suggest that they may
have made them up as the situation arose. Wilkinson issued licenses in late 1805
and next year authorized the Maha trader, Robert McClellan, to arrest anyone he
found trading without a license. Lewis meant to proceed more carefully.

3. Lewis recognized that the basically corrupt Spanish system had also infected
the Indians. For background on that experience, see A. P. Nasatir, *Before Lewis and
Clark* (Lincoln: University of Nebraska Press, 1990).

4. Lewis grasped that the trading Indians understood the economics of the
trade and they were willing to cooperate with debt-burdened traders.

5. Donald Jackson cites the exclusive Spanish license given to Manuel Lisa and
his associates, which Lisa took over in 1803. Lewis knew Lisa from the trader's
failure to deliver boatmen for the expedition and that he was not admired in St.
Louis. However, Lewis could also be referring to the trade that Pierre Chouteau had
previously enjoyed for many years before Lisa eased him out of it.

6. Charless omitted the following: "It is immaterial to the Indians how they
obtain merchandise; in possession of a supply they feel independent."

7. Lewis's understanding of the Spanish system is based on what he had been
told by St. Louis entrepreneurs. Even after the Americans took over, the influential
Chouteau family continued to ship beaver and fine peltry through the Chicago
portage/Michilimackinac connection to British exporters at Montreal.

8. The less specific original version only read "until the latter end of March or beginning of April."

9. Refers to red deerskins.

10. Lewis is writing about the Missouri River trade out of St. Louis. A credit/debt system had been employed by British traders in the Northwest for the previous hundred years. That was effective because traders became familiar with the hunting Indians and could depend upon on mutual trust in regions where there was no government authority. British traders in the Southwest brought the practice to the upper parts of Spanish Louisiana, where Americans saw it as a way of binding the tribes to a pernicious foreign influence.

11. Lewis added the Osage to this roster after he arrived in St. Louis and found that they were a nuisance to him.

12. The *Gazette* version ended at this point. Lewis told the interested merchants of St. Louis what they already knew and probably told him previously. It is curious why he felt it necessary to publicly repeat this in the local press if it was initially written for another purpose, say, discussing the licensing system. He may have shared with his new constituency to show that he recognized the flaws in the old system and intended to see them corrected. The following is taken from the version published with the narrative, as repeated in the Coues, Thwaites, and Jackson editions.

13. Compromised or prejudiced.

14. Lewis faults the Spanish for being unable to control British intrusion on the upper Mississippi, an oversight that in 1806 was threatening to renew the Indian wars.

15. Prairie du Chien, Des Moines, and Iowa.

16. When Governor Lewis arrived at St. Louis in March 1808, he was exasperated to learn that the acting governor, Territorial Secretary Bates, had allowed the British firm of Robert Dickson & Company continued access to the tribes west of the Mississippi because he feared that they would not otherwise be supplied. On June 2, 1808, Lewis wrote John Campbell, "Indian agent at Le Moin" to require proofs of a license. "I conceive it better that the Indians should be deprived of Merchandise for the present altogether than to permit them to receive it at the hands of such persons as are disposed to embroil them in war with us."

17. The British intrusion that Lewis saw at Fort Mandan in 1804–1805 reinforced his Anglophobia. That opinion would soon be strengthened when he discussed the situation on the upper Mississippi with the newly appointed Illinois Territory Indian agent John Campbell.

18. By late 1807 the threat of Indian unrest would grow into a very real danger as the Shawnee Prophet and his brother Tecumseh moved to organize tribal resistance to American expansion. British agents like the notorious Alexander McKee and Matthew Elliot actively supported unrest when they convened a council of six hundred Indians at Amherstburg, just across from Detroit. Fearing repercussions for the *Chesapeake* affair, the British were preparing for a war in which they intended to rely upon Indians. See Reginald Horsman, *Matthew Elliot, British Indian Agent* (Detroit: Wayne State University Press, 1964), pp. 157–76.

19. Lewis was in Washington as President Jefferson's personal secretary in 1802 when Congress considered revisions to previous Indian trade acts dating from 1792. Acts to "Regulate trade and Intercourse with the Indian tribes" and to "Preserve Peace on the Frontiers" on March 30, 1802, and "An Act to Relive and Continue in Force the Act of 1796" on April 30, 1802, set up boundaries between Indians and citizens, restrictions and punishments for violations. In early 1806 Congress created the Office of Superintendent of Indian Trade within the War Department. John Mason, a Georgetown merchant and District of Columbia brigadier-general of the militia, was appointed.

20. Donald Jackson points out that this was the editor's misreading of "new XY company"; Lewis's X was misread as an N.

21. Myers Michael appears to have been the St. Louis agent of the British firm G. Gillespie & Company of Michilimackinac. See Richard Edward Oglesby, *Manuel Lisa and the Opening of the Missouri Fur Trade* (Norman: University of Oklahoma Press, 1963), p. 40n16.

22. Lewis is overly apprehensive here. It was expensive competition and the increased costs of getting to ever-more-distant trading areas that forced the merger.

23. Lewis drew his opinions from observations at Fort Mandan and his return to St. Louis in 1806. The union of the North West Company of Canada and the New North West Company (Sir Alexander Mackenzie & Company) appeared to create a trading monolith poised along the northern border. The visit of two proprietors to the upper Missouri just before the return of the Corps of Discovery was alarming. However, that appears to have resulted in just the opposite, abandonment of an unprofitable trade.

24. There is a suggestion that Lewis soon learned that the loose canonneer Captain of Artillery John McClallen had already attempted it.

25. Donald Jackson is correct that Lewis saw the fur trade as the only tie with the tribes and as a future industry. This is before Lewis was informed by Jefferson of Astor's plans "for the purpose of carrying on an extensive trade with the native Indian inhabitants of America" (Jackson, *LLC* 2: 707n13). The liberal support he suggested would become his rationale for supporting the expedition of the St. Louis MFCo. in early 1809. By then he may have also known that the first adventurer to the upper Missouri had been killed by Indians under suspicious circumstances.

26. When Lewis wrote in 1807 he was unaware that the acting governor, Territorial Secretary Bates, would allow Robert Dickson & Company to continue supplying the tribes west of the upper Mississippi. Lewis's reaction when he arrived in St. Louis in March 1808 became the breaking point between the two territorial officers.

27. It does not appear that the United States had a way of taxing the profits from the fur trade and the reward was in the encouragement of commerce.

28. Donald Jackson mistook A[lexander] Henry for the former St. Louis trader Hugh Heney.

29. Robert McClellan was perpetually in debt and his partnership with Ramsay

Crooks was a series of disasters, capped with their involvement in the overland Astorian adventure. McClellan eventually died a near pauper.

30. Lewis had Clark's record of the encounter with him and probably referred to it.

31. The Congressional Act of March 30, 1802, forbade traders from following Indians to their villages or taking liquor into the Indian country. In July 1805 the British trader Robert Dickson received ninety-five eight-gallon kegs of liquor from the lake brig *Sagnah* at Michilimackinac. His trader James Aird appeared at St. Louis two weeks after Governor Wilkinson issued a proclamation limiting trade to American citizens, an insight Wilkinson may have shared with Lewis when they met in Richmond.

32. Section 11 of the Act of March 30, 1802, stated "that no agent, superintendent or other person authorized to grant a license to trade . . . shall have any interest or concern in any trade with the Indians . . . except for or on account of the United States . . . with a fine of $1000 and imprisonment not to exceed twelve months."

33. A forecast of the construction of Fort Osage.

34. Lewis meant federally designated trading licenses as required in the Indian Trade Factory Act. In the past, licenses had been a source of income for Spanish governors, but Lewis saw them as legal contracts between a trader and his government, mutually binding both parties to the law. Lewis wanted them rewritten to be more than passports for exploitation. There are surviving examples of form licenses issued by Indiana Territory governor William Henry Harrison dated December 13, 1807, and in the Bates papers for July 1807. According to the laws and regulations, Bates administered an oath and received a correct invoice of the goods before licensing the trader for a specified term to reside in a particular Indian town but not at their hunting camps. Marshall, *FB* 1: 204–206.

35. Lewis voiced a new problem that the United States had encountered as a consequence of the purchase of Louisiana. Most of the country west of the Missouri was open plains inhabited by roaming buffalo-hunting tribes, nomadic peoples of habits that the expanding nation had not previously encountered.

36. Lewis recognized that the Indian trade factory system would not work very well for most of the new dependents, but that solution was also impractical.

37. Lewis referred to James Aird, a former upper Mississippi trader affiliated with Robert Dickson who infiltrated the Missouri by declaring himself an American citizen under an unexercised clause in the Treaty of Ghent. Although the returning Corps of Discovery met Aird, who went out of his way to be hospitable, Lewis does not seem to have bought into that charade.

38. The legality of dispensing trade licenses had been a problem for Territorial Secretary Joseph Browne and for his successor, Frederick Bates. Lewis saw a trade license as a legal contract with binding obligations between the government and the recipient and wanted the language of licenses rewritten to make them more than mere passports for exploitation of the tribes.

39. Ironically, even as Governor Lewis was writing this comment, three expeditions were already moving up the Missouri River toward the Great Falls or Yellowstone River. The situation that Lewis was trying to deal with was already under way.

40. When Lewis wrote this in late summer/early fall 1807, Indians along the upper Missouri were already intercepting and robbing American fur traders.

41. Lewis failed to foresee how far he would have to go, at the risk of his own reputation, to support a competitive effort out of St. Louis.

42. This optimism was short lived as the second major expedition to penetrate to the Three Forks of the Missouri would encounter deadly resistance. However, Blood and Atsina hostility appears to have been closer to greedy opportunism than the protection of natural resources.

43. Jackson wrote in his footnote (p. 717), "From this point the manuscript is an outline of what has gone before. Biddle should have deleted it: Coues prints it with a note on its nature, and Thwaites reprints it without comment." However, Biddle did conclude, "The preceding observations of Captain Lewis, although left in an unfinished state, are too important to be omitted. The premature death of the author has prevented his filling up the able outline that he has drawn" (p. 719).

44. Frederick Bates had letters from William Clark dated July 23–24, to which he responded on the twenty-fifth with the promise to write Clark in Louisville. On August 2 Bates indicated that Pierre Chouteau was acting as Indian agent in the absence of Clark (Marshall, FB 1: 168–69). Clark was in St. Louis from early May to late July 1807, before Lewis began writing the "Observations" and should have kept his friend updated about developments on the Indian frontier.

MANUSCRIPT COLLECTIONS

Academy of Natural Sciences, Philadelphia
    Stephen Elliott correspondence, typescripts from the Arnold
        Arboretum Archives, 419 D

Archives of Ontario
    Rocky Mountain House Journal

Indiana Historical Society, Indianapolis, Indiana
    John Armstrong Papers
    English Collection
    William Henry Harrison Papers
    Mitten Collection
    Northwest Territory Collection

Jefferson National Expansion Memorial Library, National Park Service, St.
Louis, Missouri
    Grace Lewis Miller Papers, 1938–1971

Library of Congress, Washington, DC
    John Breckinridge Papers
    Thomas Jefferson Papers
    James Madison Papers

Mercantile Library of St. Louis
    M73, Joseph Philipson's account book, December 13, 1807–August 22,
1809

Missouri Botanical Library, St. Louis, Missouri
    Joseph Ewan Papers

Missouri Historical Society, St. Louis, Missouri
    Army Collection
    Astorians Collection
    John Bakeless Papers
    Bates Family Papers
    Frederick Billon Papers
    Daniel Bissell Papers
    Boone Family Papers
    George Breckinridge Papers
    Garland Broadhead Papers
    James Bruff Papers
    Harold Bulgar Papers
    William Carr Papers
    Chouteau Family Papers
    Clark Family Collection
    Coulter Family Papers
    Courts Collection
    Mary Louise Dalton Collection
    Rufus Easton Papers
    Estates Collection
    Dr. Bernard G. Farrar account books, 1807–1836
    Fur Trade Ledgers, 1804–1871
    Charles Gratiot Papers
    Samuel Hammond Papers
    Hunt Family Papers
    Kaskaskia Collection
    Kingsbury Family Papers

Meriwether Lewis Collection
Manuel Lisa Papers
Louisiana Territory, Military Command, Adjutant's Record, 1803–1805

Louisiana Territory Collection
    John Baptiste Charles Lucas Family Papers
    Morrison Family Correspondence
    Mullanphy Family Papers
    John O'Fallon Papers
    Provenchere Family Papers
    John H. Robinson Papers
    Saugrain-Michau Family Papers
    George C. Sibley Papers
    Amos Stoddard Papers
    James Wilkinson Collection

Missouri State Archives, Jefferson City, Missouri
    William Clark's Probate Records
    General Court Records, 1810–1812
    Missouri Supreme Court Records
    Territorial Supreme Court Records, 1809–1812

Museum of the City of New York
    Samuel Latham Mitchill Papers

National Archives, Archives 2, College Park, Maryland
    RG217, Records of the Accounting Officers of the Department of the Treasury
    Entry 57: Letters Received from the Accountant for the War Department
    Entry 353: Ledgers of the Accountant for the War Department (Set 1)
    Entry 366: Journals of the Accountant of the War Department
    Entry 374: Register of Warrants
    Entry 493: Letters Received by the Accountant for the War Department
    Entry 496: Miscellaneous Letters Sent by the Accountant for the War Department
    Entry 515: Audit Reports on Military Accounts and Claims

New Jersey Historical Society, Newark, New Jersey
    Dickerson Papers
    Statesman Collection

New York Historical Society, New York, New York
    Lt. Col. Daniel Bissell's Return Quarterly, 1809
    Calendar of the Albert Gallatin Collection
    US Military Philosophical Society Papers
    Orderly Books of Lt. Col. Jacob Kingsbury, 1804–1808
    General Anthony Wayne's Orderly Book, 1795
    Miscellaneous manuscripts (military)
    Gulian C. Verplanck Papers

Recorder of Deeds, City of St. Louis, St. Louis, Missouri
    Deed books A, B, C, H2, I, 1808–1839
    Land Warrants sale, deed book B, 152-7, 1808

St. Louis Circuit Court, Civil Court Archives, City of St. Louis, St. Louis,
Missouri
    St. Louis Circuit Court Case Files

Western Historical Manuscripts Collection, Columbia, Missouri
    William Clark memorandum book, 1809
    William Clark notebook, 1798–1801
    Meriwether Lewis astronomy notebook, 1803–1805
    O'Fallon Family Papers

MICROFILM

American Philosophical Society, Philadelphia, Pennsylvania
    Journals of Lewis and Clark, August 30–December 12, 1803
    Eastern Journal, film 214, reel 2

Emory University, Atlanta, Georgia
    The *Review*, 1809: Microfilm 3940

Missouri Historical Society
    Chouteau Collections
    Clark Family Papers
    Papers of Albert Gallatin, November 17, 1807–March 22, 1808, reel 15
    Meriwether Lewis Collection
    Papeles de Cuba Collection, Archivo General de Indias in Seville,
        Spain

Records of the General Accounting Office, RG217, Selected Volumes from the Accountant of the War Department, reel 14, #85

National Archives, Washington, DC
    RG46: Records of the US Senate
    M1257, Transcribed Reports and Communications Transmitted by the Executive Branch to the US Senate . . . and Transcribed Reports of Senate Committees
    M1403, Unbound Records of the US Senate for the Eighth Congress
    M1708, Unbound Records of the US Senate for the Ninth Congress

    RG56: General Records of the Department of the Treasury
    M733, Letters Sent by the Secretary of the Treasury Relating to Public Lands
    M735, Circular Letters of the Secretary of the Treasury

    RG59: General Records of the Department of State
    M40, Domestic Letters of the Department of State
    M179, Miscellaneous Letters of the Department of State
    M418, Letters of Application and Recommendation during the Administration of Thomas Jefferson

    M438: Letters of Application and Recommendation during the Administration of James Madison
    M1094, General Orders and Circulars of the War Department and Army Headquarters
    T225, Despatches from US Consuls in New Orleans, Louisiana
    T260, State Department Territorial Records, Orleans

    RG75: Records of the Bureau of Indian Affairs
    M15, Letters Sent by the Secretary of War Relating to Indian Affairs
    M16, Letters Sent by the Superintendent of Indian Affairs
    M271, Letters Sent by the Secretary of War Relating to Indian Affairs
    T58, Letters Received by the Superintendent of Indian Affairs

    RG94: Records of the Adjutant General's Office
    M565, Letters Sent by the Adjutant General's Office
    M566, Letters Received by the Adjutant General's Office
    M661, Historical Information Relating to Military Posts

M1136, Records of 1811 and 1815 Courts-Martial of Gen. James Wilkinson

RG107: Records of the Office of the Secretary of War
M6, Letters Sent by the Secretary of War Relating to Military Affairs
M22, Registers of Letters Received by Secretary of War
M107, Letters Sent to the President of the United States
M220, Reports to Congress from the Secretary of War
M221, Letters Received by the Secretary of War
M222, Letters Received by the Secretary of War (unregistered series)
M370, Miscellaneous Letters Sent by the Secretary of War

RG217: Records of the Accounting Officers of the Department of the Treasury
M235, Miscellaneous Treasury Accounts of the First Auditor

RG233: Records of the US House of Representatives
M1264, Journals of the US House of Representatives
M1267, Transcribed Reports of the Committees of the US House of Representatives
M1268, Transcribed Reports and Communications Transmitted by the Executive Branch to the US House of Representatives
M1404, Unbound Records of the House of Representatives for the Eighth Congress

New York University (NYU), Bobst Library, New York City
Albert Gallatin Papers

Tennessee State Library, Nashville, Tennessee
The *Democratic Clarion*, 1809

University of Illinois, Urbana
Bryan and Morrison Business Records, daybooks 1805–1808

University of Virginia, Alderman Library, Charlottesville, Virginia
The *Argus of Western America* or the *Frankfort Argus*, 1809: N-US, Ky-4
The *Frankfort Palladium*, 1809: N-US, Ky-10, Reel 2
Lewis, Marks, and Anderson families: M668

Western Historical Manuscripts Collection, Columbia, Missouri
  French and Spanish Archives, microfilm roll F 523

MICROFICHE

EARLY AMERICAN IMPRINTS: FIRST SERIES (EVANS)

No. 18178: Saunders, William. *Observations on the Superior Efficacy of the Red Peruvian Bark, in the Cure of Agues and Other Fevers.* Boston, 1783.

No. 21777: Currie, William. *A Dissertation on the Autumnal Remitting Fever.* Philadelphia, College of Physicians, 1789.

No. 35106: *Transactions of the American Philosophical Society* 4. Philadelphia, American Philosophical Society, 1799.

No. 36370: Stoddard, Amos. *An Oration Delivered before the Citizens of Portland, Maine and the Supreme Judicial Court of the Commonwealth of Massachusetts on July 5, 1799.*

No. 36371: Stoddard, Amos. *An Oration Delivered before the First Parish of Portland, Maine, June 24, 1799. Portland Lodge of Free and Accepted Masons in Celebration of the Festival of St. John the Baptist.*

No. 37604: Hemenway, Samuel. *Medicine Chests, with Particular Directions.* Salem, MA: Thomas C. Cushing, 1800.

No. 45776: *Lee's Genuine Bilious Pills, or Family Physic.* Prepared by Samuel Lee, of Windham, in the state of Connecticut; for which discovery he obtained a patent signed by the president of the United States, 1799.

EARLY AMERICAN IMPRINTS:
SECOND SERIES (SHAW-SHOEMAKER)

No. 3692: Ashton, Henry. *An Inaugural Essay on the Remitting and Intermitting Bilious Fever.* Philadelphia: 1803.

No. 7471: *A Bill to Amend the Laws Providing for the Organization of the Accounting Offices.* Washington: US Congress, 1804.

No. 10326: *Discoveries Made in Exploring the Missouri, Red River and Washita, by Captains Lewis and Clark, Doctor Sibley, and William Dunbar, Esq. with a Statistical Account of the Countries Adjacent.* Natchez, MS: Andrew Marschalk, 1806. (Formerly American Imprints, no. 11552.)

No. 11632: *Message from the President of the United States, Communicating Discoveries Made in Exploring the Missouri, Red River, and Washita, by Captains Lewis and Clark, Doctor Sibley, and Mr. Dunbar; with a Statistical Account of the Countries Adjacent.* New York: Hopkins and Seymour, 1806.

No. 11633: *Message from the President of the United States Communicating Discoveries*

Made in Exploring the Missouri, Red River, and Washita, by Captains Lewis and Clark, Doctor Sibley, and Mr. Dunbar; with a Statistical Account of the Countries Adjacent. Washington: A. & G. Way, 1806.

No. 11805: *John Fanning Watson. To the Public* . . . Washington: 1806.

No. 15451: *The Laws of the Territory of Louisiana.* St. Louis: Joseph Charles, 1808.

No. 16954: *Frederick Bates. Oration Delivered before Saint Louis Lodge No. 111.* St. Louis: Joseph Charles, 1809.

No. 18775: *The Travels of Capts. Lewis and Clarke.* New York and Philadelphia: Hubbard Lester, 1809. (Formerly American Imprints, no. 17911.)

No. 18893: Simmons, William. *To Inquire Whether Any Advances of Money Have Been Made to the Commander-in-Chief of the Army by the Department of War, Contrary to Law* . . . Washington: LOC, 1809. An American Time Capsule: Three Centuries of Broadsides and Other Printed Ephemera. "Public Plunder." Washington: 1809.

No. 21145: Pringle, John. *Observations on the Disease of the Army . . . with Notes by Benjamin Rush.* Philadelphia: Fry and Kammerer, 1810.

No. 21675: *Letter from the Comptroller of the Treasury Transmitting a Statement of the Accounts in the Treasury, War, and Navy Departments. William Simmons. Abstract of Accounts on the Books of the Accountant for the Department of War Which Were Unsettled on 30 September 1807 and Which Still Remain Unsettled.* Washington: 1810.

No. 22985: Heerman, Lewis. *Directions for the Medicine Chest.* New Orleans: John Mowry & Co., 1811.

No. 23216: *The Travels of Capts. Lewis and Clarke.* Germany: Hubbard Lester, 1811.

No. 24153: Duvall, Gabriel. *Letter from the Comptroller of the Treasury Transmitting a Statement of the Accounts prior to 30 September 1808.* Washington: 1811.

No. 26261: *New Travels among the Indians of North America.* Philadelphia: William Fisher, 1812.

No. 26582: *The Travels of Capts. Lewis and Clarke.* Germany: Hubbard Lester, 1812.

No. 28817: *An Interesting Account of the Voyages and Travels of Captains Lewis and Clarke, in the Years 1804–5 & 6.* Baltimore: William Fisher, 1813.

No. 32773: Simmons, William. *A Letter to the Senate and House of Representatives of the United States, Shewing the Profligacy and Corruption of General John Armstrong in His Administration of the War Department.* Washington: 1814.

Sabin, no. 40826: *Travels in the Interior Parts of America; Communicating Discoveries Made in Exploring the Missouri, Red River and Washita, by Captains Lewis and Clark, Doctor Sibley, and Mr. Dunbar; with a Statistical Account of the Countries Adjacent . . . Laid before the Senate, by the President of the United States in February, 1806, and Never before Published.* London: Richard Phillips, 1807.

NEWSPAPERS

American Citizen (NY)
American Watchman (DE)
Argus of Western America (KY)
Bridgeport Herald (CT)
Connecticut Courant (Danbury, CT)
Connecticut Herald
Democratic Clarion or Nashville Clarion (TN)
The *Democratic Press (PA)*
Eastern Argus (ME)
The *Frankfort Palladium (KY)*
Kentucky Gazette (Lexington, KY)
Louisiana Gazette (St. Louis, MO)
Missouri Gazette (St. Louis, MO)
National Intelligencer and Washington Advertiser (Washington, DC)
New-England Palladium (Boston, MA)
New York Commercial Advertiser (New York, NY)
The *New York Gazette & Daily Advertiser (New York, NY)*
Philadelphia Daily Advertiser (Philadelphia, PA)
The *Pittsfield Sun (Pittsfield, MA)*
Republican Star or Eastern Shore General Advertiser (MD)
Republican Watch-Tower (Washington, DC)
The *Review (Nashville, TN)*
The *Sun (Washington, DC)*
The *United States Gazette (Philadelphia, PA)*

WEB SITES

Annals of Congress
James Bruff, "Trial of Aaron Burr"
http://memory.loc.gov/cgi-bin/ampage?collId=llac&fileName=017/llac017.db
    &recNum=306 (accessed April 8, 2008)

Century of Lawmaking for a New Nation
American State Papers
http://memory.loc.gov/ammem/amlaw/lwsp.html (accessed April 8, 2008)

House Journal
http://memory.loc.gov/ammem/amlaw/lwhj.html (accessed April 8, 2008)

Thomas Jefferson Papers—Library of Congress
http://memory.loc.gov/ammem/collections/jefferson_papers/index.html (accessed
    April 8, 2008)
Journal of the Executive Proceedings of the Senate of the United States of America
Appointment of Ensign Meriwether Lewis
http://memory.loc.gov/cgi-bin/ampage?collId=llej&fileName=001/llej001.db&rec
    Num=187 (accessed April 8, 2008)

Lewis and Clark Journals
Moulton, Gary, ed.
http://libtextcenter.unl.edu/lewisandclark/index.html (accessed April 8, 2008)

Dolley Madison Digital Edition
http://rotunda.upress.virginia.edu:8080/dmde/ (accessed April 8, 2008)

James Madison Papers—Library of Congress
http://memory.loc.gov/ammem/collections/madison_papers/index.html (accessed
    April 8, 2008)

Senate Executive Journal
http://memory.loc.gov/ammem/amlaw/lwej.html (accessed April 8, 2008)

Statutes at Large
http://memory.loc.gov/ammem/amlaw/lwsl.html (accessed April 8, 2008)

US Supreme Court cases
Guitard v. Stoddard, 1853
http://supreme.justia.com/us/57/494/case.html (accessed April 8, 2008)

PRIMARY AND SECONDARY SOURCES

Aberbach, Alan David. *In Search of an American Identity: Samuel Latham Mitchill,
    Jeffersonian Nationalist.* New York: Peter Lang, 1988.
Abrams, Rochonne. "Meriwether Lewis: Two Years with Jefferson, the Mentor."
    Missouri Historical Society Bulletin 36 (October 1979): 3–18.
Ackerkecht, Erwin. *Malaria in the Upper Mississippi Valley, 1760–1900.* Baltimore:
    Johns Hopkins Press, 1945.
———. "Aspects of the History of Therapeutics." *Bulletin of the History of Medicine*
    36 (September–October 1962): 389–419.
Alibert, Jean-Louis. *A Treatise on Malignant Intermittents.* Philadelphia: Fry and
    Kammerer, 1807.

Allen, Henry C. *Therapeutics of Intermittent Fever.* Philadelphia: Hahnemann Publishing, 1884.

Ambrose, Stephen. *Undaunted Courage: Meriwether Lewis, Thomas Jefferson and the Opening of the American West.* New York: Simon & Schuster, 1996.

American State Papers: Finance, Foreign Relations, Indian Affairs, Military Affairs, Public Lands, Miscellaneous. 38 vols. Washington: Gales & Seaton, 1832–1861.

Anderson, Dice Robins. *William Branch Giles.* Gloucester, UK: Peter Smith, 1965.

Annals of the Congress of the United States, 1789–1824. 42 vols. Washington: Gales and Seaton, 1834–1836.

Bakeless, John. *Lewis & Clark: Partners in Discovery.* New York: William Morrow, 1947.

Balinky, Alexander. *Albert Gallatin, Fiscal Theories and Policies.* New Brunswick, NJ: Rutgers University Press, 1958.

Barker, Eugene. *Austin Papers.* 2 vols. Washington: Annual Report of the American Historical Association, 1919.

Barton, Benjamin Smith. "Facts and Observations: Natural History, Zoology." *Philadelphia Medical and Physical Journal* 2 (1805): 155–76.

Bates, Edward. "Letter Giving Sketch of Frederick Bates, February 10, 1859." *Michigan Pioneer Collections* 8 (1907): 563–65.

Bedini, Silvio. *Jefferson and Science.* Raleigh: University of North Carolina Press, 2002.

Bell, Whitfield J., Jr., and Murphy D. Smith, eds. *Guide to the Archives and Manuscript Collections of the American Philosophical Society.* Philadelphia: American Philosophical Society, 1966.

Bentley, James R. "Two Letters of Meriwether Lewis to Major William Preston." *Filson Club History Quarterly* 44 (April 1970): 170–75.

Betts, Edwin Morris, and James Adam Bear Jr., eds. *The Family Letters of Thomas Jefferson.* Columbia: University of Missouri Press, 1966.

Biddle, Nicholas. *History of the Expedition under the Command of Captains Lewis and Clark, to the Sources of the Missouri River, thence across the Rocky Mountains and down the River Columbia to the Pacific Ocean. Performed during the Years 1805–5–6, by Order of the Government of the United States.* 2 vols. Philadelphia: Paul Allen, 1814.

Bill for the Relief of the Legal Representatives of Meriwether Lewis. 20th Cong., 1st sess. House Report 282 (April 28, 1828).

Billon, Frederic L. *Annals of St. Louis in Its Early Days.* St. Louis: 1886.

"Biological Rhythms in Malaria." *Lancet* 7591 (February 1969): 403–404.

Bloom, Jo Tice. "Rufus Easton (1770–1799)." In *Dictionary of Missouri Biography,* edited by Lawrence O. Christensen, William E. Foley, Gary R. Kremer, and Kenneth H. Winn. Columbia: University of Missouri Press, 1999.

Blumgarten, A. S. *Textbook of Materia Medica, Pharmacology and Therapeutics.* New York: Macmillan, 1939.

Bordley, James, and A. Harvey, eds. *Two Centuries of American Medicine, 1776–1976.* Philadelphia: W. B. Saunders, 1976.

Boyd, Mark F. *An Introduction to Malariology*. Cambridge, MA: Harvard University Press, 1930.

———. "An Historical Sketch of the Prevalence of Malaria in North America." *American Journal of Tropical Medicine* 21 (1941): 223–44.

Boyd, Robert T. "Another Look at the Fever and Ague of Western Oregon." *Ethnohistory* 22 (Spring 1975): 135–54.

Brodie, Fawn M. *Thomas Jefferson: An Intimate History*. New York: W. W. Norton, 1974.

Brown, Everett S., ed. *William Plumer's Memorandum of Proceedings in the United States Senate 1803–1807*. New York: Da Capo Press, 1969.

Brown, William Cullen. *The Institutions of the Practice of Medicine*. 5 vols. Edinburgh, 1801.

Brown, William Mosely. *Freemasonry in Staunton, Virginia*. Staunton, VA: McClure Printing Company, 1949.

Bruce, Marian C., and Karen P. Day. "Cross-Species Regulation of Malaria Parasitaemia in the Human Host." *Current Opinion in Microbiology* 5 (August 2002): 431–37.

Brugger, Robert J., Robert A. Rutland, Robert Rhodes Crout, Jeanne K. Sisson, and Dru Dowdy, eds. *Papers of James Madison*. Secretary of State series. 8 vols. Charlottesville: University Press of Virginia, 1986.

Buckley, Jay H. *William Clark: Indian Diplomat*. Norman: University of Oklahoma Press, 2008.

Buley, R. Carlyle. "Pioneer Health and Medical Practices in the Old Northwest Prior to 1840." *Mississippi Valley Historical Review* 20 (March 1934): 497–520.

———. *The Old Northwest: Pioneer Period, 1815–1840*. 2 vols. Indianapolis: Indiana Historical Society, 1950.

Caldwell, Norman. "The Frontier Army Officer, 1794–1814." *Mid-America: An Historical Review* 37 (April 1955): 101–28.

Calendar of the Correspondence of James Madison: Bulletin of the Bureau of Rolls and Library of the Department of State. Washington: Department of State, 1894.

Calendar of the Correspondence of Thomas Jefferson. 3 vols. 1894. Reprint, New York: Burt Franklin, Inc., 1970.

Calendar of the Miscellaneous Letters Received by the Department of State to 1820. Washington: GPO, 1897.

Carter, Clarence E., ed. *The Territorial Papers of the United States*. 28 vols. Washington: GPO, 1934–1962.

———. "The Burr-Wilkinson Intrigue in St. Louis." *Missouri Historical Society Bulletin* 10 (July 1954): 447–64.

Carter II, Edward C. *One Grand Pursuit: A Brief History of the American Philosophical Society's First 250 Years, 1743–1993*. Philadelphia: American Philosophical Society, 1993.

———. *Most Flattering Incident of My Life: Essays Celebrating the Bicentennial of Thomas Jefferson's American Philosophical Society Leadership, 1797–1814*. Philadelphia: Friends of the American Philosophical Society, 1997.

Catlett, J. Stephen, ed. *A New Guide to the Collections in the Library of the American Philosophical Society*. Philadelphia: American Philosophical Society, 1987.

Century of Lawmaking for a New Nation: US Congressional Documents and Debates, 1774–1875, Journal of the Executive Proceedings of the Senate of the United States of America, vol. 1, http://memory.loc.gov/cgi-bin/ampage?collId=llej&fileName=001/llej001.db (accessed April 3, 2008).

Chandler, David Leon. *The Jefferson Conspiracies: A President's Role in the Assassination of Meriwether Lewis*. New York: William Morrow, 1994.

Charless, Joseph. *A Treatise on the Diseases Most Prevalent in the United States with Directions for Medicine Chests*. St. Louis: Joseph Charless & Son, 1830.

Chernow, Ron. *Alexander Hamilton*. New York: Penguin, 2004.

Chinard, Gilbert. "The American Philosophical Society and the World of Science." *Proceedings of the American Philosophical Society* 87 (July 1943): 1–11.

———. "Jefferson and the American Philosophical Society." *Proceedings of the American Philosophical Society* 87 (July 1943): 263–76.

Chuinard, Eldon. *Only One Man Died: The Medical Aspect of the Lewis and Clark Expedition*. Glendale, CA: A. H. Clark, 1980.

———. "The Court-Martial of Ensign Meriwether Lewis." *We Proceeded On* 8 (November 1982): 12–15.

———. "Lewis and Clark, Master Masons." *We Proceeded On* 15 (February 1989): 12–15.

———. "How Did Meriwether Lewis Die?" Part 1. *We Proceeded On* 17 (August 1991): 4–12.

———. "How Did Meriwether Lewis Die?" Part 2. *We Proceeded On* 18 (January 1992): 4–10.

Chwatt, Bruce L. J. "Ague as Malaria." *Journal of Tropical Medicine and Hygiene* 79 (August 1976): 168–76.

Clark, Sanford. "Observations on the Peruvian Bark." *Medical Repository* 3 (1812): 241–46.

Congressional Journals of the United States House of Representatives: Thomas Jefferson Administration. 8 vols. Reprint, Wilmington, DE: Michael Glazier.

Congressional Journals of the United States Senate: Thomas Jefferson Administration. 8 vols. Reprint, Wilmington, DE: Michael Glazier.

Coren, Robert W., Mary Rephlo, David Kepley, and Charles South. *Guide to the Records of the United States Senate at the National Archives, 1789–1989, Bicentennial Edition*. Washington, DC: National Archives and Records Administration, 1989.

Corner, George W. *Two Centuries of Medicine: A History of the School of Medicine, University of Pennsylvania*. Philadelphia: J. B. Lippincott, 1965.

Coues, Elliott, ed. *History of the Expedition under the Command of Lewis and Clark, to the Sources of the Missouri River, thence across the Rocky Mountains and down the Columbia River to the Pacific Ocean, Performed during the Years 1804–5–6, by Order of the Government of the United States. A New Edition*. 4 vols. New York: 1893.

———. "Notes on Thomas Meehan's Paper on the Plants of Lewis and Clark's Expedition across the Continent, 1804–1806." *Proceedings of the Academy of Natural Sciences of Philadelphia* 50 (April–September 1898): 291–315.

———. *The Expeditions of Zebulon Montgomery Pike.* 2 vols. Facsimile reprint, New York: Dover, 1987.

Coxe, John Redman. "Cinchona-Peruvian Bark." *American Dispensatory.* 5th ed. Philadelphia: Thomas Dobson and Son, 1822.

Crackel, Theodore J. *Mr. Jefferson's Army: Political and Social Reform of the Military Establishment, 1801–1809.* New York: New York University Press, 1987.

Cramp, Arthur. *Nostrums and Quackery and Pseudo-medicine.* 3 vols. Chicago: Press of American Medical Association, 1911–1936.

Crowther, Simeon J., and Marion Fawcett. *Science & Medicine to 1870: Pamphlets in the American Philosophical Society Library.* Library Publications no. 1. Philadelphia: American Philosophical Society, 1968.

Cullen, William. *First Lines of the Practice of Physic.* 4th ed., 4 vols. Edinburgh: C. Eliot, 1784.

Cunningham, Noble E. *The Process of Government under Jefferson.* Princeton, NJ: Princeton University Press, 1978.

Cutright, Paul Russell. "I Gave Him Barks and Saltpeter." *American Heritage: The Magazine of History* 15 (December 1963): 58–61, 94–101.

———. "Meriwether Lewis: Zoologist." *Oregon Historical Quarterly* 69 (March 1968): 5–28.

———. "Meriwether Lewis: Botanist." *Oregon Historical Quarterly* 69 (June 1968): 148–70.

———. *Lewis and Clark: Pioneering Naturalists.* Urbana: University of Illinois Press, 1969.

———. "The Journal of Captain Meriwether Lewis." *We Proceeded On* 10 (February 1984): 8–10.

———. "Meriwether Lewis's 'Colouring of Events.'" *We Proceeded On* 11 (February 1985): 10–17.

———. In *Explorations: Into the World of Lewis & Clark: Essays from the Pages of* We Proceeded On, *the Quarterly Journal of the Lewis and Clark Trail Heritage Foundation,* edited by Robert A. Saindon. 3 vols. Great Falls, MT: Lewis and Clark Trail Heritage Foundation, Inc., 2003.

Danisi, Thomas C. "The 'Ague' Made Him Do It." *We Proceeded On* 28 (February 2002): 10–15.

Danisi, Thomas C., and John C. Jackson. "Homeward Bound." *We Proceeded On* 33 (May 2007): 16–19.

Danisi, Thomas C., and W. Raymond Wood. "Lewis and Clark's Route Map: James MacKay's Map of the Missouri River." *Western Historical Quarterly* 35 (Spring 2004): 53–72.

———. "James MacKay: International Explorer." *Missouri Historical Review* 102 (April 2008): 154–64.

Davidson, Andrew, ed. *Hygiene & Diseases of Warm Climates*. Edinburgh: Young J. Pentland, 1893.

Davies, Nicholas E., Garland H. Davies, and Elizabeth D. Sanders. "William Cobbett, Benjamin Rush, and the Death of General Washington." *JAMA* 249 (February 1983): 912–15.

Davis, Elvert M. *The Bates Boys on the Western Waters*. Asheville, NC: Inland Press, 1960.

Davis, Richard Beale. "The Autobiography of Peachy R. Gilmer." In *Francis Gilmer: Life and Learning in Jefferson's Virginia*. Richmond, VA: Dietz Press, 1939.

Denslow, Ray V. *Territorial Masonry, the Story of Freemasonry and the Louisiana Purchase, 1804–1821*. Washington, DC: Masonic Service Association of the United States, 1925.

———. "Meriwether Lewis: Missouri's First Royal Arch Mason." *Proceedings of the 95th Annual Convocation of the Grand Chapter of Royal Arch Masons of the State of Missouri* (April 1941): 72–97.

———. "A Chronology of Missouri Masonic History Previous to 1835." *Transactions of the Missouri Lodge of Research* 1 (1943): 57–70.

———. "General William Clark: The Masonic Story of a Member of the Celebrated Lewis & Clark Expedition." *Transactions of the Missouri Lodge of Research* 1 (1943): 40–56.

Denslow, William. *10,000 Famous Freemasons*. Trenton, MO: Missouri Lodge of Research, 1957.

DeVoto, Bernard. "An Inference regarding the Expedition of Lewis and Clark." *Proceedings of the American Philosophical Society* 99 (August 1955): 155–94.

"Diary of William Joseph Clark." *Register of the Kentucky State Historical Society* 25 (January 1927): 193–206.

Dillon, Richard. *Meriwether Lewis: A Biography*. Santa Cruz, CA: Western Tanager Press, 1965.

Doren, Carl Van. "The Beginnings of the American Philosophical Society." *Proceedings of the American Philosophical Society* 87 (July 1943): 277–89.

Doren, Mark Van, ed. *Correspondence of Aaron Burr and His Daughter, Theodosia*. New York: Stratford Press, 1929.

Douglas, Jesse S. "Lewis' Map of 1806." *Military Affairs* 5 (Spring 1941): 68–72.

Douglas, Walter B. "Manuel Lisa." *Missouri Historical Society Collections* 3 (1911): 233–68.

Drake, Daniel. *The Principal Diseases of the Interior Valley of North America*, 2nd ed. Reprint, Philadelphia: Lippincott, Grambo & Co., 1854.

———. "Report on the Diseases of Cincinnati in the Spring of 1828 . . . for Ague and Fever." *Western Journal of the Medical and Physical Sciences* 2 (1828–1829): 216–19.

Earle, A. Scott, and James L. Reveal. *Lewis and Clark's Green World*. Helena, MT: Farcountry Press, 2003.

Ebert, Albert E., and Emil A. Hiss. *The Standard Formulary*. 2nd ed. Chicago: G. P. Englehard & Co., 1897.

Elliott, T. C. "The Strange Case of David Thompson and Jeremy Pinch." *Oregon Historical Quarterly* 40 (June 1939): 188–99.

Estes, J. Worth. "Changing Fashions in Therapeutics." *Caduceus* 9 (Autumn 1995): 65–72.

———. "The Medical Properties of Food in the Eighteenth Century." *Journal of the History of Medicine and Allied Sciences* 51 (April 1996): 127–54.

Evans, Charles. *American Bibliography*. 2nd series. New York: Peter Smith, 1941.

Every, Dale Van. *Ark of Empire: The American Frontier 1784–1803*. New York: Arno Press, 1977.

Ewald, Paul W. *Evolution of Infectious Disease*. New York: Oxford University Press, 1994.

Ewan, Joseph. "Frederick Pursh, 1774–1820, and His Botanical Associates." *Proceedings of the American Philosophical Society* 96 (October 1952): 599–628.

———. *Introduction to the Facsimile Reprint of Frederick Pursh's Flora Americae Septentrionalis (1814)*. Braunschweig, Germany: J. Cramer, 1979.

Ewers, John C. "Chiefs from the Missouri and Mississippi and Peale's Silhouttes of 1806." *Smithsonian Journal of History* 1 (Spring 1966): 1–26.

———. "The Influence of the Fur Trade upon the Indians of the Northern Plains." In *People and Pelts: Selected Papers. Second North American Fur Trade Conference*. Winnipeg: Peguis Publishers, 1972.

Fantus, Bernard, and G. Koehler. *Pharmacology and Therapeutics, Preventive Medicine*. Practical Medicine series. 8 vols. Chicago: Year Book Publishers, 1923.

Fausz, Frederick J., and Michael A. Gavin. "The Death of Meriwether Lewis: An Unsolved Mystery." *Gateway Heritage* 24 (Fall 2003–Winter 2004): 66–79.

Fishbein, Morris. *Frontiers of Medicine*. Baltimore: Williams & Wilkins Company, 1933.

Fisher, Vardis. *Suicide or Murder? The Strange Death of Meriwether Lewis*. Denver: Alan Swallow, 1962.

Fitzgerald, William J. "Evolution of Use of Quinine in Treatment of Malaria." *New York State Journal of Medicine* 68 (March 1968): 800–802.

Flores, Dan L. "Editor's Introduction." In *Southern Counterpart to Lewis & Clark: The Freeman & Curtis Expedition of 1806*. Norman: University of Oklahoma Press, 2002.

Flückiger, Friedrich A. *The Cinchona Barks*. Philadelphia: P. Blakiston, Son & Co., 1884.

Foley, William E. "Different Notions of Justice: The Case of the 1808 St. Louis Murder Trials." *Gateway Heritage* 9 (Winter 1988–89): 2–13.

———. "Edward Hempstead (1780–1817)." In *Dictionary of Missouri Biography*, edited by Lawrence O. Christensen, William E. Foley, Gary R. Kremer, and Kenneth H. Winn, 391–92. Columbia: University of Missouri Press, 1999.

———. *Wilderness Journey: The Life of William Clark*. Columbia: University of Missouri Press, 2004.

Foley, William E., and Carl J. Ekberg, eds. *An Account of Upper Louisiana by Nicolas de Finiels*. Columbia: University of Missouri Press, 1989.

Foley, William E., and David C. Rice. *The First Chouteaus: River Barons of Early St. Louis.* Urbana and Chicago: University of Illinois Press, 1983.

Freemon, Frank R. *Microbes and Minie Balls: An Annotated Bibliography of Civil War Medicine.* Rutherford, NJ: Fairleigh Dickinson University Press, 1993.

Frick, L. Ruth *Courageous Colter and Companions.* Washington, MO: L. R. Frick, 1997.

———. "Meriwether Lewis's Personal Finances." *We Proceeded On* 28 (February 2002): 16–20.

Friis, Herman R. "Cartographic and Geographic Activities of the Lewis and Clark Expedition." *Journal of the Washington Academy of Sciences* 44 (November 1954): 338–51.

Galen, Leennius Andreas, ed., *Claudii Galeni . . . Opera, nunc demum a clarissimus iuxt a & eruditis viris latinate donata, iam vero ordine iusto, & studio exquisitore in lucem recens edita.* Basileae, per Andream Cratandrum, mense martio, 1529.

Garnham, Percy Cyril, and K. G. Powers. "Periodicity of Infectivity of Plasmodial Gametocytes: The 'Hawking Phenomenon.'" *International Journal of Parasitology* 4 (February 1974): 103–106.

Gillett, Mary C. *The Army Medical Department, 1775–1818.* Washington, DC: Center of Military History United States Army, 1981.

Goodhart, Duane E. "Meriwether Lewis and William Clark: 'American Explorers' Freemasons." *Miscellanea* 8 (1997): 13–18.

Goodman, Nathan G. *Benjamin Rush: Physician and Citizen.* Philadelphia: University of Pennsylvania Press, 1934.

Graney, Charles M. "Colonial Medicine." *New York State Journal of Medicine* 76 (July 1976): 1123–25.

Gregg, Kate L., ed. *Westward with Dragoons: The Journal of William Clark on His Expedition to Establish Fort Osage, August 25 to September 22, 1808.* Fulton, MO: Ovid Bell Press, 1937.

Griffenhagen, George B., and James Harvey Young. *Old English Patent Medicines in America.* Washington, DC: Smithsonian Institution, 1959.

Guerra, Francisco. "The Introduction of Cinchona in the Treatment of Malaria." Part 1. *Journal of Tropical Medicine and Hygiene* 80 (June 1977): 112–18.

———. "The Introduction of Cinchona in the Treatment of Malaria." Part 2. *Journal of Tropical Medicine and Hygiene* 80 (July 1977): 135–40.

Guice, John D. W. *By His Own Hand? The Mysterious Death of Meriwether Lewis.* Norman: Oklahoma University Press, 2006.

Guide to the National Archives of the United States. Washington, DC: National Archives and Records Service, 1974.

Guitard v. Stoddard, 16 U.S. 494 (1853).

Haggis, A. W. "Fundamental Errors in the Early History of Cinchona." *Bulletin of the History of Medicine* 10 (October 1941): 417–59, 568–92.

Haller, John S., Jr. "Samson of the Materia Medica: Medical Theory and the Use and Abuse of Calomel in 19th Century America." *Pharmacy in History* 13 (1971): 27–33, 67–76.

———. *American Medicine in Transition, 1840–1910*. Urbana: University of Illinois Press, 1981.

Hamilton, James. *Observations on the Use and Abuse of Mercurial Medicines in Various Diseases*. New York: E. Bliss & E. White, 1821.

———. *Observations on the Utility and Administration of Purgative Medicines in Several Diseases*. Philadelphia: Thomas Kite, 1829.

Hastings, Donald, Jr. "Its Name Is 'Camp River Dubois.'" *Lewis and Clark Society of America*, special ed. (January 2003): 3.

Hawking, Frank. "Circadian and Other Rhythms of Parasites." *Advances in Parasitology* 13 (1975): 123–82.

Hawking, Frank, Michael J. Worms, and Kenneth Gammage. "Host Temperature and Control of 24-Hour and 48-Hour Cycles in Malaria Parasites." *Lancet* 7541 (March 1968): 506–509.

———. "24- and 48-Hour Cycles of Malaria Parasites in the Blood; Their Purpose, Production and Control." *Transactions of the Royal Society of Tropical Medicine and Hygiene* 62 (June 1968): 731–65.

Haywood, H. L. "Masonic Curiosa." *Transactions of the Missouri Lodge of Research* 25 (1968): 80–85.

Heitman, Francis B., ed. *Historical Register and Dictionary of the United States Army from Its Organization, September 29, 1789, to March 2, 1903*. 2 vols. Washington, DC: GPO, 1903. Reprint, Urbana: University of Illinois Press, 1965.

Hibbert, Wilfred. "Major Amos Stoddard, First Governor of Upper Louisiana." *Historical Society of Northwestern Ohio Bulletin* 2 (April 1930).

Hiss, Emil. *Thesaurus of Proprietary Preparations*. Chicago: Englehard & Co., 1899.

Holmberg, James, ed. *Dear Brother*. New Haven, CT: Yale University Press, 2002.

———. "Lost and Found: Discharge Papers of John Shields." *We Proceeded On* 30 (February 2004): 35–37.

Holmes, C. "Benjamin Rush and the Yellow Fever." *Bulletin of the History of Medicine* 40 (May–June 1966): 246–63.

Homberger, Esther Fisher. "Hypochondriasis of the Eighteenth Century—Neurosis of the Present Century." *Bulletin of the History of Medicine* 46 (July–August 1972): 391–401.

Honigsbaum, Mark. *The Fever Trail: In Search of the Cure for Malaria*. New York: Farrar, Straus and Giroux, 2001.

Hooper, Robert. *Medical Dictionary*. New York: Harper & Bros., 1841.

Horsman, Reginald. *Matthew Elliott, British Indian Agent*. Detroit: Wayne State University Press, 1964.

Hough, Emerson. *The Magnificent Adventure*. New York: D. Appleton and Company, 1916.

Howe, Henry. *Historical Collections of Virginia*. Charleston: William R. Babcock Co., 1856.

Humphreys, Margaret. *Malaria, Poverty, Race, and Public Health in the United States*. Baltimore: Johns Hopkins University Press, 2001.

Hunt, C. C. *The Holy Saints John*. Cedar Rapids: Iowa Masonic Library, 1923.

Hunt, Robert R. "The Blood Meal: Mosquitoes and Agues on the Lewis & Clark Expedition, Part 1." *We Proceeded On* 18 (May 1992): 4–10.

———. "The Blood Meal: Mosquitoes and Agues on the Lewis & Clark Expedition, Part 2." *We Proceeded On* 18 (August 1992): 4–10.

Hunter, Clark, ed. *The Life and Letters of Alexander Wilson*. Philadelphia: American Philosophical Society, 1983.

Index to the James Madison Papers. Washington, DC: Library of Congress, 1965.

Index to the Thomas Jefferson Papers. Washington, DC: Library of Congress, 1976.

Isselbacher, Kurt J., Eugene Braunwald, Jean D. Wilson, Joseph B. Martin, Anthony S. Fauci, and Dennis L. Kasper, eds. *Harrison's Principles of Internal Medicine*, 13th ed. 2 vols. New York: McGraw-Hill, 1992.

Jackson, Donald, "A New Lewis and Clark Map." *Missouri Historical Society Bulletin* 17 (January 1961): 117–32.

———. "On the Death of Meriwether Lewis's Servant." *William and Mary Quarterly* 21 (July 1964): 445–48.

———, ed. *The Journals of Zebulon Montgomery Pike with Letters and Related Documents*. 2 vols. Norman: University of Oklahoma Press, 1966.

———. "A Footnote to the Lewis and Clark Expedition." *Manuscripts* 24 (Winter 1972): 1–21.

———, ed. *Letters of the Lewis and Clark Expedition with Related Documents, 1783–1854*, 2nd ed. 2 vols. Urbana: University of Illinois Press, 1978.

———. "Jefferson, Meriwether Lewis, and the Reduction of the United States Army." *Proceedings of the American Philosophical Society* 124 (April 1980): 91–96.

———. *Thomas Jefferson and the Rocky Mountains: Exploring the West from Monticello*. Reprint, Norman: University of Oklahoma Press, 2002.

Jackson, John C. "Captain John McClallen." In *The Louisiana Purchase: A Historical and Geographical Encyclopedia*. Santa Barbara, CA: ABC-Clio, 2002.

———. "The Fight on Two Medicine River." *We Proceeded On* 32 (February 2006): 14–23.

Jackson, Stanley W. "Melancholia and the Waning of the Humoral Theory." *Journal of the History of Medicine and Allied Sciences* 33 (July 1978): 367–76.

———. "Melancholia and Mechanical Explanation in Eighteenth-Century Medicine." *Journal of the History of Medicine and Allied Sciences* 38 (July 1983): 298–319.

———. *Melancholia and Depression*. New Haven, CT: Yale University Press, 1986.

Jacobs, James Ripley. *The Beginning of the US Army, 1783–1812*. Princeton, NJ: Princeton University Press, 1947.

James, Thomas. *Three Years among the Indians and Mexicans*. Reprint, Lincoln: University of Nebraska Press, 1984.

Jamison, Kay Redfield. *Night Falls Fast: Understanding Suicide*. New York: Knopf, 1999.

Janson, Charles William. *The Stranger in America.* London: J. Cundee, 1807.

Jarcho, Saul. "A Cartographic and Literary Study of the Word *Malaria.*" *Journal of the History of Medicine* 25 (January 1970): 31–39.

———. "The Legacy of British Medicine to American Medicine, 1800–1850." *Proceedings of the Royal Society of Medicine* 68 (November 1975): 737–44.

———. "Laveran's Discovery in the Retrospect of a Century." *Bulletin of the History of Medicine* 58 (Summer 1984): 215–24.

———. "A History of Semitertian Fever." *Bulletin of the History of Medicine* 61 (Fall 1987): 411–30.

———. *Quinine's Predecessor.* Baltimore: Johns Hopkins University Press, 1993.

Jobe, Thomas H. "Medical Theories of Melancholia in the Seventeenth and Early Eighteenth Centuries." *Clio Medica* 11 (December 1976): 217–31.

Jones, Landon Y. *William Clark and the Shaping of the West.* New York: Hill and Wang, 2004.

Josephy, Alvin M., Jr. *The Nez Perce Indians and the Opening of the Northwest.* New Haven, CT: Yale University Press, 1965.

Journal of the Executive Proceedings of the Senate. 36 vols. New York: Johnson Reprint Corporation, 1969.

Kelsay, Laura E. *List of Cartographic Records of the General Land Office.* No. 19. Washington, DC: National Archives, 1964.

Kennon, Donald R., and Rebecca M. Rogers. *The Committee on Ways and Means: A Bicentennial History, 1789–1989.* Washington, DC: US House of Representatives, 1989.

Kline, Mary-Jo, ed. *Political Correspondence and Public Papers of Aaron Burr.* 2 vols. Princeton, NJ: Princeton University Press, 1983.

Knudson, Jerry W. "Newspaper Reaction to the Louisiana Purchase." *Missouri Historical Review* 63 (January 1969): 182–213.

Kremers, Edward, and George Urdang. *History of Pharmacy.* Philadelphia: J. B. Lippincott Company, 1940.

Kukla, Jon. *A Wilderness So Immense.* New York: Knopf, 2003.

Kvasnicka, Robert M. *The Trans-Mississippi West, 1804–1912. Part 1: A Guide to the Records of the Department of State for the Territorial Period.* Washington, DC: National Archives, 1993.

Labaree, Leonard Woods, and Whitfield J. Bell Jr., eds. *The Papers of Benjamin Franklin.* 37 vols. New Haven, CT: Yale University Press, 1959–2006.

Lavender, David. *The Fist in the Wilderness.* Garden City, NY: Doubleday, 1964.

Laws for the Territory of Louisiana. St. Louis: Charless, 1808.

Lawson, Charles F. *Remote Sensing and Archeological Testing of the Meriwether Lewis Monument and Pioneer Cemetery and the Search for Grinder's Stand.* Tallahassee, FL: National Park Service, 2002.

Lawson, Murray G. *The Beaver Hat and the North American Fur Trade.* In *People and Pelts: Selected Papers. Second North American Fur Trade Conference.* Winnipeg: Peguis Publishers, 1972.

Leden, Ido. "Antimalarial Drugs—350 Years." *Scandinavian Journal of Rheumatology* 10 (1981): 307–12.

Lewis, Grace. "Financial Records—Expedition to the Pacific Ocean." *Missouri Historical Society Bulletin* 10 (July 1954): 465–89.

———. "The First Home of Governor Lewis in Louisiana Territory." *Missouri Historical Society Bulletin* 14 (July 1958): 357–68.

Lewis, Meriwether, and William Clark. *The Travels of Capts. Lewis and Clarke from St. Louis, by Way of the Missouri and Columbia Rivers, to the Pacific Ocean; Performed in the Years 1804, 1805 & 1806, by Order of the Government of the United States . . . from the Official Communication of Meriwether Lewis.* London: Longman, Hurst, Rees, and Orme, 1809.

Loescher, Maida H. *Inventory of the Records of the Office of the Secretary of War.* Inventory 17. Washington, DC: National Archives, 1999.

Looareesuwan, Sornchai, Pravan Suntharasamai, H. Kyle Webster, and May Ho. "Malaria in Splenectomized Patients: Report of Four Cases and Review." *Clinical Infectious Diseases* 16 (March 1993): 361–66.

Loos, John Louis. "A Biography of William Clark, 1770–1813." PhD dissertation. Washington University, 1953.

Lowry, Thomas P. *Venereal Disease and the Lewis and Clark Expedition.* Lincoln: Nebraska University Press, 2004.

Macculloch, John. *An Essay on the Remittent and Intermittent Diseases.* 2 vols. London: Longman, Rees, Orme, Brown, and Green, 1828.

Mackenzie, Alexander. *Voyages from Montreal on the River St. Laurence through the Continent of North America to the Frozen and Pacific Oceans in the Years 1789 and 1793 with a Preliminary Account of the Rise, Progress and Present State of the Fur Trade of That Country.* London: R. Noble, 1801; facsimile reprint, Readex Microprint, 1966.

Mackey, Albert Gallatin. *The History of Freemasonry.* 7 vols. New York: Masonic History Company, 1898.

Maguire, Edward F. "Frequent Diseases and Intended Remedies on the Frontier, 1780–1850." Master's thesis, St. Louis University, 1953.

Majors, Harry M. "John McClellan in the Montana Rockies 1807: The First American after Lewis and Clark." *Northwest Discovery: The Journal of Northwest History and Natural History* 2 (November–December 1981): 554–630.

Malone, Dumas. *Jefferson and His Time.* 6 vols. Boston: Little, Brown, 1948–1981.

Manson, Patrick. *Tropical Diseases.* New York: William Wood and Company, 1903.

Marshall, Thomas Maitland. *The Life and Papers of Frederick Bates.* 2 vols. St. Louis: Missouri Historical Society, 1926.

Mayo, Robert. *A Synopsis of the Commercial and Revenue System of the United States.* 2 vols. Washington, DC: J. & G. S. Gideon, 1847.

———. *The Treasury Department and Its Various Fiscal Bureaus.* 2 vols. Washington, DC: Wm. Q. Force, 1847.

McKelvey, Susan Delano. *Botanical Exploration of the Trans-Mississippi West, 1790–1850.* Corvallis: Oregon State University Press, 1991.

McMurtrie, Douglas C. *Joseph Charless, Pioneer Printer of St. Louis.* Chicago: Ludlow Typography Company, 1931.

Mears, James A. "Some Sources of the Herbarium of Henry Muhlenberg." *Proceedings of the American Philosophical Society* 122 (June 1978): 155–74.

Meehan, Thomas. "The Plants of the Lewis and Clark's Expedition across the Continent, 1804–1806." *Proceedings of the Academy of Natural Sciences, Philadelphia* 50 (January–March 1898): 12–49.

Merrill, Boynton, Jr. *Jefferson's Nephews—A Frontier Tragedy.* Princeton, NJ: Princeton University Press, 1976.

Microfilm Resources for Research: A Comprehensive Catalog. Washington, DC: National Archives Trust Fund Board, 2000.

Miller, Grace Lewis. *Finding Aid to the Grace Lewis Miller Papers, 1938–1971.* St. Louis: National Park Service, 1999.

Mitchill, Samuel Latham, ed. *Medical Repository.* 12 vols. New York: 1804–1812.

———. Discourse on Thomas Jefferson, More Especially as a Promoter of Natural & Physical Science. New York: G. & C. Carvill, 1826.

———. "Dr. Mitchill's Letters from Washington: 1801–1813." *Harper's New Monthly Magazine* 58 (April 1879): 740–55.

Moore, Kathyrn. "The Lost Years of Meriwether Lewis." *Journal of the West* 42 (Summer 2003): 58–65.

Morris, Larry E. *The Fate of the Corps: What Became of the Lewis and Clark Explorers after the Expedition.* New Haven, CT: Yale University Press, 2004.

Motherby, George. *Medical Dictionary,* 3rd ed. London: George Wallis, 1791.

Moulton, Forest Ray, ed. *A Symposium on Relapsing Fever in the Americas.* Publication no. 18. Washington, DC: American Association for the Advancement of Science, 1942.

Moulton, Gary E., ed. *The Journals of the Lewis and Clark Expedition.* 13 vols. Lincoln: University of Nebraska Press, 1983–2001.

———. "The Missing Journals of Meriwether Lewis." *Montana: Magazine of Western History* 35 (Summer 1985): 28–39.

———. "New Documents of Meriwether Lewis." *We Proceeded On* 13 (November 1987): 4–7.

———. *Herbarium of the Lewis and Clark Expedition.* Lincoln: University of Nebraska Press, 1999.

Munger, Susan H. *Common to This Country: Botanical Discoveries of Lewis & Clark.* New York: Artisan, 2003.

Nicandri, David L. "The Columbia Country and the Dissolution of Meriwether Lewis: Speculation and Interpretation." *Oregon Historical Quarterly* 106 (Spring 2005): 7–33.

Nisbet, Jack. *Visible Bones: Journeys across Time in the Columbia River Country.* Seattle: Sasquatch Books, 2003.

Oglesby, Richard Edward. *Manuel Lisa and the Opening of the Missouri Fur Trade.* Norman: University of Oklahoma Press, 1963.

Osborne, Oliver T. *The Principles of Therapeutics.* Philadelphia: W. B. Saunders Company, 1922.

Osgood, Ernest Staples, ed. *The Field Notes of Captain William Clark, 1803–1805.* With an introduction and notes by same. New Haven, CT: Yale University Press, 1964.

O'Shea, J. G. "Two Minutes with Venus, Two Years with Mercury—Mercury as an Antisyphilitic Chemotherapeutic Agent." *Journal of the Royal Society of Medicine* 83 (June 1990): 392–95.

Osler, William. *The Principles and Practice of Medicine,* 2nd ed. New York: D. Appleton and Company, 1895.

Parascandola, John. "Drug Therapy in Colonial and Revolutionary America." *American Journal of Hospital Pharmacy* 33 (August 1976): 807–10.

Parker, David W. *Calendar of Papers in Washington Archives Relating to the Territories of the United States to 1873.* Washington, DC: Carnegie Institution of Washington, 1911.

Pease, Verne S. "The Death of Captain Merriwether Lewis." *Southern Magazine* (February 1894): 17–24.

Pennell, Francis W. "Benjamin Smith Barton as Naturalist." *Proceedings of the American Philosophical Society* 86 (September 1942): 108–22.

———. "Historic Botanical Collections of the American Philosophical Society and the Academy of Natural Sciences of Philadelphia." *Proceedings of the American Philosophical Society* 94 (April 1950): 137–51.

Perotti, Viola Andersen. *Important Firsts in Missouri Imprints, 1808–1858.* Kansas City, MO: R. F. Perotti, 1967.

Peterson, Merrill D., ed. *Thomas Jefferson—Writings.* New York: Library of America, 1984.

Phelps, Dawson A. "The Tragic Death of Meriwether Lewis." *William and Mary Quarterly,* series 3, 13 (July 1956): 305–18.

Philip, Wilson A. P. *A Treatise on Febrile Diseases,* 1st ed. 2 vols. Hartford, CT: Cooke & Hale, 1809.

Phillips, Henry, Jr. "Early Proceedings of the American Philosophical Society . . . from the Manuscript Minutes of Its Meetings from 1774 to 1838." *Proceedings of the American Philosophical Society* 22 (1884): 1–874.

Pickard, Madge E., and R. Carlyle Buley. *The Midwest Pioneer: His Ills, Cures, & Doctors.* New York: Henry Schuman, 1946.

Pidgin, Charles Felton. *Theodosia: The First Gentlewoman of Her Time.* Boston: C. M. Clark Publishing Co., 1907.

Pitney, W. R. "The Tropical Splenomegaly Syndrome." *Transactions of the Royal Society of Tropical Medicine and Hygiene* 62 (1968): 717–28.

Poser, Charles, and G. W. Bruyn. *An Illustrated History of Malaria.* New York: Parthenon Publishing Group, 1999.

Powell, John Harvey. *Bring Out Your Dead*. Philadelphia: University of Pennsylvania Press, 1949.

Powell, William H. *List of Officers of the Army of the United States from 1779 to 1900*. New York: L. R. Hamersly & Co., 1900. Reprint, Detroit: Gale Research Company, 1967.

"Proceedings of the Celebration of the Three Hundredth Anniversary of the First Recognized Use of Cinchona." Missouri Botanical Garden: St. Louis, 1931.

Prucha, Francis Paul. *American Indian Policy in the Formative Years, the Indian Trade and Intercourse Acts, 1790–1834*. Cambridge, MA: Harvard University Press, 1962.

Pumroy, Eric, and Paul Brockman. *A Guide to Manuscript Collections of the Indiana Historical Society and Indiana State Library*. Indianapolis: Indiana Historical Society, 1986.

Rao, U. V. Gopala, and Henry N. Wagner. "Normal Weights of Human Organs." *Radiology* 102 (February 1972): 337–39.

Ratcliffe, A. W. "The Historical Background of Malaria—A Reconsideration." *Journal of the Indiana State Medical Association* 39 (July 1946): 339–47.

Ravenholt, Reimert T. "Triumph Then Despair: The Tragic Death of Meriwether Lewis." *Epidemiology* 5 (May 1994): 366–79.

Rees, Abraham. *The Cyclopaedia; or, Universal Dictionary of Arts, Sciences, and Literature*. 45 vols. London: Longman, Hurst, Rees, Orme & Browne, 1819.

Reiss, Oscar. *Medicine in Colonial America*. Latham, MA: University Press of America, 2000.

Rinse, Gunter B. "Calomel and the American Medical Sects during the Nineteenth Century." *Mayo Clinical Proceedings* 48 (January 1973): 57–64.

Robertson, James Alexander. *Louisiana under the Rule of Spain, France and the United States, 1785–1807*. 2 vols. Cleveland: Arthur H. Clark Company, 1911.

Rocco, Fiammetta. *The Miraculous Fever-Tree: Malaria and the Quest for a Cure That Changed the World*. New York: HarperCollins, 2003.

Ronda, James P. *Lewis and Clark among the Indians*. Lincoln: University of Nebraska Press, 1984.

———. "St. Louis Welcomes the Lewis and Clark Expedition." *We Proceeded On* 13 (February 1987): 19–20.

———. "Lewis & Clark and Enlightened Ethnography." In *Westering Captains: Essays on the Lewis and Clark Expedition*. Great Falls, MT: Lewis and Clark Trail Heritage Foundation, Inc., 1990.

Rose, H. D., T. M. Golbert, C. J. Sanz, and T. H. Leitschuh. "Fever during Acute Alcoholic Withdrawal." *American Journal of Medical Science* 260 (August 1970): 112–21.

Rowland, Buford, Handy B. Fant, and Harold E. Hufford. *Records of the United States House of Representatives, 1789–1946*. Washington, DC: National Archives and Records Service, 1959.

Rudd, Velva E. "Botanical Contributions of the Lewis and Clark Expedition." *Journal of the Washington Academy of Sciences* 44 (November 1954): 351–56.

Rush, Benjamin. *An Account of the Bilious Remitting Yellow Fever*. Philadelphia: Thomas Dobson, 1794.

Rutland, Robert Allen. *The Presidency of James Madison*. Lawrence: University Press of Kansas, 1990.

Rutland, Robert Allen, Robert J. Brugger, Jeanne K. Sisson, Thomas A. Mason, Susannah H. Jones, and Fredrika J. Teute, eds. *The Papers of James Madison: Presidential Series*. 5 vols. Charlottesville: University of Virginia Press, 1984.

Rutman, Darrett B., and Anita H. Rutman. "Of Agues and Fevers: Malaria in the Early Chesapeake." *William and Mary Quarterly* 33 (January 1976): 31–60.

Rutyna, Richard A., and Peter C. Stewart. *The History of Freemasonry in Virginia*. Latham, MA: University Press of America, Inc., 1998.

Ryan, Carmelita S., and Hope K. Holdcamper. *Preliminary Inventory of the General Records of the Department of the Treasury*. Washington, DC: National Archives and Records Service, 1977.

Sabin, Joseph. *A Dictionary of Books Relating to America*. 29 vols. Amsterdam: 1961.

Saindon, Robert A., ed. *Explorations: Into the World of Lewis & Clark: Essays from the Pages of* We Proceeded On, *the Quarterly Journal of the Lewis and Clark Trail Heritage Foundation*. 3 vols. Great Falls, MT: Lewis & Clark Heritage Foundation, Inc., 2003.

Sanford, Clark. "Observations on the Peruvian Bark." 3rd hexade. *Medical Repository* 3 (1812): 244–45.

Saul, Allan. "The Role of Variant Surface Antigens on Malaria-Infected Red Blood Cells." *Parasitology Today* 15 (November 1999): 455–57.

Savitt, Todd L. *Fevers, Agues, and Cures: Medical Life in Old Virginia*. Richmond: Virginia Historical Society, 1990.

Senac, Jean. *A Treatise on the Hidden Nature and the Treatment of Intermitting and Remitting Fevers*. Philadelphia: Conrad & Co., 1805.

Seton, Anya. *My Theodosia*. Boston: Houghton Mifflin, 1941.

Setzer, Henry. "Zoological Contributions of the Lewis and Clark Expedition." *Journal of the Washington Academy of Sciences* 44 (November 1954): 356–57.

Shaw, Ralph R., and Richard H. Shoemaker. *American Bibliography: A Preliminary Checklist for 1806*. New York: Scarecrow Press, 1961.

Sherman, William F., and Craig R. Scott. *Records of the Accounting Officers of the Department of Treasury*. Inventory 14 (revised). Lovetsville, VA: Willow Bend Books, 1997.

Shryock, Richard H. "European Backgrounds of American Medical Education (1600–1900)." *JAMA* 194 (November 1965): 709–14.

———. "The Medical Reputation of Benjamin Rush: Contrasts over Two Centuries." *Bulletin of the History of Medicine* 45 (November–December 1971): 507–52.

Skelley, James W. *Some Early History of Freemasonry in Missouri*. St. Louis: Missouri Historical Society, 1943.

Skelton, William B. *An American Profession of Arms: The Army Officer Corps, 1784–1861.*" Lawrence: University of Kansas, 1992.

Smith, Dale C. "Quinine and Fever: The Development of the Effective Dosage." *Journal of the History of Medicine and Allied Sciences* 31 (July 1976): 343–67.

Smith, James Morton. *The Republic of Letters: The Correspondence between Thomas Jefferson and James Madison, 1776–1826.* 3 vols. New York: Norton, 1995.

Spamer, Earle E., and Richard M. McCourt. "The Lewis and Clark Herbarium of the Academy of Natural Sciences." *Notulae Naturae* 475 (December 2002): 2–16.

State Papers and Correspondence Bearing upon the Purchase of the Territory of Louisiana. Washington, DC: GPO, 1903.

Sternberg, George Miller. *Malaria and Malarial Diseases.* New York: William Wood, 1884.

Stewart, James. *A Dissertation on the Salutary Effects of Mercury in Malignant Fevers.* Philadelphia: Thomas & Samuel Bradford, 1798.

Stillson, Henry, and William James Hughan, eds. *History of Freemasonry and Concordant Orders.* Boston: Fraternity Publishing Co., 1892.

Sylvestris (pseud.). *Reflections on the Cession of Louisiana to the United States.* Washington City: Samuel Harrison Smith, 1803.

Thane, Elswyth. *Dolley Madison.* New York: Crowell-Collier Press, 1970.

Thwaites, Reuben Gold, ed. *Cuming's Sketches of a Tour Cumings of the Western Country 1807–1809.* 26 vols. Vol. 4, *Early Western Travels.* Cleveland: Arthur H. Clark, 1904.

———. *Original Journals of the Lewis and Clark Expedition, 1804–1806.* 8 vols. New York: Dodd, Mead, 1904–1905.

Thurston, George H. *Pittsburgh As It Is.* Pittsburgh: W. S. Haven, 1857.

Todd, Charles Burr. *Life of Colonel Aaron Burr: History of the Burr Family.* New York: S. W. Green, 1879.

Tollison, C. David, and Michael L. Kriegel. "Hypochondriasis: Does It Exist in Medical Practice?" *Journal of South Carolina Medical Association* 84 (December 1988): 575–79.

"Transfer of Upper Louisiana—Papers of Captain Amos Stoddard." *Glimpses of the Past* 2 (May–September 1935): 78–122.

True, Rodney H. "Some Neglected Botanical Results of the Lewis and Clark Expedition." *Proceedings of the American Philosophical Society* 67 (1928): 1–19.

Tyrrell, Joseph B. "Letter of Roseman and Perch, July 10th, 1807." *Oregon Historical Quarterly* 38 (December 1937): 391–97.

Underwood, Thomas T. *Journal of Thomas Taylor Underwood.* Cincinnati: Society of Colonial Wars in the State of Ohio, 1945.

United States Scientific Geographical Exploration of the Pacific Basin, 1783–1899. Publication 62-2. Washington, DC: National Archives, 1961.

Urdang, George. "The Early Chemical and Pharmaceutical History of Calomel." *Chymia* 1 (1948): 93–108.

Valencius, Conevery Bolton. *The Health of the Country: How American Settlers Understood Themselves and Their Land*. New York: Basic Books, 2002.

Van Tyne, Claude Halstead, and Waldo Gifford Leland. *Guide to the Archives of the Government of the United States in Washington*. 2nd ed. Washington, DC: Carnegie Institution of Washington, 1907.

Veith, Ilza. "Elizabethans on Melancholia." *JAMA* 212 (April 1970): 127–31.

Walters, Raymond, Jr. *Albert Gallatin, Jeffersonian Financier & Diplomat*. New York: Macmillan, 1957.

Ward, Harry M. *The Department of War, 1781–1795*. Pittsburgh: University of Pittsburgh Press, 1962.

Warren, John. *A View of the Mercurial Practice in Febrile Diseases*. Boston: T. B. Wait & Co., 1813.

Wernsdorfer, Walther H., and Ian McGregor. *Malaria: Principles and Practice of Malariology*. 2 vols. New York: Churchill Livingstone, 1988.

West Point Orderly Books. 4 vols. in one. Columbus: Ohio State Museum, Anthony Wayne Parkway Board, 1954–1955.

Will, Drake W. "The Medical and Surgical Practice of the Lewis and Clark Expedition." *Journal of the History of Medicine and Allied Sciences* 14 (July 1959): 273–97.

Wills, Gary. *James Madison*. New York: Henry Holt and Company, 2002.

Wilson, Alexander. "Particulars of the Death of Capt. Lewis." *Port Folio* 7 (January 1812): 34–47.

Wilson, Charles Morrow. *Meriwether Lewis of Lewis and Clark*. New York: Thomas Y. Crowell, 1934.

Woodruff, A. W. "Benjamin Rush, His Work on Yellow Fever and His British Connections." *American Journal of Tropical Medicine & Hygiene* 26 (September 1977, supplement): 1055–59.

Young, James Harvey. *The Medical Messiahs: A Social History of Health Quackery in Twentieth Century America*. Princeton, NJ: Princeton University Press, 1967.

———. "From Hooper to Hohensee: Some Highlights of American Patent Medicine Promotion." *JAMA* 204 (April 1968): 2–6.

Zingman, Barry S., and Brant L. Viner. "Splenic Complications in Malaria: Case Report and Review." *Clinical Infectious Diseases* 16 (February 1993): 223–32.

Index